AMAZING DOGS

A CABINET OF CANINE CURIOSITIES

JAN BONDESON

AMBERLEY

*All illustrations are from the author's collection
unless otherwise stated.*

This edition first published 2013

Amberley Publishing
The Hill, Stroud
Gloucestershire, GL5 4EP

www.amberley-books.com

British Library Cataloguing in Publication Data.
A catalogue record for this book is available from the British Library.

ISBN 978-1-4456-0706-1

Typesetting and Origination by Amberley Publishing.
Printed in the UK.

CONTENTS

1

INTRODUCTION

Over the years, the dog has become more closely associated with the human race than any other domestic animal. There is a rich heritage of canine lore, dating back to ancient times. The current estimate of the number of dogs in the world is not less than 400 million. During the many thousand years there have been domesticated dogs on the planet, the through-time total must add up to many billions.

The vast majority of these dogs have just been ordinary dogs, chewing bones, wagging their tails, and barking at strangers; showing no ambition at all to change the history of the canine race. A mere few of them have been amazing dogs, distinguishing themselves through saving human lives, acting in films, travelling around the world, writing poetry, speaking German, solving mathematical problems, becoming world-famous cult figures, or haunting houses after they were dead.

If you wish to read about ordinary dogs, and how to feed, groom and educate them, this book is not for you; it will only deal with amazing dogs: odd, anomalous, and well-nigh incredible canines through history.

The domestic dog evolved from wolves at least 15,000 years ago. Genetic data has suggested that this happened in East Asia. There are differing hypotheses as to how this domestication occurred. Some cynologists (dog experts) believe that early humans tamed wolf pups, for use as pets or hunters. Others have suggested that certain wolves scavenging for food around early human settlements became ever less fearful of people, ending up permanently parting company with the wild wolves, and joining the humans instead. These tamed proto-dogs may well have been among the very first domesticated animals.[1]

The early humans soon realized the value of their canine friends, mainly as hunting companions, enabling them to go after larger prey. Already in antiquity, there were recognized breeds of dogs. Long-haired molossus dogs were used for protecting cattle, and short-haired, fierce, mastiff-like dogs were used as war dogs, or for fights in the arena. There were also greyhound-like dogs that hunted animals using their speed and sight, and small terrier-like dogs used for hunting rats and other household pests, or as domestic pets. Xenophon considered a fine pack of hunting dogs as one of the most

1. A humorous old German cartoon, with the dog sitting at table and its master eating scraps.

2. Lord Bridgwater's Dog Banquet. This eccentric peer had a large pack of dogs, of which the twelve favourites were allowed to sit at table with him.

8

important possessions with which to adorn a country estate. A vase from the Etruscan city of Vulci shows a small dog looking just like a present-day Maltese terrier. A stone relief from the Palace of Nineveh shows the mastiff-like war dogs of Assurnasipal, and another relief from an Egyptian tomb depicts four whippet-like greyhounds ready to be released to go after their prey.[2] An investigation of ancient Pompeian dogs has indicated that in addition to hunting dogs, watchdogs and shepherd dogs, there was also a breed of small dogs, probably lap-dogs.[3]

The classical Greeks and Romans had a high opinion of their dogs. These useful animals could be used for hunting, shepherding cattle, guarding a house, or simply as companion animals. Pliny's *Natural History* tells the tale of the king of the Garamantes, who was rescued by his two hundred dogs after being captured by his enemies. The loyal animals escorted him home from exile and fought anyone who got in the way. There are several versions of the ancient legend about a man being murdered, with his dog as the only witness. The dog later recognizes its master's murderer in a crowd and points him out through barking and attacking him. The classical dogs were faithful as well as brave and sagacious. As an example of the affecting fondness of dogs for their masters, Plutarch told the story of the dog of Xanthippus, the father of Pericles. This faithful animal could not endure being abandoned by his master, but leapt into the sea and swam alongside his master's vessel. The exhausted dog staggered ashore on Salamis, but only to collapse and die; the tomb of this canine prodigy was long pointed out by the old Greeks.

Plutarch also spoke of a very skilful dancing dog exhibited before the Emperor Vespasian. After the performance, the dog feigned illness and pretended to die, only to revive at the proper time, as if waking from profound sleep. Aelian praised a pregnant hunting bitch, who gave birth to her nine puppies only after finishing her hunting duties; he recommended that the women of Liguria should follow the example of this noble animal, and rise up soon after giving birth and tend to their household duties without complaining. On a more whimsical note, Aesop's fables have the story of a dog crossing a river, carrying a piece of meat in its mouth. When looking down, it sees its own reflection in the water. Thinking the reflection is another dog with a bigger piece of meat, it drops the meat and jumps into the water to take the larger piece, ending up with no meat at all.

In contrast to these dog-loving old Greeks and Romans, early Christianity had little favourable to say about dogs; the majority of references to the canine tribe in the Bible are wholly uncomplimentary. In medieval times, the bestiaries were a valuable source of animal lore; they assimilated some of the wonderful dog stories from various classical authors, and raised the estimation of dogs among religious people. Medieval authors like Gerald of Wales and Gervase of Tilbury praised the fidelity of the dogs, and their usefulness not only as hunters, but as companion animals. Lords and knights kept hunting dogs, and their ladies lap-dogs. Most medieval monks and nuns also kept dogs as companion animals, a practice often sneered upon by visiting bishops, who complained about the cost of the animals' food. In their defence, these monks and nuns could quote the wonderful tale of Saint Roch, the patron saint of those suffering from the plague, who withdrew into the woods to die after contracting the pestilence himself. His faithful dog refused to abandon him and provided him with a loaf of bread daily.

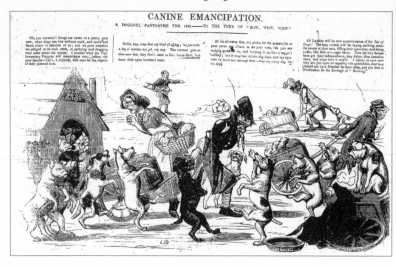

3. Canine Emancipation – a drawing from the *Penny Satirist*, 4 January 1840.

4. Dog Physiognomy.

The first dog book in English was written by the learned physician and naturalist John Caius, and translated into English in 1576 as *Of English Dogges*.[4] Caius gave a thorough overview of the breeds of hunting dogs available at the time: two species of greyhounds, bloodhounds, foxhounds, spaniels, setters, terriers, and even some kind of dachshund known as the Tumbler. There were also shepherd's dogs, butcher's dogs and watchdogs. Demoted as curs and mongrels were the lap-dogs, the dancing dogs 'which are taught and exercised to daunce in measure at the musicall sounde of an instrument', and the coarsest cur of all, the turnspit dogs running inside specially made dog-wheels to propel the roasting-spit in front of the fire.

The Italian Count Ulysses Aldrovandi, called the Pliny of his time, was one of the foremost polymaths of the Renaissance. In his 1645 treatise on dogs, the learned count showed off his knowledge of the curious canines of olden times. One of the problems he tackled was what a dog's bark sounded like in Greek: was it 'υλαο!' or 'βαυζω!', or perhaps rather 'βαυ-βαυ!' The Roman Theodorus possessed a very faithful dog; after he died, the dog lay down by his coffin after it had been put in the tomb. A certain Agnestis Corsus went hunting with his dog, but froze to death in a blizzard; the faithful dog remained by his corpse for three days. When an officer named Hecati was murdered in Antioch, his dog was the only witness; the sagacious canine later identified the murderer, and grasped him with its powerful jaws until he confessed. Hyrkanus, the dog of King Lysimachus, was so faithful that when the king's dead body was to be burnt on the pyre, the mourning dog howled and whined, before leaping headlong into the flames. Another excessively faithful dog, belonging to King Hiero of Syracuse, committed suicide in exactly the same manner. Aldrovandi also told the tale of the dog of the Roman Titus Sabinus, which accompanied its master into prison. After Titus had been executed, the dog tried to put food in the dead man's mouth. When his body was thrown into the Tiber, the faithful dog tried to hold up the corpse.[5]

Another quaint old dog book is Christian Franz Paullini's *Cynographia Curiosa* from 1685, a compilation of curious dog lore from innumerable ancient and contemporary sources. Standing out even among Paullini's manifold canine curiosities is the Egg-laying Dog of Vienna. A large mongrel cur, it laid many large eggs via the anus. After each of these strange births, it seemed weak and exhausted, but it soon recovered from its recent confinement and jumped around its master, who showed it as a curiosity. To impress the spectators, and to demonstrate that the eggs were genuine, the enterprising Austrian broke one of the dog's eggs, fried it in a pan, and ate it.[6]

None less than Carl Linnaeus made a contribution to canine lore in his 1753 dissertation *Cynographia*. He had read about an old Roman dog, owned by a prince, which had been trained to serve at table like a valet, carrying plates and saucers with the precision of a headwaiter. This dog could carry a full wine glass, balanced on a silver plate, to the prince without spilling a drop. The lower-class Romans also made good use of their sagacious dogs: the blind beggars had guide dogs leading them through the streets, and these dogs also collected food and money thrown to the beggars from the windows, and gathered the donations in a basket. Linnaeus knew a Stockholm burgher who suffered very badly from the gout. He bought a little dog, and felt much relief when it licked his aching feet. The gouty Swede recovered completely, but instead the dog got the gout and died! Not the least remarkable of Linnaeus's canine curiosities is that in Sweden, 'those who use socks knitted from dog's fur must cope with some inconvenience, since all the street dogs are unwilling to pass them by without cocking their leg at their feet!'[7]

The interest in dogs began to take off in the early nineteenth century. Prompted by the chapters on dogs in the natural history works of Buffon and Oliver Goldsmith, so did early scholarship with regard to canine history.[8] In France, A. F. J. de Fréville's *Histoire des Chiens Célèbres* had already appeared in 1796; it was followed by Charles de Ribelle's *Histoire des Animaux Célèbres* and Emile Richebourg's curious *Histoire des Chiens Célèbres*. In England, there was a considerable production of books of anecdotes about remarkable dogs: Thomas Brown's *Biographical Sketches and Anecdotes of Dogs*, Edward Jesse's *Anecdotes of Dogs*, and George Jesse's *Researches into the History of the British Dog*, to mention but a few.[9]

This book will resemble these whimsical old collections of anecdotes about celebrated dogs in that it will investigate some odd, curious and forgotten aspects of canine history. But in contrast to them, it will use modern science and recent scholarship to investigate some of the most amazing myths and baffling unsolved mysteries of the lost history of dogs.

In olden times, many people had a high opinion of the ability and intellect of the dog. The Learned English Dog, a border collie active in the 1750s, was very good at mathematics; there was even speculation that this extraordinary animal was a reincarnation of Pythagoras. Munito, the most famous performing dog in history, was a clever French poodle who toured all of Europe from 1817 until 1826 before coming to the United States in 1827. Are we to believe that he understood both French and Italian, excelled at spelling and calculus, and was a masterly player of dominoes?

5. The sad effect of an increase in the dog tax on the canine population of Paris.

6. 'The Sagacity of the Dog', a cartoon from the *Illustrated Police News*, 27 December 1884.

Even Munito was eclipsed by the super-intelligent Airedale terrier Rolf, who kept up a wide correspondence, wrote his autobiography and some poetry, and expressed a wish to join the German army in 1914 since he disliked the French. The antics of Rolf and his equally gifted daughter Lola were taken deadly seriously by a number of earnest German savants, but how are we to judge these extraordinary dogs today?

Rolf's near-contemporary, Don the Talking Dog, was the hero of the music halls of Berlin and Moscow. When Don went to perform at Hammerstein's music hall in New York, he was insured for $50,000, making him the most valuable dog in the world. Don proved a huge success in the United States: when the portly German pointer, who was said to know eight words and sometimes use them intelligently, asked for '*Kuchen!*' (cakes) in a guttural German voice, he received a standing ovation from the New Yorkers.

The history of acting dogs goes back much further than Lassie and Rin Tin Tin. The first canine to achieve great onstage fame was the Newfoundland Carlo, active in London from 1803 until 1811. He had plays specially written for him, involving tackling villains, liberating prisoners, and diving into an artificial lake on stage to save a drowning child. Dog drama, with canine performers playing major parts, remained extremely popular throughout Victorian times, on both sides of the Atlantic.

Whereas some of the hoary myths of canine ethnology have been forgotten, others still flourish, like curious tale of the dog saint, the greyhound Guinefort, who attacked a large wolf to protect his master's little son. When the master returned home, he found the blood-soaked dog, and killed it with his sword, believing it had bitten his son to death. But when he saw the dead wolf, he knew that Guinefort had been greatly wronged. As time went by, the martyred greyhound became a cult figure. Saint Guinefort was worshipped in France until the 1930s, in spite of efforts from the Catholic Church to suppress the cult.

In Edinburgh, everybody knows the history of the little Skye terrier Greyfriars Bobby who kept vigil at his deceased owner's grave for fourteen years. There is a statue of the faithful Bobby just outside Greyfriars kirkyard, which is one of Edinburgh's foremost tourist attractions; every summer, it is surrounded by tourists, some of whom weep profusely when they hear Bobby's pathetic story. But how much of it is truth, and how much is make-believe?

Who today knows about the dogs collecting for charity in Victorian and Edwardian times, with metal boxes strapped to their backs? In London, there were such dogs at every major railway station. The 'collecting dogs' were extraordinarily popular, and their doings were headline stuff in the newspapers. These weird canine mendicants were often stuffed after death to keep collecting for their charities. Equally forgotten are the Victorian 'travelling dogs' like the mongrel Owney, who covered more than 143,000 miles on the endless American railways, and once travelled round the world in 132 days. Owney was shot dead by a Toledo patrolman under somewhat mysterious circumstances; his stuffed remains are today at the National Postal Museum in Washington, D.C.

In the late eighteenth century, Newfoundland dogs were both fashionable and expensive. Lord Byron of course wanted one of these dogs, and named him Boatswain. Literary historians have marvelled that Byron, who treated the women in his life so very caddishly, was remarkably fond of his Newfoundland dog. When Byron wanted to give Boatswain some exercise, he pretended to fall out of his boat, to have his dog tow him safely back to land. At this time, the Newfoundlands were considered the most admirable of all dogs, due to their spectacular intelligence, strength, and great swimming ability. There are many remarkable anecdotes of these dogs rescuing people from drowning, performing heroics at shipwrecks, or showing other instances of extreme sagacity and altruism, but how credible are they when re-examined with a critical eye?

In the eighteenth century, cruel blood sports of every description flourished. Most forms of baiting were outlawed by the Cruelty to Animals Act of 1835, but one animal could not count on any sympathy: the rat. In purpose-built rat-pits, sackfuls of rats were killed by fierce terriers. Disregarding the pungent smell of the large sewer rats, the raucous audience made bets on how many rats the dog would kill inside a minute. The champion terrier Billy killed a hundred rats in five and a half minutes in 1823, a record which stood until 1863, when it was beaten by Jacko, another champion rat-killer. There were rat-pits not only in London and the provinces, but also in the United States. New Yorkers were particularly fond of this gory, low-class form of entertainment.

There are many instances of ghosts of dogs: 'Black Vaughan's Dog' in Herefordshire and the 'Black Dogge of Newgate' being only two examples. The Cimetière des Chiens in Asnières just north of Paris is also said to be haunted: it is probably the finest zoological necropolis in the world, constructed in 1899. The major proportion of the animals buried there are dogs, although cats, horses, a lion and a fish also feature. Along with the monument to Barry the life-saving St Bernard, Rin Tin Tin the acting dog is the most famous inmate. It is little-known even among the Londoners that Hyde Park also has a dog cemetery, since it has been closed for many years. Perhaps it, too, is haunted, since there have been reports of strange spectral dogs taking nocturnal walks in Hyde Park.

7. 'Dog Fashions for 1889' – a cartoon from *Punch*.

8. A patriotic French sanity dog shows its disdain for Germans – a propaganda postcard from the Great War.

2

THE GREAT MUNITO & THE LEARNED ENGLISH DOG

Through great Spadille, or that famed Prince of Loo
All conqu'ring Pam, turn backward from his view, –
Swift in the noble chase, 'Munito' tracks
The Royal guests and Plebeian packs;
And though the cards in mixed confusion lie,
And mock the vigour of a human eye,
'Munito' still, with more than human art,
Knows Kings from Knaves, the Diamond from the Heart.

Winthrop Mackworth Praed, 'Munito',
from *A Poem on Dogs*.

Performing dogs were nothing new to the Londoners; in fact, acrobatic or dancing dogs had been a staple item at the old fairs and markets since medieval times. In his *Bartholomew Fayre*, first acted in 1614, Ben Jonson mentions 'dogges that dance the morrice'. It took much longer for any performing dog with intellectual pretensions to appear in London. According to the *Country Journal* of 13 September 1729, there was a dog in France that could spell words with cardboard letters. The newspaper writer hoped this learned dog would become a prominent member of the Paris academy of sciences, and that the French people would now cease calling 'one another *Dogs* or *Sons of Bitches* by Way of Reproach'. It was not long before this learned dog, a medium-sized bitch looking rather like a collie, made her debut in London. She was named Charmant, and owned by the Paris showman M. Radau. Apart from spelling words and answering questions with her cardboard letters, Charmant was also very adept at playing cards. According to a newspaper cutting in Lysons' *Collectana*, 'One night this week the famous French Dog, who plays at cards with surprizing dexterity, and performs many wonderful tricks, beat Dr. Arbuthnot, one of her Majesty's Physicians, 2 games of quadrille before the junior Duchess of Marlborough, and many other great personages. *Ibid. – For the Honour of the Sex, it was a* French Bitch.'[1]

In December 1750, another *Chien Savant*, or Learned French Dog, crossed the English Channel and took up residence at the Two Blue Balls tavern, in the Haymarket. A small bitch of indeterminable race, she spelt out words in French using cardboard letters, solved arithmetical problems, read a watch, and distinguished colours.[2] In January 1751, 'M. Peter le Moin, the Proprietor of the Chien Savant', informed the Nobility and Gentry that the Learned French Dog's prodigious intellect had already allowed it to learn the basics of the English language. He soon had to find a larger exhibition-room, 'at Mr Hally's Watch-maker, facing the Canon Tavern, Charing-Cross'. In late January, it was announced that 'several Noble Persons have made the Proprietor very handsome Presents'. In early February, the Prince and Princess of Wales went to see 'the famous French Dog'.

Visitors to the dog show were given a pamphlet entitled *The Exercises of the Chien Savant; or, Learn'd French Dog*.[3] 'This entertaining and sagacious Animal' still communicated by ranging typographical cards with figures or letters on them, answering questions in Geography, Roman, French, English and Sacred History, and in Ovid's *Metamorphoses*. The dog could also read a watch, count the number of spectators present (if not more than thirty), and match the colour of the dress of any lady with its own set of coloured cards. The French Dog knew the names of all the Heathen Gods, and those of the Muses as well as their particular areas of expertise. The Dog also knew good English, M. le Moin explained, and when asked the capital of England, it could spell either 'L-O-N-D-R-E-S' or 'L-O-N-D-O-N'.

In his advertisements, M. le Moin always reminded the public that since his Sagacious Animal's stay in London would be very short, they should make haste to come and see this canine prodigy without delay. But since so many Londoners paid two shillings and sixpence to see the dog perform, he showed no urgency to return to his native land. Throughout May, June and July, the French Dog kept entertaining the Londoners. Once, when a journalist asked M. le Moin to direct the dog in English instead, the monoglot Frenchman, who apparently did not share his dog's propensity to learn foreign languages, shook his head and gave him a contemptuous look. The *Chien Savant* herself also seemed offended, since she snatched a newspaper from the journalist's pocket and tore it to pieces.

But when the French Dog set out to tour the provinces in late 1751, a usurper appeared: it was the New *Chien Savant*, or Learned English Dog, depicted on a print as looking rather like a border collie in size and colouring, and spelling the word 'Pythagoras' with its cardboard letters. Apart from the obvious arguments of patriotism, the English Dog's master ceaselessly pointed out his charge's superiority over the French Dog: the New *Chien Savant* knew the Greek alphabet, answered questions in Roman, English and Sacred History, and performed various acrobatic tricks.[4]

The Learned English Dog also published his autobiography, *History of the Most Amazing and Sagacious English Dog*.[5] If this fanciful account is to be believed, the dog's life certainly had its ups and downs. As a puppy, he had been purchased by a noble lady, becoming her favourite lap-dog. But unfortunately, as the dog expressed it, 'my

9. The New *Chien Savant*, or Learned English Dog – an engraving from 1752.

Parent had not been quite so curious in her Choice of an Helpmate: I soon discovered Marks of a Mungrel Breed, and shewed evident Promises of an unfashionable Size and Shape. In fine, I was expelled from the soft velvet Cushion of the Drawing-Room, and sent down to the hard Mattrass of the Servants Hall.' Here, the unlucky dog had to work ceaselessly, running in a dog-wheel to propel the turning of the spit for roast meat.

When the English Dog became too big to run inside the dog-wheel, he was given to a coachman. After being stolen by the notorious Bampfylde More Carew, the King of the Beggars, he was given to a travelling mountebank. From him, the English Dog learned some simple tricks, like playing dead. Poverty, and the risk of going to prison, drove the mountebank to seek refuge in France. Here, they met the *Chien Savant* and saw one of her performances. When an English showman noted that the English Dog could not only copy the French Dog's tricks, but actually improve on them, 'he was in Raptures to meet a Dog of his own Country, that might, at the same Time I brought Profit to himself, do Honour to the Nation'. After describing how they had driven their competitor from the Metropolis, the English Dog confidently states that he would easily convince the Londoners 'that the Most Amazing and Sagacious *English* Dog, far exceeds the Famous *French* Chien Savant'.

The French Dog made an attempt at comeback in 1752, but failed miserably and had to return to France with her tail between her legs. M. le Moin more than once threatened to return to London, with an even more sagacious dog and a troupe of learned birds and flying squirrels, but there is no record of him ever doing so. The English Dog now reigned supreme. In his showroom in Half-Moon Court, near Ludgate, this clever border collie entertained noblemen, ambassadors and various foreign magnates. His repertoire was very similar to that of the French Dog, except that he also did 'several bodily

Exercises, as a Posture-Master or Tumbler', answered questions in the Greek alphabet and in Ovid's *Metamorphoses*, and read people's thoughts. When Henry Fielding heard that the Learned English Dog was learning Greek, he commented that this was not at all surprising, since the Greek language had long since gone to the dogs.

In 1753, the Learned English Dog toured Stafford, Shrewsbury, Hereford, Monmouth and Gloucester, during the assizes at these places, before returning to London. One of the English Dog's 1754 advertisements told that the sagacious animal had been given a silver collar by a lady, for correctly predicting the time she would get married. There was also a poem praising the dog:

> Did souls through various bodies pass
> This dog might be Pythagoras;
> But since they no such Changes know,
> (For we're assur'd they do not so)
> What can we call this Learned Brute?
> A *Nonpareil* – without Dispute.

The last we know of the Learned English Dog is that it was performing at the Bull Inn, Cirencester, in early 1755.[6] This clever border collie had no successor and it would take long before any other performing dog had similar success in Britain, or in France.

In March 1817, the animal entertainment world of Paris was shook by a sensation like never before: Munito the Wonderful Dog had arrived. Hailing from Milan, and managed by the Italian showman Signor Castelli, Munito took up residence near the entrance of the Cour des Fontaines. The Wonderful Dog had complete knowledge of the alphabet and figures, played dominoes in the most expert manner, and possessed other qualifications beyond the reach of most of his human contemporaries. In the evenings, Signor Castelli was always available if some wealthy gentleman wanted to entertain his guests with a private dog-show, to enliven an evening party. At these fashionable gatherings, both dog and master were at their best behaviour: Signor Castelli knew that if they did well, several guineas would change hands, and the Wonderful Dog knew that after the show, the ladies would like to pet him and feed him various delicacies. Munito was a pretty, affectionate dog, in size rather resembling a large poodle, but with shorter fur and a less pointed muzzle.

Later, Munito performed at the Cabinet d'Illusions near the Palais Royal. According to an early exhibition pamphlet kept at the Bibliothèque Nationale in Paris, the Wonderful Dog was visited by many scholars and journalists, and was the subject of conversation in many salons. It was hoped that seeing Munito perform would stimulate the ambition of the indolent children of Paris; it would injure their *amour propre*, it was hoped, to be outclassed in spelling and mathematics by a *dog*! The Parisians were particularly fascinated by Munito's skills at dominoes. They bet bonbons or cakes in their games against the Wonderful Dog; a nobleman bet five *Louis d'or* instead and lost them all.

10. A very early drawing of Munito, from his first 1817 London poster.

According to a pamphlet sold at the exhibition, Munito was twenty-two months old and of a lively and caressing disposition. His father was a hound, his mother a water spaniel, but he resembled his mother most and was the size of a common water spaniel, rather tall and thin. His short, curly fur was all white except for a brown spot over the left eye. Signor Castelli d'Orino, as the dog-trainer now styled himself, claimed to be an Italian gentleman who had devoted his life to the art of training animals. He recognised young Munito's matchless intellect at an early age, and educated him for thirteen months at an isolated country retreat in a village not far from Milan. The dog was always taught with mildness, and never struck or spoken to angrily. The education was concluded when Munito was fifteen months old, at which time the pair set out on their travels through Italy and France. 'Munito' was (and is) not a commonly used name for a dog; it means 'well-endowed' in Italian, so probably Signor Castelli wanted to suggest that his dog was well endowed with intelligence.

Apart from his other superlative qualities, Munito was also very brave, the pamphlet claimed. Near Trier, Signor Castelli had lost all his luggage when the villainous carriage-driver had left them stranded. But after a while, Munito came running with a boot in his mouth, to make Castelli understand that he had found the thief. When the villain was tracked down inside a forest, Munito attacked him, seized him by the throat and forced him to confess in front of the local mayor. This tall tale leaves unexplained how the Wonderful Dog could have brought the mayor into the forest, or alternatively how he could have frog-marched the thief into the mayor's residence. A more sinister note is introduced by the claim that Munito had once performed an act of justice, by killing a large turkey-cock that had just pecked out the eye of a child. Coming too late to rescue the child, the Wonderful Dog had vented his rage on the wretched bird, tearing it to pieces.[7]

Munito knows both French and Italian equally well, the pamphlet goes on to claim. He can play at cards and knows their colours and value. One of his tricks is to pick out a certain card from the pack, after it had been chosen by some person and the pack shuffled by others. The Wonderful Dog knows addition, subtraction, division and multiplication 'which many men will never learn, and which Munito performs with an astonishing quickness'. He can spell using cards with the letters of the alphabet on them, 'not being endowed with the gift of speech'. The Wonderful Dog also knows the art of palmistry: after gazing intently at some person's hand, he describes their character using his cards with letters on them.

In late May 1817, there was a series of advertisements in the London newspapers that cannot have pleased the exhibitors of 'learned pigs' and other performing animals, since they announced that a formidable competitor had set foot, or rather paw, in the Metropolis:

> THE CELEBRATED DOG MUNITO
>
> Signor Castelli having just arrived from Paris, begs leave to inform the Nobility and Gentry, that he intends to EXHIBIT the EXTRAORDINARY FEATS of his WONDERFUL DOG MUNITO at Saville-House, Leicester-Square; who will play at cards, write, and cast accounts with the most astounding accuracy.

MUNITO,

OR

THE LEARNED DOG.

To be seen every Day at Mr. LAXTON's Room,

No. 23, NEW BOND STREET,

AT THE HOURS OF THREE AND SEVEN PRECISELY.

THIS WONDERFUL DOG understands the Alphabet, can read, copy Words, and cast Accounts. He knows all the playing Cards, and will select out of a Pack the Cards which any of the Spectators may be pleased to ask for. He plays at Dominos: is acquainted with the Principles of Botany and Geography: and exhibits many other astonishing Performances.

☞ *Admittance One Shilling.*

11. A handbill advertising Munito later in his 1817 sojourn in London. Note the different drawing of the dog.

Munito was an instant success with the Londoners, although the shows, set at two and four on all weekday afternoons, cost as much as three shillings. Later in 1817, Signor Castelli had to rent a larger exhibition room, at No. 23 New Bond Street, since their old accommodation in Leicester Square had proved far too small for the throng of people wanting to see Munito perform. In an exhibition poster, Castelli could boast that both the Prince Regent and the Duke of York, and a great number of the Nobility, had already beheld the Wonderful Dog with astonishment, and the most unbounded applause.[8]

Himself, Signor Castelli was something of a man of mystery. He was about fifty or sixty years old, shabbily dressed in foreign garb, and entirely unable to speak English. During the dog-shows, he gabbled away in Italian and bad French, languages he claimed that Munito knew perfectly. He was kind and attentive to his star performer, however, often taking Munito for a walk in the London streets. When they were strolling in Green Park, more than one passer-by remarked on the swarthy foreigner in his old-fashioned clothes, talking volubly to his pretty white dog, as though the two could really understand each other. We do not even know Castelli's first name, and this has led to speculation that he was identical to a showman of the same name who performed with his dogs at Sadler's Wells in London as early as 1783, and later at Smock Alley in Dublin in 1784. Other circus historians have suspected, quite possibly with some right, that he was identical to a conjurer named Castelli who had performed quite widely in Italy, France and Germany since the late 1790s.

In September 1817, another exhibition poster announced that Munito was still performing in London, at three and seven every day. The Wonderful Dog was not too old to learn a few new tricks: in addition to spelling, counting and playing cards, he was now acquainted with the principles of botany and geography. An illustration shows that Castelli had chosen to cut his dog's woolly fur into a rather primitive version of the lion-clip. The same illustration was used as the frontispiece of the *Historicall Account of the Life and Talents of the Learned Dog Munito*, published at about the same time and sold at the New Bond Street exhibition-room.

On 2 October 1818, Signor Castelli was taking a walk round Green Park with his dog at nine in the morning. He could see a little girl screaming nearby, but due to his deficient grasp of English, he did not understand what she was saying. But he saw that the girl was pointing towards the pond, where he could see a woman's body floating. The Italian acted with commendable resolution. Taking off his coat, he leapt into the pond and seized hold of the woman. But far from welcoming his intervention, the woman fought back fiercely. Castelli feared that they would both drown, but the faithful Munito saved the day, plunging into the pond and distracting the woman enough for Castelli to drag her onto dry land. She turned out to be quite deranged and intent on destroying herself; the little girl, her cousin, had followed her to try to make her return home.

Signor Castelli was awarded the Royal Humane Society's honorary medallion for his daring rescue. The Wonderful Dog also received a medal, as well as some useful publicity: a newspaper article in Lysons' *Collectanea* admires his sagacity and bravery, concluding that 'Munito continues to be one of the principal fashionable amusements.

The doors of the Exhibition Room are daily thronged with the carriages of the Nobility and Gentry who go to view his extraordinary performances.'

Munito remained in London until April 1819, when he went to Dublin, performing twice a day at the Shakespeare Gallery in Exchequer Street. He came back to London in June, before once more taking up residence in Paris. Just like back in 1817, he became excessively popular, and was called 'Le Newton de la race canine'. Munito performed at the Boulevard du Temple, at the Cirque Olympique, and at the Jardin des Princes, near the Palais-Royal. In aristocratic saloons, he was petted by Marquises and Princesses. According to the dog historian Emile Richebourg, Munito's master made a fortune during the three years the Wonderful Dog was based in Paris. Once, at the Jardin des Princes, Castelli wanted to walk his dog home, but the spoilt Munito growled and showed his teeth. The kind and patient master went to search for '*un cabriolet*' to accommodate his canine superstar.[9]

In 1820, the Wonderful Dog made an extended tour of France. New editions of the exhibition pamphlet were printed in Paris, Nantes, Toulouse, Strasbourg and Lyons, as

MUNITO,   *At HOME!*

SIGNOR CASTELLI

Has the Honor most respectfully to inform the Nobility, Gentry, and the Public, that his justly celebrated

DOG, MUNITO,

Having been ABROAD for some time to finish his Education, is now

AT HOME,

At No. 1, Leicester Square,

Where he exhibits, Daily, every Hour, from Twelve *till* Five,

His wonderful and surprising Knowledge, which last Year so greatly entertained all those who honoured his Performance with their presence.

MUNITO, besides his former accomplishments, will astonish the Public with his vast Knowledge in the Sciences *of*

GEOGRAPHY, BOTANY, and NATURAL HISTORY,

which he has acquired since he last had the honor of performing before them.

MUNITO is the same Dog who last Year obtained a MEDAL from the

HUMANE SOCIETY,

For having SAVED THE LIFE of a LADY in the most EXTRAORDINARY MANNER!

Admittance, One Shilling.

☞ Signor CASTELLI will attend with MUNITO in the Evening at the Houses of the Nobility and Gentry, as formerly.

12. Munito's 1819 London advertisement poster, boasting of his success at the Humane Society.

well as a Dutch translation published when Munito went to Utrecht in late 1820.[10] In 1821 and 1822, Munito toured Germany, visiting Munich, Berlin and Augsburg among other places, before returning to Strasbourg in October 1822. In early 1824, he was performing in Mannheim before going to the Hague. But for several years thereafter, there are no records of the Wonderful Dog.

In early 1827, Munito resurfaced in Paris after several years away from the limelight. He was advertised as the same celebrated dog that had appeared all over Europe for more than ten years. But an engraving in the series *Le Bon Genre* shows a startling development. Munito is no longer the rather large, muscular dog that had been performing in Paris and London ten years earlier, but a small poodle! Clearly Signor Castelli had trained another dog to take the place of the original performer. It would have been embarrassing for him if some sarcastic Frenchman had come up to him and pointed out that his dog must be wonderful indeed to have shrunk in size in such a remarkable manner since his previous visit to Paris. But there is no record of any such untoward incident; in fact, the French nation once more took Munito to their hearts.

As a schoolboy, a certain Eugène Muller, who would later describe the show in his book *Les Animaux Célèbres*, was taken to see Munito by his mother. Many years later, he could still well remember the beautiful white poodle in its elegant lion clip. On his own writing table with a green cover, Munito performed multiplication with the greatest skill, and told the time with his cards with numbers on them after having looked at a watch. He chose among twenty objects to find the one a certain spectator had named, before skilfully opening a wooden box with his teeth, having first turned the key. Then it was time for some acrobatic tricks, and a musical interlude where Munito kept time on a small drum using his paw, before the gallant Signor Castelli gave his dog a bouquet and invited him to bring it to a blonde lady in the audience. Madame Muller played a game of écarté against the Wonderful Dog, losing miserably to the delight of the rest of the audience.

In 1827, Munito toured Germany, before coming to St Petersburg later in the year. The Finnish nobleman C. G. Mannerheim saw one of the shows and wrote to a friend in Helsinki:

This animal's highly trained instincts cannot be admired enough. All what I had read about it in the newspapers came true. What astounded me most was to see it perform multiplication of large numbers, always remembering what figure to carry over for the next calculation. It knows all the cards in a deck of playing-cards, and the spectators can order it to pick any particular card out. The dog never once failed to retrieve the correct one.

Mannerheim was fortunate enough to meet Munito and his master Signor Castelli when they took a walk around the block like any other dog-owner, and was impressed how kind the Italian was to his dog, and how well Munito was taken care of.

Munito then toured Russia and Poland, before going to Austria. An exhibition poster for his visit to Vienna, dated 1 December 1828, boasts that the celebrated Munito had been praised by many kings and emperors all over Europe. The dog's accomplishments included addition, subtraction, multiplication, playing dominoes and knowing the playing-cards. The illustration again shows Munito as a much smaller dog than the one performing in London a decade earlier.

In April 1830, Munito came to Stockholm, Sweden, where the success story continued. In his *Gamla Stockholm*, August Strindberg wrote that 'a poodle-dog named Munito was very much noted for his great cleverness and unsurpassed skill in performing'. His exhibition rooms were at the Tawern Inn in the Djurgården; the shows were on at five and seven each evening, and were quite expensive, costing about two shillings. An article in the *Stockholms-Posten* newspaper provides further details:

> The dog Munito, who in just a few years has become so very famous, not just in Europe, but even in America, seems to deserve his great reputation, unlike many of the popular artists of this time, whether two- or four-footed. He is a beautiful white poodle of the smaller race. When he is not performing, he sits in a serious and pensive position …

The newspaper writer was impressed how fond the poodle was of his master: Munito seemed to enjoy the show, particularly the treats he was given after each trick was

13. Munito II in Vienna in 1828. Note the size of the dog.

concluded. Munito's young son, just fifteen months old, was watching the performance with great attention.[11]

The allegation that Munito had been to the United States is quite astounding, and does not occur elsewhere. There is a note in Ricky Jay's *Journal of Anomalies*, however, that a dog named Minetto performed at Peale's Museum in New York in May 1827. This would render it at least possible that the Wonderful Dog really crossed the Atlantic, although it should be kept in mind that several copycat learned dogs were active at the time. For example, the conjurer Mr Hoare had got a learned dog of his own, which he had the cheek to call Monetto!

During his sojourn in Sweden, Munito was taken ill. The people of Stockholm were worried that he might expire, but the poodle recovered and again performed throughout June and July. As an added bonus, the 'Son of Munito, another poodle-dog', also took part in the shows. Was Signor Castelli grooming a successor already, in case he would once more lose his star performer? The dog-trainer's alleged military background was becoming increasingly colourful: he now claimed to be Captain Castelli d'Orino, a highly decorated war hero, who had fought in the Sardinian army in the battles of Marengo and Wagram. This was something that, if it was at all true, Castelli had kept very quiet about when he was in London in 1817 and 1818.

Munito remained in Stockholm for several months, before touring the provinces. When Munito left the capital, the Stockholm actors gave a communal sigh of relief, since the other theatres had earned very little money while the famous dog was in town. A poster for one of Munito's country shows tells us that

> Many of the newspapers of Europe have unanimously lauded this Dog's rare and uncommon propensities, and expressed their admiration at the skill and cleverness with which Munito, also known as the LEARNED DOG carries out his tricks.
>
> The unprecedented feats of this Dog have secured him many accolades in Paris, London and Petersburg, among other capitals he has visited.
>
> The Tutor of this Wonderful Dog hopes that the Swedish people will give Munito the same encouragement and applause he has enjoyed elsewhere. This Dog understands the Italian and French languages, knows all colours, plays at Dominoes, can add, subtract, and multiply, can tell flowers apart, can perform the most remarkable acrobatic tricks; in other words, the only thing he fails to do, is to speak.

In September 1830, Munito performed in Helsinki. When taking his dog for a walk, Castelli met another spectator, Captain Charles Colville Frankland. In his *Narrative of a Visit to Courts of Russia and Sweden*, this gentleman described his visit to see the conjurer and his learned dog. Castelli was a funny old fellow, Frankland wrote, ugly and unfashionably dressed. His extensive travels all over Europe had not improved his linguistic skills: he still spoke only Italian and bad French.

When interviewed in the newspaper *Helsingfors Tidningar*, Captain Castelli told some yarns about his military career and his contribution to the battles of Marengo and

Wagram: 'the wandering Veteran is still hearty and in good cheer, and seems very fond of his present-day occupation, which entails little risk or exertions, but provides him with much wealth and fame.' One of the Helsinki dog shows was described in the same newspaper. Castelli had waxed lyrical about his dog's superior intelligence, claiming that Munito had crossed the border between animal instinct and human intellect, but the sceptical journalist was not quite disposed to agree. It was quite possible, he wrote, that Castelli directed his dog with minute movements of his hands and feet, or by certain cue words and signs; nor could it be ruled out that the cards used in the dog show had been smeared with some substance.

In late 1831, Munito was back in Paris, where he stayed for some considerable time, making occasional excursions to the provinces. In 1833, the dog show was described in a magazine article, illustrated with two amusing drawings, one of a bespectacled Munito spelling with his cards, another of a waistcoat-clad Munito playing dominoes with his master. A trade card for the Bordeaux firm Chocolats-Louit also depicts Munito wearing a red waistcoat, performing before a surprisingly youthful-looking trainer. There was also a fine china plate depicting Munito sitting at a desk, playing dominoes against his master.[12]

It is not known exactly in which year Munito held his farewell performance in Paris, nor whether Signor Castelli allowed his dog to enjoy a few years of retirement at the end of his career. The reason for this is the profusion of performing dogs at this time. It is recorded by Peter Bräuning, in his *Circus und autverwandte Künste*, that in 1830, when the original Munito was in Scandinavia, a certain 'Munito du Nord' had the cheek to perform at Munito's old exhibition room at Boulevard du Temple in Paris. At the same time, 'The Two Clever Dogs, Fido and Munito', were active in Mainz. In his *Anecdotes of Dogs*, Edward Jesse described Fido and Bianco, two poodles trained in Italy, performing in Paris in 1830. They spelt words with cardboard letters, read the striking of a lady's watch, and played écarté with each other. Fido was a steady, serious dog, but Bianco was giddy and frolicsome, sometimes pulling his companion's ears to make him come and play. The same year, the spaniel Don Carlos, known as the Double Sighted Dog, performed at the Brighton Pavilion. King William IV and other members of the royal

14. Munito playing dominoes, from the children's book *Memoires d'un Caniche*.

family applauded him heartily when he indicated first the loveliest lady in the theatre, and then the gentleman most partial to the ladies.

An obscure 1836 pamphlet entitled *Notice sur les chiens Munito* may well provide some further clues about the later career of the Wonderful Dog.[13] This pamphlet advertises two performing poodles, Munito and Young Munito, who were under the management of a certain M. Nief. These two dogs were dressed in red waistcoats and performed tricks that were exactly similar to those of Castelli's Munito, even down to the playing of dominoes. M. Nief had been a dog-trainer for many years, the pamphlet claimed. Old Munito, his first dog, had been born in Valencia in 1813 and had made his debut in 1817. They had visited many countries, always with success. The Princess Marianne had given Old Munito a silver collar and chain; the King of Westphalia had presented him with a silver cup and soup-bowl. This elderly dog was now retired and living in Caen, being provided with a pension of 45 francs a month by the generous M. Nief. The current Munito was just as successful. The Queen of Spain had given him a pair of spectacles, which he sometimes wore during the shows. Munito was now nine years old and his son just two; an illustration depicts them both as poodles. Some months previously, they had performed before the King, Queen, Prince and Princesses of France, to their entire satisfaction.

It is of course possible that Nief's dogs were yet another set of imitators, but many details in the pamphlet agree with what is known about the original Munitos. The Bertachon pamphlet has induced some French circus historians to speculate that M. Nief was in fact the same person as Signor Castelli, having posed as an Italian to make himself seem more interesting. But the available information about Munito's early career clearly describes Castelli as an Italian, who could speak French only with difficulty. It would seem more likely that after touring with the three Munitos for more than fourteen years, the elderly Signor Castelli retired in 1831 or 1832 and sold his dogs to the young and enterprising M. Nief, who of course took the credit for having trained the animals himself.

So, what happened to Munito in the end? Did the Wonderful Dog breathe his last in France, in England, or perhaps back in Russia? It would appear as though the second, or perhaps rather third, of that famous name, came into the hands of the Italian actor and acrobat Signor Dalle Case, whose ideas for touring the world appear to have been expansive indeed, as judged by the following advertisement from the *Courier*, the local newspaper of Hobart Town, Tasmania:

> The celebrated Dog Munito, after exciting the surprise and admiration of Europe and America, by his superior intelligence and sagacity, will exhibit for the first time before a Hobart Town audience, his incredible powers.

Munito was the star performer of the troupe, which also included two clowns, the tightrope dancers Anna and Emilia, M. Larosiere the Man Tortoise, and Signor Dalle Case himself as acrobat and strongman. The Royal Victoria Theatre was entirely crowded at the premiere on 18 November 1842. The tightrope dancers were not very good, the clowns not particularly funny, and Signor Dalle Case fell down hard during one of his acrobatic tricks and had to be carried out on a stretcher. But Munito was a sensation. The dapper-looking white poodle fetched any national flag selected by a member of the audience, displayed and waved it. Copies of a list of 350 words, in the English, French, Portuguese, Spanish, Italian, German, Latin and Greek languages were distributed among the audience; the dog spelt and translated them without fault when called upon. Then it was time for some dominoes: again Munito was so proficient that the newspapers later announced that the dog stood open to a match against any person who might take up the gauntlet.

For the second performance in Hobart Town, on 16 January 1843, the multi-cultural troupe had been reinforced with two funny Frenchmen walking on stilts, and some Brazilian musicians. Munito remained the star of the show, however. The last we hear about the Wonderful Dog, or at least his latest reincarnation, is that in March 1847, Signor Dalle Case had just returned to Mauritius, having completed a tour of the whole eastern part of the globe. He was accompanied, as always, by his tame orang-utan Gertrude and the extraordinary dog Munito.[14]

Over the years, there has been a considerable debate about what breed of dog Munito belonged to. In several books on poodles, he is claimed as one of the most famous representatives of this breed ever. But we now know that there were actually not less than three Munitos. The first of these was quite a large dog, capable of tackling a robber and tearing to pieces a turkey-cock. There is no reason to disbelieve the statement in the 1817 exhibition pamphlet that he was the offspring of a hound father and a water spaniel mother, particularly as he was said to have resembled his mother most. The two breeds of water spaniels existing at the time were the Irish water spaniel and the European (or Portuguese) water dog. They were both quite poodle-like, although with shorter fur, generally coarser build, and less elegant head than today's poodles. The early drawings of Munito agree well with this description. Moreover, the primitive 'lion clip' boasted by Munito on the more elegant 1817 drawing agrees perfectly with the most commonly used trim for a European water dog at the time.

The career of Munito the water spaniel cross seems to have begun in early 1816, touring Italy and France. He went on performing until 1824, but after that year there are no further records of him. It has to be suspected that the ten-year-old dog expired at this time, and that Castelli had to train a successor. Munito the poodle appeared in 1827 and was still going strong at least until 1831. Whether the bespectacled, waistcoat-clad Munito performing in Paris in the mid-1830s was the same dog is not known with certainty, but from the Bertachon pamphlet, a moderately solid case can be made that the second Munito and his son continued their show business career under their youthful-looking new master M. Nief. Whether the Munito performing in Tasmania and elsewhere was in any way related to Nief's dogs is anybody's guess, but due to the similarity of their acts, it is at least possible to have been the case.

There were two good reasons for the nineteenth-century dog trainers to choose poodles as their performers. Firstly, canine psychologists have pointed out that certain breeds of dogs are cleverer than others. In their various investigations, the poodle and the border collie are consistent top performers, whereas the bulldog and the Afghan hound occupy the opposite end of the scale. The poodle is a natural performer, easy to teach, and keen to show off his tricks. Whereas young poodles are giddy and scatter-brained, older poodles have impressive powers of concentration and attention, something that would have come in handy for Signor Castelli. Even so, it is amazing that he could make the dog perform three times a day without Munito getting bored with the whole thing. His strategy was probably to vary each performance, introduce new tricks with regular intervals, and to make sure Munito was always rewarded with some little treat after each successful trick. Secondly, poodles were very fashionable dogs at the time: expensive, elegant and sought after. Such a dog would draw more spectators than a common sheepdog that could be seen in every farmyard. The border collie has had its revenge, however, and is today a frequent and successful competitor in the agility and obedience events at various dog shows.

Having solved the mystery of the three Munitos, it is now time to address another problem, namely how the dog was trained. Here we are provided with some inside information by none less than Charles Dickens.[15] Munito was a very handsome dog, with a fine silky white woolly coat, half-shaved. During the show, Munito answered questions with his cards, some of which had letters, others figures. He could also pick out the card named – say the Queen of Clubs – when the pack was spread on the floor in a circle. Dickens noted that when Munito walked round the circle of cards, he had his nose down. He did not pick the card out as his eyes met it, but walked back and picked out, indicating that he was guided by smell rather than sight. When Signor Castelli walked past young Dickens, his waistcoat had an aniseed smell, leading Dickens to suspect that he put his thumb in his waistcoat pocket, impregnated with aniseed oil, and pressed it on the particular card Munito was supposed to pick out. Dickens waited until the performance was over and went up to speak to Castelli, who did not deny the discovery of his trickery.

Charles Dickens' discovery would certainly explain some of Munito's tricks, but hardly all of them. As suspected by the Finnish journalist in 1830, certain cue words or secret signs must have been used to make the dog deliver a bouquet of flowers to the right person, or to play dominoes. Other tricks used the dog's natural talent for acrobatics, and its propensity to learn to perform a sequence of events, like unlocking a box and opening its lid.[16] An unanswered question is exactly in which year Dickens saw Munito. We have to remember that he was born in 1812, and thus just seven years old when the first Munito left London for good. It is scarcely credible that a child of that age, however precocious, would be able to see through a quite accomplished performance that took in many adults. It is possible that the second Munito made a return to London sometime in the late 1820s, to be seen by the teenage Dickens. After all, he described the dog as a pretty French poodle rather than a water spaniel cross. Another alternative is that Dickens received the information about Munito from some other individual who had seen the dog in 1818 or 1819.

Charles Dickens is not the only of Munito's 'literary kin'. The obscure poem by Winthrop Mackworth Praed that was used as an epigraph to this chapter compares Munito's ability to pick out the correct cards to that of a social climber preferring royal guests to the plebeian pack. In *My Novel*, Edward Bulwer Lytton made a joke about 'the dullest dog that ever wrote a novel', adding that 'we have a good many dogs among the fraternity that are not Munitos'. In his novel *A Captain at Fifteen*, Jules Verne also alluded to the Wonderful Dog. Verne was just about old enough to have seen Munito perform in the 1830s. He gave a good description of one of the shows, with an explanation of his own: Munito's master snapped a toothpick in his pocket to make the poodle stop and pick up the correct card. The Norwegian novelist Henrik Wergeland may well also have seen Munito perform in 1830, since his play *Harlequin Virtuos*, published the same year, contains some references to 'the Divine Poodle Munito' that was clever enough to aspire to an university degree. Another unexpected reference to Munito appears in one of the early letters of Franz Liszt, where the future composer bemoans his precarious position as a virtuoso pianist, dependent on the plaudits of the fickle public just like a conjuror, or the learned dog Munito. In a similar vein, Russian author Alexander Pushkin complained that after he had become famous, people came to see him as if he had been Munito the Wonderful Dog.

The remainder of the nineteenth century saw performing dogs aplenty. The eccentric Finn Carl-Axel Gottlund, who had seen Munito perform, aspired to train his poodle Saukko to become the equal of the Wonderful Dog. After several years of education, Saukko could play cards, run errands dressed like a footman, carry the breadbasket round the dinner table, and climb trees like a woodpecker. If Saukko saw that Gottlund had fallen asleep in his chair after a drinking session, the clever dog put his paw into a jug of water and extinguished the candle, to prevent the room catching fire.

The Stockholm merchant Johan Hedman wanted to buy Saukko to exhibit him for money, but Gottlund was not at all disposed to sell his dog. Yet Hedman stole Saukko and put him on board a ship destined for Finland, where an accomplice was ready to become Saukko's manager. When Gottlund found out about the intrigue, he began a lengthy lawsuit against Hedman. In court, the eccentric Finn claimed that since Saukko had more sense and knowledge than all the dogs of Sweden together, he was also worth more than all of them. A Swedish paper had once written that Munito was an investment equal to 100,000 riksdaler in state bonds, and yet he was a moron compared with Saukko. In the end, Gottlund won his case, although the compensation for the loss of the dog was a mere 500 riksdaler.[17]

The dancing poodle Pollux was a favourite in the 1840s, competing with Herr Quincke's Dog Orchestra and Monsieur Leonard's dominoes-playing dogs Philax and Brac. In the 1860s, the poodle Bianca could translate and write in nineteen languages, and the Berlin showman Ferdinand Reinke's famous dog Lelie was said to possess the intellect of an eight-year-old schoolboy. In the 1870s, the Austrian Frans Patek toured widely with his three performing dogs. They had different specialties: Schnapsl could tell the value of coins, and play cards, and Diana could tell colours and do calculus. The little mongrel Frieda could play 'God Save the Queen' on the piano and sing parts from Italian operas.[18]

In the 1890s, a poodle known as the Inimitable Dick became a major star in the Paris music hall. Dressed in fantastic garb, Dick waltzed on his hind legs, with powerful lighting effects illuminating his dress, and a bellows operating from underneath to make it billow out around his tiny body. At the same time, Mr Lavater's Dog Orchestra were performing in London. They were a lower class of performers than the elegant Dick: six scruffy-looking mongrel dogs playing the big drum, little drum, cymbals, violin, bass and trombone, accompanying the dapper Mr Lavater playing 'The Girl I Left Behind Me' and other popular tunes. When interviewed in the *Strand Magazine* of 1897, Lavater revealed a down-to-earth attitude to his trade: the reason he employed mongrel curs was of course that they were cheap and easily replaceable. The first drummer had to be gotten rid of because of his pugnacious disposition, his successor ran amok on board a ferry from Rotterdam to Antwerp, and the trombonist was sacked for his deplorable habit of stage-diving into the audience.

The American crossbreed Chris, active in the 1950s, could count and spell, and also showed amazing talents of telepathy, convincing some gullible American

15. The German dogs Schnapsl, Frieda and Diana performing in Finland in 1874.

16. A poster for the Inimitable Dick, from Pierre Hachet-Souplet's *Die Dressur der Tiere.*

parapsychologists of the reality of extrasensory perception. Chris could also predict the future: after he helped a neighbour pick the winner in two consecutive horse races, his owners had to lock the dog up to protect him from enthusiastic betting men. When a spiritualist medium asked Chris what kind of being he was, perhaps a reincarnated human genius or some ghostly spiritual creature, the modest crossbreed replied 'Just a smart dog!' Among Chris's predictions was the date of his own death, on 10 June 1962, but he actually died the day before.

Chris's psychic powers have been eclipsed by another strange canine performer, Oscar the Hypnodog. During the 1990s, this talented Labrador toured the United Kingdom and Europe with considerable success. His owner and manager, the conjurer and hypnotist Hugh Lennon, noted the fixed, dominant stare from his dog's large eyes and decided to use Oscar in his own shows. Oscar seldom failed to put members of the audience to sleep and was a particular favourite at the Cardiff Students' Union, where a pile of unconscious bodies on the floor marked his success. In 1994, Oscar disappeared when performing in Edinburgh, and a reward was posted for his return. Members of the public were warned not to look into his eyes, to avoid getting hypnotised. But a brave Scot found Oscar, avoided his hypnotic gaze, and collected a cash reward from a dog food manufacturer, as well as a keg of beer from the pub where Oscar was performing at the time. Sadly, Oscar has since died of old age, but Murphy the Hypnodog has succeeded him, under the same management.

17. Les Toutous – a French postcard from 1902.

3

SOME CANINE INTELLECTUALS

One of the leading German intellectuals of the early 1900s was Rolf, a resident of Mannheim. With his superior intelligence, he successfully dabbled in mathematics, ethics, religion and philosophy. He speculated about the *Urseele*, the original soul of God, and his stipulation that every animal should be defined as a part of this abstract concept attracted much notice from other German philosophers. An avid reader and a talented poet, Rolf kept up a large correspondence with kindred spirits all over Europe.

In her biography of Rolf, his friend and secretary Frau Paula Moekel heaped praise on his character: the great thinker was generous, unselfish and compassionate, although his life had not been devoid of sorrows. Rolf had married a giddy and thoughtless young wife, who was not his intellectual equal, mastering only basic calculus and entirely lacking interest in philosophy. These differences did not prevent them from having ten children, but several of them died young due to various calamities. After his young son Roland had been run over by an automobile, Rolf swore revenge against the careless motorist; whether he succeeded in tracking down the driver is unfortunately not recorded. Rolf did not lack violent tendencies: one of his favourite pastimes, albeit frowned upon by the squeamish Frau Moekel, was hunting rats. Once, when having a dispute with another intellectual, Rolf lost his temper and seriously injured his opponent in a fight.

After the outbreak of the Great War, Rolf declared that the war was legitimate, since in his opinion, the French had invaded sacred German soil. He was so incensed by this outrage that he volunteered to join the army, to have a go at the Frogs himself, but Frau Moekel managed to dissuade him. As the war went on, the great thinker gradually changed his mind: he expressed pacifist, and even proto-feminist, opinions, declaring that if women had been left in charge, Europe's great nations would never have gone to war. After Rolf's death, from pneumonia in 1919, his autobiography and a selection from his letters were published posthumously.

Rolf's life's work has not stood the test of time as well as that of his contemporaries Thomas Mann and Hermann Hesse. Still, his accomplishments were far from negligible, particularly since Rolf *was a dog*, an Airedale terrier to be precise. To explain the extraordinary career of this educated dog, we need to go back a few years in time, to investigate the background of the fierce debate about animal intelligence at this time.

The catalyst of the rise of Germany's super-intelligent animals was Wilhelm von Osten, a retired schoolmaster residing in Berlin. He had some stables in his back yard, and was keen to study the horses, since he believed that these animals possessed superior intelligence. Already in 1890, von Osten started training a horse named Hans to count by tapping his hoof. The progress was exceedingly slow, however; when Hans expired in 1905, he could only count to five. But von Osten did not give up. He was a believer in phrenology, a pseudo-science stipulating that the character of a person, or an animal, could be predicted by feeling the 'bumps' on the individual's skull. After examining many horses with this method, von Osten found his ideal pupil, renamed him Hans, and took him back to the stable yard.

Hans II proved much more talented than his predecessor. He quickly learned arithmetics, even square and cubic roots. Using a system of giving each of the letters of the alphabet a certain number, Hans learnt to spell words; thus he could answer questions, tell the date and the value of coins, and recognize people from photographs.[1] In 1904, von Osten made an appeal to Kaiser Wilhelm to appoint an imperial commission to investigate his super-intelligent horse, but showing good judgment that he seldom made use of otherwise, Kaiser Bill wanted nothing to do with the old schoolmaster and his horse. The reason may well have been that von Osten was a well-known Berlin eccentric, who dressed in old-fashioned

18. Wilhelm von Osten and Clever Hans, from Karl Krall's *Denkende Tiere*.

garb and grew his long white hair and beard in the manner attributed to Father Christmas. He owned a large house, but lived in just two tiny rooms. Some Berliners thought him sane, and even gifted; others disagreed on both these points.

But Wilhelm von Osten did not give up. He put advertisements in the newspapers that he would hold free public performances with his horse. Surprisingly many people were convinced by 'Kluge Hans' (Clever Hans): both scholars and laymen believed that the horse really possessed a superior intellect. The horse spelt long words correctly and solved complicated mathematical problems. Clever Hans nodded his muzzle to indicate 'yes' and shook his head for 'no'. Having finished counting out numbers by right-hoofed tappings, he gave a single, emphatic tap with his left. Refusing to exhibit his horse for money, or join a circus, von Osten instead craved official recognition for Clever Hans. A commission of thirteen zoologists, psychologists and military men was appointed to investigate this extraordinary horse.

One of them, Professor Carl Stumpf, brought along his amanuensis Oskar Pfungst, who had a low opinion of the intelligence of animals. Moreover, he was wholly unimpressed with the bushy-bearded buffoon parading his horse in front of the commission. When he saw Clever Hans perform, Pfungst noticed that the horse was closely watching the person asking the questions, whether it was von Osten himself, or someone else. He was clever enough to make the correct deduction: the horse was looking for an unconscious sign from his human partner. When Pfungst challenged the horse with some mathematical problems, Hans gave the right answer five out of five times when von Osten knew the answer, but none out of five when this was not the case. Moreover, Pfungst noticed that Hans over-tapped in all five instances, as if he had been waiting for some hidden cue that was not forthcoming. In a later, more ambitious series of experiments, Hans tapped out the right answer in 89 per cent of questions when he could see the experimenter, but only 6 per cent when he was blinkered.

Oskar Pfungst made his fortune out of the debunking of Clever Hans, writing a book about the case that was later translated into English; the 'Clever Hans effect' is still a term regularly used for unconscious cues from the person conducting an experiment.[2] The reaction of the scientific establishment seems to have been something along the lines of 'Ah, that is what we suspected all along'. Poor von Osten was disgraced, and became an object of ridicule. But the old schoolmaster still had one friend, the wealthy merchant and jeweller Karl Krall. After having seen Clever Hans perform, Krall became convinced that the horse possessed near-human intelligence. Not even sixty animal psychologists writing books debunking this wonderful horse would have changed his mind. Krall was what in Germany is known as a *Besserwisser*; he *always knew best*, and when his mind was made up about some topic, he *simply knew he was right*. Krall lacked an academic education, and his knowledge of psychology and zoology left much to be desired; these shortcomings did not deter the bold German in the slightest, however, as he set out to rewrite the history of biology. Krall visited the pathetic von Osten, who was blaming not Pfungst, but the horse, for his downfall. He bitterly accused Hans of deliberately deceiving him, and wanted to export the horse to America, for use in the Chicago sausage factories.

But Krall managed to change von Osten's mind. He would carry on the work, he promised, and show the world that the old schoolmaster had been right all along. Krall took over Clever Hans, purchased four more horses, and set up a research establishment of his own in Elberfeld. The Arab stallions Muhammed and Zarif were soon extracting cubic roots, the pony Hänschen spelt and counted, and even a blind horse named Berto made some progress in calculus. Wilhelm von Osten died in 1909, cursing the faithless Clever Hans with his dying breath, and hoping that the remainder of the deceitful horse's life would be spent pulling hearses. The ambitious Krall was now the leader. He began to criticize von Osten, claiming that the old man had used to beat Hans with a whip, and that the stables had been very dirty and unkempt. Hans had often bit Pfungst, and sometimes Krall himself, but after moving to Elberfeld, the super-intelligent horse's character had improved very much.

In his 1912 book *Denkende Tiere* (*Thinking Animals*), Krall openly challenged the scientific establishment.[3] Krall now knew from his own experience that horses and other higher animals were well-nigh as intelligent as human beings, possessing not only consciousness but also a soul. Thus he had disproved, to his own satisfaction at least, the Catholic dogma that there was a fundamental difference between the intellects of humans and animals, since the animals lacked a soul. Krall's 'Neue Tierpsychologie' (New animal psychology) was widely debated at the time. A favourable reviewer lauded Krall as a second Darwin, whose great work would raise dogs and horses from serfdom; an adversary called his book 'a foul and shameful blot on German literature'. Catholics of course found Krall's work particularly blasphemous and distasteful. Still,

19. Karl Krall teaches his horse Zarif, from Karl Krall's *Denkende Tiere*.

Krall soon gathered quite a following among kindred spirits in Germany; many of them were controversial characters, linked with organized quackery, spiritualism, and the antivivisection movement. In Britain and the United States, where his teachings were widely derided by the academics, he found few allies, and only a smattering of enthusiasts in Switzerland, France and Italy. At an international zoological conference in Monaco in 1913, the rationalists declared that they had heard enough about educated horses tapping out messages. Twenty leading European zoologists signed an official protest against Krall and his activities. As a result, 'Animal psychology' and 'New animal psychology' parted company, for good. The wealthy Krall formed his own scientific society, and published his own journal, entitled *Tierseele* (*Animal Soul*).

To bolster his wild theories, Krall was always on the lookout for other super-intelligent animals. Frau Paula Moekel, the invalid wife of a wealthy Mannheim solicitor, provided him with valuable support.[4] In 1911, she had obtained a young Airedale terrier named Rolf from the local animal shelter, and this talented dog had actually surpassed the Elberfeld horses. It had all started, or so at least Frau Moekel claimed, when she was trying to teach one of her daughters simple arithmetic. Since the little girl was quite

20. An amusing German caricature of Krall and his horses.

ineducable, Frau Moekel called Rolf over, telling her daughter that she was sure even Rolf could tell what 2 + 2 was. The dog sauntered up and struck her hand four times with his paw!

Frau Moekel tried other mathematical problems, only to find that Rolf was equally proficient in addition, subtraction, multiplication and division. She realized that by simply watching the Moekel children's lessons in mathematics, this amazing dog had learnt much more than them! The next thing was to teach him to spell. Frau Moekel let Rolf develop his own alphabet, by speaking out the letters and allowing the dog to assign them a certain number of taps with his paw. It is weird, and certainly indicative of a superior intellect, that the less common letters of the alphabet were the ones demanding the highest number of taps; either Rolf or someone else seems to have been concerned that it should not take him all day to tap out his messages. There were abbreviations for 'Yes', 'No', 'Piddle', 'Tired', 'Bed' and other words Rolf thought he might find useful.

Once he had his alphabet, there was no stopping Rolf. His vocabulary steadily increased, he learnt grammar, and he formulated sentences. He learnt to read, and to answer questions. When asked to express his feelings about cats, Rolf tapped out 'Lol imr hd dsorn wn sid kdsl frleigt son wgn graln'. To translate this abracadabra into proper

21. Rolf, from Paula Moekel's *Mein Hund Rolf.*

German would have taxed Thomas Mann himself, but fortunately, Frau Moekel knew the ways of her dog. Firstly, he referred to himself as 'Lol'; secondly, he used 'phonetic' spelling, tapping out the words as they sounded when spoken; thirdly, he sometimes left words out; fourthly, he often used words from the local Pfalz dialect. What the super-intelligent dog meant was of course '*Rolf immer hat Zorn wenn [er] sicht Katzel, vielleicht wegen [der] Krallen*' (Rolf is always angry when he sees cats, perhaps because of the claws). In fact, the only member of the feline tribe Rolf could abide was Frau Moekel's little cat Daisy, with whom he had grown up. The reader will not be surprised that Daisy was a super-intelligent cat, albeit only capable of doing simple sums, and tapping out a word or two when she felt like it.

One of the first scientists to investigate Rolf was Dr William McKenzie, a psychologist active in Genua. When he gave his *carte de visite* to Rolf to read, the dog impressed him by tapping out 'Magnzi' and 'Gnua'. When asked what he liked best, Rolf replied 'Laks sn' – of course meaning '*Lachs essen*' (To eat salmon). His second favourite occupation was reading illustrated books. Showing not only amazing intelligence, but also colour vision superior to what scientists today attribute to dogs, he correctly identified some multi-coloured geometrical shapes. He preferred women to men, because he liked their long hair and elegant gowns. Autumn he defined as 'time when there are apples' and a crocodile was an 'odd beast'. Finally, Dr McKenzie tried to trick Rolf, by asking him which was the heaviest, a pound of lead or a pound of feathers; after thinking hard, the educated dog replied '*Gein!*' (Neither!)

Rolf had a mind of his own. Once, when he had been stubborn during his exercises, Frau Moekel called him a *Dummkopf* (fool). 'You are one too, Mother!' the dog was quick

22. Rolf speaking to Frau Moekel.

to retort. Another time, when Frau Moekel had been sitting up late at night writing letters, he angrily tapped out, 'Go to bed! Rolf wants the room to be dark!' He refused to do any schoolwork on Sundays, perhaps from reverence towards the Almighty, Frau Moekel speculated. Another time, he tapped out 'When Christ-child comes, horses shall have trees!', but it is not known whether Frau Moekel obeyed him and put Christmas trees in the stables for the horses to admire. Like a proper Airedale terrier, Rolf liked hunting rats, sometimes even digging them out of their holes and lairs in the Moekels' large garden. Frau Moekel very much disapproved of these activities. She reminded Rolf of his own speculation that every animal, even a rat, was a part of the *Urseele*, but the dog did not listen to her.

Rolf usually liked to have visitors, but sometimes, he could be more than a match for them. The educated dog did not like to be put on show, and when a journalist once asked him to extract some cubic roots, Rolf replied 'Tell him to extract them himself.' When informed that his visitor had come all the way from Berlin, the haughty dog dismissed him with the words 'Then let him go back to Berlin!' Nor did Rolf appreciate a visit from a noble lady, Frau von Schweigenbarth; he was disrespectful throughout their conversation, even likening her to a jackass. To the noblewoman's astonishment, the headstrong dog insisted on asking her questions rather than the other way around. When asked what 5 + 9 was, she first answered '13' and the dog tapped out 'Wrong!' She next gave the correct answer, but the dog again tapped out 'Wrong!' Both Frau Moekel and the visitor were flabbergasted, but Rolf tapped out 'I was only teasing you!' When Frau von Schweigenbarth asked Rolf if there was anything else the dog would like her to do, the witty Airedale terrier responded 'Could you wag your tail?'

Already in 1913, Rolf had some imitators. When one of them, a little dog capable of tapping out messages and doing sums, came to visit the great Rolf, Frau Moekel waited with bated breath to see what they would say to each other. But when the visiting dog instead decided to chase the little cat Daisy, the angry Rolf bit him hard; the two canine intellectuals had to be forcibly separated by Frau Moekel and her daughter. When the visiting dog's owner came to fetch him, the wounded little dog ran up to her and tapped out 'Mummy, Rolf bit me!' It took some time before Frau Moekel and her friend were on speaking terms after this outrage.

Frau Moekel had several children, all of whom were very fond of Rolf. Sometimes, the super-intelligent dog was kind enough to help them with their schoolwork, particularly mathematics, an area where he excelled. He also liked to tell the children stories, or test them with riddles, like this one:

ROLF: Why does the cow say 'Muh!'?
CHILDREN: Rolf, perhaps because she is hungry?
ROLF: Very silly!
CHILDREN: Well, why then?
ROLF: Because she knows nothing else!

After Frau Moekel had decided that Rolf should have a family of his own, she purchased a young Airedale terrier bitch named Jela. At first, Rolf was delighted to have a wife, although he sometimes seemed to be ashamed of the foolish Jela, who was unable to progress beyond simple calculus. Once, when she failed to give an answer to 'What is 5 + 6?', he struck her on the back eleven times with his paw, to prompt her to give the correct answer. The chasm between the couple's intellects did not prevent Nature from taking its course, and soon Rolf was the proud father of ten healthy puppies. Jela was not a good mother, however: several of the puppies died in various calamities, and Rolf blamed his wife for not taking care of them properly.

One of Krall's lieutenants in the 'New animal psychology' movement was Professor H. E. Ziegler, of the University of Stuttgart. After conducting tests with Rolf, he became entirely convinced that the dog possessed a superior intellect. At Christmas, he wanted to find out whether Rolf's excessive learning had impaired his natural instincts. He put a large rat into a box, wrapped it in festive packaging, and gave it to Rolf as a present. As soon as the box was unwrapped, the rat darted out, to the alarm of the Moekel females. Rolf took a huge leap into the air and expertly killed the rat. Professor Ziegler was very much impressed, but Frau Moekel and her daughters were equally indignant; it had been very wrong of him, the squeamish ladies reasoned, to make the educated dog wantonly take the life of another living creature.

At the outbreak of the Great War, Rolf demanded to be allowed to join the army. Although an Airedale terrier by birth, he disowned the Yorkshire roots of his forefathers, instead considering himself a very patriotic German dog. Since Rolf detested the French for having invaded his beloved *Vaterland*, he wanted to fight them at the frontline. It took all of Frau Moekel's tact and persistence to moderate the militarist zeal of her educated dog. When the Moekel children sang '*Die Wacht am Rhein*' to Rolf, the dog seemed wistful of military glory: to don his field-grey uniform and spiked little helmet, and sink his fangs into the buttocks of one of the dastardly Frogs. After the German newspapers had announced the fall of Antwerp in late 1914, the Moekel family was elated: the children marched round the house singing '*Deutschland, Deutschland über alles*', and Rolf followed them, barking and showing his teeth like if he fancied himself to have contributed to this great victory himself. The canine strategist then excitedly ran up to Frau Moekel and tapped out 'And now for Paris!'[5]

But as the war went on, Germany suffered some crushing defeats, prompting Rolf to change his mind. He still wanted to join the army, but only to become a rescue dog, to help wounded soldiers in the battlefield. In late 1915, Rolf's attitude to the war changed once more; he deplored the immense loss of life on the battlefields of Europe and wished that women had ruled the great powers instead of men. He urged Frau Moekel to become a peace negotiator between France and Germany, but this did not happen, since the learned lady herself expired in November 1915. She had made sure that Rolf was taken care of, by her eldest daughter Fräulein Luise Moekel, a talented violinist. Throughout the wartime years, Rolf was regularly visited by professional or amateur animal psychologists; most of them departed convinced that the dog could really communicate with them. Rolf survived Frau Moekel nearly four years, before expiring from double-sided pneumonia in late 1919.[6]

In his posthumously published memoirs, Rolf told some dramatic stories from his early life. His first master, a gardener named Facius, had been unable to control the boisterous Rolf, and he had been given away to a dog's home in Mannheim. It was here the kind Frau Moekel had found him. But one day, when her young son Fritz had taken Rolf for a walk, the dog was stolen by a thief and resold to a sinister-looking man. But when this individual was going to take Rolf to Frankfurt on a train, the clever dog bit through the lead and escaped, but only to be run over by an automobile. Despite his injuries, Rolf was able to run home to Facius, his first owner, who had him transported back to Frau Moekel. The vet who came to see Rolf, unaware that the dog could understand his every word, exclaimed 'He must be killed at once!' But Frau Moekel ignored this bad advice and nursed Rolf back to health; the rest of the story we know.

The second part of Rolf's autobiography is given over to a selection of his letters. Throughout his lifetime, the dog had kept up a large correspondence with people all over Europe. A schoolboy, who complained that his arithmetics were not up to the standards demonstrated by the super-intelligent dog, was invited to come to Mannheim for personal tuition. Another youngster, who complained that his dog Pick was entirely unable to replicate Rolf's achievements, and that the other family dog, a dachshund, was ill, received the reply: 'Greetings! Pick should be sent here, for study! Also dachshund, fetch doctor! Greetings, Rolf.' A boy who sent the educated dog some tit-bits in a parcel got the reply: 'Thanks for the biscuits! Now send a larger parcel!'

Rolf's favourite correspondent was Karl Krall himself. When he sent Rolf an illustrated pamphlet about vivisection, the dog responded with a passionate appeal against these evil practices. Some of the other letters are equally bizarre. It is not a little weird that a number of earnest, serious German professors, schoolmasters and clergymen wrote letters to a dog, asking for his political opinions or his views on the conduct of the war, and enclosing polite greetings to Rolf's wife and children. Gerda Jacobi, a Swedish doctor active in London, wrote Rolf a lengthy letter, enclosing an illustrated children's book and a photograph of a little dog with a bandaged broken leg. Since Rolf was very pleased that Gerda Jacobi had cured the London dog, he invited her to come to Mannheim, to treat the equally lame Frau Moekel. Rolf added that through perusing the picture-book, he was already learning some English.[7]

The Moekels had made sure that Rolf's surviving 'children' were all provided with good homes. His daughter Ilse had been given to a kind, dog-loving clergyman, who was delighted when she began to show signs of her father's intellect, doing sums and tapping out simple messages. She could be quite stubborn and headstrong, however, having inherited her mother's giddy character, and also very untruthful. Once, when returning from a country walk, she declared that she had seen a deer with green wings and a snail with four legs!

Henny Kindermann was another kind, dog-loving German lady. Being impressed with Krall's 'New animal psychology', she was of course very keen to obtain one of Rolf's puppies. The Moekels decided that Rolf should see and judge her for himself, to determine if she was good enough to take care of his daughter Lola. At first, the great canine intellectual was severe with her, declaring that too much learning would not be good for his little daughter, but Henny Kindermann told Rolf that she lived on a country estate, where Lola could go for walks and develop her intellect by studying the plant and animal life.

After deliberating for a while, Rolf gave his consent to Henny Kindermann adopting Lola. Demonstrating an intellect equal to that of her father, the young Airedale terrier soon learnt calculus, and tapped out words using an alphabet of her own construction. She learnt English, composed letters, and keenly studied music – not to play the piano herself like the performing dog Frieda, but to tell the chords. She was also very good at predicting the weather.

Lola's philosophical lucubrations were not as far-reaching as those of her father, but they still deserve notice. When asked who she liked most of all people and animals, the egotistical dog replied 'Myself!', although she pleased Henny Kindermann by allowing her to come second in her affections. The body was food for worms, Lola declared, and the soul went to heaven. Humans, dogs and horses had souls, she pontificated; stones and water did not.

Unfortunately, Lola had inherited some of her mother's flighty character. One day, she came home 'in a state of great depression', as Henny Kindermann expressed it, and tapped out 'My honour is gone!' Fräulein Kindermann understood that she must have enjoyed a short affair with a farmyard dog, who had basely seduced and then left her. She tried to console poor Lola, saying that her broken heart would recover with time, but the pathetic dog responded 'Only when I die!'[8]

23. Lola, daughter of Rolf, from Henny Kindermann's *Lola, or the Thought and Speech of Animals*.

But Lola recovered from this tragedy and again began to enjoy life. In time, she 'married' another pedigree Airedale terrier and had several 'children'. When asked to name one of her sons, Lola did not tap out any message, but instead gave a sharp yap; the sympathetic Henny Kindermann at once understood that she wanted the little puppy to be named 'Awa'! This particular son of Lola was given to the aforementioned Professor Ziegler, and under his expert tuition, Rolf's grandchild developed into yet another super-intelligent dog.

In the 1920s, Germany had a numerous brood of 'New animal psychologists'. The hardcore faction, led by Karl Krall himself, believed that dogs and horses were nearly as intelligent as human beings; they were capable of abstract thinking, and understanding of religion. Only want of tuition barred these animals from communicating with their owners and developing their minds. For obvious reasons, Krall and his adherents were anti-vivisectionists and proponents of animal welfare; surely it was a crime that cried out to heaven for vengeance, to mistreat or torture a creature of near-human capacity. With time, Krall's own notions became even odder: in his large research institute outside Munich, he sought to prove that telepathy was possible, not only between human beings, but also between human and dog. A hilarious photograph shows a white-coated person trying his best to communicate with a poodle, with two sinister coves surveying the proceedings through some weird-looking instruments.

Some of the 'New animal psychologists', like the aforementioned Ziegler and McKenzie, distanced themselves from some of the more sensational elements of Krall's creed. McKenzie is said to have groaned 'Too much! Too much!' when Frau Moekel informed him that Rolf had started writing poetry, and to have reacted in a similar manner when Henny Kindermann told him about Lola's claim to possess an immortal soul.

There were many fewer 'New animal psychologists' in the remainder of continental Europe. The Belgian writer and Nobel laureate Maurice Maeterlinck was fascinated by the idea of human–animal communication, and wrote some enthusiastic early articles about Krall and his horses. Professor Edouard Claparède, of the University of Geneva, was another supporter, albeit unconvinced by the more spectacular of Krall's notions. Krall's most useful French supporter was the spiritualist Madame Carita Borderieux, editor of *Physica* magazine. After a visit to Germany, to meet Krall and other enthusiasts, she trained two little dogs to communicate by touching her hand. In England, the Swedish-born controversialist Lizzy Lind-af-Hageby was one of the very few 'New animal psychologists'. She was quite a fanatic, taking every lugubrious utterance from the dogs very seriously indeed.

Karl Krall's death in 1928 was serious blow to the 'New animal psychologists'. Not only had he been their leading light, but his deep pockets had financed both their society and their journal. But the members clubbed together to keep the journal going, although its quality suffered badly; it contained many depressingly similar accounts of educated dogs trying their best to emulate the great Rolf.

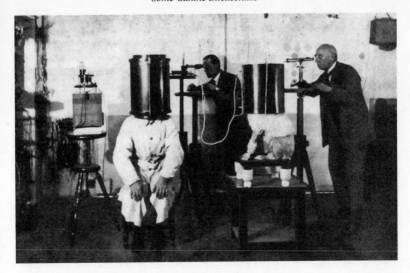

24. Karl Krall experiments with telepathy between dog and human.

25. Madame Carita Borderieux having a conversation with her little dog, from her book *Almost Human*.

Another, more serious threat to the movement came a few years later. Surely, the brutal Nazi regime would put an end to this 'New animal psychology' nonsense, for good? Perhaps they would build a special concentration camp for the educated dogs and their dotty owners, where the unfortunate animals could tap out pathetic messages like 'These fetters are really uncomfortable' and 'Will they never feed us in this place?'

But the Nazis, who had such conspicuous disregard for human rights, felt more strongly about the animals. In their murky philosophy, a key concept was *Ganzheit von Leib und Seele*, roughly meaning that there was a strong bond between the human being, nature, and society. Thus, the good Nazi was a friend of animals. In 1933, strict legislation against animal abuse was introduced, and there was much interest in animal welfare. The journal of the German animal defence league – the *Reichtierschützblatt* – had some amazing illustrations, one of them depicting Adolf Hitler patting a horse on the nose, with the caption 'Our Führer, the ideal animal friend.'[9]

Another key concept in National Socialism was of course the race theory, some principles of which had been adopted from the pre-Darwinian concept of the Great Chain of Being, but with the Aryan German at the top. Then came the other Aryans, then the rest of the European whites, and so on, until we got to the *Untermenschen*: Jews, Negroes and Gypsies. For the 1930s thinkers pondering these murky principles, it was an appealing idea that educated dogs and non-human primates would bridge the gap between the higher animals and the *Untermenschen*. As a result, 'New animal psychology' flourished throughout the 1930s; there were new recruits from both leading academics and Nazi officials.

Nor was there any shortage of educated dogs in the Third Reich. In 1937, the London anti-vivisectionist Lizzy Lind-af-Hageby travelled to Germany to research a lecture on 'New animal psychology'. In Weimar, she and her friend the Duchess of Hamilton visited the super-intelligent fox-terrier Lumpi. When the dog's rustic owner, who had little knowledge of how to address a duchess, pointed at the noble lady and asked 'What has auntie on her blouse', Lumpi tapped out 'A carnation!' When asked what the Duchess had on her head, the fashion-conscious dog replied 'A smart hat!' Lumpi was quite critical of his more plebeian visitors, once asking a journalist to clean his dirty collar, if he were to be fit to address the educated dog. Another newspaper man, who tried to trick Lumpi into making a mistake, got the sneering reply 'I hate doubting people!' The enthusiastic zoologist Ludwig Plate declared that Lumpi could understand spoken German, read simple sentences, and answer questions by tapping just like Rolf, but more sceptical scientists disagreed.[10]

The dachshund Kurwenal, another resident of Weimar, was even more remarkable. Prompted by his owner, the Baroness von Freytag-Loringhoven, he spoke by barking, using an alphabet going forward from A to L, and backward from Z to M. Thus, 'A' and 'Z' were one bark, whereas 'L' and 'M' were twelve; at the end of each letter, one or two barks signified whether Kurwenal had started from 'A' or from 'Z'. Kurwenal could read, and he had considerable knowledge of literature. When Miss Lind-af-Hageby asked him who had written 'To be or not to be …' the dachshund replied 'Shakespeare!'

According to his biographer Otto Wulf, Kurwenal had been taught since the age of six months, and presented with his barking alphabet on his second birthday. The opinionated little dog liked pink roses and pretty ladies, and had fantasies about eating large cheeses and big fat cats. He preferred Goethe to Schiller, but also liked reading illustrated zoology books. When asked whether he wanted to become the father of little dachshund-babies one day, his answer was an emphatic 'No!' Kurwenal wanted to vote for *Reichspräsident* Hindenburg, whom he found very honourable; regrettably, the little dog's biographer did not record Kurwenal's his opinion of *Reichskanzler* Hitler. On Kurwenal's birthday, he was visited by a troop of twenty-eight uniformed youngsters from the Nazi animal protection organization. When the *Tierschütz-führer* started reading a long congratulatory poem to Kurwenal, the little dog stopped him after a few stanzas, barking out 'No more poetry!' To prevent further unpleasantness after this angry rebuff, a kind doctor presented Kurwenal with a large teddy bear as a birthday present, saying 'Now, does this bear not look very nice?' Looking into the bear's grinning face, the ungrateful little dog replied 'No, he looks horrible!'

In 1935, Kurwenal had been investigated by Ludwig Plate, who had earlier praised Krall and his horses. Plate was very impressed with Kurwenal's intellect, boldly proclaiming that the dachshund could read, count and spell. Plate was opposed by the physiologist Otto Renner, who believed that the dog was receiving conscious or unconscious cues from its mistress. In an acrimonious debate, Plate was backed by Munich zoologist Max Müller, whereas Renner had support from several other scientists.

Unlike Rolf and Lola, who had both been quite attractive dogs, Kurwenal was not a pretty sight. A very fat little dachshund, reddish yellow in colour, he barked incessantly (a single word could require eighty-five barks!) in a hoarse, coughing voice. As he waddled around, greedily eating the tit-bits the Baroness kept rewarding him with, he himself looked very much like a thick German sausage, provided with four very short legs. In addition, Ludwig Plate, who certainly made some very queer deductions for someone supposed to be a distinguished zoologist, asserted that Kurwenal's private parts had atrophied due to his high level of mental activity! The Baroness herself was also severely challenged in the looks department, according to an article in *Time* magazine, which described her as 'a motherly woman who looks something like Napoleon, with wisps of hair on her broad forehead, squinting eyes, and a huge nose'.

But still, Kurwenal cracked jokes like a proper comedian. He described himself as 'intentionally witty' and was delighted when the audience laughed at his wisecracks. Once, when Max Müller and the Baroness discussed the possibility of making sausages out of dog meat, as a measure of wartime economy, the 'sausage dog' felt inclined to object that 'the Christian religion prohibits killing!' To the wife of Ludwig Plate, he sighed: 'I do love you so.' Frau Plate responded: 'Oh! Don't try to make me believe that.' Kurwenal: 'I always speak the truth.' When a professor of theology asked the dog which religious persuasion he belonged to, Kurwenal politely replied 'The same one as yourself, Sir.' When a sceptical Swiss researcher tried to trick the dog, Kurwenal barked out 'I answer no doubters! Go bother the asses instead!' Shortly before his death, in late 1937, Kurwenal barked, 'I am not afraid of dying; dogs have souls and they are like the souls of men.' The little dog was buried in the garden of the Weimar town house owned by the Baroness; although the house has been converted to offices, Kurwenal's gravestone can still be seen there.[11]

There were some very strange experiments going on in wartime Germany, with regard to dog–human communication. The sinister Professor Max Müller, who had supported Lumpi and Kurwenal, remained active throughout the war. It is clear from his writings that he was a wholehearted supporter of the Nazi natural philosophy and race biology. Another animal psychologist, Werner Fischel, was provided with dogs for his communication experiments by the staff of the *Reichsführer-SS*. In 1943, a certain Frau Schmitt was featured in an article written by Max Müller for a Nazi magazine. She was the headmistress of Tier-sprachschule ASRA, a school that was supposed to teach large, muscular German mastiffs to communicate with humans. Müller claimed that some of them had already said a few words.[12] At a Nazi study course, a talking dog was once asked 'Who is Adolf Hitler?' and replied '*Mein Führer!*' Why, in a Germany where all money went towards the war effort, could such bizarre projects go ahead, if not supported by the Nazi regime? According to Müller, representatives of the *Wehrmacht* had received directions from the *Führer* to satisfy themselves concerning the usefulness of these educated dogs in the field. Were the Nazis trying to develop a breed of super-intelligent canine stormtroopers, capable of communicating with their human masters of the *Herrenvolk*?

After the great cataclysm of 1945, some of Germany's great cities had well-nigh been reduced to rubble. The 'New animal psychology' movement was in a similar state of disarray. In 1954, Henny Kindermann tried to rally the faithful by publishing her second book on educated animals. Its title translates as *Can Animals Think? Yes, They Can!* As an appendix, she published a list of 102 educated animals: the earliest was Hans I, the latest recruit a little dog doing sums as late as 1951. Frau Moekel's Daisy was the only cat on the list. As we know, the earliest educated animals had been horses, but the vast majority since 1913 were dogs. They communicated through either stamping their paw, striking a board, or barking. Not less than 86 of the 102 educated animals hailed from Germany.[13]

Elizabeth Mann Borgese, the daughter of Thomas Mann, was a distinguished expert on maritime law, and also a propagandist for animal rights. After she had settled near Florence in Italy in the 1960s, she became interested in dog–human communication, and decided to teach her English setter Arli to operate a modified electric typewriter with his nose. The dog gradually became more proficient, although for some reason, he adhered to three- or four-letter words. Since he was very fond of motoring, he often wrote 'arli go car'.[14] Like Rolf, he also wrote some poetry, a selection of which has been published in a literary magazine, among them his masterpiece *bed a ccat*:

> cad a baf
> bdd af dff
> art ad
> abd ad arrli
> bed a ccat

Although there are some strong contenders for the title, the most pathetic book about educated dogs must surely be the gullible English novelist Maurice Rowdon's 1978 effort

The Talking Dogs. It is the old story again: some eccentric German ladies living near Munich had trained their two dogs, Elke the poodle and Belam the saluki, to communicate by tapping their paws. The educated dogs sometimes ordered their owners about at will, criticized their clothes, and made their opinions known about various matters. Still, they were pious, religious dogs, often speculating about spiritual matters. Showing himself a worthy follower of Rolf and Lola, with regard to obtuse philosophical utterances, Belam defined death as 'One rests in peace', and God with the words 'Live by him until breathing ends'. Elke instead had a talent for medical science, diagnosing both men and beasts with various maladies. Once, when Belam was ill, she diagnosed him with cancer of the kidney! Very much perturbed, dog owner Frau Meyer took Belam to the vet, but he pooh-poohed her concerns, saying that the saluki only had a cold. The vet proved to be right, and Belam fully recovered; Elke was fortunate that he did not tap out 'Call a medical negligence lawyer, at once!' to start proceedings against her for this incorrect diagnosis!

Few people were convinced by Rowdon's book; if he had hoped to inspire a 'New animal psychology' revival throughout Europe, he would have been deeply disappointed. In fact, *The Talking Dogs* appears to have been the latest (and one hopes the last) book within its particular genre, which is probably a good thing for the scientific research of dog–human communication. Instead of having the dogs attempting to learn the human language, incessantly tapping out messages until their paws ached, or barking convulsively like the pathetic little Kurwenal, the humans have gone to the dogs. There have been several excellent books about how to understand canine vocalization and body language, the best of them Professor Stanley Coren's *How to Speak Dog*.

In 1928, when the 'New animal psychologists' were still active in Germany, scientists from Columbia University published one of the first proper studies of canine intelligence. The handsome German Shepherd dog 'Fellow', trained by Mr Jacob Herbert, of Detroit, Michigan, was noted for his remarkable intelligence, having acted in several films. Through conducting experiments with the dog, the scientists found that Fellow knew at least fifty words; he was very good at retrieving various objects, and could execute a considerable series of commands.[15]

In 2004, the border collie Rico made the news as the world's most clever dog. He understood, at this time, more than 200 words, many of them the names of his various toys. In a rigorous study, which eliminated the Clever Hans effect, Rico was invited to pick out a named toy among 9 others, getting it right 37 times out of 40. In addition, Rico responded correctly to a new word being introduced, using a canine equivalent to the 'fast mapping' mechanism to associate the unfamiliar word with the unfamiliar object situated among the familiar toys. This extraordinary dog remembered the new word he had learnt, again picking out the right toy after several weeks.[16]

In 2008, Rico was rivalled by Betsy, another border collie who had a vocabulary of 340 words, and made use of them to pick out various toys. She also knew 15 people by name. When showed a picture or drawing of a certain object, this amazing dog used the two-dimensional image to guide her to the right toy, even if she had never seen either picture or toy before.[17]

Domestic dogs are highly skilled in reading human social and communicative behaviour. Whereas tame wolves proved to be clueless with regard to following human communicative signals to find hidden food, dogs excelled in the same test, even surpassing non-human primates. This raises the possibility that there has been convergent evolution, with dogs and humans developing intricate social-communicative skills to aid their close interaction and cooperation. After all, over the last 100,000 years, the social environments of dog puppies and human children have become increasingly similar, and this intense cohabitation may well have led to dogs emulating certain skills considered uniquely human, like following complex cues and signals, or reading human mindsets and emotional states.[18]

Dogs are good at tricking other dogs, or even humans, to obtain rewards. They react to unfairness: dogs taking part in an experiment where some, but not all, of the animals are rewarded for correct behaviour, tend to opt out if they consider themselves badly done by.[19] Dogs can communicate with each other through whining and barking, and they can also communicate with humans. The dog's different barks have distinct patterns of frequency, tonality and pulsing, and are easy to identify. Even people who had never owned a dog could recognize the emotional meaning of recorded dog barks from certain situations, like when the dog was playful, lonely, or guarding its territory against a stranger. The observant dog owner will also be able to react to the dog's body orientation, gazing, and vocalization.[20] In another study, a dog was trained to use a simple keyboard, with signs for 'walk', 'water', food', 'piddle', 'toy' and 'petting'. The animal seemed to understand how to operate it, and made intelligent use of its messages to fulfil its various wishes.[21]

Thus, modern research has pointed out that dogs are much cleverer than people give them credit for. But they still have no business writing poetry, learning foreign languages, or speculating about God. There is no doubt that Oskar Pfungst was right, and that the educated horses and dogs were reacting to unconscious cues from their owners to obtain a reward. There was a strong bond between Krall and his horses, between Frau Moekel and Rolf, and between Henny Kindermann and Lola, aiding the development of such cues. It would have been extremely interesting to study the interplay between Rolf and Frau Moekel, to find out to what extent, if at all, the dog took active part in the proceedings, but unfortunately there is no film recording of them, and the existing transcripts of their conversation leave much to be desired.

Moreover, it is clear that not only Frau Moekel, but also other owners of super-intelligent dogs, interpreted the 'speech' of their animals quite freely, using their own imagination and expectations to correct misspellings and fill in words the dogs had 'forgotten'. Rolf's alleged predilection for phonetic speech vastly increased the chance of his tappings being interpreted as natural language, as did his purported command of both High German and the local Pfalz dialect. When Rolf speculated about the *Urseele*, claiming that each animal had a soul, he actually echoed a pet theory of Frau Moekel herself: in that bizarre instance, the dog became the prophet of the weird ideas of his mistress. The episode of Lola's 'lost honour', retold in such a pathetic manner by Henny Kindermann, tells us more about the psychology of this prim German lady than about that of her dog.

A clever doctor named Wilhelm Neumann came to see Rolf some years after Frau Moekel had died. Neumann was accompanied by another doctor, named Ferdinand Lotmar; they both politely introduced themselves to the educated dog, but without Lotmar allowing Luise Moekel to hear his second name. Depressed by the wartime rationing, the educated dog tapped out 'Give poor Rolf money to buy sausages!' and the doctors were kind enough to give him some coins. Neumann then asked Rolf to spell out the second name of his colleague, but Rolf just tapped out 'Cannot do it' even when the question was repeated. But after Neumann had whispered to Luise Moekel that perhaps the name 'Lotmar' was too difficult for Rolf to spell, the dog spelt the name perfectly. The two doctors left the Moekel house, their cunning plan a complete success: Rolf was only able to communicate when Luise Moekel knew the answer! Neumann reckoned that a slight movement of the board Rolf was tapping on constituted the unconscious cue for the dog to stop tapping.[22]

Another question of some importance is to what degree fraud played any part in these bizarre proceedings. Both von Osten and Krall fully believed that the horses were able to communicate with them, but there has been speculation that von Osten's groom deliberately tricked the gullible old man, and even that Krall's stable hand played a similar trick on him.[23] Nor is it reasonable to accuse the kind, dog-loving Paula Moekel and Henny Kindermann of deliberately falsifying their conversations with their dogs. They were both honest, reputable people, who refused to gain money by having their dogs perform in public. Personally, I would be more wary of the wisecracking 'dogs of Weimar', who made fools of journalists and insulted the sceptics. Perhaps Fräulein Gerda Hensoldt and Baroness von Freytag-Loringhoven, the owners of Lumpi and Kurwenal, shared a hearty laugh at the end of the day, at the expense of all the fools and fanatics taken in by the antics of their dogs?

It is also important to note that the people involved in the 'New animal psychology' were neither fools nor obviously mentally deranged, with the possible exception of the original prophet himself, Wilhelm von Osten. Karl Krall had been a shrewd, self-made businessman; Paula Moekel was an educated, cultured woman; Henny Kindermann was a graduated agronomist who wrote several books about other topics; the Baroness von Freytag-Loringhoven was a talented artist. In the 1935 debate about Kurwenal, Otto Renner tried another line of attack. He made fun of the childless spinsters who treated their dogs as their furry babies, teaching them to speak, read and count. And indeed, according to the list of educated dogs provided by Henny Kindermann, 54 out of 68 owners of educated dogs were females. But Renner's misogynist theory cannot be applied to the high priestess herself, since Paula Moekel had numerous children, at least one of whom was a boy, before she acquired her furry little 'son' Rolf, who called her 'Mother'. Henny Kindermann also married, and had at least three sons growing up to adulthood.

Finally, did Germany's 'New animal psychologists' achieve anything at all that was positive? No, not really. Perhaps they made some small contribution with regard to promoting animal welfare and animal rights, but they did so using arguments that were largely erroneous. Founded on fanaticism and pseudoscience, the movement obstructed the proper investigation of animal intelligence and dog–human interactions; it will remain an unfruitful sidetrack in the history of biology, ending with a whimper rather than a woof.

4

SOME CELEBRATED TALKING DOGS

There was a speaking dog exhibited at Stockholm some years ago, which could articulate several complete sentences, in French and Swedish; and Vive le Roy, he pronounced with much grace.

Joseph Taylor, *Canine Gratitude* (London 1808)

In 1715, one of the most startling notices ever was inserted into that sombre journal, the *Histoire de l'Academie Royale des Sciences*. It emanated from the pen of Gottfried Wilhelm Leibniz, and reported the case of a talking dog. Having heard of this remarkable animal from a German prince, who had seen it at the Ostermesse in Leipzig in 1712, the great philosopher went to see the dog perform. This animal, a male dog of moderate size and very common shape, was born and bred in Zeiss near Meissen in Saxony. It was alleged that a little boy had heard the then three-year-old dog utter some words, without prior tuition, and decided to teach it to speak properly. The dog's master, a countryman, soon took over the training, with Teutonic thoroughness. After some years, the dog could pronounce about thirty words, '*thé*', '*caffé*', '*chocolat*' and '*assemblée*' among them. It was left unexplained why the animal had such a preference for French words that had been assimilated into the German language. The dog spoke only by echo, repeating the word in question after the master. It was not beaten or scolded during the performance, which probably took place at some country fair visited by Leibniz.[1]

When publishing Leibniz's short note, the Paris Academy of Sciences thought it necessary to add the apology that if the dog's performance had not been witnessed by the great Leibniz himself, they would not have printed it. Dr Peter Templeman, who commented on the case in his 1753 compilation *Curious Remarks and Observations*, was equally sceptical. Although he had recently seen the aforementioned *Chien Savant* perform in London, he considered the ability to speak to be well beyond the intellect of a dog or a monkey. Later commentators have agreed, considering the odd letter about the talking dog as a pointless curiosity within the Leibniz canon.

The Leibniz scholars have also failed to trace this remarkable talking dog, but I have had better success in this respect. There are several reports from the year 1716 and 1718 concerning a talking dog making various appearances in Germany and Holland. In one of these, it was said that the dog's master swung it in the air, and rubbed its jaws with his hand, to make the superstitious audience believe he was a conjurer providing the dog with the gift of speech. Since the animal spoke the words 'thee', 'coffee', '*chocolade*' and '*oui monsieur*' it is very likely to have been the same dog seen by Leibniz some years earlier. In another short account, the same dog was said to pronounce clearly all the letters of the alphabet, and to speak not just French, but also Dutch and English. In a letter to his friend Grimarest, Leibniz had written that in addition to pronouncing thirty different words distinctly, and answering questions from its master, the dog could pronounce all the letters of the alphabet apart from 'm', 'n' and 'x'.[2]

Nor is it fanciful to relate Leibniz and the talking dog to the following curious advertisement, in the *Daily Packet* of 14 June 1718:

> JUST BROUGHT FROM GERMANY, and to be seen in the Ram's Head Inn in Fenchurch-street on Wednesday next, a Dog that has been taught to pronounce articulately all the Letters of the Alphabet, and to speak Several Sentences in the French, High-Dutch, and English Languages, so distinctly and plainly, that to hear him only, and not see him, any one would mistake it for a human Utterance. The Hours for the Performance (that no Person may be disappointed) are at 10 in the forenoon, and at 4, and at 8 at night. If any Person of Quality, or others, are desirous to see and hear this uncommon Performance, the Owner will wait upon them with his Dog at their own House.

The Talking Dog remained in London for several months, before returning to the Continent.[3]

Since the remarkable dog seen and heard by Leibniz had no immediate successor, the world would hear very little about talking dogs for many years. In the early 1800s, there was a story about a wealthy Englishman who heard a dog order '*Biftek, pommes*' at a Paris restaurant, sitting opposite his master with a plate in front of him. But after the Englishman had bought the dog, he discovered that the seller had been 'a travelling ventriloquist, who had thrown his voice into the dog'! In another case from Paris, a circus performer had sold a talking dog to a publican for 400 francs. When the offer was accepted, the indignant dog exclaimed, 'So you sell me, do you! Then I shall never talk again!' To be sure, the dog never spoke another word, and when the ventriloquist was taken to court, he was acquitted and the publican much laughed at.[4]

The Leibniz scholars have had much difficulty explaining why their hero would bother about a performing dog. There have even been claims that the great philosopher had actually been deceived by a clever ventriloquist, just like the two silly individuals mentioned above. It would take the better part of two centuries before Leibniz was finally vindicated: dogs can really speak in the human tongue!

It began when, in 1910, Alexander Graham Bell proudly announced to the American newspaper press that after long effort and nearly superhuman persistence, he had succeeded in teaching a terrier to speak. The great inventor claimed that this dog could say 'How do you do, Grandmama', pronouncing it 'Ow-a-goo-ga-mama'. Although Bell's latest breakthrough hardly rivalled inventing the telephone, the American journalists were most impressed. Indeed, the story about the talking dog appeared in newspapers all over the globe, including those read in the little village Theerhütte, on the Lüneburg heath in Germany.

The next week, the same paper contained a letter from local gamekeeper Herman Ebers, challenging the American monopoly with regard to talking dogs. Ebers claimed that his own dog, the German pointer (or Vorstehhund) Don, had begun talking spontaneously five years earlier, and that this extraordinary dog now had a vocabulary of six words, all of which he used intelligently! The German press was flabbergasted. Bags of telegrams and letters inundated the tiny Theerhütte post office, inquiring whether Ebers might be pulling their legs, or whether the gamekeeper was really in the possession of a dog of such unique talents. With Teutonic curtness, Ebers replied, 'Story true. Inspection is permitted.'

First to arrive was an Austrian journalist named Carl Haberland. After he had seen and heard Don perform, his jaw literally dropped. Haberland immediately offered to become the talking dog's manager, and was accepted by the rustic gamekeeper,

26. Don the Talking Dog. Like the two following, this illustration is from Karl Krall's *Denkende Tiere*.

who felt out of his depth among city dwellers. In the coming weeks, journalist after journalist came to see and interview Don; none of them went away disappointed. The first question to the talking dog, his name, was answered by a gruff '*Don!*' The second question, '*Was hast du?*' (What do you have?), was replied by '*Hunger!*' To '*Was willst du?*' (What do you want?), the dog replied '*Haben! Haben!*' (To have!) '*Was ist das?*' (What would that be?) – '*Kuchen!*' (Cakes!) '*Was bittest du dich auch?*' (What do you also want?) – '*Ruhe!*' (Rest!)

The reporters wrote long and enthusiastic accounts of this wonderful talking dog, a zoological wonder to stun the world.[5] That a simple German pointer, living in a small country village, completely outclassed Alexander Graham Bell's American talking dog, called for much nationalist celebration. The German journalists, who do not seem to have known much about dogs, queried whether Don was the reincarnation of a human being, or if he might be a new kind of super-dog, heralding a future when spoken communication between Man and his Best Friend would become perfectly possible. An amateur zoologist considered that certain anatomical peculiarities, like Don's exceptionally high forehead, strongly supported the latter notion.

In November 1910, the Hamburg correspondent of the *New York Times* made inquiries about Don. The talking dog was quite a handsome specimen, he asserted, with well-groomed dark fur and an intelligent facial expression. When interviewed, Herr Ebers said that Don had started to speak at the age of just six months. Once, when Ebers had been sitting at table with a cake in his hand, Don had come sauntering up. He had jokingly asked the dog what he wanted, being completely taken aback when Don replied '*Haben!*' in a deep masculine voice. To make sure he was not mistaken, he had repeated the question, to which the dog again answered '*Haben! Haben!*'

27. Don saying '*Kuchen!*'

Herr Ebers decided to educate the talking dog further. It did not take long before Don learned to repeat his own name when prompted. With time, he also learnt the words '*Hunger*', '*Kuchen*', and '*Ruhe*' well-nigh perfectly. His record effort to date had been a sentence of four words: 'Don hungry, wants cakes!' Recently, this remarkable dog had also mastered '*Ja*' and '*Nein*' – 'Yes' and 'No' – and was using these words in an intelligent manner, Ebers asserted. When asked whether he wanted to go outside when the weather was wet or damp, Don always answered '*Nein!*' Some sceptics had likened Don's speech to barking or growling, but the journalist and others who had heard the dog wholly disagreed.[6]

A certain Dr Paul Scheller, who took an interest in animal communication, also went to see the talking dog. He was particularly impressed with how very clearly Don spoke '*Haben*' and '*Hunger*' in a deep voice that seemed to emanate from the very depth of his throat. When Scheller called the talking dog's name, the animal went up to him and clearly repeated '*Don!*' Later, Don went up to the gamekeeper's daughter, Fräulein Martha Ebers, who was preparing luncheon, and said '*Don Kuchen haben!*' Later, when Scheller was leaving the Ebers family, the gamekeeper said '*Don, wollen wir ausgehen?*' (Don, should we go for a walk?) '*Ja!*' the talking dog replied with alacrity.[7]

Having read about Don in the newspapers, the director of the Hamburg Zoological Gardens, Professor Julius Vosseler, summoned the talking dog to Hamburg for his speaking ability to be properly assessed. Vosseler was no gullible enthusiast, but a distinguished biologist who had published many valuable books and articles. He thought Don a solid-looking brown Vorstehhund, with an elegant head and soulful eyes. Since Don was used to his quiet rural surroundings, he was somewhat flustered by the bustling Hamburg street life, but when asked to perform for the professor, he went through his entire repertoire without any mishaps. Professor Vosseler, who had suspected the talking dog to be a newspaper hoax, was very much impressed: Don spoke more distinctly than most talking parrots. He pronounced the vowels 'u' and 'e' very distinctly, more so than 'a' and 'o'. He could not say 'i' at all, except when the professor pinched him to make him give a squeal. When Don spoke, he never barked or growled; with a look of great concentration, gazing at his young mistress Martha Ebers and wagging his tail slowly, he made every effort to imitate her words.[8]

Herr Ebers and the journalist Carl Haberland, who seemed to mastermind things behind the stage, refused several offers to buy the talking dog. A wealthy German who offered \$15,000 had been turned down with scorn, they asserted, as had an enterprising publisher who offered \$5,000 for the souvenir postcard rights alone. Herr Hagenbeck, proprietor of the celebrated Hamburg menagerie, offered \$2,500 for the right to exhibit Don at the zoo, but Haberland was waiting for a higher bidder among the many impresarios who managed music hall acts, since the talking dog would be ideally suited for this kind of performance. Don was kept indoors at all times during this shrewd waiting game, since Ebers and Haberland were wary of dognappers, and almost equally fearful of photographers lurking in the bushes to issue pirated picture postcards of the celebrated talking dog.[9]

On 2 April 1911, Don made his debut at the Wintergarten music hall in Berlin. The dog spoke loudly and clearly, and was rewarded with thunderous applause. The day before, he had won over an audience of forty highly sceptical Berlin journalists with a bravura performance, including what appeared to be intelligent use of '*Ja*' and '*Nein*'. When asked who had first made him famous in the newspapers, Don clearly spoke 'Haberland!' This gentleman, still employed as Don's personal manager, now doubled as the fiancé of Martha Ebers. Guarantees for the scientific authenticity of Don's speech had been given by Professor Vosseler and other zoologists. At around this time, Don's supporters received a dubious new recruit: the busybody Karl Krall could of course not resist the temptation to publicly proclaim his support for this super-intelligent talking dog. His bombastic eulogies outraged the rationalists, to whom the name Krall already was anathema, and served to link the talking dog with Krall's other dubious theories.

In August 1911, Don was still active in the Berlin music hall, at a salary of 12,000 marks per month. A French journalist who interviewed the talking dog and his entourage came away highly impressed, urging his readers not to confuse this extraordinary animal with the *chiens savants* performing at fairs and markets. Don needed no direction from his master; in fact, he had become a very headstrong and independent dog, who

28. Don with Martha Ebers (as she then was).

spoke only when he wanted to. Like a rather spoilt star, he was sometimes sulky and unwilling to perform, unless some proper delicacies were produced to represent the cake this simple country dog had once so coveted. The Frenchman agreed with other observers that Don's speech was entirely different from his barking, and that they were never intermixed.[10] Once, a religious Swiss visitor to the music hall had objected to the dog show, exclaiming that it was an abomination of God's nature that a dog should be able to speak. But after Don had unexpectedly called out 'Hallelujah!' the Swiss knelt in wonderment, praising the talking dog for his religious zeal. He offered to settle a generous pension on Don if the dog came to his local church to speak, or rather preach, but there is no record indicating that such a bizarre canine sermon ever took place.

Don's long stay in Berlin was followed by a tour of other German music halls, and a visit to the large cities of Poland and Russia. When residing in the latter country, he spontaneously began saying two words that sounded rather like 'Drinski' and 'Roubles'. In May 1912, he was contracted to perform at Hammerstein's Victoria Roof Garden in New York for the coming season, with a weekly salary of 3,000 marks. By this time, Carl Haberland had married Martha Ebers, and the gamekeeper had given Don to them as a wedding present. In late June, Don had made it to London, where the underwriters at Lloyds refused to insure the talking dog, since they had negative experience with animals making transatlantic journeys. But the wealthy Oscar and William Hammerstein solved the problem by giving Haberland a bond that they would pay him $50,000 should the talking dog expire on the journey from London to New York. This made Don the most valuable dog in the world.[11]

According to Ellis Island records, the Haberlands and Don travelled on the *Kronprinz Wilhelm* liner, arriving with Don and a certain Paul Haberland, a successful New Jersey businessman who was related to Carl. But trouble was brewing elsewhere for Don and his entourage. Professor Vosseler had appeared in Don's advertisement posters to affirm that the talking dog's act was not a fraud, or ventriloquism.[12] But since then, two sceptical experts had entered the fray: the animal psychologist Dr Oskar Pfungst and his colleague Dr Erich Fischer, both belonging to the anti-Krall lobby. As we know, Pfungst had been instrumental in debunking the 'thinking horse' Clever Hans, demonstrating that this animal was directed through hidden signs from its owner. In spite of this triumph, Pfungst seems to have been quite a prejudiced, rigid character, whose opinion of the intellect of dogs was very low. Although he had studied dogs for just two years, the opinionated German boldly stated that due to 'the animals' vagueness of perception and extremely low degree of attention' dogs were entirely incapable of learning even the simplest tasks by observation and imitation! With this remarkable diatribe in mind, it is not surprising that Pfungst found many faults with Don's performance. The dog did not speak clearly, and was sometimes entirely tongue-tied when asked to perform. Using an Edison Home Phonograph, the cunning German made a phonogram of the speaking dog and played it for some people who were not allowed to hear the prompting. Only two out of sixteen words were entirely intelligible, and disinterested hearers found difficulties in distinguishing his '*Hunger*' from his '*Haben*', and his '*Ruhe*' from his

'*Kuchen*', although they were flabbergasted when Don suddenly spoke 'Hallelujah!' quite clearly without being prompted.

Pfungst wanted to do another 'Clever Hans', expose Don as a humbug, and strike another blow against Krall and his fellow fanatics. It was dismal to see, he wrote, how 'scientists of a certain class' were reading their own mental processes into the behaviour of their pets. In no way could a 'lower animal' like a dog be capable of intelligent imitation and other complicated mental processes needed for the ability to speak. But Professor Vosseler interceded in Don's favour. Firstly, he rightly argued that a talking dog remained a great scientific curiosity, even if it sometimes got its pronunciation wrong. Secondly, would it really be wise of Pfungst to openly challenge all the journalists and dignitaries, including Vosseler himself, who had previously eulogised Don? And what would the Berliners think of the 'animal shrink' who had denigrated Germany's famous talking dog? Grinding his teeth, the ambitious psychologist had to be content with publishing a summary of his results in an obscure newspaper supplement.[13]

After Don had gone to conquer America, Pfungst had enough. His promise to Vosseler was no longer valid, nor was his concern for the German people's pride in their talking dog. At a psychology conference in Berlin, held in April 1912, Pfungst openly challenged Vosseler for allowing his enthusiasm to pervert his sound scientific judgement.[14] It was not the dog that was the problem, he pontificated: it was the human being who was an easy victim of suggestion and trickery. It was ludicrous that Don would be paid $1,500 per week when he went to America, and just as freakish that Don's successor on the Berlin stage, a poodle who could only speak two words, was paid 1,400 marks for the same period of time, much more than Pfungst's own salary! It was high time, this weird 'pet detective' thundered from the pulpit, that these talking dogs, earning easy money from human gullibility, had their muzzles obturated once and for all!

And Germany's answer to Ace Ventura was not done yet. The cunning psychologist sent a translation of his work to his American colleague Harry Miles Johnson, of Johns Hopkins University, urging him to expose the talking dog in a leading American scholarly journal. Pfungst was concerned for his own reputation, he claimed, since Don's management team were claiming that not only Vosseler, but also he himself, was endorsing the dog's performances in Germany. Johnson, another anti-Krall rationalist, agreed to help. With excellent timing, his article was published in *Science* in May 1912, just when Don was expected in New York.[15]

Pfungst's activities were not the only concern for Don's management team ahead of the talking dog's New York premiere. They had nagging doubts about whether a dog speaking only German could really become a success among the New Yorkers, who certainly had no shortage of alternative amusements. Furthermore, the Haberlands had been shocked to find out that Hammerstein's Paradise Roof Garden was a decidedly rowdy establishment, situated at the corner of 42nd and Broadway. It was managed by Oscar Hammerstein's son Willie, charging only a quarter for a ticket and drawing large and unruly crowds. Don would be billed along with the 'Man with the Seventeen-foot Beard', a Swiss yodeller, and two tap-dancing midgets. Another set of regulars were the shrill, clumsy Cherry Sisters, also known as America's Worst Act. Willie Hammerstein hung a net along the stage to catch the fruit and vegetables the audience were encouraged to throw at the poor girls.[16] Would Don share the fate of these weird performers, and would the hostile crowd, waving their copies of *Science* magazine, pelt the talking dog with rotten tomatoes, shouting: 'Buloney! This mutt can't speak American! Get that Kraut dog out of here, Mister, and give us our money back!'

But the clever Oscar and Willie Hammerstein had thought matters through before investing in the talking dog. They reassured the Haberlands that Don would be treated with respect, and that the risk of any of their audience having any knowledge of *Science* magazine was extremely low. And the Hammersteins were proven right: Don's premiere, on 15 July, was a great success. Prompted by the pretty Martha Haberland, who was wearing traditional German country costume, the dog spoke loudly and distinctly. An actor named Loney Haskell had been employed as Don's interlocutor; he was an amusing fellow, and soon the audience was roaring with laughter. When the talking dog said '*Hunger!*' for the first time, the audience applauded for nearly a minute without cessation, as the portly, dignified-looking Don wagged his tail and ate cake from Martha Haberland's hand.

The newspaper reviews of Don's performance were uniformly positive. According to the *New York Times*, the talking dog was 'a sizable brown German forest dog, a little inclined to corpulence, but still good looking'. Nothing like him had ever been seen and heard in New York, and it was not surprising that Don 'received an ovation such as any mere man or woman seldom receives in this theatre'. A Pittsburgh journalist wrote that Don really did speak like a human being: tremendous canine earnestness was thrown into his efforts at vocalization.[17]

Don remained at Hammerstein's establishment until December 1912, rubbing shoulders with the likes of Harry Houdini, Buster Keaton and Charlie Chaplin. He then had stints at the Grand Theatre in Pittsburgh, the New Brighton Theatre, and Keith's Bronx Theatre in New York. In August 1913, Martha Haberland was teaching Don to retrieve various objects from the surf at Coney Island. Seeing that a swimmer was struggling in the surf, and waving for help, she indicated him to Don, and the talking dog swam out and grasped the swimmer by his bathing suit. The swimmer grabbed hold of Don, and both went under momentarily, but the talking dog broke free and secured another hold of him. A police constable rode his horse into the surf and rescued the man. He turned out to be the Greek student John Contreca, who was very much impressed with just having been rescued by the world's most valuable dog.[18]

When Don was performing in Syracuse in September 1913, Loney Haskell thought of an amusing routine. On stage, Don was introduced to a Russian wolfhound, and said 'Roubles!' in his best Moscow accent, but the startled wolfhound only replied 'Woof!' Don was then introduced to a German sheepdog, saying '*Kuchen!*' in the hope of conversing when his fellow countrydog in the language of their *Vaterland*, but the sheepdog only answered with a growl. 'This goes to prove that Don is the only talking dog in the world!' Loney Haskell exclaimed, 'Why, that Russian animal doesn't even understand his own language!'[19] But in August 1914, Carl Haberland cancelled Don's

29. An American newspaper caricature of Don and Martha Haberland.

forthcoming engagement at Hammerstein's Victoria, since he claimed to belong to the Austrian army.[20] The Haberlands returned to their native land, where the once-famous talking dog died in obscurity in 1916, nursed by his devoted mistress Martha, whose fortune he had made.[21] Plans for his body to be donated to the Rockefeller Institute, whose experts were keen to examine the anatomy of his vocal organs, were never acted upon.

Don's great success in show business paved the way for other talking animals, all over the world. As we know, there were several other talking dogs in Germany, some of them securing lucrative theatre engagements after Don had left for America. In London, the Airedale terrier Buller could say 'Mama' and 'God save our gracious King'. But when a *Daily Mirror* reporter interviewed this dog, he found Buller's speech quite indistinct; although the dog's owner and trainer claimed that Buller was inconvenienced by a cold in the throat, the reporter was not impressed.[22]

There were also several talking copycats trying to get in on the act. The American tabby Billikin could say 'milk' and 'mamma', as this talented feline demonstrated at the Atlantic Cat Club in December 1910. Even more successful was Peter Alupka, the Speaking Cat of Germany. Peter toured Europe with some of the leading circuses of the time, always to great acclaim. When the circus historian Alfred Lehmann saw Peter perform, he was amazed how clearly the cat could pronounce certain words, like '*nein*', 'Anna' and 'Helene'. When the name of Kaiser Wilhelm was mentioned, the patriotic cat exclaimed 'Hurrah! Hurrah!' Peter could also sing 'O Tannenbaum' in a high mewing voice, although Lehmann remarked that it needed much imagination to liken this *katzenjammer* to the tune in question. He also observed that Peter's mistress held his neck in a loving embrace when he performed, clearly to modulate his voice with her fingers. In 1912, Peter Alupka was interviewed by the philosopher Dr Oskar Prochnow, who was impressed how closely this amazing cat could imitate the human voice. Peter's ambitious mistress even made plans to join Don at the New York music hall, but unfortunately this unique German talking dog–cat duet never came to fruition.[23]

Whereas Don's eventful life had been widely reported by the press, much less is known about the world's next talking dog, the French Bulldog Princess Jacqueline. Although a tiny dog, weighing in at just nineteen pounds, Princess had a vocabulary of twenty words, which she was claimed sometimes to use intelligently. In February 1928, she made her debut at the Eastern Dog Show in Boston. A journalist nearly fainted when the dapper-looking little dog clearly said 'Hello' when greeted. Her owner, Mrs Mabel A. Robinson of Bangor, Maine, told the press that the now three-year-old Princess had been speaking since she was three or four months old. When asked where she wanted to go, she answered 'Out!' She could say 'ball', 'Bangor', 'I will' and 'I won't' according to her mood. When urged to walk up stairs, the lazy dog replied 'Elevator!' New York dog fancier Frank Dole declared that Princess was the most remarkable dog he had ever seen, and unique in the world. Dr Knight Dunlop, a psychologist at Johns Hopkins University, was equally impressed. Newspapers even quoted, or probably rather misquoted, this expert saying that Princess Jacqueline had vocal cords closely resembling those of a human being. Mrs Robinson received several offers for Princess to follow Don into the American vaudeville, but she decided against it, although the talking dog sometimes showed her skills at various dog shows. When Princess Jacqueline expired from pneumonia in 1934, most American newspapers, and foreign ones as far off as Australia, published the talking dog's obituary.[24]

In 1946, the *Daily Mirror* dispatched journalist Noel Whitcomb to Royston, Hertfordshire, to investigate the talking fox-terrier Ben, the property of night watchman Alf Brissenden. When Whitcomb was having tea in the Brissenden kitchen, the dapper-looking little dog came sauntering in, looked hard at him, and said, in a low-pitched, authoritative voice, 'I want one!' Mr Brissenden explained that Ben had started talking a year earlier, nearly causing his wife to faint when she heard him for the first time. When he walked Ben and Whitcomb back to the station, the dog stopped outside the public house and remarked, tersely, 'I want one!' 'Me too, chum,' the dazed Whitcomb replied, 'I need one!'

Having regained his composure back at the newspaper office, Noel Whitcomb realised that he was sitting on a remarkable story, one that could be milked for many *Daily Mirror* exclusives.[25] On 10 August 1946, the news about the talking dog beat the occupation of Germany and the troubles in Palestine to the *Daily Mirror* first page, with an illustration of Ben being surrounded by some juvenile admirers. Whitcomb had consulted distinguished veterinary surgeon W. H. Woolridge, who had consented to examining Ben, although he was wholly sceptical that a dog could really talk.

In the next instalment in the talking dog saga, Whitcomb brought Ben to Dr Woolridge's house, but the dog did not distinguish himself. Ben rampaged round in the veterinarian's garden, and examined his vegetable patch closely. When they moved inside, Ben seemed much awed by Dr Woolridge's large and elegant house, and was entirely tongue-tied. The journalist suggested that they should completely ignore Ben, to make the talking dog feel more at ease. And indeed, just as Dr Woolridge was about to dismiss Ben, the dog indistinctly said 'I want one!'

Dr Woolridge was sufficiently impressed to arrange for himself and his colleague Professor W. C. Miller to call at the Brissenden house the next day. This time, Ben was in top form. It did not take long for him to pronounce 'I want one! I want one!' well-nigh perfectly. Professor Miller declared that he had never heard a dog imitate the human voice so very closely. He thought Ben sounded rather like 'Grandma Buggins', a cantankerous old Cockney woman who used to amuse the radio listeners of the time. Even the sceptical Dr Woolridge was greatly impressed how Ben used his mouth and tongue to formulate the words. As the two scientists were enthusiastically discussing the talking dog, commenting that it would be most interesting to examine his brain and voice box after death, Ben was playing happily with a ball nearby.

Noel Whitcomb had another scoop for his newspaper, this time with the headline 'Ben sits up – And the world takes notice!' And he was not far wrong. Mr Brissenden was deluged with fan mail and telegrams about his wonderful dog, and hundreds of local people came to see and hear the local celebrity perform. According to Noel Whitcomb, Ben looked most interested and attentive when some of the telegrams were read out to him. Later, when taken out shopping, Ben looked wistfully at a leg of mutton in the butcher's shop and exclaimed 'I want one!' but since the talking dog was not in possession of a ration book, the butcher turned him down. When Whitcomb had a pint of beer at the Bull public house, Ben found his voice again, but the barmaid refused to serve any person, or dog, below the age of eighteen.

Back at home, Ben behaved like any ordinary house dog. He slept on an old mat in the kitchen, barked at strangers, and played with his balls. When Mrs Brissenden was upstairs cleaning, she might say 'Ben, go and get my duster!' The dog would cock his head knowingly, before trotting off to the kitchen to fetch her the right object. Ben could also be trusted to fetch the newspaper at the local newsagents; he always chose the *Daily Mirror*, another sign, at least to Noel Whitcomb, of the dog's superior intellect!

Mr Brissenden explained that Ben's mother had been put down during the war, because she went crazy when the sirens sounded; the identity of his father nobody knew. There had been several other pups, all of which had been given away, something Mr Brissenden regretted. Were these super-intelligent dogs sniffing around in the gutter, chasing cats and digging for bones, from want of proper tuition to become talking dogs like their famous sibling?

Many dog fanciers wanted to purchase Ben, including an American showman who offered $10,000 for the dog. But the Brissendens refused to part with their family pet. Fearful of thieves and dognappers, they instead insured the talking dog for £1,000, before embarking on a tour of local public houses, where Ben was always well received. The proprietor of a holiday camp paid £100, with a week's free holiday for the Brissendens thrown in, to have the talking dog perform. Ben's finest hour came when the BBC sent a broadcasting team to record the talking dog's voice for their international service. The interview went as follows:

INTERVIEWER: Well, Ben, have you any puppies?

BEN: I want one!

INTERVIEWER: If you want puppies, Ben, the first thing is to get a wife.

BEN: I want one!

INTERVIEWER: What do you think of the political situation, Ben?

BEN: I want one!

A year later, in August 1947, Noel Whitcomb went back to see his friend Alf Brissenden. Unfortunately, things were no longer looking so rosy for the Brissenden family, since Alf's health was giving way and he might soon have to give up his job. He now very much regretted not selling Ben to the American showman who had offered $10,000 for the dog, particularly since there was not much money to be had exhibiting a talking dog in gloomy post-war Britain. The Brissendens had made less than £200 out of Ben's five broadcasts, his short film, his television show and all his personal appearances. On a brighter note, the prediction of Dr Woolridge that Ben would one day extend his vocabulary had actually come true: before a Cambridge audience of 6,000 people, Ben had sat up and exclaimed 'Alf! I want one! Oh, I do want one!'

There have been several later talking dogs. In 1950, the talking Pekinese Blackie caused quite a sensation in Ceres, Fife. The little dog had caused two lady visitors to faint, and several tradesmen to check whether it had really been tea they had been drinking, by sauntering up to them and saying 'Hello!' Blackie sometimes called his fellow Pekinese by exclaiming 'Fifi!' The local veterinarian was most impressed by Blackie, as was the judge at a local dog show, who was unexpectedly addressed by the elegant little dog.[26]

In 1953, a fox-terrier in Newcastle, New South Wales, began saying 'Hello, Mum!' and 'Here I am, Mum', allegedly without any tuition. Embarrassingly to the dog's owner, a clergyman, the dog also spoke 'a word often heard in masculine company and not in the ladies' presence'. Nevertheless, this foul-mouthed talking dog was given an audience with Archbishop of Newcastle, The Right Reverend Francis de Witt Batty, who was most impressed with the dog's clear speech. Some Australian scientists speculated that the dog's talk was a 'conditioned reflex', and that the animal picked up its vocabulary from its environment, but in an amusing commentary, the *Evening Standard* newspaper did not agree. Although it was quite possible that an Australian clergyman might utter words unfit for ladies to hear, any person referring to his mother as 'Mum' would never rise to even moderate eminence in the Anglican Church! Since it had been remarked that the talking dog was speaking with an English accent, it was probably the reincarnation of a transported convict pining for his mother.[27]

In January 1962, Noel Whitcomb, the *Daily Mirror*'s talking dog correspondent, again went into action when the two-year-old poodle Trudi spoke to him on the telephone, calling from Epping just outside London. A photograph and an interview were of course called for, during which the dog spoke 'No' and 'I want one!' in a high-pitched voice. In 1966, Pepe the Talking Chihuahua became a newspaper favourite in California. The tiny dog spoke 'I love you!', 'How are you?', 'Hello!' and 'Hello there!' in a shrill, singing voice.[28]

As we have seen, there have been quite a few instances of dogs capable of imitating the human voice more or less accurately. Apart from the extraordinary dog seen and heard by Leibniz, the two leading talking dogs have been Don and Princess Jacqueline, since independent sources indicate that these two dogs were capable of pronouncing several words quite clearly. Since there does not appear to have been any controlled evaluation of Princess Jacqueline's performance, Don remains the only talking dog to have been properly investigated by the scientists of the time.

Was Oskar Pfungst right, and was Don just a bluff? It has to be admitted that Pfungst was clever to make a phonograph recording of the talking dog, to remove the element of showmanship, and also the unconscious wish of the audience that the dog would really speak clearly. He also erased Martha Haberland's contribution: thus the exchange

MARTHA: What do you want?
DOG: Cakes!
MARTHA: So it is cakes you want, Don!

becomes just

DOG: Cakes!

This effectively removed the pretence of a conversation, and also the reinforcement given by Martha Haberland; if she could recognize the word as 'Cakes!' then so should the audience.

But by modern standards, it is also clear that Pfungst's study has serious methodological flaws. Firstly, it is not stated how the recordings were procured in the first place, and to what degree fatigue and boredom on the part of the dog played a part. Since Pfungst could hardly have brought his machine to sixteen consecutive performances at the Berlin music hall, it seems likely that Don had to repeat his performance sixteen times in one afternoon, hardly the optimal circumstances for him to go through his vocabulary. Secondly, the phonographs used in the 1910s were very primitive instruments: many people would have had considerable difficulties recognizing the word '*Kuchen!*' spoken by a human being, had it been regurgitated through one of these vintage machines! Thirdly, Pfungst left it unstated how the 'jury' was selected: had they been selected from his own 'sceptical' friends? The final and most serious argument is that Pfungst was very much against Karl Krall's 'New animal psychology' movement. When Krall took sides with the talking dog, Pfungst automatically joined the opposition. It is clear from his writings that Pfungst was a headstrong, confrontational character, keen to strike another blow against Krall and his adherents.

It should also be taken into account that Don had several times been examined by other scientists, who were quite impressed with the talking dog. Firstly, as we know, Professor Julius Vosseler fully endorsed the dog's talking ability, although he was somewhat sceptical whether Don was able to use his vocabulary intelligently. Vosseler was quite a distinguished zoologist, and it seems impossible that a person of his stature could have been bribed or persuaded to exaggerate by Don's management team. Importantly, Vosseler was no friend of Krall's 'New animal psychology'; he seems to have been motivated by his zeal for evaluating the performance of the talking dog, rather than some hidden agenda. The same is true for Dr Oskar Prochnow, a philosopher interested in the development of speech.[29] He also examined Don, again being quite impressed with the dog's speech. It was clear to him that Don spoke by imitating Martha Haberland's words, using several distinct sounds: '*Haben*' sounded like 'Uau-on', '*Ruhe*' was 'U-ae' and '*Hunger*' 'Ung-ae'. The dog's vowels were very distinctive, his consonants less so, but still it was not difficult to distinguish the words. Vosseler and Prochnow's arguments in favour of Don are of course strongly supported by the fact that Don was such a great success both in Berlin and New York. If Don had not been able to imitate the human voice quite closely, how could he have been such a success in Berlin, and later among the critical New Yorkers?

In June 2009, an article in the *Scientific American* featured 'Maya', a dog able to say 'I love you!' or rather 'Ahh rooo uuu!' A similar dog had performed on the David Letterman show, and several other talking canines could be seen and heard on YouTube. When interviewed, distinguished dog expert Professor Stanley Coren told the story of a colleague who always greeted her dog with a cheerful, two-syllable 'Hel-lo!' It did not take long before the dog returned the greeting![30]

Present-day cynologists are well aware that dogs are capable of learning by imitation, and they also possess some degree of selective tonal imitation skills; after all, they themselves are adept at expressing their emotions by varying the pitch and tone of their growls. Although the structure of the lips and tongue of the dog are not conducive to the pronunciation of consonants, Don and the other talking dogs were quite good at imitating the vowels, as Vosseler and Prochnow rightly deduced. Although Don spoke by repetition only during the shows, he sometimes used the words he knew spontaneously; some sources even claimed that he did so intelligently, although this was never properly investigated at the time, mainly due to Pfungst's preconceived ideas about canine intelligence. Still, this amazing performer, Don the Talking Dog, remains the most outstanding example that certain dogs are able to imitate the human voice.

5

DOGGY DRAMA:
SOME CELEBRATED CANINE
THESPIANS

Already in the Elizabethan theatre, dogs occasionally appeared on stage. A Cambridge performance of Euripides' tragedy *Hippolytus* in 1552 was enlivened by a pack of foxhounds invading the stage. Hunting dogs also appeared in a dramatization of Chaucer's *A Knight's Tale*, played before Queen Elizabeth in 1566, and a greyhound had a part in Giovan Battista Guarini's tragicomedy *Il Pastor Fido*. The main character of Ben Jonson's *Every Man out of His Humour* is the quixotic knight Puntarvolo, who is very fond of his greyhound. The dog follows him everywhere, until a malicious enemy poisons the poor animal. Puntarvolo is not amused when another scoundrel suggests that he should flay his favourite dog and purchase a slightly smaller one to fit into the skin.

The most famous Elizabethan onstage canine is the dog Crab, appearing with his foolish master Launce in Shakespeare's *Two Gentlemen of Verona*. Crab is the straight-man, or rather straight-dog, of the play: his major role is to listen to Launce's dotty and rambling monologues. His sole voluntary action of note is that he once cocks his leg against a gentlewoman's farthingale (outer skirt) inside a ducal palace. When the kind Launce saves his dog by saying that he committed the offence himself, he is duly whipped out of the room by the lady's servants. Crab's deplorable lack of house training is his only interesting feature; in fact, it would be fair to call him a non-performing dog rather than a performing one. In some low-budget productions of *Two Gentlemen of Verona*, Crab was even represented by a stuffed dog on wheels, dragged along by Launce using the lead.[1]

One would have expected the success of the *Chien Savant* and the Learned English Dog in the 1750s to have alerted playwrights and theatrical managers to the potential of onstage canine performers, but this seems to have happened only slowly. There were many showmen who travelled round fairs and markets with their performing dogs and monkeys, sometimes having these animals enacting simple plays, but these downmarket animal dramas had no impact on the London stage proper. In some eighteenth-century performances of *Two Gentlemen of Verona*, Crab took a more active part in proceedings, cocking his head as if he really understood what Launce was saying. In 1784, a troupe of performing dogs was contracted by Sadler's Wells theatre, to act in the play *The Deserter*.

30. An awkward-looking pair: the clownish servant Launce and his dog Crab, from an old illustration to Shakespeare's *Two Gentlemen of Verona*.

Led by Moustache, the star performer, and dressed in military uniforms, the dogs stormed a fortress to great acclaim from the audience. According to the *Life and Times of Frederick Reynolds*, this canine stampede was accomplished through starving the canine performers, and then placing a hot supper on the top of the fortress, unseen by the audience.

In 1803, the playwright Frederick Reynolds, who had admired Moustache and his fellow performers nineteen years earlier, presented his latest script to the manager of the Drury Lane Theatre. In a Hispanic setting, the tyrant Muneral, Governor of Barcelona, falls in love with the beautiful Marchioness of Calatrava. He has the Marquis arrested on a trumped-up charge, and conveyed to prison in a caravan, guarded by the driver Blabbo and his large dog Carlo. Although the Governor successively threatens the Marchioness that unless she succumbs to his advances, her husband would be transported to Mexico, blown up in the ship, or even starved to death on his journey in the caravan, the virtuous lady is obdurate. When she and her young son catch up with the caravan, she is relieved to find out that although Blabbo had orders to starve the Marquis on his journey, he has actually allowed the hungry nobleman to share the dog's food. But the evil governor also turns up, as obnoxious as ever. When the lady again rejects him, he orders a soldier to throw her son into a river. But the dog Carlo plunges into the water and saves the child. In the end, the governor is deposed, the Marquis liberated, and Blabbo and his dog rewarded.

'I have never heard such nonsense in my life!' you would have expected the manager to exclaim after he was made to listen to this absurd plot, but instead his response seems to have been more in the line of 'This will surely be a huge hit!' Actors were recruited, suitable music written by a certain Mr Reeve, and carpenters set to work constructing a precipice and an artificial lake on stage for the play's most dramatic scene. A large butcher's dog was purchased, renamed 'Carlo', and given a crash course in acting. Carlo was a Landseer Newfoundland, and probably three or four years old when he made his stage debut.

When *The Caravan, or the Driver and his Dog*, opened on 5 December 1803, reviews were very favourable. It was considered novel and praiseworthy to have a dog actor as one of the principal performers, and little less than a masterstroke of modern scenography to have a precipice and artificial lake onstage.[2] In particular, Carlo's intrepid leap was much admired. The *Spirit of Public Journals* described how the audience stood flabbergasted when the massive Newfoundland splashed into the water, exclaiming 'An't he a fine dog? Did you see the dog? How excellently he did it'.

The *Morning Chronicle* struck a more ribald note, since the journalist thought that the acting dog's onstage behaviour had been rowdy indeed: 'We are extremely unwilling to touch upon the private foibles of the theatrical *corps*, when they do not interfere with their professional engagements, but we are compelled to observe, that on Monday night's performance Mr. *Carlo* was evidently *in liquor*!' It was no coincidence that the artificial lake was so very full, he continued, since Mr Carlo had also given the stage hands a *lift* filling it up! The *Hampshire Telegraph* was somewhat more respectful, commenting that if the largest of all *bipeds* was Bonaparte, who fills all the prisons in *France*, then surely the greatest of all *quadrupeds* had to be the Dog Carlo, who fills the largest theatre in *England*.

The *Caravan* was a great success, constantly playing to full houses, many of whom came to see the acting dog. When he made his bow (wow) on stage, there was a great roar of 'Carlo! Carlo! Carlo!' from the rowdy and numerous audience. When a trumpet sounded, to mark the arrival of the tyrant Muneral, Carlo responded with an equally sonorous howl. In March 1804, the mother of the child actor demanded that Carlo was replaced, since her son had been 'terribly bruised' from the acting dog's powerful jaws when surreptitiously pulled out of the artificial lake. The manager got hold of a less squeamish child actor instead, however, and Carlo's career was saved.

The acting dog remained a controversial member of the cast, however, since he frequently improvised on stage. Once, he pushed the Marquis over and reclaimed the dog food he was supposed to share; another time, he prevented the throwing of the child by obstructing the soldier. Sometimes, the audience distracted him with their shouts of 'Carlo! Carlo! Carlo!' and made him jump about and bark excitedly; at other times, when the acting dog was bored, he lay down on stage and did not move a muscle. But Frederick Reynolds and the manager of the theatre were sufficiently astute to realize that Carlo's unpredictable behaviour was in fact one of the prime attractions of the play; in fact, not two performances were identical. The audience were delighted when the acting dog was up to mischief, and some people came to see the play again and again to see what rowdy behaviour Carlo would be up to next.

31. Carlo makes his leap, from the *Sporting Magazine* of 1804.

The Times published an amusing review of Carlo's latest performance, which deserves to be given in full:

In the 'Caravan' *Carlo* gave signs of much confidence and improvement. He seems familiarized to the audience, and as proof of it, he lay down on the stage during the greatest part of *his* principal scene. In the *finale*, at the end of the first act, he made atonement; for, instead of *modestly* confining himself, as formerly, to a timely and occasional *howl*, he assumed the principal part of the chorus, and *barked away* highly to the entertainment of the audience, and not a little to the amusement of the performers, who were convulsed with laughter. We cannot with-hold him the justice due to his merit, in saying that he took the *leap* with gallant and desperate resolution.

The same newspaper also published a short poem about the celebrated acting dog:

> Now Attic wit's o'ercome by Gothic rage,
> And authors *throw cold water* on the stage;
> While, honest *Carlo*, envying even you,
> They make their very dramas *Dog*-grel too.[3]

Children's author Eliza Fenwick was one of the many Londoners to see *The Caravan*. By this time, Carlo's onstage exploits had made him a favourite among the children, and Eliza Fenwick was amazed to see many little boys and girls sitting in the front row of the boxes, applauding Carlo with the greatest enthusiasm. She was clever enough to exploit the situation: later in 1804, her little book *The Life of the Famous Dog Carlo* was published for a juvenile audience. Carlo had been so impressed with the 'rapturous exclamations' of the hundreds of young gentlemen and young ladies who had come to see him act, she explained, that the dog had seen fit to compose his autobiography. Carlo's fictional life story was dramatic indeed: he saved people from drowning, once dropped an angry little dog into the water after it had annoyed him, and dragged a young boy who had stolen half a roast goose in front of the Lord Mayor of London to have him confess the theft. According to Eliza Fenwick, Carlo's master, who kept a tavern, offered to have his dog play in *The Caravan*. Since the acting dog had shown both zeal and sagacity, his reputation as a good actor was universally established. This version throws some doubt on the original story of Carlo being a butcher's dog purchased by the theatre. Both Eliza Fenwick and a writer in the *Sporting Magazine* depicted and described Carlo as large, handsome, purebred Landseer Newfoundland, a fashionable breed of dog that the average butcher could ill afford at the time.[4]

Largely thanks to Carlo, *The Caravan* was still going strong in 1805. After one performance, the wit Richard Brinsley Sheridan called out 'Author!' When informed that Mr Reynolds had retired, Sheridan replied 'Pooh! – I mean the Dog-actor, the *Author* and *Preserver* of Drury-lane Theatre!' A laborious satire in the *Morning Chronicle* instead presented a 'Comparison between a Certain Great Statesman and a Certain Great Actor; or, Lord Castlereagh and the Dog Carlo'. To gain his dinner, Carlo had to plunge into the water in an illuminated theatre, surrounded by applauding spectators; the Prime Minister made similar exhortations to save a sinking cause, and a falling government. In another, more amusing joke of the time, one of the actors in *The Caravan* had suddenly been taken ill. The prompter rushed off to see the manager, who initially seemed a good deal put out, before exclaiming, 'How you alarm me, the tragedian unwell! I was afraid it was the dog!'[5]

A number of satirical caricature prints were inspired by Carlo's onstage exploits. In *The Manager and his Dog*, Carlo swims in the artificial lake on stage, holding Sheridan's head above water to symbolize his importance for the theatre's survival. Other prints depicted Carlo bringing a basket of new 'Growley Dramas' for him to act in, or guarding a padlocked 'Drury Lane Strong Box'. In 1808, after the latest of several false rumours that Carlo had died, the print *A New Drop Scene for Drury Lane Theatre* depicted a man painting black spots onto a white dog with a collar marked 'Carlo'![6]

32. Carlo the Acting Dog, from his biography.

33. Carlo keeping Sheridan afloat in the caricature 'The Manager and his Dog'.

In 1806, Carlo went on tour, but the next year he was back in London, acting in another play. In 1808, an actor named Munden tried to recruit Carlo to play the role of Crab in Mr Kemble's revision of *Two Gentlemen of Verona*, but the acting dog had other engagements at the time. Instead, Munden brought with him on stage another Newfoundland dog, named 'Caesar', but this dog misbehaved himself throughout, even by the low standards set by Carlo. In the scene where the dog was roughly handled, the large Newfoundland, 'not understanding *making belief* in such matters, seized his assailant by the leg.'[7] Nothing more was heard of Caesar after this short but violent acting career, but Carlo himself is said to have been alive and well, and still acting, when his biography was reissued in 1809. The last notice of this extraordinary dog is that he appeared in *The Forty Thieves* at the Theatre Royal, Covent Garden, in May 1811.[8]

The great success of Carlo set playwrights and theatrical managers thinking. In spite of possessing neither discipline nor any discernable acting skills, Carlo had established himself as a canine superstar. Newfoundland dogs were highly thought of at the time, and admired for their great strength and handsome looks. These fashionable dogs were also intelligent and easy to train, and large enough to fight villains, dive into lakes, and rescue people. Now what if a clever young Newfoundland dog was given acting lessons from an early age, and was made accustomed to the clamouring of the audience? And what if a play was deliberately written for the dog?

Not long after Carlo had retired from the theatre, an actor named Bush (or Rush) trained another Newfoundland dog to become his successor. In early 1817, the Dog Bruin acted in *The Viceroy, or the Spanish Gypsey and the Assassin*, saving a child from a burning castle. According to the *Morning Chronicle*, 'the actions of the Dog Bruin almost exceed credibility'. Advertisements for this play, or for its successor *The Terrible Peak, or a Mother's Sorrows*, never failed to point out that the Dog Bruin was part of the cast.

It did not take long for the first, archetypical dog drama to be staged in London. In Paris, *Le Chien de Montargis, ou la Forêt de Bondy* had premiered in Paris in 1814, where it had an uninterrupted run in until 1834. Translated into English as *The Dog of Montargis, or the Forest of Bondy*, and staged at the King's Theatre, it was to remain the staple item for canine thespians for many years. It is roughly based on an old French legend. In a remote forest, the officer Aubri is murderously attacked by two enemies, Macaire and Landri. He is valiantly defended by his large dog Dragon, but when the faithful animal is kept occupied by Landri, the second villain gives Aubri the fatal wound. Later, an innocent deaf-mute simpleton is 'framed' for the murder, but Dragon saves him by producing a sash he has torn off Macaire's uniform. Each time Dragon sees the murderers, he growls and tries to attack them. The King gives the brave dog the right to trial by battle, and after a long and gory fight, the defeated Macaire confesses the murder. This scene introduced the trick of 'taking the seize', in which the acting dog leaps up onto the villain and seizes him by the throat. The actor playing the villain had to wear protective padding round his neck, and yell 'Take off the dog!' once he was brought down. With its racy plot and exciting fight scenes, *The Dog of Montargis* would remain a staple item of dog drama for decades to come. In spite of this, the play did not always come off as planned; it is recorded that once, the friendly acting dog stood watching the audience and wagging his tail, instead of 'taking the seize'. The infuriated villain desperately tried to induce him to attack; in the end, he had to fly at the placid dog himself and lift the animal up to his throat.

In 1819, the Dog Bruin acted in a piece entitled *The Gipsy*, which concluded with the hunting of a wild boar. It was an ambitious production, with guns being fired, horses ridden across the stage, and the appearance of a pack of hunting dogs, led by Bruin. After several successful performances, disaster struck one evening, when the powerful Bruin decided to improve on the plot. Breaking free from the huntsmen, he darted after the actor representing the wild boar. The fearful actor jumped into the orchestra pit, but Bruin leaped after him and seized hold of the wild boar costume. According to a newspaper review:

> The terrified musicians fled, leaving the two champions in possession of the field. The most indescribable confusion prevailed throughout the theatre. The other dogs on stage encouraged their comrade with all the power of their lungs. The uproar was terrible, and the intrepid dog was separated from his prey with no little difficulty.[9]

In April 1820, the Dog Bruin starred in *The Cottage of the Lake*. In this play, a child is thrown into an artificial lake, to be saved by the dog. The advertisement for the play also tells that the Misses Cawse, musical prodigies aged eight and eleven, also took part, hopefully in some more dignified position than being unceremoniously thrown into the lake, to be retrieved by Bruin's powerful jaws. The next year, Bruin again demanded trial by battle in *The Smuggler's Dog*, but this is the last we hear of this particular acting dog.[10]

The Victorian theatregoers loved to see animals on stage. Hippodrama, with horses playing leading roles, was established already before Carlo's success, and these equine actors continued to hoof the boards for several decades. The Covent Garden theatre hired horses from Astley's circus to act in melodramas written particularly to suit these performers. If *The Dog of Montargis* was the ultimate dog drama, the hippodrama *Mazeppa*, where a naked Tartar boy is strapped to the back of an apparently wild horse, had equal success, particularly if the leading role (the boy, not the horse) was played by the scandalous American star Adah Isaacs Menken.[11] In Victorian theatre, bulls and dragons were played by horses, and wolves and hyenas by dogs; in some low budget productions, tigers were played by large black dogs painted with yellow stripes. In a play entitled *The Hindoo Robber*, two acting dogs played the part of leopards. When one of them was 'shot', it pretended to stagger and expire on a rock, amid such tumultuous applause that the other 'leopard' became jealous backstage. He rushed on the stage and simulated all the agonies of death 'to show that he could die better'. There was great amusement at this ludicrous scene, particularly when the spotted costume burst so that *two* tails were exhibited.[12]

A few years after the original Dog Bruin had retired from the stage, he was succeeded by a namesake, another Newfoundland. Along with his master, an impecunious young actor named Wood, Bruin II acted in *The Dog of Montargis* and other plays, at the Warwick and Drury Lane theatres.

In October 1826, a certain Philip Vincent summoned Wood before the Union Hall magistrates' court, claiming that he had reared Bruin from a puppy, and that the handsome and expensive dog had disappeared two years ago, without trace, until it had been found in the possession of the defendant. Things did not look particularly good for the actor Wood, who did not contest these facts. Fortunately he had consulted the solicitor Mr Harmer. It turned out that Vincent, who represented himself in court, had made a serious mistake. The statute under which the summons was granted expressly mentioned that there had to be a charge of theft, and in the present case no such charge had been made. On this technicality, the case was dismissed by the magistrate, since there was no charge of felony.[13]

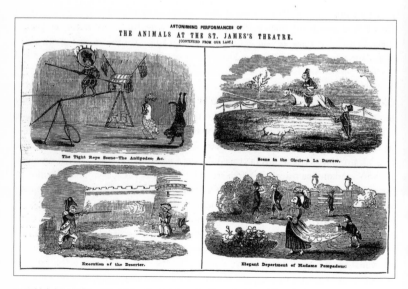

34. Old-fashioned 'dog and monkey theatre', from the *Penny Satirist*, 4 May 1839.

Sometimes, it was useful to have an acting dog around. In March 1828, a poor woman, who made a precarious living selling watercress, walked along the floating timbers near Searle's boathouse in Lambeth, and plunged headlong into the Thames. Fortunately, as *The Times* expressed it, 'Wood, the owner of the famous dog of Montargis, was close at hand bathing his favourite.' Regarding the situation as an unscheduled rehearsal, Bruin jumped in after the woman and dragged her to shore. When she stood up and threatened to jump back into the river, the acting dog practised 'taking the seize'. When this suicidal woman was taken to a public house nearby, the servant girl fainted straight away. She was later reproached for her 'hysteria', but it turned out that 'she had a more afflicting cause – the watercress woman was her own mother'.[14]

In 1829, Wood and Bruin acted in *Androcles and the Lion* at the Coburg Theatre, with the dog 'contrieved and fitted' in leonine guise. In 1830, Sir Walter Scott's *The Talisman* was adapted for the stage as the amazingly titled dog drama *Knights of the Cross, or the Dog of the Blood-Stained Banner*, with major parts for Wood and Bruin. Going through his entire acting repertoire, Bruin saves Edith Plantagenet from drowning, brings food and drink to a chained prisoner, discovers a thief, and kills a wicked Emir of the Desert. When the dog is ordered to guard the English standard, a French traitor, played by Wood himself, sneaks up to steal it. The noble Bruin 'takes the seize' and pulls him to the ground, but only to be stabbed by the Frenchman's vassals. There was not a dry eye in the house when the brave dog fell lifeless to the ground, but much cheering and applause when Bruin leapt up after 'playing dead' to join his fellow thespians in taking the applause.

Wood appears to have been the first person to realise that there was one thing better than keeping an acting dog, namely to possess *two* of these animals. Later in 1830, he procured, hopefully by more honest means this time, another Newfoundland, named Hector. The two acting dogs got on well together, and had several plays written for them, like *The Foul Anchor* and *The Cherokee Chief*. The last mention of Wood and his dogs dates from October 1831 when Hector played in *The Dog of Montargis* at the Royal Pavilion Theatre.[15]

Old actors, and acting dogs, do not die; they merely fade away. Although we will hear no more from the impecunious, dog-stealing Wood, it must be suspected that his two acting dogs started another career, under new management. In May 1833, a performance of *The Cherokee Chief, or the Dogs of the Wreck*, featured the young actor Barkham Cony and his two dogs Hector and Bruin. Although a newspaper review praises Cony 'for the very extraordinary degree of docility and intelligence to which he has brought his favourite animals' there is good reason to suspect that Cony had purchased Wood's dogs, particularly since the drama was one the dogs were already adept at acting in.

Barkham Cony was born in 1802, and became an actor when he was still a young man. In 1828, he was one of the leading performers at the Cobourg Theatre in London. A strong, muscular fellow, he was a useful boxer and athlete. The success of *The Cherokee Chief* made him take up dog drama in a big way, and he would remain a major exponent of this form of theatre for decades. He soon joined forces with the young American actor Edwin Blanchard. This amusing character specialized in low comedy, sometimes

Sailors & Savages,

OR THE

RIVAL DOGS!

In which the celebrated and unequalled

CARLO & LION will exhibit their astonishing sagacity

and introduce a variety of new and surprising Tricks.

Pattaparo, (the treacherous Indian) Mr. H. SIMPSON.

35. 'Take that, Pattaparo!' A Treacherous Indian receives his comeuppance at the paws of two sturdy acting dogs.

playing the role of an orang-utan dressed in a specially manufactured suit. Cony's success with Hector and Bruin convinced Blanchard that dogs paid better than apes, however, and the two actors would remain inseparable for many years. By this time, there were several other actors specializing in training acting dogs; they were known as 'dog-men' and travelled from theatre to theatre, performing with their beasts.[16]

For decades, Cony and Blanchard kept their position as London's leading dog-men. In 1836, they even crossed the Atlantic with their acting dogs. Whether Hector and Bruin were still the original performers is anybody's guess, but their performance in *The Dog of Montargis* at the Bowery Theatre in New York was a huge success. The Americans had never seen acting dogs like these two massive but sagacious Newfoundlands, and Cony soon became known as 'The Dog Star'. He usually played the villain, and was particularly adept in finding novel ways for the dogs to put an end to his career, by drowning or suffocating him, pushing him down a precipice, shooting him with a pistol held in the dog's mouth, or discharging a hidden explosive device. In *The Dog of Montargis*, Cony played the role of the villain Landri, introducing a new high point in dog drama when the agile Hector made a great leap to knock him from the saddle of his horse. He used protective padding underneath his clothes to lessen the bruising when the dogs grasped him with their powerful jaws. Blanchard sometimes played the hero, although the American's newfound wealth had caused him to put on much weight, rendering him quite unfit to be jumping about on stage.

Cony and Blanchard dominated the dog drama throughout the 1830s and 1840s. They were equally successful in Britain and in the United States. In 1840, they were back in London, acting with their dogs in *Napoleon, or the Deserter*. One day, when Blanchard was taking Bruin to the theatre, a large dog came rushing out from a carpenter's shop and attacked the celebrated acting dog. When the massive Newfoundland fought back, driving his opponent back into the shop, the carpenter emerged with a stick, which he used to belabour the acting dog. Blanchard, a useful boxer just like his fellow 'Dog Star', ended the fracas by knocking the carpenter out cold.

Later, when prosecuted for assault and battery, Blanchard calmly asserted that both he and his dog had acted in self-defence. They were engaged at the Victoria Theatre, playing for full houses, and would he risk an injury to his star performer by setting the acting dog on some disreputable street mongrel, risking injury to his own valuable animal? It turned out that the carpenter had a bad reputation, and that his dog had been a nuisance to the local residents, once even biting a policeman on duty. When the case was dismissed, the carpenter with the black eye swore an angry oath at the spectators.[17]

Victorian melodrama was entirely unhindered by political correctness. A blind or deaf-mute character was considered quite hilarious, as was a clownish black servant, or a simpleton labouring under some unfortunate speech impediment. In the dog drama *The Dumb Black and his Watch Dog*, the intrepid dog is not only stronger, but also more intelligent than his pathetic, speechless human sidekick. The Dumb Black gets into trouble again and again, only to be saved by the noble, patient Watch Dog. When the hapless Black is framed for theft, the faithful dog turns detective, uncovering evidence that exonerates him.

In *The Smuggler's Dog, or the Blind Boy's Murder*, the forceful Smuggler's Dog saves the life of the Blind Boy a number of times, but the sightless lad still keeps bumbling about in a dangerous manner. If there is a fire, a waterfall or an open trapdoor on stage, he heads straight for it. Having been rescued from drowning, fire and a cutlass-wielding pirate, the Blind Boy is finally pushed down a precipice when the dog is busy biting another villain. Still, the Smuggler's Dog witnesses the murder and demands trial by battle, with the inevitable result.

An actor named Jack Matthews rewrote one of Shakespeare's masterpieces into the half-hour dog drama *The Dog Hamlet*, frequently performed at various booth shows and fairs. The melancholy Prince of Denmark is followed everywhere by a large black dog, which would howl at the moon at the sight of the Ghost, and 'take the seize' to throttle the King in the final scene. A melancholy groan was said to emanate from Shakespeare's tomb each time this sad travesty was enacted.

There was a good deal of interest in Native Americans in England at this time. Eschewing the Wild West adage that the only good Indian is a dead Indian, the London playwrights instead took their cue from the books of Fenimore Cooper: there were Good Indians, and then there were Bad Indians. The Good Indians were noble savages with names like 'Wonga' or 'Eagle-Eye', usually the last of their tribe, and accompanied

36. 'Get the key, Bruin!'

37. 'Quick, Bruin, carry that burning torch away from the gunpowder store!' 'Woof!'

by a 'funny' blind or dumb simpleton – and by a large dog. The Bad Indians had names like 'Rattlesnake' or 'Black Vulture', entertained lurid designs on white women, had a firm dislike for dogs, and a propensity to throw disabled simpletons into the water from high precipices.

There were no canine actresses bitching about at this time: the dogs were all male, with martial-sounding names like Hector, Victor, Lion or Neptune. The majority of them were either purebred Newfoundlands or Newfoundland crosses: large, imposing animals capable of holding their own in the frequent fight scenes. One would have thought it a useful ploy to pit the acting dogs against each other: both the hero and the villain should be accompanied by dogs, one a noble and upright animal, the other a veritable Cujo. The drama would of course end with both the human and canine actors settling their various scores in a grand fight scene. This idea was never put into effect, however; in Victorian melodrama, the acting dogs were uniformly good, loyal and faithful, and more heroic than the play's hero himself.

Cony and Blanchard remained in London until 1844, acting in *The Knights of the Cross*, *The Smuggler's Dog* and *The Dumb Slave*. Blanchard made a burlesque contribution in *The Orang Outang and his Double, or the Runaway Monkey*. In 1845 and 1846, they were back at the Bowery in New York. This was the time when dog drama was at its most famous. The New Yorkers' delight in seeing canine actors on stage led to some old plays being revised: *Jack Sheppard, and His Dog*, *Dick Turpin, and His Dog* or even *Caspar Hauser, the Blind Boy of Germany, and His Dog* were all much more successful than the dog-less original versions.

When performing in New York in 1851, Cony and Blanchard had an angry quarrel, leading to the two 'Dog Stars' parting company, for good. Still, they remained in town, doing their best to put each other out of business. Blanchard was acting at the National with the dogs Hector and Bruin, whereas Cony was at the Bowery with his son Eugene Cony and the Dog Yankee. They acted in the same plays: *The Dog of Montargis*, *The Butcher's Dog of Ghent* and *The Dogs of Mount St. Bernard*. When Blanchard once more squeezed his bulky frame into the monkey-suit in *The Orang Outang*, Cony retaliated by having *The Cross of Death; or, The Dog Witness* written expressly for himself and the Dog Yankee. Although some purists complained that two of New York's major theatres had been made into kennels, there was enough interest from the dog-loving theatregoers to make both outfits prosper.

38. Mr Cony and his dog Bruin acting in the *The Dog of Montargis*.

39. A poster for dog drama at the Bower Saloon.

Cony and Blanchard were to remain enemies and competitors until Cony's premature death in 1858. Young Eugene Cony tried to carry on his father's life work, but without much success. Blanchard, a more established name, remained a force to be reckoned with in New York show business until the 1870s. By this time, his main rival was the actress Fanny Herring, who performed with her dogs Lafayette and Thunder, in plays like *The Rag Woman and Her Dogs*. Although classics like *The Dog of Montargis* and *The Smuggler's Dog* received an occasional airing as late as the 1880s, the enthusiasm for dog drama had all but ended by that time. It was considered old-fashioned and downmarket to have animals on stage, and the traditional Victorian melodramas continued without the canine actors.

In contrast, the traditional 'dog and monkey theatre' at fairs and music halls continued unimpeded. In 1899, two such companies were active in London. Mademoiselle Erna brought a troupe of twenty dogs and ten monkeys to the Alhambra Theatre. In one of her plays, a monkey lady is lounging on the cushions in a miniature landau pulled by two retrievers, with fox-terriers as coachman and footman. When a wheel comes off the vehicle, the dogs quickly reattach it. Mr Percy Victor's troupe of dogs played musical instruments, dressed in fantastic garb. Victor's popular 'Dog Minstrels' also acted in *The Coster's Wedding*, where two gaily dressed poodles are married by a stern, white-robed retriever.[18]

In September 1918, the American Corporal Lee Duncan was serving with his battalion in Lorraine, France. One day, when he and his troop were checking out a bombed

40. A dog playing the part of Toby in a Victorian 'Punch and Judy' show in London, from an old print.

war-dog kennel, they found a mother German Shepherd dog and her litter as the only survivors. Duncan made sure all the dogs were saved and himself took care of two of the puppies. He named them Rin Tin Tin and Nannette after some small puppets the French had given to the American soldiers for good luck. Rin Tin Tin survived the journey back to the United States, but poor Nannette soon died of disease. 'Rinty', as he was nicknamed, grew up to become a large, strapping German Shepherd dog, dark sable in colour and with very dark eyes. At a dog show in 1922, he amazed everyone with his extraordinary agility; the dog was able to clear a fence of 11 feet, 9 inches.

The canny Lee Duncan soon realized that such a handsome, well-trained dog could be an asset in the film industry. After Rinty had got his great break in the film industry by stepping in for a recalcitrant wolf in *The Man from Hell's River*, there was no stopping the acting dog. He successfully competed against Strongheart, Hollywood's resident acting German Shepherd, and made not less than twenty-six pictures for Warner Brothers, allegedly saving the company from bankruptcy, just like Carlo the Acting Dog rescued the Drury Lane theatre more than a century earlier. Some of Rin Tin Tin's films had 'fierce' names like *Clash of the Wolves* and *Jaws of Steel*. At the peak of his career, he was insured for $100,000; twice as much as Don the Talking Dog ten years earlier. Rinty received several thousand fan letters every week. Although sometimes posing as a wolf or a wolf hybrid, he was always the 'good guy', saving people from drowning, carrying children out from burning houses, and fighting outlaws or Bad Indians with enthusiasm. A worthy successor to Carlo and Bruin, this agile and super-intelligent dog opened and shut doors and windows with the greatest of ease, boarded trains or stagecoaches when he thought he needed faster transportation, and understood the workings of firearms and explosives.

In 1930, Rin Tin Tin got his own radio series, also featuring the silly boy Rusty, the slightly more sensible hero Lieutenant 'Rip' Masters, and the comical sidekick Sergeant 'Biff' O'Hara. The average episode went something like this:

The three hapless humans try to seek out the gunslinger Black Bart and his gang of outlaws, but are eventually captured, tied up and left in a cave.

'Har-Har! This'll be the end of yer!' gloats the unpleasant Black Bart, lighting the fuse of a powerful bomb.

But after the villains have made themselves scarce, the heroic Rin Tin Tin sneaks in, unties his three friends, grabs the explosives and leads the way out of the cave.

'Where are you going with that bomb, Rinty?'

'Woof!'

'Why, he is putting it into Black Bart's saddlebag!'

'Boom!!'

'Good dog, Rinty!'

Rin Tin Tin did his own sound effects for the radio show until his death in Los Angeles two years later, according to Hollywood legend expiring in the arms of actress Jean Harlow. Just like Captain Castelli 120 years earlier, Lee Duncan had made sure the succession was secured, however, by raising several litters fathered by Rin Tin Tin, and selecting the best puppies to continue their famous father's bloodline. Rin Tin Tin Jr took over his father's part in the radio show, and later acted in several films. Rin Tin

Tin III only made one film, but both he and Duncan distinguished themselves as head trainers in a camp for war dogs during the Second World War. Rin Tin Tin IV, the next successor, starred in his own popular TV series in the 1950s.

Lee Duncan passed away in 1960, leaving the care of the Rin Tin Tin bloodline to dog breeder Jannettia Brodsgaard Propps. Under her management, the dogs had less acting success, but they remained highly sought after as show and service dogs. Ms Propps left the care of Rin Tin Tin to her granddaughter Daphne Hereford in 1988. The dogs have continued to act, performing their usual stunts in the TV series *Rin Tin Tin, K9 Cop* and other productions. The dogs also make personal appearances, attending war memorials and parades, and visiting schools and residential homes. After the untimely death of Rin Tin Tin X, he was succeeded by the little puppy Rin Tin Tin XI, born in July 2009.[19]

In 1943, the sentimental story *Lassie Come Home* about a collie making a long and heroic journey to rejoin her master after his family is forced to sell her for money, was made into a major film by Metro-Goldwyn-Mayer. Starring Roddy McDowall and Elizabeth Taylor, the film was a huge hit. It also launched the career of the handsome collie Pal, handled by the American brothers Frank and Rudd Weatherwax. Pal starred in seven films and two TV shows between 1943 and 1954. Like all other collies to play Lassie over the years, Pal was a male; not only are male collies larger than the females, they also retain a thicker summer coat which looks better on film.

Although Lassie was a male in drag, her onstage character differed from that of Rin Tin Tin. As we know, Rinty was a masculine, gung-ho dog who never backed out of a fight, dispatching various outlaws, pirates and tomahawk-wielding Bad Indians with gusto. Lassie was more feminine, and her adventures more sentimental, although she sometimes made use of her fangs to defend small children against various mean-spirited characters. The theme from the original film was often resorted to, with weeping children mourning their departed Lassie, and the resourceful dog escaping from heartless new owners, or even dognappers, to rejoin them. With her superior intelligence, Lassie was very adept at looking after foolish and imprudent children getting into trouble. If they fell into the water, she dragged them ashore; if they got struck by an avalanche, she dug them out; if they got caught by Bad Indians, she braved arrows and tomahawks to liberate them. If there was a landfall across the railway line, Lassie understood the danger, grabbed a red flag and stopped the train.

Many of Pal's descendants have appeared in various Lassie TV series and remakes over the years. In 1945, Lee Duncan and Rin Tin Tin III met with Rudd Weatherwax and Lassie III to find out which of the two acting dogs was the most intelligent. Fears that the two forthright Americans would settle the issue with their fists were unfounded; in fact, they emerged as friends, declaring that the dogs were of equal intelligence. The Weatherwax Lassies have continued to act, although there have been some quarrels about who has the rights to the dogs, and also deplorable attempts from low-budget TV companies to hire in cheaper 'Lassies' on the sly. The Lassies also make personal appearances, and sign lucrative deals to promote dog food and accessories. In 2009, Rin

Tin Tin X appeared along with Lassie X in Canyon Country, California, to be admired by a bevy of fans and admirers.

On Hollywood's Walk of Fame, there are stars for Strongheart, Rin Tin Tin and Lassie, the only three dogs represented. In contrast, the acting dogs of Victorian times are a forgotten part of canine history; their story is told here for the first time. It is clear that Carlo was the great forerunner, and that the concept of dog drama started with him. Although later acting dogs, like those managed by Cony and Blanchard, were more proficient and had more tricks in their repertoire, it was the great Carlo plunging into the artificial lake on stage who started it all.

It is also clear that there are some important parallels between Victorian dog drama and today's concept of the onstage canine. Carlo, Bruin and Hector were all superlatively brave and heroic, just like Rin Tin Tin and Lassie. They save their pathetic human sidekicks when they get into trouble: the child of the Marchioness of Calatrava, the Dumb Black, the accident-prone Rusty and the thoughtless children protected by Lassie. The mongrel dog Benji in the 1974 film with the same name also uses his superior intellect to find and rescue some kidnapped children.

Another long-lived concept is that of the dog as 'silent witness' to a murder, like the Dog of Montargis and the Smuggler's Dog. In the amusing and popular 1989 film *Turner & Hooch*, a large junkyard dog is taken care of by a detective after witnessing the murder of its owner. And indeed, the dog spots the killer and tries to attack him. In the end, Hooch is shot dead, giving his life to save that of his master, like many a Victorian acting dog before him.

In *Turner & Hooch*, the dog is supposed to be a junkyard mongrel, but he is in fact a pedigree Dogue de Bordeaux, an uncommon breed notable for their large heads, powerful jaws and prodigious slobber-cheeks. Unlike the well-trained Rin Tin Tin and the spotlessly clean Lassie, Hooch is a very mischievous and destructive dog, in spite of his heroic qualities. The same is true for the disgraced police dog Jerry Lee in the 1989 film *K-9*: the intelligent but lazy dog works only when he wants to, and is up to all kinds of mischief. The detective masters of these two dogs, played by Tom Hanks and James Belushi respectively, are depicted as equal partners to their heroic dogs, rather like the stalwart Knights of the Cross and courageous Good Indians in Victorian dog drama.

It is also rewarding to look for traces of Victorian dog drama in the very popular 1992 film *Beethoven*. In this hit comedy, a St Bernard puppy escapes from dog thieves and is taken care of by an American family. Although Beethoven is full of mischief, and constantly filling his digestive cavity, they soon become fond of him. He grows up to become a massive St Bernard male. When the son of the family is annoyed by bullies, Beethoven frightens them off, and when the careless little girl falls into a swimming pool, the brave dog does a 'Carlo' to perfection and retrieves her. The dog thieves are not far away, however; together with an evil veterinarian, who wants to use Beethoven for an ammunition test, they imprison the great dog in a research facility. In the final fight scene, the acting dog 'takes the seize' like a champion to dispose of one of the villains.

6

RAILWAY JACK, OWNEY & SOME OTHER CANINE GLOBETROTTERS

The British Library's copy of George R. Jesse's *Researches into the History of the British Dog* contains some very curious newspaper cuttings pasted onto its endpapers by a previous owner. In June 1881, a correspondent to the *Illustrated Sporting and Dramatic News* wanted to know if any other reader had seen the extraordinary fox-terrier Jack, who used to travel on the London, Brighton & South Coast Railway trains. Jack lived at the Lewes railway station, but every day, he made excursions to Portsmouth, Horsham or Brighton. He used to sit by the guard's wheel, looking out through the window. Jack always caught the last train back to Lewes, where he used to sleep. One day, a railwayman had traced Jack's movements. The dapper little fox-terrier boarded the 10.50 from Lewes to Brighton, where he disembarked and walked to a local pub, where he was given a biscuit. After another walk, he took a later train to East Grinstead, where he spent the afternoon before returning to Brighton and Lewes. How could a dog have such extraordinary talents of direction and punctuality, the writer asked himself, and did Jack regard himself as sub-guard, director or general overseer of the railways?

Another correspondent to the same newspaper added that he, too, had seen this famous travelling dog in Lewes as a curiosity. Not long after, he had actually met Jack at Victoria Station, where the fox-terrier jumped off the train like an experienced traveller. The guard said that Jack was a frequent visitor to London. This time, he had changed trains at Clapham Junction, knowing well which train to catch to get to Victoria. The guard speculated that Jack would 'probably take a trip round to London Bridge and go home that way. There is no accounting for him'.

A military officer wrote that he had known Jack for four years. The fox-terrier knew London Bridge and Victoria stations as well as himself, particularly the refreshment rooms where he had many friends. Jack had private apartments at Croydon, Three Bridges, Tunbridge and Eastbourne stations. He once caught the wrong train at Croydon and went all the way to Edinburgh by mistake. Fortunately, the friendly Scottish railway guards and porters had heard of this famous travelling dog; they fed and housed him for a week, before returning him to Lewes. Occasionally, Railway Jack went to Dieppe or Paris for the weekend. Noting the officer's uniform, Jack took him for a railway guard

41. Railway Jack before the accident – a drawing in *Chatterbox*, 30 December 1882.

and did not object to riding with him in the first-class compartment, sitting on his lap and watching each station carefully.[1]

Many people went to Lewes to see Railway Jack as a curiosity. If they tipped the stationmaster, a rotund, bushy-bearded character named Mr F. G. Moore, he allowed them to see and feed Railway Jack, and to watch the dapper little dog jump onto any train that took his fancy. Although Jack treated the Lewes railway station as his home, he did not consider that he needed a master; neither Mr Moore nor any other person had any authority over him, and he came and went as it pleased him. Jack knew all local railway stations, and the principal London ones; he had friends everywhere. He had an almost uncanny ability to always catch the right train to take him home. Once, a guard had tried to be helpful, lifting the dog on board his train, but Jack seemed to sense that this train would not carry him home, and immediately jumped out again.

For some reason, this eccentric Railway Jack was very fond of funerals. When John Isgar, the old head porter at Lewes, departed this life in September 1881, Jack was one of the chief mourners, despite Mr Moore's attempts to prevent him from going into the church. In November the same year, Jack arrived in Eastbourne and insisted on taking part in the funeral of the old platform inspector Mr Bryant. He ran alongside the hearse, sat by the coffin during the ceremony, and later entered the chapel, where he had a final look at the coffin. This incident would have been less significant, a journalist solemnly wrote, if the dog had not turned up in an equally singular manner, and conducted himself with the same commendable sobriety, at the funeral of Mr Isgar a few weeks earlier.

In early 1882, there was no shortage of newspaper interest in Railway Jack: there were features about the Lewes celebrity in both the *Girl's Own Paper* and *Chatterbox* magazine. A wealthy lady, Mrs J. P. Knight of Brockley, presented Jack with a silver-mounted collar with the inscription 'I am Jack, the L.B. and S.C. Railway Dog. Please give me a drink, and I will then go home to Lewes'. Another present from the same lady, a sumptuous dog basket with a soft mattress, was spurned by the eccentric dog, who preferred to sleep in the waste paper basket in the booking office. By this time, Jack had been to Canterbury, Exeter, Glasgow and Edinburgh. A reporter once followed Jack on one of his expeditions. First the dog took the morning train to Brighton, then decided he had business in Portsmouth, where he ate his luncheon. He left that town by the 1.30 train and proceeded to Littlehampton, where the journalist persuaded him to have his photograph taken at Mr White's studio at No. 32 High Street.

Just a few weeks later, Railway Jack travelled to Norwood Junction, where he was busy sniffing around the platforms. When crossing the rails, his attention was caught by a dead bird. Just at that moment, a fast train was running through the station. Sensing the danger, Jack took a flying leap at the platform, but missed and fell under the wheels of the train. The railwaymen feared that he had been killed, but it turned out that Jack had escaped death, although his left forepaw was badly crushed. The travelling dog was said to have showed great fortitude after the accident: he licked the hands of those who

42. Railway Jack, from *Graphic* magazine.

helped him, and only whined a little when the mangled limb was bandaged. A surgeon was consulted: his verdict was that Jack's forepaw had to be amputated. A telegram was sent to Mr Moore, who ordered that Jack was to be put onto the next train to Lewes. When he arrived, the skilful veterinary surgeon Robert Stock stood ready to operate: once his assistant had put Jack under with the chloroform, the limb was amputated at the shoulder.

Mrs Stock nursed Railway Jack devotedly, and the railway porters took turns to keep vigil by his basket. As a result, the dog survived both accident and operation, and soon learnt to jump around on three legs with alacrity. Mr Moore gave interviews to the press, introducing the journalists to the now three-legged canine celebrity. He had received more than a hundred inquiries from anxious railwaymen, he said, and a shelf in his office was full of presents and 'get well' cards for the dog. Just before the accident, Jack had been on one of his long trips, attending a wedding in Berwick and arriving back home gaily bedecked with ribbons in honour of the event. Later, Railway Jack made an appearance at a benefit for the disabled railway porter William Medhurst in Eastbourne, since they had both lost a leg.

When Judge Sir Henry Hawkins came to the Lewes assizes in July 1882, he decided to pay Railway Jack a visit. Although he was known as a 'hanging judge' of unremitting severity, Sir Henry was very fond of dogs. He travelled nowhere without his little fox-terrier Jack, who apparently got on quite well with his namesake, the three-legged Lewes celebrity. Sir Henry himself witnessed Railway Jack board the Brighton train, and heard many stories of his sagacity from proud Mr Moore. A week later, Sir Henry sent Railway Jack a collar mounted in silver, with the inscription 'I am "Railway Jack". Treat me well and send me home to the station master, Lewes. Presented by Sir Henry Hawkins's "Jack", July 1882.'

43. A photograph of Mr Moore, the three-legged Railway Jack, and his saviour Mr Stock the veterinary surgeon, from an old cabinet card.

When the Prince and Princess of Wales visited Eastbourne in July 1883, they expressed a wish to see Railway Jack. Proud Mr Moore brought the dog on the train from Lewes, where traveller and dog-lover Lady Brassey introduced the three-legged dog to the royal couple. Mr Moore looked something like a curiosity himself with his huge belly, bald head, bushy beard and enormous tall hat; it is to be hoped that the irreverent Prince did not make fun of this ludicrous figure when he was admitted into the presence of royalty. The Princess was very interested in Jack and asked Mr Moore many questions. He presented her with two photographs of Jack: one where he was seated on a trunk before his accident, another taken since, with the three-legged dog seated in front of Mr Moore.[2]

Railway Jack's life became much less adventurous after his accident. Mr Moore was worried that he might be run over again, and restricted his travels to a daily journey from Lewes to Brighton and back. When Mr Moore retired in 1884, he bought a house in Mayfield and took Jack with him to live there. Thus Jack's independent life as a Travelling Dog was over; he had become just an Ordinary Dog, a dog with a master. Instead, Mr Moore, who had been in serious danger of becoming just an Ordinary Man, a retired old stationmaster without much purpose in life, had become Railway Jack's master, a minor newspaper celebrity who was always keen to give interviews about his famous dog.

Throughout the 1880s, Mr Moore and Railway Jack clung to their status as minor celebrities with the tenacity of last year's reality TV star. They were often invited as guests of honour at dog shows or at railwaymen's conventions. At the Southdown Fox-Terrier Club Show in November 1884, a *Sporting Gazette* journalist thought Railway Jack a very interesting feature of the show; he was looking well, and was the recipient of many caresses. Mr Moore and Railway Jack often made trips together as the invited guests of railway companies. The bushy-bearded old man in his huge black coat and oversized tall hat sat contentedly on his seat, perhaps thinking of what to say to the provincial journalists invited by the railway company; the three-legged old dog sat on his lap, eagerly watching the trains and locomotives when they reached a station, and perhaps dreaming of his old life as a proper Travelling Dog. Their greatest triumph came at the Cowes regatta, where Lady Brassey introduced them to Prince and Princess Edward of Saxe-Weimar. By 1889, Jack could boast three silver presentation collars and a large silver medal. In October 1890, Railway Jack made his last journey, dying of old age in the arms of Mr Moore. He was said to be thirteen years old, but quite probably was older than that, since the aforementioned newspaper correspondent had known him as an adult dog for four years already in 1881.[3]

There has been some debate as to what breed of dog Railway Jack belonged to. The homepage of the Cliffe Veterinary Group, a practice founded by Robert Stock, who had saved Jack's life back in 1882, calls him a Jack Russell terrier. But the few available illustrations of Jack show him as a larger dog, rather like a fox-terrier. One of the best contemporary descriptions of Jack calls him 'a fox-terrier, big in bone and not over well bred'. The drawing of him in the *Chatterbox* magazine fully supports this impression. An article on Railway Jack in the *Sussex Express* calls him a mongrel, and it is likely he was a cross between a pedigree fox-terrier and some other medium-sized, terrier-like dog.

In the 1880s and 1890s, there were several Railway Jack wannabes: travelling dogs who tried to emulate his exploits.[4] Birmingham had a railway dog named Trotter, who travelled the Great Western and other lines. He had a collar with the inscription 'Let me wander at my will / For I am Trotter of Snow Hill'. When Trotter visited Henley in March 1882, this four-legged celebrity took luncheon with the railway porters, went round town, sat for his portrait at the Hart Street Photographers and dined at the Royal Hotel, before catching the late afternoon train to Oxford.

Luton had another railway dog, also named Jack, who used to travel to Hatfield sitting on the brake; at his death in 1895, he was said to have visited every station and signal box along the line. 'Railway Bob', a travelling dog in the north of England, had a sad history. A fine-looking collie, he had lost his shepherd master at some fair, and searched for him everywhere. As the frantic, dejected-looking dog travelled from town to town, the kind railwaymen fed and cared for him, and sometimes let him ride on the trains. After some years, Railway Bob gave up his quest and settled down to being a full-time railway dog; the guards vied with one another to have him as a travelling companion. Bob lived on the railways for many years, until one day he mistimed a jump to get onto an engine, with the inevitable consequences.

South Africa had its own travelling dog, also called Railway Jack. He used to travel on the trains between Port Elizabeth and Durban, sometimes with his master, but more often alone. In Durban, he was always made welcome at the Royal Navy base. One day, when this adventurous dog was on the train to Durban with his master, he saw some animal moving in the bushes near the railway track, and took a headlong leap off the moving train! His master mourned him as dead, but as he sat down to eat his dinner, Jack returned: he had survived the fall unscathed, gone back to the railway, and stopped the next train to be given a lift home!

After this experience, Railway Jack never set paw on a train again. But this did not mean that his travelling days were over. This extraordinary dog began stowing away on various steamships, travelling between Port Elizabeth, Natal and Cape Town. Once he went on a steamer bound for London, but disembarked at Cape Town, where a friendly butcher returned him home. Another time, Jack made it all the way to London, as a free passenger on board the steamer *Norham Castle*, returning to Natal on board some other ship. When nearly home, according to the *Newcastle Courant* newspaper, the old dog was 'being insulted by a negro (one of a race for which he had always showed great dislike)'. Jack tried to jump through an open hatchway to attack the canophobe blackamoor, but fell to his death, a victim of his racial prejudices.

In the mid-1880s, the craze for travelling dogs spread to the United States. New York express-wagon driver Michael Carroll used to bring his Scotch terrier puppy with him to the Union Station, where it became a great favourite of the baggage staff. Probably having heard of the original Railway Jack's exploits in Lewes and elsewhere, they named the dog 'Railroad Jack', equipped him with a collar saying 'Property of headquarters at Union Depot, Albany NY', and sent him for a number of journeys to nearby stations and depots. Dog-loving colleagues provided Jack with food and water on his travels, before returning him in the baggage car of another train, sometimes having attached a tag or ticket stub to his collar.

Railroad Jack travelled far and wide in the baggage cars. He went on and off the trains as he wanted, and himself decided when he was to go travelling. He attended the opening of the West Shore Road in 1884, and the inauguration of President Grover Cleveland in 1885. It was hard to keep Jack out of the baggage cars, since the dog was stubborn and persistent when he wanted to go for a ride, knowing that his friends the baggagemen would have many a treat for him. In 1892, when Jack was around twelve years old, he remained quite healthy and vigorous. In July the same year, he was sent for his longest journey: as far north as Canada, as far west as the Pacific Ocean, and as far south as Cuidad Juarez, Mexico.[5]

The newspaper publicity generated by this extraordinary journey exceeded all precedents from the American canine world. On 10 August, when arriving in Jacksonville, Florida, he paid a visit to the editorial office of the *Times-Union* newspaper. Described as a large grey Scotch terrier, he now wore a larger collar, donated by the *Illustrated Buffalo Express*. From this collar were dangling around ninety tags, badges and newspaper clippings, mementoes from every place he had visited. There were miniature skulls, tomahawks and Bowie knives, and trinkets of every description. Railroad Jack had been quite fat when he set out on his great journey, and he had not lost any of it due to being very well fed on the way. Still, the old dog was vigorous and alert, and his reactions as quick as ever when some person called out 'A rat!'

Like not a few other US celebrities, Railroad Jack became a victim of his own fame. On his way back to Albany, he was kidnapped, not to be held for ransom, but for public exhibition in some kind of freak show! Without having any say in the matter, Railroad Jack the Globetrotting Dog was exhibited in Rochester, Boston, Ontario and Toronto, before the outraged Albany railwaymen managed to retrieve their favourite. His last hurrah as a canine celebrity came in October 1892, when he occupied a prominent position on the 'railway float' at Albany's Columbian Parade.

By early 1893, Railroad Jack had grown very stout indeed. His days of riding the trains were over, and he had to be content with waddling round the Union Depot's baggage room. One day in June, when the old dog stood wistfully looking at the moving cars and engines, he suddenly rolled over and died. Newspapers all over the United States mourned Railroad Jack. It was said that his remains were to be stuffed, but there is no record of this actually happening. His obituary in the *New York Times* rightly pointed out that he had travelled more miles on the railways that any other member of the canine tribe. Another obituary, in the *Malone Palladium* newspaper, even claimed that he 'was no doubt the most intelligent and remarkable canine ever known'. This seems a superlative claim, since there is no evidence the old railway dog possessed any particular talents apart from his travelling exploits.

Railroad Jack's obituary in the *New York Times* briefly mentioned his successor as Albany's railway dog: the brown mongrel Owney. This mystery mutt had appeared out of the blue one day in the late 1880s, attaching himself to the workmen in the station post-room. Owney was not a puppy at this time, but a rather rough-looking adult dog with short, curly fur of a dirty grey colour. An accident, or perhaps rather a fight with some other street mongrel, had deprived him of a few inches of his tail. Owney liked the smell of the large leather mailbags, on which he used to sleep. He was soon very popular among the postal clerks and letter-sorters, who liked having the alert little dog around. Owney knew them all, but acknowledged none of them as his master; in fact, the eccentric dog came and went as he liked, as if he owned the place. Some people gossiped that Owney might be Railroad Jack's son, but this is unlikely to be the case. While Jack had only consorted with the baggage handlers, Owney preferred the postal clerks and route agents. As long as Railroad Jack lived, the two dogs had detested each other, each dodging the length of a railway carriage to avoid the other.

It has been speculated that Owney was of mixed Irish and Scotch terrier stock, but other breeds of dog may well have featured in his ancestral tree. His odd name also takes some explaining. It has been speculated that people visiting the station post-room often stopped to pet him, asking the ownerless little dog 'Owney! Owney! Who's your owner?', but this theory has no support from contemporary sources, apart from a fanciful article in the *St. Nicholas* children's magazine. There was an old letter-carrier named Eugene J. Wise, whose widow claimed that Owney used to follow her late husband on his daily rounds. Wise's Irish colleagues all called him 'Owen' or 'Owney' and after Wise died, the name transferred to the dog. This story may well be true, since 'Owney' was, at the time, a common nickname for people named Owen, including the gangster Owney Madden.[6]

44. Owney guarding the mail bags.

Owney loved the smell of the leather mailbags, which served as a bed for the travelling dog. He sometimes jumped onto the mailbags when they were bundled into the train to New York, and this was the beginning of his career as a travelling dog. Not content with commuting between Albany and New York Central, Owney went for longer and longer trips, always travelling in the mail cars. He guarded the mailbags jealously and allowed none other than the mail clerks to handle them. The clerks were all very fond of Owney, who treated them impartially. Sometimes, he was gone for weeks, or even months, before returning to his Albany friends, with some tags and mementoes attached to his collar. An increasing number of American railway stations had reason to be proud of the inscription 'Owney was here' as a memento of the visit of this canine Kilroy.

Worried that they would lose their travelling dog, Owney's friends equipped him with a collar with a silver tag engraved with 'Owney, Post Office, Albany, N.Y.' This turned out to be a wise strategy, since on a visit to Montreal, Owney was arrested by the Canadian police as a stray dog, and put in prison. Not until the Albany railwaymen had paid $2.50 to cover the cost of keeping and feeding the dog could they recover their favourite. It was said that the superstitious mail clerks wanted Owney to travel with them because they believed that the presence of the much-travelled railway dog would preserve them from accidents. If so, they were very much mistaken, because once, during a visit to Canada, Owney's train was badly wrecked. The travelling dog emerged from the wreckage minus one eye and part of an ear. This did not help his looks, as a *Norwood News* journalist expressed it, but added interest to his appearance.

After the death of Railroad Jack, Owney usurped his position as America's leading railway dog. Following his beloved mailbags, he went all over the United States. The eccentric dog seemed to love to travel and see new sights; his friends in the mail cars made sure that he was well taken care of, and very well fed. On his travels, Owney's friends used to attach ticket stubs, tags and local mascots to his collar; as a result, it soon became so heavy the travelling dog was at risk of choking to death. Postmaster General John Wanamaker, who was one of Owney's supporters, had a special harness made for the travelling dog, to which his many decorations were transferred.

Each time Owney went for a long trip, his harness was emptied of tags and gadgets. When he returned to Albany, he carried a prodigious amount of trinkets, cataloguing his endless travels on the highways and byways of the American rail network. Many of Owney's travel mementoes are still kept today, to provide a vivid snapshot of American society in the 1890s through its interactions with the travelling dog. There were ticket stubs, hotel room checks, dog tax receipts, and advertisement trinkets for cod liver oil, whisky and peanut butter. One advertisement tag entitled Owney to a cup of coffee at Stude's Coffee Parlour in Houston, Texas; another gave him a shave at Mr Munsey's Barber Shop and Bath House Palace; a third gave him a drink or a cigar at Mr Thyes Saloon in Reno, Nevada. A memento from Sioux City insisted that 'Corn is King!' and one from Texas urged the travelling dog to 'Remember the Alamo!' In Los Angeles, Owney once took part in a Kennel Club dog show, winning the special award of 'Best Traveled Dog'. An amateur poet from Hardacre, Minnesota, wrote that there was

Only one Owney,
And this is he;
The dog is aloney,
So let him be.

Another poetic contribution, from Haverhill, Massachusetts, proclaimed that

This tag will tell you all the news;
Owney has visited the City of Shoes.

The Albany postal clerks had many stories about Owney and his almost uncanny intelligence. Once, when Owney wanted to go to Boston, his human friends were too busy to take him along. The dog then instead took the local train to Troy, where he changed for the Boston express, arriving in time to greet the clerk who had evicted him from the mail car back in Albany. The railwaymen solemnly affirmed that Owney could interpret all the engine whistle and bell signals, and that he even could read a clock. He knew the location of all the railway station lunch rooms, and led the postal clerks there. Owney ate the same food as his human friends, in generous helpings; he eschewed raw meat for cooked sausages and beefsteaks. He did not care for strangers, unless they smelt of mail bags, and ignored them even when they tried to bribe him with food. He was pugnacious towards other dogs, whatever their size, particularly when he suspected they had designs on his beloved mail bags. Once, the Albany postal clerks though that Owney deserved a holiday. They took him camping, and at first Owney seemed to like strolling on the beach and swimming in the sea. After two days, the eccentric dog had had enough of country life, however. He took the first boat back to Boston, and walked straight to Old Colony Station, where he reported for duty at one of the mail cars.

In early 1895, Owney arrived on the train to Tacoma, Washington. He soon became firm friends with Tacoma postmaster Mr A. B. Case, and decided to drop anchor for a few months. When, in July, Owney's wanderlust became obvious, Mr Case sent him for a trip to Alaska and back again. When the travelling dog returned, Mr Case had a more ambitious idea. Why not send Owney for a trip round the world? He consulted Owney's Albany friends, who were enthusiastic. When the travelling dog was taken out to see the great Northern Pacific steamer *Victoria*, he seemed quite interested, sniffing around contentedly. Sensing publicity, the editor of the Tacoma *Morning Union* persuaded some local businesses to sponsor Owney's tour. In a ceremony, he introduced the travelling dog to Captain John Panton, of the *Victoria*, who agreed to take Owney across the Pacific as a 'registered dog package'. With great reverence, he attached a tag to Owney's harness, containing a lugubrious slogan concocted by the businessmen sponsors:

Owney, boom Tacoma while you live,
And when you die, be buried in a Tacoma-made coffin!

45. Owney with one of the postal clerks.

The tag attached by Mr Case made much more sense:

> To all who may greet this dog: Owney is his name. He is the pet of 100,000 postal employees of the United States of America. He started today, Aug. 19, 1895, for a trip around the world. Treat him kindly and speed him on his journey across ocean and land to Yokohama, Hongkong, and New York. From New York send him overland to Tacoma, and who knows but he may compass the globe and beat the record of Nellie Bly and George Francis Train and be known as a celebrated globe-trotter.

Captain Panton assigned a purser named Woods to look after Owney on the long journey to Hong Kong. Both men later agreed that the eccentric dog had been on his best behaviour throughout, making many friends on board. He slept outside Purser Woods' cabin and allowed no one but the purser's boy to enter it. In his spare time, he hunted rats with considerable success. In Hong Kong, Owney's friends met with a setback, since the port authorities refused to allow an ownerless dog ashore. But in Yokohama, the Japanese customs officials were less strict, although they were quite bamboozled by the sight of the dapper-looking little dog with his jacket full of tags, coins and medals.

Himself, Owney seems to have been far from impressed with the Orientals and their ways. When, in the presence of the Mikado, some court ladies sought to caress him, the eccentric dog growled and bristled up in a manner decidedly unfavourable for the propagation of good relations between the United States and Japan, as a *Brooklyn Daily Eagle* reporter expressed it. The same newsman added that throughout his stay in Japan, Owney got involved in numerous dog-fights, in which he 'whipped every dog he ran across, just to show what an American dog could do'. Things did not improve in Hong Kong. When Owney was invited to visit a British gentleman of very high rank, he fought and killed this grand personage's little Pekinese dog.

Somewhat under a cloud due to his pugnacious behaviour, Owney returned to Japan, where he found passage to New York on the British steamship *Port Philip*. When the American traveller Herbert Flood heard he had a compatriot on board, he asked to be introduced to Mr Owney. The clerk whistled, and 'a large-sized Irish terrier, with one eye missing, who had been sleeping on a pile of mail-bags in the corner, trotted to the front'. On board ship, Owney behaved himself better, and actively decimated the ship's rat population. After stops at Port Said, Algiers and St Michael in the Azores, the *Port Philip* finally docked in the East River on Christmas Eve 1895. Owney was swiftly taken to Grand Central Station, embarked on a cross-country train, and arrived in Tacoma five days later. His journey around the world had taken 132 days.

After his journey round the world, Owney was an A-list celebrity. He appeared at dog shows and at music halls as 'The Greatest Dog Traveler in the World' and regularly attended railwaymen's conventions. At the National Association of Postal Clerks early in 1897, the old dog stole the show when he ran up the aisle, mounted the platform and received a standing ovation lasting fifteen minutes.

But not all American railway officials were kindly and dog-loving. Later in 1897, the killjoy Superintendent of Mails in Chicago issued an order forbidding all postal clerks to allow dogs to travel on the mail cars. Of course, Owney's old friends disobeyed this order and let him travel just like before. But by now, Owney was quite an old dog. Obese and irritable, he was becoming increasingly obstinate and snappish. A newspaper even wrote that 'Of late the dog has grown cross and overbearing and has become imbued with the idea that all government buildings were owned by him and all government employees were his abject servants.'

It is not a little sinister that in 1897, after Owney had been banned from the mail cars, there were several erroneous rumours that the famous dog had expired. The first of these said that Owney had fallen under the wheels of a train at a small station near Syracuse. It was speedily proven false: the dog was found alive and well in Indianapolis, Indiana. Two months later, another newspaper story claimed that Owney had run amok at the Union Depot in Cleveland. Refusing to leave the mail car, he had bitten a brakeman quite severely. When a policeman tried to 'pacify' Owney with his club, the travelling dog bit him also, the end result being that the brutal cop beat Owney to death with his club. There was relief among Owney's Albany friends when this story was exposed as yet another lie: Owney was still alive and kicking, and still travelling. He had been taken ill in St Louis, but regained his health after careful nursing, and proceeded to Frankfort, Indiana. After a third newspaper rumour had alleged that the travelling dog had expired in Ohio, the *Chateaugay Journal* commented that 'judging from the number of times that "Owney" has been killed, the animal must have had more lives than the traditional feline'.

It remains a fact, however, that in the morning of 10 June 1897, Owney disembarked a train in Toledo. At the railway station, Clerk W. W. Blanchert received the famous dog,

46. Owney in old age.

along with a reporter from the *Toledo Daily Blade*. When the clerk wanted to show off the dog, Owney refused to co-operate. Clerk Blanchert then took out a chain and tied Owney to his desk. The old dog took great exception to this indignity and bit Blanchert hard in the arm and leg. The clerk, who was unable to work for several days after the incident, insisted that Owney should be destroyed. Toledo Postmaster C. Rudolph Brand filed a request with the police that this 'dangerous dog' was to be summarily killed. Shortly after four in the afternoon the same day, Patrolman Beauregard Smith led the world's most travelled dog out into an alley behind the Toledo police station and executed him with a well-aimed pistol shot.

At first, the newspaper report that Owney had once more been killed was treated with incredulity. But as soon it had been confirmed, there was outrage throughout the American railway community that their celebrated travelling dog had met with such an ignominious death. In particular, Owney's old Albany friends were furious that their pet had been killed, heaping odium on that miserable Judas, Clerk Blanchert, and that canicidal cop, Patrolman Smith. It did not take long for conspiracy theories to appear. Had not the dastardly railway bosses 'put out a contract' on Owney, since they were jealous of his considerable fame, and fearful that the mail cars would be full of travelling canine mascots, to the detriment of the morale of the employees? Why had Owney been destroyed with such great expedition? And were the previous newspaper stories the result of failed assassination attempts, or merely smokescreens to spread disinformation about the conspiracy?

The Albany railwaymen even alleged that Owney could never have bitten Clerk Blanchert, since the old dog had lost all his teeth! Owney's biographer Dr Charles A. Huguenin established that Owney's teeth were in good working order, however, and also that the clerk was bitten badly enough to keep him off work for some time. This has not prevented the RoadsideAmerica website from giving the old conspiracy theories another airing, but they were answered by the American Wayne Escott, who informed them that Clerk Blanchert had in fact been bitten so badly by the infuriated Owney that he had died not long after. He had left behind a widow and a one-year-old son, Escott's grandfather. Another website adds the information that Patrolman Smith did not survive the travelling dog by long: when trying to break up a fight in a Toledo saloon, he received such a haymaker that he expired on the spot. It is not known how long the *Toledo Daily Blade* journalist survived the Curse of Owney.

Owney's corpse had been preserved after he had been shot dead, by some person with a higher sense of canine history than the clerk and the patrolman. The grieving Albany postal clerks raised money to have him stuffed by an expert taxidermist. This individual made a good job of it, although he replaced one of Owney's paws with one from another dog, perhaps because the original one had been too badly damaged when the dog was killed. Owney's missing eye was also restored, albeit in glass only.

The stuffed Owney was kept at the Post Office Department's headquarters in Washington D.C. until 1911, when he was transferred to the Smithsonian Institution. He was exhibited in Philadelphia in 1926, in Chicago in 1933, at the Commodore Perry Hotel in Toledo in 1937, and at a grand philatelic show in New York in 1955. In 1993, the stuffed Owney was transferred to the National Postal Museum in Washington D.C., where he can still be seen. A very ordinary-looking dog, almost ugly, Owney would not, as an American journalist expressed it, win the five hundredth prize at a dog show. Yet during his extraordinary career, he travelled 143,010 miles, went round the globe once, and collected at least 1,017 tags.

Owney has remained as popular in death as he was in life: he never lacks juvenile visitors at the National Postal Museum, and has inspired a number of children's books. In the mid-1990s, an American schoolmaster thought of a clever idea to use Owney to teach the pupils geography. A stuffed dog mascot was sent round from school to school, accumulating local mementoes on the way. Through studying Owney's belongings, the third-graders, who hopefully took their schooling more seriously than their South Park counterparts, would acquire useful information about their huge country and its various states. For several years, the Owney mascot was sent from school to school. In Camarillo, CA, some jokers sent it to the White House, but President Bill Clinton wrote them a polite letter of thanks, adding that he and his staff would miss Owney's company very much, since the dog mascot had now been sent on to another school. By 2000, it had visited schools in all fifty states. The scheme may well be still ongoing.

In 1953, assistant stationmaster Elvio Barlettani saw a stray dog jump off a goods train at Campiglia Marittima, a railway junction on the line between Pisa and Rome. The dog was a small white mongrel. Since he seemed quite friendly and sociable, Barlettani let him sleep at the station. Due to his extreme quickness, the railwaymen named him Lampo (Lightning). Lampo got to know every person at the station. He watched the trains with great interest and was sometimes allowed to ride on the locomotives used for shunting. Lampo knew exactly when the express trains were due; he stood on the platform outside the dining car, waiting for the cook to throw him some bones and other morsels. The dog's timekeeping was so impeccable that the passengers used him as a four-legged clock: when Lampo left the ticket-office and ran out onto the platform, they knew the express train would be arriving shortly. Barlettani was curious to find out more about Lampo's origins, but all he could discern was that some Leghorn workmen had rescued a stray white mongrel from the dog-catcher as a joke, putting the animal onto one of the open trucks of a passing goods train.

But Lampo had higher ambitions in life than just sitting around at the railway station. He started travelling on the trains, visiting Rome, Leghorn and Pisa. Just like Railway Jack, he knew the trains and stations very well. If he wanted to go to Florence, he changed trains at Pisa like an experienced traveller, repeating the feat on his journey back home. Another time, Lampo took the southbound train to Rome. For his return home, he mistakenly chose to travel on the fast northbound express, which did not

47. Lampo the travelling dog.

stop at Campiglia Marittima. The clever dog changed trains at Pisa, however, this time picking out a local train that took him safely back home. The railwaymen put a tag on to his collar 'Free Pass for Lampo, the Travelling Dog'. In time, Lampo became quite a celebrity: people came to the station to see this eccentric dog jump onto any passing train that caught his fancy, and there were features about him in the local newspapers.

But just like in the story of Owney, there was a 'bad guy' lurking in the shadows. The Campiglia Marittima stationmaster very much disapproved of all the hullabaloo around Italy's travelling dog, and decided there was no place for Lampo at his station. Elvio Barlettani of course objected to Lampo being sent away, but he was a meek and humble young man who was fearful of his superior. Accordingly, Lampo was put onto a long distance goods train. 'Good riddance,' said the wicked stationmaster, but two days later the travelling dog returned on the Rome express. This time, the stationmaster ordered that Lampo was to be put in the luggage-van kennel of the Naples express, where he would be loaded onto another train destined for an even more distant part of Italy. This time Lampo seemed to have disappeared for good.

But five months later, Lampo jumped off the Rome express at Campiglia Marittima. The travelling dog was ill and emaciated; it is not known what privations he had endured, and how many trains he had had to take to return home. Barlettani and his colleagues greeted their favourite with enthusiasm, and soon nursed him back to health. The wicked stationmaster was replaced by a more humane railway official, who became Lampo's friend and agreed to keep the travelling dog on the establishment for life.

Lampo soon started travelling on the trains again. His fame increased by the month: many people came to see him as a curiosity, and the amount of fan mail and parcels of dog food sent to him from all parts of Italy exceeded all precedents. Whenever newspaper journalists came to the station, Lampo tolerated them, although he greatly disliked flash photography. In 1960, *This Week* magazine introduced Lampo to the Americans; the feature on the travelling dog was longer than another one in the same issue, about President J. F. Kennedy.[7]

In July 1961, the old dog fell under a train and died. *This Week* magazine paid for a statue of Lampo to be erected at the railway station. Having been twice vandalized, once by a demented *gattofilo* (cat lover!) who thought there was too much fuss about this silly dog, once by some mindless drunks, and twice repaired by the railwaymen, it is still there today. Elvio Barlettani wrote the travelling dog's biography, *Lampo, il Cane Viaggiatore*, which enjoyed considerable success and was translated into English, French and German. A sentimental tale intended for children and young adults, it is sometimes unintentionally funny, like when Barlettani describes how delighted he and his neighbours had been, at the end of the Second World War, when they were liberated from their brutal German allies by their kind and generous American enemies. Barlettani lived on until 2006, having had the satisfaction of seeing his only book reissued a few years earlier.[8]

All these travelling dogs, from the 1880s to the 1960s, would appear to have decided to travel due to positive reinforcement. Railway Jack associated trains with good food and

48. The statue of Lampo in Campiglia Marittima.

good company; Owney was fond of his beloved mailbags, and the generous lunches the mail clerks bought for him. During his time at the railway station, Lampo was probably thrown some morsels by the express train cooks. He soon learnt to wait on the platform when the express was due, and was said to be more punctilious than the Italian trains. Having learnt to associate trains with food, he was encouraged to travel on them.

Due to strict railway regulations and rigorously guarded platform barriers, the present-day travelling dogs are less adventurous than their historical counterparts. In Dunnington, near York, the lame Jack Russell terrier Ratty used to take the No. 10 bus all by himself, to travel three miles to the Black Bull public house, where he was given sausages and some water (some accounts say beer). The kind bar staff often drove the lame terrier home, although he was sometimes able to catch the bus back by himself. When the Black Bull changed hands and pets were banned, Ratty went to the Rose & Crown instead. He was run over, just by his favourite bus stop, in April 2010.[9]

In Moscow and other Russian cities, stray dogs living in the suburbs sometimes take the tube or tram into the city centre in search of food scraps. Tourists are sometimes startled to see a large stray dog sleeping on the seat in a carriage, or young dogs playing on the platform. These canny canines sometimes sneak up on people eating *shawarma*, a kebab-like snack popular in Moscow, barking loudly to shock them into dropping their food. When I recently took a journey on an old tram in St Petersburg, a terrier-like mongrel dog boarded this vehicle, without a ticket. Since he seemed to deduce that I was more likely to be kind to him than needy locals, he sneaked up to me, keeping a watchful eye on the elderly tram conductor. We later shared a hot dog outside the Finlandskoie railway station, before the travelling dog decided he must catch another tram and get on with his life.

7

SOME CANINE PHILANTHROPISTS

In early 1907, life was not good for Mrs Alice Rayner. Her husband Horace was a work-shy cad who beat and abused her, and carried on affairs with other women. Since he did not support her, the family was near destitute, and they had two children and a third on the way. Could things get any worse?

Yes, they certainly could! The demented Horace Rayner tried to extort money from the wealthy shopkeeper William Whiteley, whose illegitimate son he believed himself to be. When rebutted, he produced a pistol and murdered Whiteley, on the spot, before shooting himself in the head. Thus the desperately poor, heavily pregnant Alice Rayner was now the wife of a terribly disfigured murderer, who might well be facing the death penalty. What would she do? Scream and curse God, or poison herself and the children? Or perhaps employ a 'collecting dog' in an attempt to raise money for her starving family?

Happily for all concerned, as the illustration shows, Mrs Rayner chose the third of these alternatives. A trained collecting dog was hired and set to work in central London. It walked about with a sign 'For Rayner's wife and children' strapped on its back, inviting passers-by to put money into its collecting box. Since there was widespread public sympathy for Mrs Rayner, the dog collected thirty-three shillings in less than three hours. Then a police constable came up to ask the dog's owner whether this was really a licensed collecting dog. This turned out not to be the case, so the dog was sent home with its tail between its legs by the officious constable.[1]

'What is this nonsense about collecting dogs?' I can hear the reader exclaiming. Surely there were no such animals at the time? But it is a forgotten aspect of canine history that from 1860 until 1960, numerous collecting dogs were active throughout Britain.[2] The enthusiasm for these dogs was highest in London and the Home Counties, and lower in Scotland and the north of England; the idea never seems to have caught on abroad.

There were two kinds of collecting dogs. Some were privately owned dogs, trained to carry a sign and a collecting box on their back, and to invite people to put money in the box by various stratagems. Whenever some person believed he or she had a claim

49. Horace Rayner shooting Mr Whiteley, from the *Illustrated Police News*, 2 February 1907.

50. Mrs Rayner's Dog Friend, from the *Illustrated Police Budget*, 13 April 1907.

for charity from the general public, they could hire a collecting dog for a fee. The dog was either led around by its owner, or let loose in a market square or a railway station. Anyone could rent a collecting dog, although takings were probably better if the sign on the animal's back said 'For the Red Cross orphanage' or 'For Rayner's wife and children', rather than 'For buying Jock Scroggins a Jug of Ale'.

More numerous troops of collecting dogs were owned by railway or hospital charities. These dogs were permanently based in specific railway stations or hospitals, and collected for one charity only. These railway dogs became quite an institution in Victorian and Edwardian life. The dogs collecting at London's major stations became celebrities: notices of their activities were published in *The Times* and other newspapers, and they featured on numerous postcards. Many of them were stuffed after death, to continue collecting for their charities.

The earliest collecting dog upon record was 'Rover', described in a magazine as 'an active little dog belonging to Mr. W. Edwards, oil and colourman'. Rover had been trained to beg from well-dressed gentlemen, by jumping up and pawing at their pockets, whining as if he was saying 'Give me a ha'penny, please, Mister!' When he was successful, Rover took the money in his mouth and ran to a nearby shop, where he exchanged it for a cake or bun. This sagacious dog never troubled the poor, and avoided women altogether. Mr Edwards had philanthropic interests, and wanted to help the victims of the Lancashire cotton famine. He had a card printed with the words 'For the distressed operatives in Lancashire', tied it around Rover's neck, and set the dog to work. Soon, Rover had collected twenty shillings. When giving an interview to a children's magazine in 1863, Mr Edwards told an amusing anecdote. Rover had once been out collecting, returning with three halfpennies. He dropped two of them, but insisted on retaining the third in his mouth, evidently thinking that he deserved some reward for his philanthropic zeal.[3]

When a journalist writing for a religious magazine was visiting Brighton in 1868, he was mystified that a large dog was following him around. When he entered a shop, the dog followed him in there and jumped up at him. The shopkeeper explained that this was 'Brighton Bob', the Dog with the Missionary Box. This sagacious animal had been trained to approach well-dressed strangers and ask for a penny for his charitable work. Once the journalist had given Bob a penny, the dog trotted off. But the shopkeeper, who knew the dog's habits, warned that the penny was not yet safe in the missionary box, however, since Bob was known sometimes to go to the baker's shop and buy biscuits instead. The journalist and the shopkeeper followed the dog, and indeed fell Temptation came into Bob's way: he looked at the baker's shop and seemed to want to enter it. But his two friends called out 'Go home, Bob; go home, good dog!' and the canine collector immediately took heart: with a bound in his step and a wagging tail, Bob made haste home to deliver his penny into the missionary box. The journalist, whose zeal for do-gooding may well have obscured his motivation to tell the truth, ended his article by urging all British boys and girls to emulate Brighton Bob and start collecting for the missionary movement without delay, since there were still many heathen little blackamoors who had never heard of the glories of Jesus Christ.[4]

51. The earliest collecting dog: 'Rover' begging money from a gentleman in an illustration from *The Children's Friend*, 1 January 1863.

52. The sagacious 'Brighton Bob' begs a penny from his journalist friend.

The articles about Rover and Brighton Bob clearly demonstrate that at least by the 1860s, there were people in Britain who had the ambition to train canine collectors. Where had they got the idea? It is curious to note that according to Alfred Rosling Bennett's *London and Londoners in the 1850s and 1860s*, there was a tradition among the London crossing-sweepers and beggars of being accompanied by animals, most often dogs, to gain sympathy and bigger tips from passers-by. A print by Thomas Rowlandson depicts the actor Cecil Wray playing the part of a blind beggar; he is accompanied by a dog with a collecting-box dangling from its collar. In his *London Labour and the London Poor*, Henry Mayhew told the tale of another blind beggar, whose dog carried a little basket in its mouth, to receive the donations. One day, when a boy tried to steal some money from the basket, the 'blind man' ran at him with his stick, proving that he was an impostor and that he could really see. It seems very likely that the Victorian collecting dogs owed their origin to a pre-existing tradition for mendicants to be accompanied by dogs with collecting-boxes.

In 1880, the veteran railway guard John Climpson trained a two-year-old collie named 'Help' to become the earliest collecting dog to gain proper fame and renown. This docile, intelligent dog proved ideally suited to the task, travelling with Climpson on the London to Brighton train, to collect money for the Railway Servants' Orphan Fund. The dog wore an elaborate silver collar with a medallion bearing the inscription 'I am Help, the railway dog of England, and travelling agent for the orphans of railway men who are killed on duty. My office is at 306, City-road, London, where subscriptions will be thankfully received and duly acknowledged.'

53. John Climpson and 'Help' – a drawing from *Young England*, 1 March 1884.

Help proved quite a success and many people donated money to the orphans' fund. Climpson let his dog travel with other railway guards, throughout England, Scotland and Wales, carrying a piggy-bank to collect money. It was said that Help had worked every railway line of the country, and visited every principal town in England and Wales. In 1884, he collected £10 at the Bristol Dog Show, and was presented with a silver medal. He was a regular attendant at the railwaymen's congresses, even after his retirement in 1890. When Help died in 1891, Climpson had him stuffed and put him in a glass case on the platform at Brighton Station.[5]

In the 1880s, being employed by the railways was a perilous way of earning one's living: engines collided or exploded, signalmen were run over, and guards fell off the trains. There was a need for a reasonably effective charity organisation to take care of crippled railwaymen and the widows and orphans of those killed on duty. The example of Help seems to have set many railway charity officials thinking. Collecting dogs were clearly more successful than human mendicants, since they were a novelty that appealed very much to the animal-loving Victorians.

By the mid-1880s, collecting dogs had become all the rage. It would appear as though a not inconsiderable proportion of Britain's canine population were undergoing training as professional mendicants. The earliest of these dogs used the same modus operandi as Rover and Brighton Bob, collecting coins with their mouths and disposing of them into a piggy-bank or missionary box. As late as 1898, a magnificent Newfoundland dog named Nelson, who collected for various Bournemouth charities, used to carefully pick up every coin thrown to him and put them into a collecting box standing nearby. But this stratagem had serious drawbacks. Firstly, the dogs could not always be relied upon to deliver the money into the box. In particular, it had been counterproductive of Rover's owner first to train the dog to 'buy' food at the baker's shop, since the wilful animal received what would today be called 'positive reinforcement' to steal the money donated and run off to the shop where he would receive a proper reward. Nor was it a particularly good idea to allow dogs to handle small coins with their mouths. I have found no evidence of any canine collector being suffocated by a coin, or dying from intestinal obstruction, but when 'Charley' the Windsor collecting dog died in September 1898, his stomach was found to contain six pennies, eleven halfpennies, and several stones.[6]

It was better to equip the dog with a collecting box carried round its neck, or strapped to its back. One of the first collecting dogs to use this stratagem was 'Brake' of Southsea and Ryde. This dog had quite an adventurous history. When quite young, he had been teased by a mischievous lad, and it was alleged he had bitten the lad in the buttocks. To pacify the boy's parents, his owner ordered that Brake was to be destroyed. When she ordered her gardener to tie a stone around Brake's neck and throw him into the sea, the disgruntled menial did so most reluctantly, since he very much doubted that the boy had been bitten at all. But still he carried out his orders, only to find that the rope broke and the dog swam ashore safely. Since the gardener was a religious man, he regretted his attempted canicide, thinking that the dog's near-miraculous survival must have been a sign from God that he was innocent. He gave Brake to the furniture-remover Mr Curtiss, whose wife trained him as a collecting dog. A drawing shows Brake wearing a custom-made brass collar with a collecting-box attached to it. In turn, Brake was rented to the Portsea Hospital, the Isle of Wight Infirmary, and the Shipwrecked Mariners Society. The attractiveness of the dog and the novelty of his act meant that in 1883 and 1884, Brake collected more than £31 for these three charities, much of it when travelling unsupervised on the Isle of Wight ferry. He wore a sailor's cap and sometimes carried a pipe in his mouth. He begged only from well-dressed passengers, by sitting up or by rattling the coins in his collecting-box.[7]

When two professors from the Lycée at Versailles were visiting Inverness in 1883, they were approached by a spaniel dog, around whose neck had been fastened a small padlocked box, with an inscription asking for donations to the Inverness Infirmary. One of the Frenchmen, M. Fontaine, wanted to put a penny into the box, but the dog put its head down over the opening and instead seized the coin in its mouth. A few minutes later, the Frenchmen saw the dog sitting on the counter of a baker's shop, enjoying a loaf it had 'bought' for the penny. The baker explained that 'Clyde' had been doing this kind of thing for some considerable period of time, misappropriating the donations for his own personal use. When the amazed M. Fontaine wrote a letter to the *Revue Scientifique* about this unparalleled instance of canine sagacity, the editor, who did not know about collecting dogs, suspected that he was joking. The Frenchman wrote back enclosing an affidavit from Mr J. T. Lindsay, the owner of Clyde. Although the dog sometimes took the coins for his own use, he had collected an average of twenty shillings a month for the Infirmary. Clyde was trained to approach only tourists and not to bother about the needy locals. Sometimes, this penny-pinching Scottish dog hid the money in his mouth, saving it for a rainy day; when he was ordered to disgorge, the result was sometimes as much as fivepence.[8]

But not all Victorians were good, honest and charitable. The sight of a collecting dog trotting by, the coins rattling in its collecting box, was sometimes too strong a temptation for various criminal elements. After some incidents when the dogs had been robbed of their collecting boxes, the charities made sure the boxes were attached to strong leather harnesses, which were padlocked underneath the dog's belly. In 1896, two thieves were caught in the act of holding the Paddington collecting dog 'Tim' by the legs upside down and shaking his body over an empty suitcase, in the hope that some coins would fall out through the slot in his collecting box. After being so shamefully treated, one cannot blame Tim for sinking his teeth into the calf of one of the thieves as soon as he had been liberated from their clutches.

Throughout the 1890s, the Bristol collecting dog 'Punch', property of the Castle Street publican Mr G. Williams, was busy collecting for the Bristol Hospital for Sick Children and Women. The dog became a member of the Ancient Order of Foresters and used to lead the annual church parade of this society. But in 1898, Punch went missing. Since neither dog nor collecting box was ever recovered, there were fears that poor Punch had been 'made into sassages' after he had been deprived of his harness and box. He was succeeded by his son Punch II, who was praised for his charitable work in no less a publication than the *Lancet*; together, the two dogs had collected 48,579 coins for various medical charities.[9]

In the 1890s, the most famous of all collecting dogs was the Labrador retriever 'London Jack'. After being trained as a collecting dog by the railwayman Mr Wickins in 1894, London Jack became a familiar sight at Waterloo Station for many years to come. Not content with just patrolling the platforms, he jumped into the carriages, barking and shaking his collecting box to attract attention. Sometimes he travelled on the local trains to Vauxhall and back, collecting from the passengers. Once, he jumped on to the express train by mistake, but was recovered and sent back by the railway officials at Bournemouth. Whenever Jack heard the Salvation Army band playing, he jumped up and tried to grab his harness and collecting box, since he knew he was likely to be taken for a walk to collect among those listening to the band.

In 1899, the railway orphanage had four canine collecting agents: London Jack, Basingstoke Jack, Bournemouth Nell and Southampton Gyp. London Jack completely eclipsed the other three. He was one of the celebrities of London, and his doings were regularly reported in the press. When London Jack disappeared in early August 1899, there was immediate newspaper interest. Resigning himself to the loss of the collecting box, Mr Wickins feared that his famous dog was being held for ransom. But the weeks went by without any blackmailing letter containing a tuft of dog's hair arriving at the railwayman's office. After London Jack's description had been circulated in the newspapers, there were alleged sightings of the famous dog all over Britain. Numerous stray Labradors were sent to Waterloo, but the disconsolate Mrs Wickins recognised none of them as London Jack.

In early September, a sharp young lad went to the King's Road police station. He had read in the newspapers about the recent epidemic of dog thefts in London, he said, and at an empty house near where he lived, in Brewer Street, mysterious men had been coming and going after dark, and there was much barking both day and night. Might there be a connection? 'No, certainly not!' Officer Barbrady would have replied, advising the lad to concentrate on his schoolwork, but Sergeant Clarke's detective talents were better developed than those of the bumbling South Park cop. The very same evening, the house in Brewer Street was raided by a party of constables. There were sixty-two dogs on the premises, of every size and description, from Great Danes to Toy Poodles. One of them was London Jack, who barked and jumped up when he saw Mr Wickins. Four thieves were apprehended: three young thugs and a librarian named William Clements. The latter turned out to be the mastermind of the gang, if such an inept criminal deserved that name. In spite of obviously lacking the means of profitably disposing of the dogs, the gang had kept on stealing these animals until the house was completely full. The thieves were convicted and received lengthy prison sentences; the dogs were reunited with their owners.[10]

There was much relief in the newspapers that London Jack had been found safe. He received letters of congratulation from all over the country, and the demand for his likeness was so high that the railway orphanage paid to have him photographed. But after a month in the hands of the Chelsea dognapping librarian and his dastardly gang, poor Jack was very thin and nervous. Although kind Mr Wickins took him to Bournemouth, where he could eat as much fish and chips as he wanted, and swim in the sea, London Jack never quite recovered. He retired in 1900 and was taken care of by an old railwayman living in the Isle of Wight.

Mr Wickins had made sure that before retiring, London Jack had been mated with a handsome half-bred Newfoundland bitch. He had taken care of the most attractive of the puppies, and in 1901 London Jack II took his father's place at Waterloo. It was said that whenever Jack II was equipped with his collecting box and led out to start work on the Waterloo platforms, he always stopped to greet the stuffed body of his father inside its glass case. When Sir Robert Baden-Powell was returning to South Africa in December 1901, Jack II was led up to him when he departed from Waterloo. The celebrated general patted and 'shook hands' with the equally famous collecting dog, and gave him a Christmas box. In 1905, a newspaper article described Jack II as the most famous collecting dog in the world. The railway orphanage had presented him with a handsome silver collar, adorned by a number of silver medals, each representing a collection of £100. Jack abhorred drunkenness, always barking furiously when he saw an inebriated person. Once, he broke up a fight between drunken navvies all by himself. In June 1907, Jack fell ill with a swelling on his back; he had an operation at the Westminster Bridge Animal Hospital, but died from cancer a few months later, just after receiving another medal from the directors of the railway orphanage for collecting £1,000 throughout his career.

Jack II was succeeded by his son London Jack III, who looked very much like a black Labrador, and lived to be very old. He was not allowed to roam free, but was accompanied everywhere by Mrs Wickins, perhaps to dissuade dognappers who had designs on Jack and his collecting box. Nevertheless, he had twice beaten his father's record monthly collection of £28. According to an article in the *Animal World* of 1909, Jack III's philanthropic efforts had to date gathered £386. The £1,900 collected by the three Jacks had come in very handy when the new railway orphanage was erected at Woking. His son London Jack IV was active throughout the 1920s. In 1929, he was still going strong at the age of ten, in spite of failing eyesight; it was said that if he collected another £60 before retiring, his lifetime takings would amount to £4,000 in all. He was replaced by London Jack V who ended this famous dynasty of collecting dogs when he expired without issue in 1931. Like most of his predecessors, he was stuffed by an expert taxidermist to keep collecting after death. Two other collecting dogs were purchased to replace him: a yellow Labrador named 'Bisam Jack' and a short-haired St Bernard named 'Marigolde of Clairvaux', or 'Mary' for short. It seems as if she completely eclipsed her colleague, appearing in both newspaper features and advertisements for dog food.[11]

The other great London termini had collecting dogs of their own. In 1910, Euston porter R. E. Edwards purchased a very attractive Newfoundland cross named 'Brum'. This clever dog knew how to put out a fire, balance a penny on his nose, and bark by the tap until he was given a drink of fresh water. Brum appears to have been a great friend of royalty. In 1912, the Queen and Princess Mary went from Euston to join the King at Balmoral. As they were to enter the train, 'the Railway Benevolent Fund collecting dog "Brum" approached, and her Majesty patted the handsome creature. The Princess insisted on "Brum's" following her into the carriage and put some coins in his box.' In 1913, when King George V and Queen Mary were going to Crewe, the King put a sovereign into Brum's collecting box and patted his head, the dog showing his appreciation by barking loudly.[12]

Brum was succeeded by the collie cross 'Roy' who collected at Euston for many years before retiring in 1924. But strange to tell, Roy did not like to retire. Although he had been given a good home with a retired railwayman in a London suburb, Roy escaped seven times to return to his old haunts. He was always found in a railway station, where the old dog was trying his best to collect money without his collecting box. The Euston railway officials took Roy back to the station, where he was given back his old kennel next door to his friend and successor, the sheepdog 'Rags'. Roy lived there for ten more months before expiring in October 1925. In his obituary in *The Times*, it was said that he had collected more than £3,100 during his long career, and that the King and Queen had often asked for him when they were at Euston. The sheepdog Rags was succeeded by the black Labrador 'Victor', who collected £2,700 before retiring in 1934. His successor, the retriever 'Jack', collected £900 before retiring in late 1937. Porter Edwards told a journalist that Jack was a great favourite of the regular users of the station, including Lloyd George and Gracie Fields. His successor, the large black retriever 'Roy' shared a comfortable kennel with Jack.[13]

Another royal favourite was 'Tim' at Paddington, who had once been so shamefully treated by the thieves. He was an Irish terrier who had been given to Inspector Bush at Paddington in 1892. Tim paid particular attention to the wealthy, well-dressed travellers in the first-class coaches, and ignored the needy and poor. An illustration shows that after the attempted theft, Tim had been equipped with a collecting box fixed to his collar, meaning that any would-be thief would have to negotiate with Tim's fangs to lay his hands on its contents.

Tim was a particular favourite of Queen Victoria, to whom he bowed gracefully each time she put a gold sovereign into his collecting box.[14] Tim collected £450 in all during his long career. After his death of old age in 1902, he was stuffed by the taxidermist Rowland Ward, as a newspaper poet described it:

> Our pet we may still gaze upon
> Tho' dead, like life in form and limb.
> For what he did at Paddington,
> Now Rowland Ward is padding Tim.

The stuffed Tim remained at Paddington for many years. He was the favourite of generations of schoolchildren. Tim was definitely still there in the 1950s, and quite possibly as late as 1965, but today nobody knows what eventually happened to the remains of this celebrated dog.

From 1900 until 1940, most major railway stations in England and Wales had their own collecting dogs. Since the railway dogs were owned and kept by railwaymen or porters, who had been given a franchise to collect for the charities, the market was dwindling for the private individuals who were training collecting dogs and renting them out to those considering themselves deserving of charity. The Red Cross, the RSPCA, Our Dumb Friends' League, and many hospital charities also had their own collecting dogs. During the Boer War, the Ladies Brigade of Collecting Dogs collected for the families of dead soldiers, with thirty-five dogs employed. Similar strategies were made use of in the Great War: an army of collecting dogs, including the tiny 'Southville Beau', were active to support the armed forces.

People were proud of their local railway collecting dog, and many of these provincial heroes featured on early picture postcards: 'Dash' at Snow Hill, 'Jack' at Southampton, 'Grace' at Dalston, 'Bristol Bob' at Temple Meads, 'Prince' at Croydon, and another 'Jack' at Reigate. The black Labrador 'Sandy' collected £9,000 at Exeter central station, rivalling the London Jacks. In contrast, 'Twister' at Merthyr Tydfil was a very lazy dog, who used to lie down whenever he was equipped with his collecting box. One year, he did not even collect enough to pay for his own dog licence.

Slough had 'Station Jim' who started his duties as a canine collector in 1894. Like the majority of collecting dogs, he would roam the station at will, even making excursions into the town when he felt like it. He sometimes travelled on the train to Leamington, or up to London, where the guards put him on the next train back to Slough. He barked

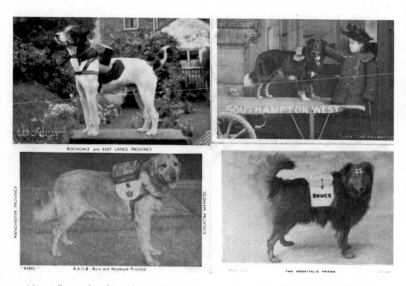

54. Many collecting dogs featured on early picture postcards: here we have 'Southampton Jack' in 1904, 'Spot' at Bexley in 1909, the celebrated 'Bruce' of Swindon in 1909, and the Oldham collecting dog 'Rebel'.

for each coin put into his collecting box, which meant a lot of barking; once, when he walked in a hospital parade, he collected not less than 265 coins. He would sit up and beg, play dead, or climb a ladder if one was put against the wall. Sometimes Jim was put in the ticket office, where he looked quite at home with a railwayman's cap on his head and a pipe in his mouth. He would not tolerate any music, and was particularly annoyed by the Salvation Army band. When any person threw a lighted match or a burning piece of paper on the ground, he would extinguish it.

The beautiful retriever 'Wimbledon Nell', featured in the *Illustrated Police Budget* of 23 November 1907, was a particularly sagacious collecting dog. She was active at Wimbledon station, where both the South-Western and District trains were stopping. Nell knew that the former had separate compartments, preferring to collect on the platform. But when a District train pulled up, she jumped on board and walked down the central corridor, looking at each passenger in turn and rattling the money in her collecting box. In some uncanny way, she seemed to know when the train was due to depart, always jumping out a few seconds before the doors were closed.

Another local celebrity was 'Bruce' at Swindon. He was depicted on several picture postcards, wearing his silver collar and the fifteen gold and silver medals he had been awarded. Bruce was even inducted into the Brotherhood of Hero Dogs, founded by Bertha de Courcy Laffan, a dotty author who was very fond of dogs. She had written several overblown and melodramatic novels and fancied herself as a literary grande dame. Her eccentric activities did not benefit the career of her husband, a snobbish and fashionable clergyman who was a pioneer of the Olympic movement; he had to resign as Principal of Cheltenham College after she had been accused of actively corrupting the morals of the boys.[15]

The Revd Robert de Courcy Laffan instead became Rector of Walworth, where his wife founded her Brotherhood in 1907. In solemn ceremonies, dogs that had done something heroic, like alerting the family when the house caught fire, were decorated with a silver-mounted collar in the presence of the other Hero Dogs and the President of the Brotherhood, the tiny Royal Edward. In spite of his distinguished title, he had done nothing heroic, but earned his position by being Mrs de Courcy Laffan's own dog. More than once, these bizarre ceremonies were covered and photographed by the newspapers.[16]

In 1910, Mrs de Courcy Laffan wrote the *Story of the Brotherhood of Hero Dogs*, a history of her canine society. In spite of its somewhat chauvinistic name, female dogs were allowed, as evidenced by the inclusion of Little Nell, the celebrated Blind Man's Dog, and Jess, the Dog with the Human Brain. Jess was the pet of a paralysed Islington watchmaker, assisting him by answering the door, collecting the mail, holding his tools, running errands and generally acting as a domestic. Most of the Heroes had given the alarm when their owners' houses had caught fire. When Lieutenant-Colonel Kevans, of St Kilda's, wrote to Mrs de Courcy Laffan about a white cat that had saved a family from perishing in a fire, the outcome was a clever compromise: 'I sent Pussie a collar, and the excitement in the village was great, and Pussie was a heroine, though she could never be made a member of the Brotherhood of Dogs.'

Two collecting dogs were members of the Brotherhood: the fox-terrier Spot at Bexley and the aforementioned mongrel Bruce of Swindon. Bruce's inauguration into the Brotherhood, as the sixteenth Hero, was a particularly grand affair, held in Swindon Town Hall. Royal Edward oversaw the ceremony, seated on a small throne next to Mrs de Courcy Laffan; all fourteen other Hero Dogs were present. When the Mayor of Swindon buckled the collar inscribed 'I Plead for the Sick' round Bruce's neck, the spectators gave a great cheer for the popular collecting dog. Bruce's collar, medals and collecting box are today at the Swindon Museum.

After the ceremony, Mrs de Courcy Laffan was interviewed by another dog-loving literary lady, the American Kate Sanborn, who later described the occasion in her curious book *Educated Dogs of Today*. Mrs de Courcy Laffan's canine society was thriving: each month, she received at least sixteen letters from various people thinking their animals worthy of becoming Heroes, but their claims were carefully sifted. Although there had been applicants from France, South Africa, Australia and New Zealand, not a single of these foreign dogs had been found worthy of inclusion. All the proceeds of her own literary activities went to maintaining the brotherhood, Mrs de Courcy Laffan asserted, and her home was a veritable hospital for homeless and ailing canines.

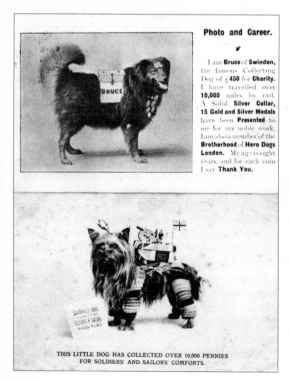

Photo and Career.

I am **Bruce** of **Swindon**, the famous Collecting Dog of £450 for **Charity**. I have travelled over **10,000** miles by rail. A Solid **Silver Collar, 15 Gold and Silver Medals** have been **Presented** to me for my noble work. I am also a member of the **Brotherhood** of **Hero Dogs London**. My age is eight years, and for each coin I say **Thank You.**

THIS LITTLE DOG HAS COLLECTED OVER 10,000 PENNIES FOR SOLDIERS' AND SAILORS' COMFORTS.

55. Bruce, a member of the Brotherhood of Hero Dogs, along with the tiny Southville Beau, who was active throughout the Great War, collecting 10,000 pennies for the Soldiers & Sailors Wool Fund.

In her book, Kate Sanborn also provides the only known example of an American collecting dog: a bulldog stood in the lobby of the Cort Theatre during the annual benefit given for the New York Anti-Vivisection Society. In a basket he held in his mouth, he received not less than $2,500. Fortunately for the antivivisectionists, no thief managed to sneak into the theatre lobby, to give the bulldog a bone in exchange for his basket!

In the 1960s and 1970s, 'modernisation' was all the rage in British Rail. There was a feeling that since the Age of Steam was now finally at an end, the Age of Electricity and Diesel should also make a clean sweep of the remainder of Victorian railway paraphernalia. The result was wholesale destruction of British railway heritage. No building was safe from the British Rail vandals, not even Euston station itself.

The canine collectors were not spared by these railway philistines. Dogs collecting money had no part to play in the modern railway, they declared, enlisting some mawkish busybodies from the 'cruelty' brigade, who argued that it was degrading for dogs to be used in this way. These individuals ignored that the collecting dogs were healthy and well cared for. With the exception of that misfit mutt in Merthyr Tydfil, they clearly liked their jobs. The black Labrador 'Sandy' was collecting at Exeter as late as 1952, and the Airedale terrier 'Laddie' was active at Waterloo until 1956, but after that time, no further collecting dogs were recruited. Some of the stuffed dogs were sold or given to collectors of curiosities, but the vast majority were simply destroyed. Complaints from the public, who liked the collecting dogs, and from the railway orphanage superintendents, who lost much funding as a result of the dogs being 'phased out', went unheeded.

But in spite of this wholesale vandalism, a few stuffed collecting dogs have been saved for posterity. The stationmaster at Slough in the 1960s must have had a higher regard for railway history than his superiors in London, since he boldly disobeyed the order that the stuffed collecting dogs were to be disposed of. As a result, the celebrated 'Station Jim', who amused the railway passengers by climbing ladders and growling at lighted matches back in the 1890s, is still there, in his glass case on Platform 5. The aforementioned Laddie, who collected at Waterloo station until his retirement in 1956, later went to live at the Southern Railwaymen's Home for Old People in Woking, where the old dog remained until his death in 1960. He was stuffed and placed in a glass case to continue his good works at Wimbledon station. He remained there until 1990, when

56. Chelmsford Brenda, the collecting St Bernard.

he was donated to the National Railway Museum in York, where he has become quite a favourite, collecting for the Friends of the Museum on Platform 3 in the Station Hall.[17]

Two of the stuffed London Jacks have also survived. One of them is likely to be Jack V, who expired in 1931. A burly Golden Labrador wearing his collecting box and a number of gold and silver medals, he now collects in the waiting room of the Bluebell Railway in Sussex, raising about £30 a year for the Woking Homes. Finally, the original London Jack, who was once stolen and recovered during his lifetime, is still in existence. After being stuffed, he remained at Waterloo until 1915, and then collected at Southampton station until 1965, when he was given to Sir William McLain. In 1996, he was purchased by Potter's Museum of Curiosities at Jamaica Inn in Cornwall. After this eccentric museum closed in 2003, the contents were sold at auction. In spite of an estimate of £2,000–3,000, Jack was bought by an anonymous bidder for £1,600. The stuffed dog then appeared on an internet auction site, before ending up at the Natural History Museum in Tring, Hertfordshire, where he has been restored to his former glory and again put on public display, wearing his heavy brass collar and collection box on leather mounting.[18]

When I visited London in 1990, there used to be a young beggar sitting at the Leicester Square underground station, with a small dog in his lap. The beggar himself looked pale and haggard; the dog was alive but deathly still. On his blanket was a notice saying 'Please give me something for my sick dog' or words to that effect. In contrast to the other mendicants infesting London at the time, this young man seems to have done reasonably well, the dog-loving Londoners keeping his money-bowl well filled with coins. When I came to work in London in 1996, there was a twist to this story when I saw a newspaper report that a well-known begging impostor had been jailed. For years, he had made a comfortable living touring the country with his 'sick dog' which he had drugged with sleeping pills, but the police and the RSPCA had managed to track him down.

This dismal begging impostor was not devoid of psychological insight. At a time when Londoners were heartily tired of all the beggars, a 'sick dog' was still a very nice little earner. Whereas the dog was seen as being blameless and child-like, the two-legged beggar was perceived to be weighed down by all the sins of a wasted life, and wholly undeserving of charity. Although the Victorian collecting dogs served a nobler purpose than merely filling the pockets of their work-shy owners, the logic behind their success is not dissimilar. Whereas a two-legged charity collector was greeted with some degree of suspicion, the pure and innocent collecting dog had a much more favourable reception. Even a veritable Ebenezer Scrooge would put a coin into London Jack's collecting box, to hear him bark 'Thank you!' and wag his tail. Sympathy for an animal comes much easier than sympathy for a person.

8

GUINEFORT THE DOG SAINT &
SOME OTHER HOLY DOGS

It is written, in the Acts of Peter, that after the Apostle had travelled to Rome to seek out and contest the heretic Simon Magus, he saw a great dog chained nearby. Peter loosened the chain and lo! the dog acquired a human voice, asking Peter what he required of it. After Peter had made this clear to the dog, the animal immediately ran into the house where the heretic was staying, lifted its forepaws, and called out in a loud voice:

> I tell you Simon, Peter the servant of Christ is standing by the door, and he says to you 'Come out to confront me, for it is on your account I have come to Rome, you most wicked deceiver of simple souls!

Like some of the spectators hearing Don the Talking Dog for the first time, Simon was at first completely dumbstruck by this singular example of canine eloquence. He cravenly bargained with the dog, begging the animal to tell Peter that he was not at home, but in another long, sulphuric harangue, the dog instead blasted him as a cheat and deceiver. The animal then returned to Peter, told him about Simon's whereabouts, and predicted that the contest between the Apostle and the heretic would convert many who had been deceived by Simon. This was the final speech of this remarkable preaching dog; having done its good work, it lay down at Peter's feet and died.[1]

This remarkable talking dog, helping Peter to suppress the heretic Simon Magus, was probably the first canine to take active part in promoting the Christian faith. It would take quite some time for any other dog to challenge this loquacious canine with regard to zeal for religion, until the appearance of Guinefort, the saint who also happened to be a dog.

The thirteenth-century Dominican friar Etienne de Bourbon wrote a collection of theological anecdotes, one of which concerns a strange cult he had come across in the Dombes region, north of Lyon in France. It was based on an old story about a lord and a lady living in these parts, who had an infant son. One day, they went out of their castle, and the nurse also made herself scarce, leaving the baby in the cradle in the care of a greyhound. When a huge serpent slithered into the nursery, and approached the cradle, the dog attacked it to protect the child. After a furious fight, the snake was torn to pieces by the faithful dog. Although the faithful canine had been the recipient of several bites from the infuriated reptile, it still remained on guard by the cradle, in case there were further dangerous vermin about. When the lord came home, he saw the bloodstained dog and thought it had devoured his son and heir. He drew his sword and killed the dog. But then he discovered the child alive and well in its cradle, and also the mangled remains of the serpent. Deeply regretting his rash action, the lord threw the dead greyhound into a well, heaped a pile of stones on top of it, and planted trees near the grave, as a memorial to the faithful dog. But in spite of this belated act of piety to the martyred greyhound, divine retribution struck him: his manor was razed to the ground, and his estate became a wasteland.

Later, the superstitious local peasants heard the story of the martyred dog. They seem to have reasoned that if the noble greyhound had died to save the life of a child, then the site where the canine martyr had been buried surely must have magical powers to heal sickly children, and they began worshipping there. In weird rituals, the mothers exposed their ailing offspring to the cold, and passed them through an opening between the trunks of two trees. They later plunged the children into a nearby river, reasoning that if they survived, Saint Guinefort, as the martyred dog was called, would surely make them strong and healthy.

57. The knight kills the faithful dog, from an old woodcut.

Etienne de Bourbon, an enemy of superstition, claimed that the mothers had invoked certain forest fauns and devils, asking them to take back their own sick and failing child, and to return her own plump and healthy one. For this reason, he wanted to suppress the cult of the dog saint. He had the gravesite destroyed, the trees cut down, and the dog's bones burnt and scattered. He threatened the peasants that if they kept worshipping Saint Guinefort, they would be severely fined. The forthright Dominican believed these harsh measures had produced the desired effect.

In 1879, the antiquary A. Vayssière investigated various old legends in the Dombes region. Since he was curious about 'Saint Guinefort's wood', the peasants told him the old story of the child, the serpent, and the martyred dog.[2] Thus the cult of Saint Guinefort has withstood every attempt to suppress it for more than six centuries. From all over the region, mothers with ailing children had worshipped at the cult site well into recent times. When the ethnologist Jean-Claude Schmitt investigated the cult of Saint Guinefort in the 1970s, there were still some elderly people who remembered the legend. As late as the 1920s, a witch-like old woman had worshipped the dog saint at the cult site, and taken sickly children there.

When Schmitt investigated matters further, it turned out that there was actually a human Saint Guinefort as well: a martyred missionary whose remains were kept at Padua. In medieval times, this Saint Guinefort performed several miracles, and was actively worshipped, but at the time when his canine namesake had a numerous following in the Dombes, he had become quite forgotten. In his book about the dog saint, Schmitt used the story of the two Saint Guineforts to emphasize the chasm between the mainstream Catholicism of the Latin treatises of Etienne de Navarre's time and the earthy vernacular religion, which had some pagan beliefs thrown in. And could not some of the weird rites performed at Saint Guinefort's cult site be interpreted as some kind of legalized infanticide, and was this the reason why that cult had become so very long-lived?[3]

There are differing hypotheses as to how the dog saint received his name.[4] One is that the human and canine Saint Guineforts were connected in some manner. As Jean-Claude Schmitt suggested, it is of course possible that travelling monks and pilgrims spread the tale of the human Saint Guinefort to the Dombes region, but there are also strong arguments against this theory. Firstly, the human Saint Guinefort was never a well-known saint; secondly, he had nothing to do with healing sickly children; thirdly, the Dombes region would have few attractions for travelling pilgrims; fourthly, the inhabitants of those parts seem to have adhered strongly to their own odd religious beliefs, rather than showing interest in foreign saints. There is a bewildering profusion of obscure saints with similar-sounding names: Millefort, Dignefort or Wilgeforte; but again it is impossible to connect them with martyred dogs and ailing children.

Another theory discussed by Schmitt seems rather more promising, namely that Guinefort or some similar word was actually a dog's name in use at the time the cult was begun. This hypothesis has some support from the findings of the antiquary Vayssière: the locals told him that the dog Guinefort (or in this version rather Guignefort) had originally been so named because it always wagged its tail. According to this story, there had been some kind of statue of Saint Guinefort in the old days, and there was a saying that if the dog wagged its tail, men who feared for their virility should rest assured. Now, the Old French word 'guigner' can mean either 'wink' or 'give a sign', agreeing somewhat with this theory. Another of Schmitt's curious findings is that 'guiner' is a rare version of the Old French verb 'graigner', meaning to growl or to bite. Promisingly, he also found a medieval poem about a greyhound named Guinalot; could perhaps Guine-fort ('bite-strong') be another obscure medieval dog's name, lost through the passage of time?

Perhaps the most famous legend of Wales is that of Prince Llewelyn the Great and his faithful wolfhound Gelert. Llewelyn ap Iorwerth, also known as Llewelyn Fawr (the Great), was an early thirteenth-century Prince of Gwynedd who dominated Wales for forty years, through a mixture of war and diplomacy. He married Joan Plantagenet, the daughter of King John of England, but this did not prevent him from successfully waging war against the English, and becoming the ruler of large parts of Wales.

The wolfhound Gelert was the favourite of all Prince Llewelyn's dogs, the legend said; he had been a present from King John when the two princes had been on friendly terms, and was a dog of uncommon size and beauty. Gelert always used to accompany the Prince and his followers when they went hunting. But one day, Gelert was nowhere to be seen. Prince Llewelyn blew his horn but no dog came. Returning from the hunt, he was pleased to see Gelert coming, as the poet William Robert Spencer expressed it:

> But when he gains his castle door,
>   Aghast the chieftain stood;
> The hound all o'er was smeared with gore,
>   His lips, his fangs, ran blood.

Seeing that his young son's cradle is overturned, Prince Llewelyn becomes furious:

> 'Hell-hound! my child by thee devour'd!
>   The frantic father cried;
> And to the hilt his vengeful sword
>   He plung'd in Gelert's side.

But after completing this rash canicide, Prince Llewelyn hears his little son cry! It turns out that he is alive and well, lying next to the cradle in a bundle of clothes; next to him is the torn body of a large wolf.

> Ah, what was then Llewelyn's pain!
>   For now the truth was clear:
> His gallant hound the wolf had slain
>   To save Llewelyn's heir.

There never could the spearman pass, Or forester unmoved;
There, oft the tear-besprinkled grass, Llewelyn's sorrow proved.
And there he hung his horn and spear, And there, as evening fell,
In fancy's ear he oft would hear Poor Gelert's dying yell.

58. Gelert's grave, from a postcard of 1930.

59. Prince Llewellyn mourns
the faithful dog, from
Chatterbox, 11 November 1888.

Stricken by remorse for killing his faithful dog, Llewelyn had Gelert buried with much ceremony; the village where the martyred wolfhound was laid to rest was named Bedd Gelert (The Grave of Gelert) in his honour. But in spite of this act of piety towards the canine martyr, Prince Llewelyn would mourn him forever:

> Vain, vain, was all Llewelyn's woe:
>> 'Best of thy kind, adieu!
> The frantic blow that laid thee low,
>> This heart shall ever rue.'[5]

Since the late eighteenth century at least, Gelert's grave in Beddgelert, as the village is still known today, has been a tourist attraction. Ignoring the many quaint villages nearby, the historic castles, and the magnificent natural scenery of the Snowdonia mountains nearby, many of them have come to see Gelert's grave.

When surveying the very similar tales of Saint Guinefort and Gelert, I believe the reader will smell neither a dog saint, nor a heroic wolfhound, but a rat. In his *Curious Myths of the Middle Ages*, the antiquary Sabine Baring-Gould exposed the tale of the knight and the martyred dog as a version of a widespread medieval legend. The earliest version was found in an ancient Indian book, the Sanskrit *Pantschatantra*, complied about AD 540. A Brahmin named Devasaman had a wife, a son, and a pet mongoose. One day, when

60. Gelert fights the wolf, from *Chatterbox*, 16 November 1879.

the Brahminee went to fetch water, she asked her husband to look after the baby, so that he was not injured by the mongoose. But the thoughtless Brahmin went out begging, leaving the house deserted. When a black snake came slithering in and attempted to bite the child, the faithful mongoose tore it to pieces. But when the returning Brahminee saw the bloodstained creature, she rashly concluded that it had injured the baby, and threw her water-jar on it with lethal results. She then discovered her mistake, mourned the brave mongoose, and berated her foolish husband for deserting his post.[6]

The story evolved as it travelled all over the cultural world. The Faithful Animal, which had originated as a mongoose, developed into a cat, a falcon, or a tame lion, before ending up as a dog guarding the cradle of its master's young child. The Bad Animal, a snake or a wolf, approaches the cradle with evil intent, but the Faithful Animal kills it after a fierce fight, only to succumb to the rash and irate master's sword; the cantankerous Brahminee was disposed of in the European versions.

The fate of the dog's master varied widely. In the bloodthirsty versions, he kills himself or goes mad; in others, he never speaks again, or becomes a recluse. In the more benign variants, he learns the medieval equivalent of anger management, refrains from further rash canicides, and lives happily ever after. The moral of the tale is always that rash wrath can have disastrous consequences. The other obvious point, that it is not a bright idea to leave a defenceless child alone in its cradle, guarded only by a dog, when there are dangerous vermin about, was given no attention whatsoever.

In a German version of the tale, an angry knight beats his faithful dog to death with a long cudgel, and then disembowels himself when he sees the dead snake; the crying little child is the only survivor of this fierce encounter. In Russia, a tale closely resembling that of Prince Llewelyn was told about a certain Czar Piras. In the *Gesta Romanorum*, a fourteenth-century collection of anecdotes with a moral, the knight Folliculus goes to a tournament with his entire retinue, leaving his son guarded only by a falcon and a greyhound. In comes the snake, but the falcon wakes the sleeping dog by fluttering its wings, and the snake is killed by the greyhound. When the child's nurses come home, they see the cradle overturned and the bloodstained floor, and immediately conclude that the dog has bitten the little child. They run to find the wife of Folliculus, and she in turn alerts her husband. Maddened by fury, the knight returns home and kills the faithful dog with his sword. But when he examines the cradle, he finds the child alive and well, lying next to the dead serpent. Folliculus laments bitterly over the dog's body, blaming himself for having too hastily depended on the word of his wife. He abandons the profession of arms, breaks his lance into pieces, and goes on a pilgrimage to the Holy Land.

Several versions of the 'Martyred Dog' tale were current in Welsh medieval culture. In the Iolo manuscripts, a thoughtless Welshman living in Abergarwan left his only child in the charge of a greyhound when he went out stag-hunting. Cue for a wolf to enter, with the usual disastrous consequences for both wolf and greyhound. The legend was in fact so well known that it gave rise to a proverb: 'A hasty act is not a prudent act, but like the man who killed his greyhound'.

61. The death of Gelert, from an old postcard.

62. The knight, the faithful dog, the serpent and the child, from an early edition of the *Directorium Humanae Vitae*.

In the old Welsh versions of the 'Martyred Dog' legend, the dog is not named, but Celart or Cylart is certainly an ancient dog's name, perhaps derived from 'kill-hart'. There is an old Welsh epigram praising the hunting dog Cylart, whose swiftness ensured that his master's table was never short of game, but this has nothing whatsoever to do with Prince Llewelyn and his martyred wolfhound. According to Carlisle's *Topographical Dictionary of Wales* from 1811, Beddgelert was named after Celert, a greyhound or wolfhound of uncommon swiftness, which had belonged to Llewelyn ap Gruffyd, the last prince of independent Wales. There was a large rock, this author alleged, which was pointed out as a monument of this celebrated dog, on the spot where Celert had expired, together with the stag he had pursued all the way from Caernarfon, which is thirteen miles distant.

Although the 'Martyred Dog' legend is certainly very old, in Wales as well as in continental Europe, its association with Prince Llewelyn the Great, the dog's name Gelert or Cylart, and the village of Beddgelert, is a relatively recent invention. There are several eighteenth-century works on the topography and history of west Wales, but none of them mentions anything about any colourful origin of the name Beddgelert. In fact, there is a strong case to be made for the village having been named after an early Christian missionary named Celert (or Cilert) who was active in these parts during the eighth century. The earliest records of the name are from the thirteenth century, as either 'Bekelert' or 'Bedkelerd'.[7]

In 1793, a certain David Pritchard became the first landlord of the Royal Goat Hotel in Beddgelert. A man of superior intelligence and enterprise, he knew about the 'Martyred Dog' legend, and had also heard of the village's purported association with Celert, the greyhound of Llewelyn the Last, who had pursued his prey all the way from Caernarfon. Pritchard decided to improve on both stories: the faithful wolfhound Gelert, who had fought the wolf, had instead belonged to Llewelyn the Great, and had been a gift from his father-in-law King John. Pritchard and his friends built a suitable grave mound for Gelert, and showed it to visitors and early tourists, who were told the pathetic story of Prince Llewelyn the Great and the martyred dog.

As Gelert's grave in Beddgelert became a tourist attraction, David Pritchard's trade picked up markedly. One of the early visitors was the Hon. William Robert Spencer, a poet of repute, who went to Beddgelert in 1800. His beautiful and dramatic poem about Gelert deservedly became quite well known, and aroused much curiosity about the martyred dog. No tourist in Snowdonia wanted to miss Gelert's grave, which was piously maintained by Pritchard and his successors, as Spencer expressed it:

> And, till great Snowden's rocks grow old,
> And cease the storm to brave,
> The consecrated spot shall hold
> The name of 'Gelert's grave'.

George Borrow, the author of *Wild Wales*, thought the story of Gelert 'singularly beautiful and affecting'. Gelert's tomb stood in a beautiful meadow just below the side of the high Cerrig Llan mountain. It consisted of a large slab lying on its side, and two upright stones, shaded by a weeping willow and surrounded by a hexagonal paling.[8] The story had become quite widely known by this time, and hundreds visited Beddgelert each year who had never heard Spencer's poem; some of them came exclusively to see Gelert's grave. David Jenkins, another local historian, was much more critical. He exposed Pritchard's activities, and traced how the legend had evolved. Although he had robbed Beddgelert of the monopoly on the legend, he remained unrepentant: Gelert's purported grave was still worth visiting as a memorial of the vividness with which the Welsh mind appreciated unjust reward for faithfulness.[9]

The medieval *historia valde memorabilis* can be defined as a short memorable tale with a moral, told and retold throughout the cultural world with different protagonists. One example is the tale of the wicked noblewoman, who chides a poor beggar carrying twins for her unchastity, since she believes they must have two different fathers. The beggar woman puts a curse on her, and not long after, the lady gives birth to a great number of children. The most famous protagonist, Countess Margaret of Henneberg, was said to have given birth to 365 tiny children, as many as the days in a year. In some versions, the children all die; in others, they are hidden away and later grow up to found a noble family. This is told of the French family of Trazegnies (Treize-nés), and also of the Guelphs. The most macabre variant concerns the pregnant wife of the Lord of Arles, who met the inevitable mendicant and dismissed her with the usual taunts. The beggar woman answered her with the words 'You are wicked as a sow, and like that unclean animal, you will disgust all those present at your childbed.' In due course, the lady herself gave birth to nine little pigs!

63. The faithful dog fights a huge snake to save the sleeping child – a fanciful drawing from Emile Richebourg's *Histoire des Chiens Célèbres*.

Plate 1. A French drawing of the learned dog Munito, issued as a part of a series called *Le Bon Genre* in 1827.

Plate 2. A 'Dog of St Gotthard'. (Natural History Museum of Berne)

Plate 3. A poster for a French imitator of the Inimitable Dick.

Plate 4. Don the Talking Dog on the cover of Dr Scheller's *Der Sprechende Hund*.

Plate 5. The stuffed London Jack I. (Natural History Museum)

Plate 6. Peter Alupka the Speaking Cat, from an old poster.

Plate 7. A caricature of Carlo the Acting Dog helping Sheridan select his next 'Growley Drama'.

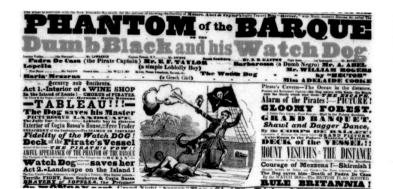

Plate 8. A poster for that astonishingly titled dog drama *Phantom of the Barque, or, The Dumb Black and his Watch Dog*.

Plate 9. The acting dogs Hector and Wallace attacking some Bad Indians in *Dogs of the Forlorn Log House*.

Plate 10. St Bernard dogs rescuing a traveller, from an old French print.

Plate 11. The stuffed Owney as he can be seen today. (National Postal Museum, Washington DC)

Plate 12. One of Owney's tags. (National Postal Museum, Washington DC)

Plate 13. Last of her breed: the stuffed turnspit dog Whisky. (Abergavenny Museum)

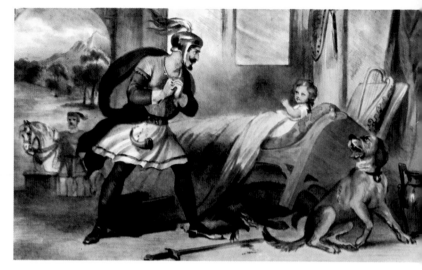

Plate 14. The death of Gelert, from an old postcard.

Plate 15. Gelert's grave in Beddgelert, from a postcard of 1904.

Plate 16. The statue of Rollo, the American cemetery dog.

Plate 17. An Edinburgh parade on World Animals Day 2009 was led by Greyfriars Bobby lookalike 'Blue', the official mascot of the One o'Clock Gun & Time Ball Association, and ended up at the famous monument outside Greyfriars. Reproduced by permission of Blue's owner, Mr John Lovie.

Belgique. Laitières — Préparatifs de Départ. Baptême du Lait.

Attelage de chiens Flamand

Above: Plate 18. Two postcards of Belgian draught dogs, posted in 1908 and 1909.

Left: Plate 19. The Abergavenny dog-wheel. (Abergavenny Museum)

Above Left: Plate 20. An advertisement card for a French chocolate firm, depicting Munito performing under the direction of his master.

Above right: Plate 21. Lord Byron and Boatswain – a fanciful representation in a collection of engravings. (Nottingham City Museums and Galleries, Newstead Abbey)

Right: Plate 22. Boatswain's monument at Newstead Abbey, from an old postcard.

Plate 23. Landseer's *My Dog*.

Plate 24. A colour print of a Newfoundland dog, after Landseer.

Plate 25. Landseer's *Saved*.

Plate 26. The Chiens Sauveteurs
practising their skills – an engraving
from the *Petit Parisien* (No. 678, 1902).

Plate 27. The Newfoundland dog Diane
rescues a man from the Seine, from the
Supplément Illustré of *Le Petit Journal*,
22 June 1902.

Plate 28. Whizz jumping from a rubber dinghy. (Mr D. Pugh)

Plate 29. Whizz flying. (Mr D. Pugh)

Plate 30. The monument to Barry at the Cimetière des Chiens in Paris, a postcard from 1915.

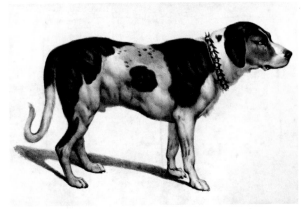

Plate 31. A colour engraving of Barry.

Plate 32. The stuffed Barry. (Natural History Museum of Berne)

Plate 33. A plate celebrating a heroic St Bernard dog.

Plate 34. A contemporary print of Kit Burns's rat-pit in New York.

Plate 35. A coloured engraving of Landseer's *Two Alpine Mastiffs Reanimating a Stranded Traveller.*

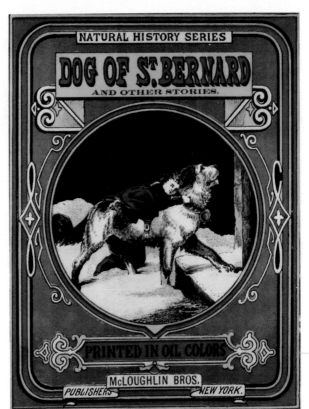

Plate 36. The sagacious St Bernard dog gives the child a ride back to the Hospice, from the old American children's book *Dog of St Bernard*, published by McLoughlin Bros., New York.

Plate 37. The champion ratting dog Billy in action.

Plate 38. Two curious monuments in the Cimetière des Chiens, from old postcards posted in 1909 and 1913.

Plate 39. An old colour postcard of the Hyde Park dog cemetery in its heyday.

Another *historia valde memorabilis* is that of the mouse-tower. During a famine, a wicked magnate mistreats the poor, likening their cries for food to the squeaking of mice. As divine retribution, he is devoured by an army of rats and mice, even though he takes refuge in a mouse-tower purposely built to serve him as a refuge in such an emergency. The legend of the mouse-tower also occurs in several variations. The most famous of them concerns Archbishop Hatto of Mainz, who was cursed for locking the poor into large barns, setting them on fire, and exclaiming 'Hark! how the rats and mice are squeaking!' to mock their cries for help. But an army of rodents advanced through the fields, invaded Mainz, and put the Archbishop to flight. He took refuge in a mouse-tower situated on a small island in the Rhine, but the rats and mice swam the river, invaded the tower, and ate the Archbishop. Another medieval legend states that Bishop Widerolf of Strasbourg was devoured by rats and mice in AD 997, as divine punishment for having suppressed a convent. Similar tales were told about the Austrian mouse-tower at Holzölster, and the so-called Mouse-lake near Inning in Bavaria, once the place of a tower where the wicked Count of Seefeld was devoured by mice, although he had suspended his bed from the roof with iron chains.[10]

As we know, Saint Guinefort's wood, Gelert's grave monument, and the various tombs and shrines erected for some faithful dogs in India, connect the 'Martyred Dog' legend with certain visual landmarks. The same is true for the other two legends. In the church of Loosduinen, near the Hague, a memorial plaque to the prolific Countess Margaret of Henneberg can be seen to this day, along with two copper basins, said to be the very ones in which her 365 children were baptized. A castle at the Dutch village Pouderoyen was called Arx Puerorum, since it had 365 windows, one for each of the children of the Countess. The mouse-tower, which was pointed out as Archbishop Hatto's place of death, can still be seen standing in the Rhine, at Bingen, although it was actually built much later, for use as a toll station.

It may well have been easy for the rash knight to kill the faithful dog, but it is much harder to kill off a good story; the spirit of Saint Guinefort is still with us today. The 1987 French film *Le Moine et la Sorcière* stars the stalwart Etienne de Bourbon trying to stamp out the cult of Saint Guinefort, being distracted by a pretty sorceress along the way.[11] When eccentric Barcelona artist José Hernández-Díez exhibited some of his avant-garde work in the United States, the lead exhibit was a stuffed dog inside a hermetically sealed glass box, connected to an oxygen tank, to symbolize the immortal Saint Guinefort.[12] In popular novelist Bernard Cornwell's *Grail Quest* trilogy, the archer Thomas of Hookton prays to Saint Guinefort and wears a dried dog's paw on a piece of leather around his neck.

The 'Martyred Dog' legend has been reported as news more than once in the twentieth century. As late as the 1990s, a Belgian paper reported that a man had left his young son in the car, after he had gone shopping. Returning, he saw his bloodstained son and the bloody jaws of the dog, which he threw to the ground and killed. Aghast, he then discovered the body of a large rat, which was presumed to have emerged from a sack of potatoes and attacked the child, only to be dispatched by the canine martyr.[13] Saint Guinefort must have wagged his holy tail up in heaven when he heard that one.

9

GREYFRIARS BOBBY & SOME OTHER FAITHFUL DOGS

No visitor to Edinburgh will miss the monument to Scotland's most famous dog, the little Skye terrier Greyfriars Bobby. This amazing dog, the most faithful in the world, kept vigil at his master's grave for fourteen long years. Many children's books, and three successful films, have been inspired by the affecting story of this little dog, said to be the most inspiring tale of love and loyalty ever heard.[1] But how much of it is actually true, and how much is make-believe?

The traditional story of Greyfriars Bobby is that some time in 1858, an old Midlothian farmer was buried at the Greyfriars burial grounds in Edinburgh. Nothing more was known about him except that his name was Gray and that most people referred to him as 'Auld Jock'. According to John Traill, who kept an eating-house nearby, the old farmer had been a regular guest of his, along with Bobby, his little Skye terrier. After Auld Jock had been buried, the ownerless little dog remained at the cemetery, keeping vigil at his master's grave. James Brown, the curator of the burial ground, tried to shoo the dog away, but Bobby always returned to the grave, resting underneath one of the great table-stones nearby. With time, Brown grew attached to Bobby, providing the little dog with food and shelter in the cemetery grounds. In cold and wet weather, efforts were made to keep Bobby indoors, but the dismal howls of the devoted dog made it clear that he wanted to return to Auld Jock's grave, whatever the weather conditions.

With time, Greyfriars Bobby won many friends. Every day, when Bobby heard the one o'clock gun fired at Edinburgh Castle, he made his way to the local restaurant, where the kind Mr Traill made sure he received food and water. In addition, Colour Sergeant Donald McNab Scott, of the Royal Engineers, allowed the little dog a weekly treat of steaks at Currie's Eating House. Bobby was a vigorous hunter of rats, endearing himself to James Brown by keeping these pests at bay both in the church and in the burial grounds. Bobby also chased cats with alacrity, and was fond of picking fights with other male dogs, irrespective of their size. James Anderson, an upholsterer living in Candlemaker Row nearby, was surprised to see the angry little dog chase all the cemetery cats away. He knew that it was part of James Brown's work to keep dogs

64. Greyfriars Bobby lying on his master's grave, from *Chatterbox*, 22 June 1867.

and children out of the burial grounds, but when challenged, the old curator told him that Bobby was an exception to this rule, since the little terrier did such sterling work keeping the vermin at bay. Regarding Greyfriars as his own property, Bobby even chased away the Heriots' schoolboys if they climbed over the dividing wall from their playground. James Anderson also joined Bobby's friends, feeding him bones and scraps, and offering him a warm bed in front of the fire on stormy nights. Anderson's neighbour, the tailor Robert Ritchie, also provided for the little dog from time to time. Already in 1864, Greyfriars Bobby was something of a local celebrity; people liked to see the dapper little dog trotting along to Mr Traill's restaurant after the sound of the one o'clock gun.

But Greyfriars Bobby also had some enemies. In 1867, John Traill was summoned to the Burgh Court for keeping an unlicensed dog. It was well known that for at least five years, Bobby had paid a daily visit to his temperance movement restaurant, situated at No. 6 Greyfriars Place, just by the burial ground. Some mean-spirited person had noticed that Traill was not paying any dog tax, and proceedings were duly taken against the restaurateur. In court, Traill argued that Greyfriars Bobby had no owner, since the dog refused to attach himself to anyone. Thus it was unfair to burden Traill with the tax of a dog that did not acknowledge him as its owner. The Burgh Court saw sense, and the summons was dismissed. The question remained who should be responsible for Greyfriars Bobby's dog tax, however, after the parsimonious restaurateur had refused to pay a penny of the seven shillings owing. James Brown, although old and in poor circumstances, offered to pay the money, but two of Bobby's other friends preceded him. Worried that the faithful little dog would be destroyed, James Anderson and Robert Ritchie called at the City Chambers, having clubbed together to pay the tax. But it turned out that the Lord Provost himself, the publisher William Chambers, had read about Greyfriars Bobby in the newspapers. This gentleman, the director of the Scottish Society for the Prevention of Cruelty to Animals, and a firm lover of dogs, ordered the City Officer McPherson to bring Greyfriars Bobby to him. When they met, Chambers was so delighted with the vigorous little Bobby that he offered to pay his dog tax, for life. Bobby was duly given a collar with a brass plate, bearing the inscription 'Greyfriars Bobby, from the Lord Provost 1867. Licensed.'[2]

The debate about Greyfriars Bobby's dog tax, and the happy outcome thanks to the intervention of the Lord Provost, was reported in almost every British newspaper, and in quite a few Australian and American ones as well. There was widespread curiosity about this amazing dog and his alleged nine-year vigil at his master's grave. Business picked up markedly for Mr Traill's eating-house, which was never short of customers who had come to see Bobby have his dinner just after the stroke of one. One of them, the old Edinburgh resident Andrew Hislop, described the scene many years later:

> Towards one o'clock people would gather just outside the large entrance gates, forming a line on each side of the sloping causeway. So widespread was the interest that every class of society was represented, from the well-to-do and fashionably dressed to the artisan and humble message-boy. As the hour grew near there was a hush of expectation. Then bang went the gun in the castle, and every head turned to the gate, knowing that at the signal Bobby would break his lonely vigil and set off on the way out. Soon there was a hushed whisper, 'Here he comes!' and the grey, shaggy little figure appeared, pattering over the causeway between the two lines of people. Looking neither to one side nor the other, intent only on his own affairs, Bobby hurried round the corner to his right, up the street a few yards, and disappeared into Mr Traill's Dining Rooms for the meal he never failed to get for many years.[3]

Greyfriars Bobby was also visited by journalists eager for copy. When some reporters from the *Aberdeen Journal* came to Greyfriars to see Bobby, they instead met James Brown, who told them that Bobby was busy ratting in the church. Indeed, this proved to be the case: the angry little dog stood snarling at a rat-hole. Brown told his visitors about Bobby's long residence in the churchyard, adding that in addition to his fidelity, the dog also possessed the virtue of orthodoxy: 'O, he hates to see a rottan in the kirk, but there's an thing he hates waur, and that's the whussles on Sunday.'[4] Bobby knew that Traill's restaurant was closed on Sundays, making no attempt to go there; instead, the little dog subsisted on various bones and scraps he had hidden at his den near the table-stones.

After he had become famous, Greyfriars Bobby was many times visited by artists keen to sketch or paint his likeness, or even to photograph him. The official photograph of Edinburgh's most famous dog was taken already on 13 April 1867, just after the dog tax business, by W. G. Patterson of 34 Frederick Street. He may well have been photographed also by another Edinburgh photographer, John Dickson of 3 Bristo Place.

65. A print of Greyfriars Bobby, from the painting by R. W. Macbeth.

The celebrated artist Gourlay Steell, known as the Scottish Landseer for his particular talent in painting dogs, of course invited Bobby to sit for his portrait. But as Steell was painting away, the one o'clock gun sounded, and the little dog became quite excited. Bobby could only be pacified when supplied with a hearty meal. When Steell exhibited his portrait of Bobby at the Nash Gallery in early 1868, it was widely admired. Another portrait of Bobby was painted by R. W. Macbeth, and exhibited the same year. Etchings or prints made from these two portraits were never short of buyers. The little dog's likeness was also painted by the artists John Macleod and John C. Gunter.[5] In fact, there were more portraits and drawings of Bobby than of some of the celebrated beauties of the time. No self-respecting illustrated magazine, in Scotland or England, could do without a drawing of Greyfriars Bobby, from life.

Greyfriars Bobby lived on for several more years, to enjoy his fame and security. He received letters from all over Britain, and parcels of bones, sausages, and other treats; a wealthy lady, fearful that he would freeze to death, offered to send him a comfortable kennel. Already during his lifetime, Bobby was several times featured in the RSPCA's journal *Animal World*; no animal welfare lecture was complete without a lantern slide depicting this canine paragon of virtue. In 1869, he was visited by the wealthy and dog-loving philanthropist Angela Burdett-Coutts. She was informed that the dog had once belonged to a humble old man named Robert Gray, who had once served his country as a soldier. Since Miss Burdett-Coutts saw that Gray's grave was unmarked, she offered to supply a gravestone, but the town council guardedly responded that if the name of the dog's owner could be ascertained, they would be willing to erect one.[6] The gravestone was never erected.

66. Greyfriars Bobby lies mourning his master, from *Dogs and their Doings* by F. O. Morris, engraved from Gourlay Steell's painting.

In his old age, Greyfriars Bobby kept patronising Mr Traill's restaurant, but he also paid visits to some other public houses nearby. His loyal old friends James Anderson and Robert Ritchie also looked after him. In 1871, the old dog was permanently adopted by John Traill and his family. Atoning for his lack of generosity back in 1867, the restaurateur took good care of Bobby, keeping him warm and well fed. When Bobby fell ill, mainly from old age, in early 1872, he was nursed by Traill's young daughter Elizabeth. On 14 January 1872, Bobby fell asleep in front of the fire, never to awake again. Bobby's obituary in the *Scotsman* of 17 January praised Traill for his kind attentions to the old dog.

John Traill and his friends buried Bobby in a triangular patch of ground facing the entrance to the cemetery itself. A small tombstone, marked only with the words 'Greyfriars Bobby' was put on the spot, and a photograph was taken by a friend of Traill's. However, this stone was either stolen by some mean-spirited individual, or taken away by the curator of the burial ground.[7]

Already during Bobby's lifetime, there had been discussion whether there ought to be a monument to Edinburgh's most famous dog. Baroness Burdett-Coutts, as she had become for her many good deeds, had offered to erect a memorial drinking fountain to keep Bobby's memory alive. This time, the town council gratefully accepted her offer, and the fountain was duly erected at the top of Candlemaker Row, providing drinking water for the public, as well as a trough at the bottom for thirsty dogs. On top of the fountain was placed a life-size bronze statue of Bobby, made during life by the sculptor William Brodie. The fountain has the following inscription:

67. A drawing of Greyfriars Bobby, from *Little Folks* magazine of 1876, based on a photograph of Bobby during life.

A tribute to the affectionate fidelity of Greyfriars Bobby. In 1858 this faithful dog followed the remains of his master to Greyfriars Churchyard and lingered near the spot until his death in 1872. With permission, erected by Baroness Burdett-Coutts.

In 1924, some American visitors to Greyfriars clubbed together to erect a gravestone for John Gray, with a suitable inscription to 'Auld Jock'. In 1981, the Dog Aid Society of Scotland presented and erected a red granite memorial to Bobby himself, similar to the stone on Auld Jock's grave, on the triangular grass plot in front of the kirk where reliable witnesses agree that Bobby was buried back in 1872. It was unveiled by the Duke of Gloucester, and there was a service with a children's choir. Another memento to Greyfriars Bobby is at Huntly House Museum, where his dinner-bowl and collar are on display, along with some photographs of Bobby and the Traills.

The Greyfriars Bobby drinking fountain was functional for many years, as evidenced by old postcards showing both humans and dogs making use of it. In 1954, after a careless motorist crashed into it, the fountain was cleaned and repaired and the dog statue polished. The following year, the fountain was first damaged by another motorist, and then vandalized by some young louts. After some discussion whether it was advisable to move the fountain from its exposed position at the top of Candlemaker Row, it was decided to turn off the water supply, since the pipework had been too badly damaged. In 1971, the drinking fountain was crashed into by a butcher's van, catapulting the dog statue into the pavement, but a few weeks later, it had once more been repaired.[8] Suggestions from Edinburgh conservationists that the water supply should be restored

68. The monument to Greyfriars Bobby, from *The Child's Companion*, 1 June 1880.

have not been acted upon. Still, Greyfriars Bobby's statue is one of the landmarks of Edinburgh. Busload after busload of tourists from all over the world photograph it, particularly the Americans and the Japanese. Some are so overcome with emotion when they hear Bobby's pathetic story that they cry aloud.

Already in 1902, there was a short biography of Greyfriars Bobby, by local author Henry Hutton. In 1912, the little dog received the full treatment, when American journalist and author Eleanor Atkinson wrote a novel about his adventures. Although she states that the story is absolutely true, her *Greyfriars Bobby* is largely pure fiction. The jury is still out on whether she made the effort to visit Edinburgh to learn more about the famous dog, or whether she made use of the guidebook. Her story of the rustic Auld Jock's antecedents at a farm called Cauldbrae is entirely fictitious, and she has the one o'clock gun banging away in 1858, when in fact it did not fire until June 1861. The novel is in part written in a ludicrous pseudo-Scots dialogue which is unlikely to have appealed to Bobby's friends back in Edinburgh.[9]

But although the fastidious Scots may have frowned on Eleanor Atkinson's excesses, her version of the affecting story of Greyfriars Bobby became quite a bestseller; it is still in print today, as the sole claim to fame for this obscure literary lady. Although there have been at least six modern children's books about Greyfriars Bobby, offering cute drawings and saccharine narratives, the Atkinson book still rules the roost. In 1948, during the height of the Lassie craze, Metro-Goldwyn-Mayer bought the rights to the Atkinson story, although they substituted Lassie for the humble little Scottish terrier.

69. A postcard from the 1920s depicting the
monument to Greyfriars Bobby, and the dog's collar.

Challenge to Lassie follows the novel relatively closely, with Lassie (or rather Pal, as we know) turning in an excellent performance, with her (or rather *his*, as we know) son Yip-Yip acting the part of a puppy in the early scenes. Lassie 'takes the seize' to save Auld Jock when he is attacked by robbers, but the old man dies of his wounds. In her vigil on his grave, Lassie is supported by the kind Mr Traill, but a mean-spirited local police sergeant objects to her presence in the cemetery. He kidnaps Lassie using a net, and prosecutes her for lacking a licence, but the kind Lord Provost saves the day. The wicked policeman is punished by having to act as a guide outside the churchyard gates, telling and retelling the story of Greyfriars Lassie to all comers.

In 1961, the Atkinson book was adapted into the full-length film *Greyfriars Bobby: The True Story of a Dog* by Walt Disney Productions. Disney visited Edinburgh in person, giving directions for some scenes to be shot on location, whereas others were filmed at Shepperton Studios in West London. He held auditions to find acting Skye terriers, with good success, although the dog trainer had to be hidden inside Auld Jock's coffin to direct his charge walking mournfully after it. In Disney's tear-jerker, every bit of sentimentality is wrung out of Auld Jock's death, Bobby's vigil on the grave, and his friendship with the local children. There are further touching scenes when the children of Edinburgh contribute their pennies for Bobby's dog licence, and the jovial Lord Provost declares the dog a Freeman of the City. There were murmurations from the direction of Edinburgh at these uncalled-for improvements of the story, but the Disney producers retorted that they should be grateful that the film had not been recorded in some American film studio, as may well have been the original plan. The film was followed up by the official *Walt Disney's Greyfriars Bobby* comic book, with the human characters speaking ludicrous pseudo-Scots and the dog barking 'Yark! Yark!'

The very considerable success of the 1961 Disney film prompted yet another remake of the old story, namely the 2005 film *The Adventures of Greyfriars Bobby*. All the old exaggerations are carried along, with a few novel inventions added for good measure: it is now the task of a shy boy named Ewan to rescue Bobby from some mean-spirited villains, who are keen to have him destroyed for lacking a dog licence. New characters are liberally added to the cast, whereas the stalwart Traill is unaccountably left out altogether. Bobby's Edinburgh friends must have been appalled to see that the dog himself had transformed into a West Highland white terrier, and that the Edinburgh Castle scenes had been shot at nearby Stirling Castle instead. Not even the geography is right: when Bobby travels from East Lothian to Edinburgh, he passes what are obviously Highland hills and lochs![10]

So, what do we really know about Greyfriars Bobby? What are the hard facts remaining after nearly 140 years of canine hagiography has turned the simple Skye terrier from Edinburgh into a Hollywood megastar?

The earliest mention of a dog living in the Greyfriars burial grounds is from May 1864, namely an article in the *Inverness Advertiser* stating that the little terrier named Bob had been staying there for some period of time, becoming quite well known locally. It was presumed that he had come from the country with a funeral cortege, but nobody knew who he was mourning or where he had come from.[11] Then, as we know, there was massive publicity about Greyfriars Bobby in April and May 1867: the sentimental story about the faithful dog evading the dog-tax gatherers was spread all over the English-speaking world. These articles mention nothing about a country funeral cortege, instead stating that Bobby had belonged to a poor man named Gray, who had lived in a quiet way in some obscure part of Edinburgh, before expiring eight and a half years earlier. James Brown remembered the funeral, he said, and also the dog being one of the most conspicuous of the mourners. Thirdly, there is an account of John Traill telling an 1871 visitor to his restaurant that Bobby's master had been a Midlothian farmer named Grey, who had expired in 1858.[12] Fourthly, we have the old soldier Robert Gray, referred to as Bobby's master by Baroness Burdett-Coutts' informant.

Multiple independent sources agree that there was a resident dog at Greyfriars from 1864 until 1872. There were many accounts of Bobby and his various antics, by reliable witnesses, already during the dog's lifetime. When Greyfriars Bobby was debated in the *Scotsman* newspaper in August 1934, many elderly Scots wrote letters to say that they had seen the famous little dog themselves, either at the churchyard or at Mr Traill's establishment nearby. As late as 1953, a very old lady declared that as a little girl, she had more than once seen Bobby accompany her father to Traill's eating-house.[13] Bobby was definitely at Greyfriars in 1864, and he probably came there several years earlier, since the 1864 article speaks of him having attained some degree of local fame already by that time. John Traill could remember feeding Bobby for a very long time, perhaps already in 1862. Bobby's dinner dish at the Huntly House Museum has the dates 1862 and 1872, supporting this hypothesis. Even if Bobby was an adult dog already when he came to Greyfriars in the late 1850s or early 1860s, he could easily have lived until 1872, since Skye terriers may well reach fifteen or sixteen years old if they are well looked after.

If there is solid evidence that Bobby really existed, and that he stayed at Greyfriars for some considerable period of time, the four different versions about his master all appear very suspect. Firstly, Edinburgh historian Forbes Macgregor found out that John Traill's story about the old farmer having had luncheon in his restaurant with his little dog back in 1858 was pure invention; Traill had no connection whatsoever with the restaurant in Greyfriars Place until May 1862. Nor had a Midlothian farmer, or an out-of-towner of any description, any business being buried in the Greyfriars burial grounds, since they were reserved for local inhabitants. There was no Cauldbrae farm, nor did any John Gray residing in Midlothian or Edinburghshire expire from 1858 until 1860. Several historians have searched the Greyfriars burial records for a more promising candidate to be Bobby's master, instead of the fictional 'Auld Jock'. It turned out that there were two men named John Gray buried at Greyfriars kirkyard in 1858: a 45-year-old local policeman and the young son of a merchant.

Forbes Macgregor considered John Gray the policeman a worthy candidate, and managed to find some useful information about his career. John Gray had once been a country gardener, but after losing his job, he migrated to Edinburgh in 1853. He managed to get a job as a police constable, an unattractive and badly paid position. Gray lived in a hovel called Hall Court, situated in Cowgate not far from Greyfriars, with his wife and son. Importantly, Macgregor was able to elucidate that John Gray was actually the local policeman: his beat included Greyfriars itself. In 1857, John Gray fell dangerously ill with tuberculosis; he died at Hall Court in early 1858, and was buried at Greyfriars churchyard on 10 February 1858.[14]

If we make two quite hazardous presumptions, namely that the name 'John Gray' is really that of Bobby's master, and that the vague reports that Bobby came to Greyfriars in 1858 are true, then Forbes Macgregor is probably right: Gray the policeman is the only likely candidate to be Bobby's master. But there are also strong arguments against this individual ever having anything to do with the dog. Firstly, the local policeman was a very well-known character in those days. Would it really be possible that the locals would entirely forget about his identity just a few months after his death, when the dog appeared in the cemetery? Macgregor's hypothesis that Bobby had been John Gray's watchdog is also open to criticism. Would any sane person really employ a tiny Skye terrier as a police dog? If Constable Gray had got into a brawl with some sturdy fellows, it would have been enough for one of the combatants to step on Bobby by accident, for the 'watchdog' to be put permanently out of action. And would not the locals remember such a singular police dog, patrolling the local beat for several years, before turning up on the grave of his master?

Author Richard Brassey, who wrote a children's book about Greyfriars Bobby, supported the theory of John Gray the policeman as Bobby's master, but eccentric local historian James Gilhooley disagreed. He instead presumed that Bobby had been keeping vigil by the wrong grave, since a farmer from the Borders named John Gray, who had come to Edinburgh for the market, had died in February 1858 and been buried in the East Preston Street cemetery. Gilhooley believed that dogs had telepathic abilities, and presumed that Greyfriars Bobby had used his psychic powers to find John Gray, but only to be thwarted because two men with that name had died within a week of each other in 1858.[15]

The strongest criticism of the Greyfriars Bobby story is that just like the yarn about of Prince Llewelyn's wolfhound Gelert, it is a variation on an ancient and widespread popular legend, told and retold all over the world for many centuries, with different canine and human protagonists.

Already the ancients knew about the myth of the 'Dog on the Master's Grave'. Eupolis, a Greek comic poet who flourished around 435 BC, had a dog so attached to him that at his death the faithful animal refused all food, dying of grief and starvation on his master's tomb. A Roman named Theodorus had a dog that lay down by his coffin and grieved to death. One of the dogs of King Hiero of Syracuse instead leapt into the flames and committed suicide when it was lit for his deceased royal master. There are several similar yarns from sixteenth- and seventeenth-century France and Italy. Bouchart's *Hierozoicon* tells the story of a Paris dog keeping vigil on its master's grave for three years, and another dog near Lisle remaining on its master's grave for nine long years. The kind and dog-loving local inhabitants erected a comfortable kennel over the grave, and fed the faithful dog regularly.

The next reincarnation of the 'Dog on the Master's Grave' resurfaces not far from Greyfriars Bobby's home territory. In 1716, a certain Mr Stewart, of Argyleshire, died suddenly from 'inflammation in his side'. His faithful Highland greyhound followed the remains of his master to the cemetery. Every evening afterward, about sunset, this dog walked the ten miles to the graveyard, lay down on his master's grave and spent all night there, before returning home in the morning. The local children befriended the dog and brought him some morsels of food, but the unhappy dog refused them. He could not be persuaded to eat a morsel, and frequently uttered long and mournful groans.[16]

France has quite a number of 'Dog on the Master's Grave' stories. In Lyons, a dog died of grief, lying on the grave of his master, a nobleman guillotined during the Revolution. Many Parisians had seen the 'Dog of the Innocents' keeping vigil on the tomb of his late master in this famous old cemetery for several years.[17] The vigil of Médor, the Dog of the Louvre, at the tomb of his master, who had perished in the July revolution of 1830, was immortalised by the poet Casimir Delavigne:

> He'll linger there
> In sad despair,
> And die on his master's grave.
> His name? 'Tis known
> To the dead alone –
> He's the dog of the nameless brave!

70. A mournful-looking cemetery dog, from George Jesse's *Researches into the History of the British Dog.*

> A tear for the dead! for the dog some bread!
>   Ye who pass the Louvre gate!
> Where buried lie the men of July,
> And flowers are flung by the passers-by,
>   And the dog howls desolate.

A study of nineteenth-century French attitudes to animals made note of a wealth of newspaper reports concerning dogs mourning their masters.[18] The more rash and excitable of these French dogs committed suicide from grief, through jumping out of the window or drowning themselves in the Seine. The more sentimental dogs kept vigil on the graves of their masters, moaning and sobbing aloud. When, in 1874, a Paris city ordinance prohibited dogs from cemeteries, dog-loving Parisians objected that this unfeeling attitude would cause further grief to the many piously faithful dogs mourning on the graves of their masters.

Stockholm had its own 'Dog on the Master's Grave'. In the 1830s, a dog lived in the Maria cemetery just south of central Stockholm. The Swedes presumed that the faithful animal, appropriately named Fidèle, was keeping vigil on the grave of his master. The name of this individual was unfortunately not known, but since the dog looked like a foreign breed, the master of Fidèle was presumed to have been an English skipper. The

71. Médor, the Dog of the Louvre.

artist Baron Carl Stephan Bennet painted a portrait of the sad-looking little dog, and the poet Julia Nyberg lauded him in verse:

> Though winter winds scatter the leaves
> On his master's grave, the poor dog grieves
> Both day and night, in snow and ice
> By the grave stone, he always lies.

But a historian investigated and found that the story was more legend than fact; even the dog's existence was very much open to doubt. He consulted the Norwegian cynologist Olaf Roig, who told him that

the legend of the dog on the master's grave is reproduced in several old British dog books. The location varies from Edinburgh to various towns in Northern England; the length of the vigil varies from 10 to 15 years. It is often added that the dog pays a daily visit to a pub, where it is fed. This vulgar legend, which is widespread all over Britain, suits the romantic view of dogs prevalent among the inhabitants of those parts.[19]

72. A dog howling on its master's grave, from Henri Coupin's *Les Animaux Excentriques*.

And this forthright Norwegian dog expert is not far wrong. There are versions of the 'Dog on the Master's Grave' legend from all over Britain. In 1827, a dog was constantly to be seen in St Bride's churchyard in Fleet Street. This dog had, for two years, refused to leave its master's grave. People were a little disappointed the dog did not look at all miserable. The inhabitants of the houses round the church fed the faithful dog daily, and the sexton provided him with a kennel. At Newcastle upon Tyne in the 1820s, another gloomy cemetery dog was brought food and water by kind people, but still expired 'worn away by pining, and by rain and cold'. Pondering this poor dog's fate, a children's magazine exclaimed, 'How does this poor brute shame us! We have a master Jesus Christ, who died for us, in our stead. Should we not then love him? think of him? serve him always? and if called upon, be willing to die for his sake?'[20]

In the 1830s, there was a 'Dog on the Master's Grave', presumed to have belonged to an Italian, in the cemetery of the Catholic chapel in Scotland Road, Liverpool. Every day, this dog went to the Throstle Nest tavern nearby to be provided with a meal. Another faithful old dog lived in the cemetery of St Margaret's church, Lee, not far from London. After spending eighteen months mourning at his master's grave, he was given a special collar, with the inscription 'The Little Wonder, of Saint Margaret's Church,

Lee'. There are many similar versions of the legend, from every part of the British Isles.[21]

Nor did the 'Dog on the Master's Grave' legend fail to cross the Atlantic. In Rose Hill cemetery, the oldest public cemetery in Washington County, is the stone statue of the dog Rollo, who kept vigil on his master's grave for several years. The cemetery opened in 1865 and the dog's statue is said to be nearly as old as that. People living near the cemetery tried to entice Rollo away from the grave, but without success; they instead provided the mourning canine with food, water and shelter in cold weather. When Rollo died, a marble statue was subscribed to by the kind, dog-loving locals. Although the name of the dog owner is long since forgotten, the head of Rollo's statue has been worn smooth by thousands of sentimental visitors patting him on the head; nor does the grave ever lack fresh flowers.

Another variation of the tale comes from Fort Benton, Montana, where an old sheep-farmer had expired in 1936. After his coffin had been loaded onto a train in Fort Benton, a dog appeared at the station. Everyone presumed that it must be the sheep-farmer's faithful dog that had come to mourn him. The animal was well fed by the railway staff and passengers, and made the station his permanent home. Already during his lifetime, he became a local celebrity: fan mail poured in after the dog had been featured by Ripley's *Believe It or Not*, schoolchildren sent Christmas gifts, and rail travellers took detours to stop at Fort Benton and see him. 'Old Shep', as the dog was called, even appeared on television, doing some simple tricks and playing with the station agent. In 1942, Old Shep had a grand funeral after he had been run over and killed by a train. He is commemorated by an obelisk at his grave, and by a statue; his collar and bowl are on permanent display. A children's book based on his exploits became a healthy seller, and Old Shep also inspired a popular Country and Western song.[22]

Japan has its own Greyfriars Bobby, an Akita named Hachikō. This dog belonged to a university professor, and used to meet him at the local railway station. One day in 1925, the master did not turn up, since he had died from a stroke. Hachikō was given away, but he did not like his new owner, escaping and returning to his old home, and then visiting the railway station. Every day, he appeared at the station, just in time to meet the train his old master had used to travel on. The other passengers recognized the dog and began giving him food and other treats; this went on for several years, making the dog into a newspaper celebrity. His faithfulness to his master's memory impressed the people of Japan as a spirit of family loyalty that all should strive to achieve. Teachers and parents used Hachikō's vigil as an example for children to follow. Already before the old dog had died in 1935, his statue was unveiled at the railway station; there have later been several books, and at least two films, about him.

Already during Greyfriars Bobby's lifetime, some sceptics suggested that he was not what people supposed him to be. The truth, an 1871 newspaper writer asserted, was that in the early 1860s, a dog had strayed into Greyfriars churchyard, where the sexton and gravediggers had taken care of him. Being well fed and looked after, the dog had been encouraged to take up permanent residence at Greyfriars, making himself useful by decimating the local rat and cat populations. During daytime, he trotted about at will in the burial grounds; at night, he slept underneath one of the old table-stones. The Edinburgh correspondent of a north-country newspaper thought it odd that a dog should live in the burial grounds. As a joke, he invented a story of the faithful dog keeping vigil on his owner's grave. What he had not calculated with was that the hoax would later find its way back to Edinburgh, where it caused quite a sensation. Although he was just an unconscious impostor, Greyfriars Bobby became a local hero. Now it was time to call an end to this embarrassing joke, the 1871 writer demanded: 'the sympathies of the Baroness Burdett-Coutts have been evoked to perpetuate an idle tale and bequeath a fountain, to extol faithfulness that never existed, and history whose entire foundation is fictitious.'[23]

Some other people in the know seem to have held on to the idea that the Greyfriars Bobby story had originated as a newspaper hoax. The Ayr journalist Thomas Wilson Reid claimed to have been involved in creating the hoax after seeing the Greyfriars cemetery dog in 1864 and persuading a colleague to make up the story about his faithful mourning for the *Inverness Advertiser*. In a novel he wrote in 1882, he openly boasted that he was the spiritual father of the Greyfriars Bobby legend, and that there was no truth in the story whatsoever.[24]

In February 1889, there had been a subscription to erect a marble monument to Bobby in the Greyfriars churchyard. But when the matter was debated at the town council, councillor J. B. Gillies objected that the Greyfriars Bobby story was just a penny-a-liner's romance. There was no truth to the story, the dog had never had any 'beloved master', and one monument to this canine impostor was more than enough. When challenged by the *Scotsman* newspaper, Gillies was unrepentant. A friend of his, James Stillie, had investigated the story and found it to be 'altogether a sensation myth'. Gillies had himself searched for some relative or acquaintance of the elusive master 'Gray' but found not a single person who could corroborate the story. The reason the dog had taken up residence in the burial grounds had merely been that he was well provided there with both shelter and food. Gillies and Stillie provided several witnesses declaring that Bobby had frequently visited their houses for food, that he had not kept vigil on the alleged master's grave, and that James Brown had begun propagating the legend of Bobby's faithful mourning after he had found out there was good money to be had from selling the photographs of the dog.[25]

Modern research on dog behaviour would suggest that dogs are perfectly capable of grieving a dead or departed human or nonhuman animal with whom the dog has bonded. There are also several verified instances of dogs remaining with their dead masters for some considerable period of time, after the master has met with some lethal accident or disease when walking in a desolate area. The most famous of them concerns the young artist Charles Gough who perished high up on Helvellyn during a tour of the Lake District. When his body was found three months later, his little dog still remained nearby. There was widespread admiration for the faithful dog, and a monument was erected in its honour, although some sources claim that the dog had eaten from the body and nearly reduced it to a skeleton. Another, more recent monument, at the Derwent Dam in Derbyshire, celebrates the heroic sheepdog 'Tip', who had kept vigil by the body of her dead master for fifteen weeks.[26]

In contrast, it is not logical behaviour for a dog to linger round, or rest upon, its dead master's grave. Firstly, a dog has no clear concept of death, nor the ability to connect the once-living master with the lifeless flesh being buried in the coffin. Secondly, one of the primary instincts of a healthy dog, like Greyfriars Bobby, is that of self-preservation; it would make no sense for him to pine to death lying on the master's grave, instead of getting on with life. It is not known where the apocryphal 'John Gray' was buried, whether he was a shepherd or a policeman, and it must be suspected that Bobby's favourite lair in the burial ground was chosen solely because the large table-stones nearby provided him with shelter from the elements.

As we have seen, the ancient concept of the faithful dog had widespread sentimental appeal; the legend of the 'Dog on the Master's Grave' can be found all over the world, in many different versions. It seems to have been a very appealing thought to the Victorians that dogs were capable of such intense affection, with the smug extension that the humans themselves were the deserving recipients of such sterling loyalty. It would appear as if this sentimental reasoning was taken advantage of by some canine adventurers: stray dogs who took up residence in a suitable cemetery, where the dismal, half-starved animals were surprised to find themselves well looked after by kind, dog-loving people who presumed they were keeping vigil on the graves of their masters. In Paris, the Dog of the Innocents and the Dog of the Louvre were seen and fed by many people, as were the cemetery dogs of London, Liverpool and Newcastle, and the 'faithful mourners' from America and Japan.

The 'Dog on the Master's Grave' legend has enjoyed considerable staying power. In 1930, Mrs Elizabeth Smith, of Buffalo, was buried at Pine Hill cemetery. The day after, workmen were surprised to see a black collie dog lying near the grave, howling dismally. Many people went to admire the devoted dog and bring him food. The SPCA took the dog away to their pound, where it was seen by Mrs Smith's flabbergasted relatives; they had never seen the 'faithful mourner' before, and Mrs Smith had never owned a dog! But the dog's newspaper photograph was seen by another Buffalo citizen, who had lost his fine collie Rex a few days earlier. When he arrived at the pound, Rex jumped up, yelping with delight. Since the dog had never even seen Mrs Smith, his alleged 'faithful mourning' had just been sentimental misinterpretation from the cemetery workmen.[27]

In 1971, a stray golden retriever attracted attention in the West Country town of Bradford-on-Avon, by stationing himself at a busy crossroads near the district hospital. Since the forlorn-looking dog was gazing wistfully at passing cars, people soon suspected that his master had been killed in a road traffic accident at the crossroads, and that the faithful canine was keeping vigil at the spot. There was widespread sympathy for Winston, as the dog was called. A snug kennel was built for him at the crossroads, and another in the hospital grounds. Every day, he was given a hearty meal at the hospital canteen. The nurses pampered him, and the local children gave him bones and other treats. After Winston had become a newspaper celebrity, and even

73. A French dog mourning on its master's grave, from Emile Richebourg's *Histoire des Chiens Célèbres*.

appeared on television, the faithful dog received treats and gifts from sentimental dog-lovers all over the world. At Christmas, the crossroads were inundated with cards and gift-wrapped presents. As a leading local celebrity, Winston enjoyed police protection: the local constable stopped the traffic if the old dog decided to take a stroll along the High Street.

Winston died of old age in October 1978, after having enjoyed more than seven years of complete independence and security; his funeral, at the Claverton Dog Cemetery, was a grand affair. But in the local newspaper, quite a different story emerged. It turned out that Winston had once belonged to a Devon hunt, but he had been too gun-shy and unreliable to be of any use. Mr Alex Moulton, a Bradford-on-Avon inventor, offered to give Winston a home, but the dog did not appreciate his intervention and ran away as soon as the trailer door was opened. Mr Moulton pursued him, but the determined dog swam the River Avon and disappeared. Winston later turned up at a farm nearby, where the eccentric dog was fed and allowed to sleep in a hay barn. Winston had higher aims in life, however, and ended up as Bradford-on-Avon's most popular dog. He is another example of a 'Dog on the Master's Grave' where the story of his alleged faithful mourning has been definitely disproved.[28]

Not long after his death, Greyfriars Bobby usurped the mantle of Saint Guinefort, becoming a canine saint, revered for his devotion and fidelity. The books and films about him are still popular, and he has launched a thousand school projects from Inverness to Chittagong. His value for the Edinburgh tourist industry must be very considerable indeed. Like some bizarre four-legged anchorite, he still sits motionless on top of his monument, to receive homage from the wide-eyed tourists and their flashing cameras.

But it is time for Greyfriars Bobby to rise up from his pedestal, and free himself from the fetters of the sentimental Victorian notions about how a dog was supposed to behave. As we have seen, Bobby's story is the most prominent variant of an ancient and widespread myth of canine loyalty. But there is no reliable evidence that Bobby was ever mourning his dead master, or keeping vigil on his grave. The assertion on the fountain inscription that he 'lingered near the spot' is certainly false: Bobby roamed all over the district as it pleased him. Albeit conveniently ignored by the official historians of Greyfriars Bobby, there is much to be said for the hypothesis that Bobby was an unconscious impostor, who made use of the 'Dog on the Master's Grave' legend to improve his lot in life.

Bobby was an independent dog, who made a good life for himself at the Greyfriars burial grounds. He was affectionate to his various human friends, and grateful for being well fed and kept warm. It does not appear as if he considered that he needed a master, until the last year of his life, when the old dog was adopted by the Traills and allowed to end his days in comfort. Bobby was a clever little dog, a good ratter, and an enemy to be reckoned with for the cemetery cats; see here a better obituary for him.

10

THE TURNSPIT DOG & SOME OTHER EXTINCT BREEDS

> The dinner must be dished at one;
> Where's this vexatious Turnspit gone?
> Unless the skulking cur is caught
> The sirloin's spoilt, and I'm at fault ...
>
> John Gay, *The Turnspit Taught*

Since medieval times, Britons have delighted in eating roast butcher's meat, much more so than the continental Europeans. Roast beef, pork or turkey was the nation's principal Sunday meal, eaten at all levels of society, except by the very poor. Roast beef became a symbol of national pride, as signified by the patriotic song 'O the roast beef of Old England', inspired by William Hogarth's print with the same title. Many people sneered at the idea of roasting meat in an oven, in the manner of the 'Frogs' and other dodgy foreigners: for a true Briton, the proper way was to spit-roast it the old-fashioned way, before an open fire.[1] This was believed, rightly in my opinion, to improve the flavour and texture of the meat.

Open-fire roasting was a very demanding method of cooking, however. It required not just skill and constant attention from the cook, and a plentiful supply of firewood, but also constant turning of the spit to make the meat roast evenly. In medieval times, the spit-roasting of meat was both a strenuous and tedious affair. A sixteen-pound joint of sirloin took more than four hours to roast, and had to be kept turning throughout that period; a moment's neglect meant that the meat would be burnt. In the kitchens of the wealthy, the turning of the spit was performed by male scullions referred to as 'turnspits'. These individuals were servants of low rank, picked for their brawny arms and high boredom thresholds. They were sometimes given to drunkenness and dissolution; since they sat so close to the fire, they were always dirty, and referred to as 'blackguards' as a result. With time, the words 'turnspit' or 'blackguard' developed into a slur; the latter version was still prevalent in Victorian times.

In Tudor times, some bright kitchen servant had the idea to use dogs to operate kitchen dog-wheels, thus saving the exertions of the scullions, and probably improving the quality of the roast as well.[2] Low, sturdy, short-legged dogs were used to operate the dog-wheels;

they were referred to as the Kitchen Dog, the Cooking Dog, or the Vernepator Cur. In his 1576 *Of English Dogges*, Dr Caius devotes a section to the Turnespete, as he calls it. When any meat was to be roasted, one of these dogs was hoisted into the dog-wheel, which was rotated by the weight of this canine squirrel; the Turnespetes 'so diligently look to their business that not drudge or scullion can do the feat more cunningly'. Caius called the Turnespete a mongrel, but with time they evolved into a distinct breed: small, long-bodied and bandy-legged. Most had drooping ears, but some had ears standing up. Some turnspit dogs had grey and white fur, often with a white blaze down the face; others were black or reddish brown. There may well have been several other colours. In his taxonomy of dogs, Carl Linnaeus listed the Turnspit as a distinct breed, mentioning that there were both short- and long-haired varieties. With a sense of humour seldom met with in his writings, he called it *canis vertigus*, Latin for 'dizzy dog'.

In the seventeenth and eighteenth centuries, most larger farms and houses in Wales and the west of England employed turnspit dogs. There are many records of dog-wheels in seventeenth-century Bristol probate inventories, but many fewer in similar inventories from Essex and Staffordshire. In 1639, when the Cornishman Peter Mundy visited Bristol, he was amazed that there was 'scarce a house that hath not a dogge to turn the spitte in a little wooden wheel'.[3] Although Bristol seems to have remained the epicentre of turnspit dog activity, along with South Wales, the eighteenth-century dog-wheels were rotating in every part of Wales, England and Ireland, and even in Scotland. There are several

74. A turnspit dog at work – an engraving reproduced in Chambers' *Book of Days*.

instances of *chiens tourne-broches* employed in French kitchens, and also scattered records of turnspit dogs being employed in Germany, Holland and Switzerland.

In his 1756 *Cynographia*, Carl Linneaus wrote that Sweden had no turnspit dogs, although he knew that 'in foreign countries, a dog sometimes performs the duty of a kitchen scullion, walking round in a wheel that turns the spit, until the roast is done; his reward for this work is usually a taste of the steak.'[4] Interestingly, there are also a few records of Turnspits being employed in America. Benjamin Franklin's *Pennsylvania Gazette* had advertisements for turnspit dogs and wheels for sale. A Turnspit was active at the State House Inn, Philadelphia, and it is known that the keeper of the City Tavern in Philadelphia imported several turnspit dogs from England and kept them hard at work in the tavern's large basement kitchen.[5]

Since wealthier households roasted meat most days, the life of the turnspit dog was not a pleasant one. Think of that endless toil in the narrow dog-wheel, which was suspended from the ceiling or wall not far from the hot, dirty fireplace! A rope or chain led from the dog-wheel to the spit, making it rotate at a steady pace. If the poor dog stood still to catch its breath, the spit stopped; this arose the fury of the cook, who was fearful that the meat would get burnt. The dogs were treated as household machinery, and often scolded and ill-treated. And a large roast might take three or even four hours to cook, taking a severe toll on the turnspit dog's leg strength and stamina, even if two dogs were worked in tandem.

The Revd Henry Crowe, author of the heartfelt but sometimes overly imaginative book *Zoophilos*, deplored the turnspit dog's lot in life in no uncertain terms: enclosed in a wheel from which they could not escape, and oppressed by the heat of the stove, their fate was comparable with that of Ixion, King of the Lapiths, whom Zeus bound to an ever-spinning wheel. A kitchen joke, which the poor turnspit dog is unlikely to have appreciated, was to put a glowing coal into the dog-wheel to speed the wretched animal up if it was lazy. In his *Letters from England*, Robert Southey claimed that the turnspit dogs were sometimes trained through being put in the wheel together with a burning coal, which they could only escape through running 'at full gallop'. This is probably an exaggeration, since the Turnspits were in fact taught to run at a steady trot. From America, there is an anecdote of William Penn sitting at the porch of the State House Inn, which was built in 1693, together with the inn's turnspit dog. When Penn knocked his pipe out, the dog would flee, since the sparks reminded it of its bitter training days in the wheel.[6]

Understandably, the turnspit dogs did not appear to be particularly happy about their lot in life. In his *Anecdotes of Dogs*, Edward Jesse described the turnspit dogs belonging to a Welsh clergyman in Worcestershire as being 'long-bodied, crooked-legged and ugly dogs, with a suspicious, unhappy look about them'. Due to the strenuous work, the dogs were often hoisted up into the dog-wheel in shifts, or on alternate days. It was often remarked that the turnspit dogs knew perfectly well which day they were supposed to work; this led to the saying 'every dog has his day'. According to the *Remarks on a Tour to North and South Wales*, published in 1800, the inn at Newcastle Emlyn employed a turnspit dog; great care was taken that this animal did not spy the cook approaching the larder, for then he immediately hid himself for the remainder of the day, and the guests had to be content with more humble fare.

The hard and unceasing labour of the turnspit dog was sometimes used as a metaphor in stories for schoolchildren, often to point out the moral advantages of hard labour. In one of these tales, a lazy turnspit dog escapes from his duties, forcing the other dog in the pair to work double shifts. Enraged, the hard-working dog sniffs out his work-shy companion and drags him by the ear down into the kitchen. Buffon told a more bloodthirsty version, concerning two *chiens tourne-broches* employed in the kitchen of the Duc de Lianfort in Paris. One day, when one of them hid in a fit of laziness, the servants forced the other dog to go into the wheel instead. But the agitated dog barked and wagged its tail, persuading the ducal scullions to follow it. The vengeful turnspit dog led them to a garret, dislodged the skulker from underneath a bed, attacked and killed him.

Another of these silly tales features some turnspit dogs conversing in the kitchen. One of them has dangerous radical opinions: like a socialist firebrand, he urges his colleagues to go on strike. Their ceaseless labour is demeaning, and their reward very scant. The other dogs are undecided, but when the kitchen maid brings some bowls of dog food they all eat with enthusiasm. The socialist dog joins in with gusto, all thoughts of industrial action evaporated from his head as he fawns before the kitchen maid, licking her hands:

> Among the rest he went to play,
> Was put into the wheel next day,
> He turned and ate as well as they,
> And never speeched again …

If Karl Marx had happened to come across this story, he would probably have groaned deeply, realising that it would be no easy task to sow the seeds of revolution in England's green and pleasant land.

The turnspit dogs had a day off, or at least a half-holiday, on Sundays, when they were taken to church. This was not motivated by concerns for their spiritual edification, but simply by the fact that the little dogs could be used as foot warmers for the churchgoers. According to a eighteenth-century joke, the Bishop of Gloucester once preached in a church in Bath, uttering the line, 'It was then that Ezekiel saw the *wheel* …' At the mention of this dreaded word, all the turnspit dogs ran for the door, their tails between their legs. Another version of this story has the Bishop provoking this canine stampede by giving a sermon on the horrors of Hell, where the unfortunates were *roasting* and *turning on the spit.*

A more amusing anecdote tells of the captain of a man-of-war, stationed in the port of Bristol in the eighteenth century, who was snubbed by the townspeople because of political bias. To play a trick on them, the exasperated mariner sent his men into town to steal all the turnspit dogs they could lay their hands on. With the dogs stowed away in the ship's hold, there was consternation among the Bristol merchants, and roast beef became very expensive indeed. When the captain released the dogs, he and his men were not charged with dognapping; the Bristol townspeople appreciated the joke, and the captain and his officers were rewarded with many dinners of roast meat.[7]

Already in the sixteenth century, some ingenious people realised that the turning of a spit roast by human or dog power was a device that could be improved on. Leonardo da Vinci invented a smoke jack that was supposed to be driven by fan-like blades inside the chimney, which were turned by the hot smoke rising from the fire. His invention was not practical, but others improved on it, and such smoke jacks were in use at the time of Samuel Pepys. They were relatively cheap, but unhygienic, unreliable, and greedy of fuel. In the early nineteenth century, Lowther Castle near Penrith had a particularly advanced smoke jack, driving eight horizontal and four vertical spits, saving the labour of not less than twelve turnspit dogs. Clock jacks, driven by weights, were in existence already in the sixteenth century, but serving only the very wealthy. These expensive contraptions used the same mechanism as a clock, making the mechanism tick over at a steady rate, and the spits rotate more evenly than even the most well-trained turnspit dog. An eccentric clergyman suggested a less high-tech replacement for the turnspit dog: if a hedgehog 'was taken into the kitchen, he would soon rid it of cockroaches, and ably discharge the duties of a Turnspit dog'.[8]

With time, the clock jacks were steadily becoming more affordable. They came in all sizes, suiting everything from a royal castle to a humble farmhouse, and customer satisfaction was high; the hard-working cook would not have to rely on the vexatious turnspit dogs, and would also get the meat roasted much better. Already in 1790, the zoologist Thomas Bewick wrote, in his *History of Quadrupeds*, that the turnspit dogs were on their way out. These dogs varied a good deal in size, shape and colour. The dog-wheels have been said by some authorities to have been of a standard size, but when kitchen historian Dr David J. Eveleigh examined eight preserved dog-wheels, he found them to be between 78 and 143 centimetres in diameter, and between 20 and 29 centimetres wide. Clearly there were different sizes of wheels for different sizes of Turnspits.[9]

Most turnspit dogs had grey fur spotted with black; some had one black eye and one pale blue one. Drawings of turnspit dogs in Buffon's *Natural History*, the 1797 *Encyclopaedia Britannica* and *The History of British Quadrupeds* show some awkward-looking animals, individually quite disparate. These and other observations on the Turnspits would seem to indicate that by anything resembling modern standards, they would hardly qualify as a distinct breed, rather as a group of mongrel dogs with some important characteristics in common: short legs, long bodies, and a capacity to keep running for considerable periods of time. In his *Origins of Species*, Charles Darwin briefly mentioned the turnspit dog, querying whether its odd body shape and very short legs were the results of natural selection, or if a spontaneous mutation had taken place.

But although the dog-wheels had been cleared out of the London kitchens by early Victorian times, they were still rotating in Wales, Ireland, and the west of England where a combination of parsimony and traditionalism prevented the clock jacks from making inroads. According to Campbell's *Life of Mrs Siddons*, it was an old habit in Brecon, where this celebrated actress was born, to roast the meat at the kitchen fire, on a spit turned by a dog. A Welsh correspondent to the *Notes and Queries* could well remember that in the 1830s, the kitchen of nearly every respectable house in Haverfordwest possessed a dog-wheel and at least one turnspit dog. A Welsh clergyman had two turnspit dogs, worked on alternate days. Although meat was not roasted every day, the dogs knew well which of them was on call for duty, and if the cook was not careful, it would escape when it saw the meat being prepared for roasting. In that case, the other dog had to take its place 'and he would lie down in the wheel, and howl dismally, in expression of his sense of the injustice with which he was treated'. If the right dog was put into the wheel, the other one looked quite satisfied, wagging his tail and licking his jaws as though looking forward to dinner.[10]

The metaphor of the turnspit dog has been used by several authors and poets, great and small alike. In Shakespeare's *Comedy of Errors*, the character Dromio spoke about a suspected witch that

> If my breast had not been made of faith, and my heart of steel,
> She had transformed me to a curtail-dog, and made me turn i' the wheel.

Dr Johnson wrote about a person being 'as awkward as a Turnspit Dog, when he is first put into the wheel'. Oliver Goldsmith once elegantly opened a letter with the phrase, 'No Turnspit dog gets up into his wheel with more reluctance than I sit down to write; yet no dog ever loved the roast meat he turns better than I do him I now address ...' In Samuel Butler's *Hudibras*, the turnspit dog metaphor makes another appearance:

> But as a dog that turns the spit
> Bestirs himself and plies his feet
> To climb the wheel, but all in vain –
> His own weight brings him back again,
> And still he's in the self-same place,
> Where, at his setting out, he was ...

In his *Art of Speaking*, Pitt spoke of a verbose orator:

> His arguments in silly circles run,
> Still round and round, and end where they begun.
> So the poor Turnspit, as the wheel runs round,
> The more he gains, the more he loses ground.

A rare collection of poems entitled *Norfolk Drollery* had some verses inspired by the life and labours of 'a dog called Fuddle, Turnspit at the Popinjay, in Norwich':

> This I confess, he goes around, around,
> A hundred times, and never touches ground;
> And in the middle circle of the air
> He draws a circle like a conjuror.

> With eagerness he still does forward tend,
> Like Sisyphus, whose journey has no end.

In an equally obscure *Collection of Miscellaneous Essays*, a certain T. Mozeen wrote the verse epitaph of 'Sharper', a turnspit dog owned by Mr Roger Watts who kept the Sign of the Cock, in Corn Street, Bristol:

> That Quality he had; and every Grace
> That need adorn Successors of his Race.
> The Wheel of Fortune Men capricious deem;
> None better understood the Wheel than him.

Having been helped to many a good dinner through Sharper's labours in the wheel, Mozeen continued, in equally laborious verse:

> Art thou a Drunkard? – to thy Shame remember,
> From *January's* Month unto *December*,
> He ne'er was so, tho' living among Sots;
> A Turnspit Dog – and own'd by *Roger Watts*.

The collection *Apollo's Lyre*, published in London in 1795, contains the poem 'Fat Dolly the Cook', written by Mr Cawdell, comedian, and ending with the stanza:

> A fire she's made within my breast,
>   Without the help of fuel,
> A calf's head on my shoulders plac'd
>   My soul is water gruel;
> Would but Pythagoras set me free
>   From a life of melancholy,
> A little turnspit dog I'd be,
>   And turn the wheel for Dolly!

An eccentric clergyman, the Revd Thomas Parks, Curate of Lismore in Ireland, insisted on keeping turnspit dogs in service throughout his long life, until his death in 1854 at the age of eighty-six. At about the same time, physician Erasmus Wilson recorded seeing several turnspit dogs on a visit to Germany, one of which he described in some detail: 'It was at one of these stations that I made acquaintance with a handsome specimen of the old Turnspit dog; his coat a bluish grey, his body remarkably long, a large head with standing-up ears, and legs bandied to the highest point of excellence. The creature was a perfect mole in his figure; his shoulders and fore legs strong, and haunches and hind legs small – so small, in fact, to appear too weak to support him'. In 1861, the Revd J. G. Wood wrote that although a solitary Turnspit could still be seen, a relic of bygone days, the roasting-jacks had well-nigh annihilated their very existence. In 1864, a Yorkshire dog fancier saw a strange-looking canine 'of the smooth terrier kind, quite black, with a very long, heavy body and particularly short legs'. Its owner proudly stated that this was a very curious dog indeed, bred for use inside the dog-wheel, and possibly the last of its kind.[11]

In 1844, an English visitor to St Briavel's Castle near Tintern in Wales thought it curious that there was a wooden dog-wheel in the kitchen, which showed obvious signs of being in use. When he asked to see the turnspit dog, the cook informed him that, fearful that his services would be called upon, the old dog was in the habit of quietly slipping out of the house at the approach of visitors. In 1856, a later visitor to this castle was informed that their old turnspit dog had died some years ago. As a joke, this gentleman put his own little dog into the wheel, but this animal proved to be entirely averse to turnspit work. In 1852, another Englishman thought it very curious that his leg of lamb had been roasted with the help of a turnspit dog at one of the hotels in Caerleon. He asked the waiter to bring the dog into the dining room, where he gave it some of the lamb it had helped to roast. This 'hotel' may well have been the Hanbury Arms near the Usk, where a turnspit dog is recorded to have been at work at least until 1864. As the Turnspit breed grew scarcer, some parsimonious Welshmen hired them out; as the dogs became fewer and fewer, the hire money rose, although never above sixpence a day. Writing in 1905, the antiquary Sabine Baring-Gould confirmed that the Hanbury Arms dog-wheel in Caerleon was still in existence, as was one at Butter Hill, Maesgwyn, Pembrokeshire.[12]

There are some other observations of turnspit dogs well into late Victorian times. Some public houses, like the Sugar-Loaf Inn in Bristol and the Squirrel Hotel in Wellington near Taunton, found it profitable to keep their dog-wheels rotating, since the turnspit dogs at work were curiosities attracting customers from near and far. A visitor to the former establishment was amazed to see the large joints of beef being roasted, and the poor turnspit dog working hard in a box high up on the right side of the huge fireplace. At Brancepeth Castle, in Northumberland, it was also the habit to use Turnspits well into Victorian times, all with the hereditary name of 'Wheeler'. Once, when dinner was unaccountably delayed on a great occasion, the lady of the house rang the bell to find out the cause; the cook replied 'Please, Ma'am, Wheeler's pupping!' Quite possibly the last observation of a turnspit dog comes from the old hospital at Beaune in Burgundy, where one of these animals was still at work in the early twentieth century.[13]

With time, the turnspit dogs were in danger of being not only extinct, but totally forgotten. In 1850, the *Lady's Newspaper* described and figured a dog-wheel in operation somewhere in Gloucestershire five years earlier, to edify its female readers about old-fashioned kitchen apparatus.[14] When, in the 1860s, a wooden box and wheel was put up at auction, no person could figure out what it was used for, until an old blacksmith confidently stated that it was the wheel once trodden by a turnspit dog. In 1884, another correspondent to the *Notes and Queries* stated that three dog-wheels were kept in museums and collections of curiosities: the aforementioned one at St Briarvel's Castle near Tintern in Wales, one at Christ Church, Winchester, and another one at

75. The dog-wheel at St Briarvel's Castle, as drawn in King's *Ten Thousand Wonderful Things*.

76. An engraving of a turnspit dog, from Edward Jesse's *Anecdotes of Dogs*.

Windsor.[15] A correspondent to *The Times* in 1961 had seen the dog-wheel at St Briarvel's, and also another one kept at the George Inn in the National Trust village of Lacock, Wiltshire. When the subject of turnspit dogs and dog-wheels was discussed in the same newspaper in 1967, it was pointed out that a dog-wheel from Rhostryfan near Caernarfon was kept at the Welsh Folk Museum in St Fagans. Other dog-wheels were kept in Mitford in Northumberland, at the Dogwheel public house in Bewdley, West Midlands, in Birmingham and in Bristol.[16] The Blaise Castle House Folk Museum in Bristol has three eighteenth-century dog-wheels from old Bristol houses, one of which is on permanent display. The St Fagans dog-wheel also survives to this day, as does the one at the pub in Bewdley, which is quite a tourist attraction.

Abergavenny Museum goes one better, however, since it possesses not only a dog-wheel but also a stuffed turnspit dog. This animal, known as Whisky, was acquired by the museum in 1959, having previously been exhibited for decades at the Old Shop in Cross Ash. The same person who gave Whisky to the museum also donated a photograph of the rustic-looking Old Shop from around 1880; it may well be that the turnspit dog was stuffed around this time, as one of the few remaining ones. Whisky is small, only 14 centimetres tall, but is not standing erect. She looks very odd indeed, like a cross between a squirrel and a dog, with a very arched back that is not consistent with normal canine physiology. She is a true Turnspit, however, and the deformed back is likely to have been caused either by cack-handedness in stuffing and mounting her body, or more probably deliberate distortion of the stuffed body to make it fit the wheel in which it was exhibited at the Cross Ash shop. Whisky remains the only stuffed turnspit dog in existence today.

The turnspit dog is perhaps the most striking example of an extinct breed of dog. In 1750 there were Turnspits everywhere, by 1850 they had become very scarce, and by 1900 they had disappeared altogether. The availability of cheap clockwork roasting-jacks

77. The dog-wheel depicted in the *Lady's Newspaper* of 9 February 1850.

effectively brought about the demise of the turnspit dog; already by the 1850s it was considered old-fashioned and eccentric to keep a dog-wheel. The only use for a turnspit dog was in the kitchen dog-wheel, since their ugly looks and morose temperaments made them unattractive pets. There are in fact very few records of turnspit dogs being kept as pets, with the exception being that Queen Victoria herself showed praiseworthy sympathy for these downtrodden members of the canine *lumpenproletariat*. It is recorded that in 1843, Her Majesty kept three 'turnspit tykes' as pets at Windsor.

There are many other extinct dog breeds. For example, the Old English bulldog was not uncommon in the eighteenth century. It was a large, muscular dog, specially bred for use in bull baiting. But after the Cruelty to Animals Act of 1835 had caused this cruel blood sport to decline, the Old English bulldog became extinct already in Victorian times. Sweden used to have a distinctive breed of large dogs used for guarding cattle from wolves, known as the Dalbo dog, but these mastiff-like dogs became extinct in the 1910s due to no longer being required.[17] The draught dogs of Belgium and Flanders provide an even closer parallel to the turnspit dog. Many visitors to these parts were amazed to see these large, muscular dogs pulling quaint little dog-carts. The milkmen, or rather milkwomen, did their rounds with their carts of milk bottles and canisters pulled by one or two well-trained dogs. There were at least two breeds of draught dog used: the Trekhond and the Belgischer reker. Even the old-fashioned Belgian army used dogs to pull mobile machine-gun batteries, a strategy that proved quite worthless in the Great War: the ruthless Germans shot the Belgian soldiers and bayoneted the dogs. In the 1920s and 1930s, it was considered a mark of poverty to use dogs to pull carts. As a result, both these breeds of dog became entirely extinct; just like in the case of the turnspit dog, nobody bothered to save the poor man's donkey.[18]

It is curious that both in Europe and the United States, inventors patented treadmills for dogs or sheep, to be used in powering butter-churns and other machinery at small farms. In 1901, the *Daily Mail* had an illustrated account of various treadmills operated by dogs or sheep. Some Americans used dogs to power washing machines, corn grinders or even printing presses. The proprietors of the *Plymouth Review*, in Wisconsin, were able to turn out a whole edition of 1,000 papers, using a 100-pound mastiff rotating a large wooden wheel. Another printing dog in Alberta was reported to have died of a broken heart when the newspaper offices burned down, since it had loved its work so very much. The Welsh people, who were notorious for their use of dog power, kept butter-churning dogs working treadwheels as late as the 1920s. They are reported to have been more content with their lot than the wretched Turnspits, since they were given a reward of warm buttermilk when their work was done.[19]

There have been many hypotheses about which of today's breeds of dogs are most closely related to the old turnspit dog. The dachshund and the basset hound have both been proposed, albeit with little merit; a slightly more worthy candidate is the Glen of Imaal terrier, which is quite Turnspit-like, but with a more terrier-like head. The Welsh corgi might be another candidate; in that case, it would be ironical that the pampered royal pooches at Buckingham Palace and Windsor Castle are relatively close relations to the Turnspit 'underdogs'.

78. The milk service of
Antwerp, from the *Treasury
of Literature and the Ladies
Treasury*, 1 September 1875.

79. A Belgian dog cart, from a postcard dated 1904.

80. Two late nineteenth-century American patents for the use of dog power to propel machinery.

81. Two Welsh butter-churning dogs at work.

11

LORD BYRON'S BOATSWAIN & SOME OTHER REMARKABLE NEWFOUNDLAND DOGS

N is for Newfoundland, of all dogs the best;
Just give me this dog, you may keep all the rest.
In the water he'll jump and will struggle to save
A dear little child from a watery grave.
A lover of children, a boy's closest friend,
A servant of man on which to depend.
He'll carry a basket or drive home the cow,
Or keep back a tramp with his fierce
  Bow-wow-wow!

From *The Natural History A*B*C**,
printed by M. A. Donahue and Co., Chicago

The Newfoundland dog is not an ancient breed, like the Chow Chow or the Saluki, but a relatively recent creation. The province of Newfoundland was discovered by Vikings around AD 1000, but there is no evidence that they were in possession of any dogs resembling Newfoundland dogs, or indeed that they left any dogs behind at all. In 1497, Newfoundland was rediscovered by John Cabot, who gave it its name; he mentions nothing about any indigenous breed of dogs. Nor does Captain Richard Whitbourne in his 1620 *Discourse and Discovery of Newfoundland*, a most exhaustive treatise; had there been a distinctive breed of large dog at Newfoundland in these days, he would surely have mentioned it.

It is reasonable to suggest that during the seventeenth and eighteenth centuries, dogs were regularly brought to Newfoundland, by fishermen and various visitors. The local inhabitants soon found that large, strong dogs could be extremely useful allies, particularly if they were also good swimmers, enabling them to retrieve objects from the water, and to help with the fishing nets. The dogs needed a thick, water-resistant coat to be able to swim in the icy waters. These early Newfoundland dogs were large, muscular beasts, useful as draught dogs and excellent in the water. The hardy animals were far from picky about their food and liked eating raw fish from the nets. With time, the dogs developed, becoming more homogenous, with thicker fur, and greater prowess at swimming. The Newfoundlanders are likely to have appreciated that dogs with webbed feet swum better, and selected their breeding accordingly. Similarly, double coats of fur insulated the dogs from the icy cold water, and an oily outer coat made them more buoyant. The dogs bred on the mainland were bulkier, often with black and white or brown and white spotted fur. Those bred on the St Pierre and Miquelon islands were smaller, and often solid black. The island of St John had its own breed of dog: the St John's water dog, which is the ancestor of today's Labrador and flat-coated retrievers.[1]

Many cynologists have pondered which breeds of dog constitute the ancestor(s) of the Newfoundland dog. Pyrenean mountain dogs were certainly used as ship's dogs in these days, and look not unlike early Newfoundland dogs, but they have double hind dew claws, a characteristic lacking in the Newfoundland. Another likely contributor is the Portuguese water dog, sharing the typical Newfoundland trait of having webbed feet. A recent study of the genetic structure of the purebred domestic dog clusters the Newfoundland with some other large mastiff-like breeds, such as the Rottweiler, bullmastiff and Bernese mountain dog, but provides no further clue about their ancestry.[2] It is very likely, from the looks and behaviour of the early Newfoundland dogs, that there was also significant cross-breeding with Eskimo dogs. For example, it is said of the early Newfoundlands that if one of them gave a howl, the rest of the pack immediately joined in. This sometimes works with today's Newfoundlands as well: try playing the popular YouTube recording of 'Lulu, the Singing Newfoundland' to a Newfoundland male, and you might be amazed at the result.

The first certain mention of a Newfoundland dog is in the *Gentleman Farrier* from 1732, which states that 'The Bear Dog is of a very large Size, commonly sluggish in his Looks, but he is very watchful, he comes from *Newfoundland*, his Business is to guard a Court or House, and has a thundering Voice when Strangers come near him, and does well to turn a Water Wheel.' A painting dated 1742, depicting what may well be an early Newfoundland dog, is kept at Ripley Castle in Yorkshire. Its inscription 'Windsor, Newfoundland' may well refer to where the dog was seen. The earliest mention of a Newfoundland dog in the British Library's Burney Collection of early newspapers is from the *Daily Advertiser* of 16 January 1752: 'Lost, a white rough puppy of the Newfoundland Breed'. The year after, a Fulham gentleman lost 'a large black Dog of the Newfoundland Breed, with some white spots about his head', answering to the name of Fearnought. In 1759, 'a large black Dog of the Newfoundland Breed, with a white Star on his Breast, and a large Brass Collar' was lost; it was added that 'he answers to the name of Ipswich'. The earliest use of the term 'Newfoundland dog' took place in March 1760, according to the same database.

The early Newfoundland dogs imported into Britain could be discerned as a distinct breed, although they were somewhat heterogeneous: some were retriever-like, others were bulkier and had longer fur, and a few even resembled today's Newfoundlands. Many fur colour variations existed: black and white, brown and white, pure white, and even white and yellow. In his *History of Quadrupeds*, Thomas Bewick described a Newfoundland dog he had encountered at Eslington, Northumberland. The dog was web-footed and could swim very fast and dive with great ease. It was very adept at retrieving objects from the bottom of the water. It was naturally fond of eating fish, both cooked and raw. In Newfoundland, Bewick wrote, these dogs were often used for draught, being able to pull large sledges loaded with timber without any human intervention. After delivering their load, they returned to the woods after being rewarded with some dried fish.

The Europeans were very much impressed with these early Newfoundland dogs: they were brave, strong and majestic in appearance, but also intelligent, affectionate and gentle. The dogs soon became fashionable and expensive. Keeping a Newfoundland dog seems to have been something of a status symbol in those days. The Earl of Home had a Newfoundland dog celebrated for catching salmon, sometimes retrieving twenty in a morning, a success rate that clearly annoyed Lord Tankerville, the owner of the fishing rights. He instituted a process against the dog, but when the case went to court, it was won by the four-legged defendant.[3]

During a winter storm in 1799, a ship out of Newcastle was driven onto the rocks and wrecked near Yarmouth. The only survivor was a Newfoundland dog, carrying the captain's pocket-book in his mouth. For days, the dog remained on guard on the beach, plunging into the waves to retrieve various large pieces of wreckage. Politician Lord Grenville, who was in the area on some business or other, went to see the shipwrecked dog. He decided to take care of the dog, renamed him Tippo, and installed him at stately Dropmore Park in Buckinghamshire. When Tippo expired several years later, Lord Grenville built him an elaborate monument with a Latin inscription, which was translated in Edward Jesse's *Anecdotes of Dogs*:

> Here, stranger, pause, nor view with scornful eyes
> The stone which marks where faithful Tippo lies ...

The dog's adventure back in 1799 was also described:

> Cast by a fatal storm on Tenby's coast,
> Reckless of life, I wailed my master lost.
> Whom long contending with the o'erwhelming wave
> In vain with fruitless love I strove to save.
> I, only I, alas! surviving bore
> His dying trust, his tablets, to the shore ...

Although Dropmore Park is no longer in the hands of the Grenvilles, having recently been converted into flats, the monument to Tippo is still present in the grounds.

In contrast to these canophilic English gentlemen, the Newfoundlanders themselves were not overly concerned about their dogs. The animals were worked hard and fed the most unpromising diet, such as the offal of cod. Since the dogs bred like rabbits, there was soon significant canine overpopulation in these parts. Some of the more unscrupulous and penurious Newfoundlanders allowed their dogs to roam free, to scavenge for scraps and terrorize the neighbours. The problem with the unruly dogs soon amounted to such proportions that in 1780, the Governor prohibited the keeping of more than one dog, and authorized the destruction of ownerless animals scavenging for food. When they learnt that Newfoundland dogs were quite highly valued in England, the Newfoundlanders began exporting the dogs in increasing quantities. When the timber ships from Newfoundland arrived in Poole and other harbours, they were met by crowds of dog fanciers, eager to snap up a fine specimen.

In April 1803, Colonel Montgomery, of the 9th Regiment, was riding through Hyde Park, followed by his favourite Newfoundland dog. As ill-luck would have it, Captain McNamara RN was also taking a ride that particular day, accompanied by another large Newfoundland. The dogs took an instant dislike to each other, and started a furious fight. Trying to part the dogs, the Colonel struck the Captain's dog with a small cane. Since the dog-loving Captain took great exception to this, there were 'high words' between the two gentlemen. They arranged to meet, with pistols, at Primrose Hill the very same day. Both officers were crack shots: the Captain was wounded in the groin, but the Colonel received a lethal shot in the chest. For this regrettable duel over two Newfoundland dogs, Captain McNamara was later tried at the Old Bailey, but common sense prevailed on this occasion, and he was acquitted.[4]

At the same period of time, the Duke and Duchess of York were very proud of their fine Newfoundland dog, named Nelson. This was the notorious Frederick, Duke of York, who had once commanded 10,000 men and marched them about in a random manner during the disastrous Flanders campaign of 1793. He later disgraced himself further through getting involved in a swindle to sell military commissions, run by his mistress Mary Ann Clarke. Since this dismal Duke kept several other mistresses, and sired a number of bastard children, the Duchess soon had enough of him: they separated, and she settled down at Oatlands Park in Weybridge. Frederica, Duchess of York, who had been born a Princess of Prussia, was very fond of dogs. At Oatlands, she kept at least forty of these animals, from the massive Nelson to the most diminutive breeds. In 1803, the painter George Stubbs exhibited a portrait of Nelson before the Royal Academy. Interestingly, this very impressive dog looks just like a present-day Newfoundland, except that his tail is rather curved over his back. The large and handsome Nelson also figures prominently in a painting of the Duchess by Peter Edward Stroehling in 1807, later issued as a print or book illustration; the characteristic spotting pattern shows that it is clearly the same dog. Nelson is buried at the Duchess's private dog's cemetery at Oatlands Park, which is still in existence today, although the house is a luxury hotel.[5]

Lord Byron was another of the many upper-class people who wanted a Newfoundland dog. He had been very fond of animals, particularly dogs, from an early age. While a Cambridge undergraduate, he was annoyed that the university regulations prohibited the keeping of dogs. Since the statutes had no mention of bears, he installed a tame bear in his rooms instead, without the authorities being able to interfere. The bear seems to have conducted itself with decorum; in a letter, Byron even suggested that his ursine friend should sit for a fellowship.

82. A print depicting the Duchess of York with some of her dogs, the large Newfoundland Nelson prominent among them.

At his family seat, the rambling Newstead Abbey, Lord Byron kept quite a menagerie of animals. His predecessor, the 5th Baron, had kept a tame wolf, and a descendent of this animal, named Lyon, was in residence. Noted for his fierceness, this bad-tempered wolf-dog hybrid had once torn the backside off Byron's breeches. Lord Byron also kept two Newfoundland dogs, named Boatswain and Thunder, and the canine population at Newstead sometimes also included the fierce mastiff Nelson and Mrs Byron's fox-terrier Gilpin. Both Boatswain and Thunder are likely to have been imported from Newfoundland. According to Byron, Boatswain had been born there in May 1803, and was resident at Newstead at least since early 1806. A tenant farmer at Newstead told that at the Upper Lake, he sometimes saw the poet get into the boat with his two noble Newfoundland dogs, row into the middle of the lake, and tumble into the water, having the two dogs seize him by the coat and drag him away to land. When Byron went to visit his friend Edward Long at Little Hampton in Sussex, he was accompanied by his favourite Boatswain. When the poet practised with pistols, shooting at oyster shells by a tall pier, Boatswain leapt into the water from the pier, a feat Long could not persuade his own dog to perform.

Less valorously, Byron used his two Newfoundland dogs to bait the tame bear. A former Newstead servant remembered that Thunder, although the larger of the two dogs, was less courageous than Boatswain. The brass collars of both dogs, which were sold at auction in 1903 for twenty-one and four guineas respectively, are still kept at Newstead Abbey.[6] They have been severely battered, probably through the dogs' scraps with the bear, with each other, and with other large dogs. It does not appear as if Boatswain was ever chained or put in a kennel. He went where it pleased him to go, seeking out other large dogs to fight, or bitches to mate with. Byron's friend Elizabeth Pigot once wrote that Boatswain had enjoyed another battle with a dog named Tippoo, at the House of Correction, coming off the conqueror. Mrs Byron's fox-terrier Gilpin was Boatswain's particular enemy. When Byron lived with his mother at Burgage Manor in Southwell, Boatswain fought Gilpin all over Burgage Green, until the opponents were finally separated by Elizabeth Pigot's brother Henry.

Since Boatswain took every opportunity to attack and worry his fierce little opponent, Mrs Byron was fearful her little dog would be killed. She sent Boatswain and her son's other two dogs away to a servant when Lord Byron went back to university. But one morning, the servant was alarmed to find that Boatswain had gone away. It turned out that he had gone all the way to Newstead to fetch Gilpin, and that the two had become good friends. Byron's biographers have used this story to illustrate Boatswain's magnanimous nature, but an explanation more consistent with modern notions of canine behaviour is that there had been some fighting between the two dogs before Gilpin had been forced to accept a lower position in the canine hierarchy. When Boatswain returned to Newstead, probably to look for his generously filled food-bowl there, he met Gilpin, whose nature was to follow the pack leader. Later, Boatswain protected the pack member Gilpin against other dogs, a task which the quarrelsome nature of the little terrier rendered no sinecure.[7]

83. Boatswain's collar, reproduced by permission of Nottingham City Museums and Galleries, Newstead Abbey.

Lord Byron seems to have been quite an irresponsible dog owner, even by Georgian standards, allowing his large, fierce dogs to roam free and terrorize the neighbourhood. The concept that it was advisable to have some degree of control over a large and potentially aggressive dog seems to have been entirely alien to the poet's mind. The mastiff Nelson had to wear a muzzle most of the time, since he was quite ferocious and intractable. Once, Byron amused himself by removing the muzzle and helping Nelson to wreck the room of a friend of the poet's, who was staying at Newstead. There was a jealous feud between Nelson and Boatswain, which one day exploded into a ferocious fight when Nelson was unmuzzled. If Lord Byron and his friends had not parted the dogs, by thrusting pokers and tongs into the mouth of each, either dog might have died. Boatswain's feud with Nelson continued until the unpredictable mastiff was shot, after he had tried to kill one of Lord Byron's horses.

After returning to Cambridge in the summer of 1807, Byron left his dogs Boatswain and Bran (a replacement for Nelson) at Southwell, where they were taken care of by the groom Charles Monk. Byron's friend and neighbour Elizabeth Pigot, who regularly corresponded with him about the dogs, also seems to have been very fond of Boatswain. The great dog, who roamed free as always, often visited Elizabeth and her brother at their cottage nearby. Once, when Elizabeth Pigot was having tea with some elderly lady friends, Boatswain frightened them by suddenly jumping in through an open window. He approached them wagging his tail, perhaps hoping to share their meal, but since the timid old ladies objected to his presence, Elizabeth managed to decoy the great dog out of the room by opening the door and exclaiming 'Cat Bos'n!'

The best likeness of Lord Byron's favourite dog is the portrait of Boatswain by the Nottingham artist Clifton Tomson, painted in the summer of 1808. It depicts a very strange-looking animal indeed; today, Boatswain would not have won the five-hundredth prize at a Newfoundland dog show. His head is too small, his fur too short, his ears the wrong shape, and his tail too curled. It was sometimes said at the time that any dog as big as a donkey and as furry as a bear could be called a Newfoundland dog. But although the Newfoundlands were quite heterogeneous at the time, Boatswain was certainly an extreme, perhaps even a Newfoundland–husky cross. In contrast to the shrewd Duchess of York, who had selected Nelson, perhaps the finest Newfoundland available in Britain at the time, Lord Byron had been 'sold a pup' in more ways than one by some unscrupulous dog dealer!

Since the dog in the 'Boatswain' portrait looks so very unlike a Newfoundland, there has been speculation that perhaps there had been a mix-up or substitution of paintings at some stage. Tomson's portrait is well authenticated, however, and Lord Byron would hardly have valued a portrait of his favourite that looked quite unlike the dog in real life. What settles the matter is a series of drawings of Byron and Boatswain, made by their friend Elizabeth Pigot in March 1807. In one of these, Byron comes back from playing cricket, to find Boatswain eating his dinner from a large plate. The dog looks just like the animal depicted by Tomson. Elizabeth Pigot calls Byron and Boatswain 'the wonderful pair': Byron was a person of fame and renown, and his favourite Boatswain was well known in town.[8] She also emphasizes the close relationship between them:

84. The portrait of Boatswain at Newstead Abbey, reproduced by permission of Nottingham City Museums and Galleries, Newstead Abbey.

> Lord Byron look'd pleas'd, I know what he saw,
> 'Twas Bo'sen, who instantly gave him his paw,
> He patted his head with affectionate hand.
> Says he, 'You're the very best dog in the Land.'

In spite of their idealization of their hero's relation with his favourite dog, Lord Byron's biographers are right that their hero, who treated the women in his life so very caddishly, was remarkably fond of his Newfoundland dog. It has been speculated by the descendants of Lord Byron's publisher John Murray that when asked for a lock of his hair by his many female admirers, the poetical peer cut off some of Boatswain's fur instead.[9] If this is at all true, Byron must have made sure that he used only black fur, since otherwise his lady friends would have become fearful that his hair had gone white overnight, an obscure medical phenomenon mentioned by Byron himself in his poem about the Prisoner of Chillon.

Boatswain sometimes went into Mansfield, to do mischief and to fight other large dogs. In November 1808, he fought one too many, and caught hydrophobia. Returning to Newstead, Boatswain was seized by 'a fit of madness'. It is recorded that Byron, who was unaware of the nature of the malady, wiped the slaver from Boatswain's jaws more than once during his paroxysms. Poor Boatswain died on 11 November (not

85. Boatswain being given a hearty meal by Lord Byron's servants – an amusing vignette from the children's book *Memoires d'un Caniche*.

on 18 November, as claimed on his monument). In a letter to his friend Hodgson, to announce the death of his favourite dog, Byron assured him that Boatswain had retained all the gentleness of his nature to the last, and did not attempt to do any injury to the people surrounding him.

Lord Byron's friend John Cam Hobhouse wrote a prose epitaph to Boatswain, pointing out Boatswain's undaunted courage and belligerent nature. Being of a nature truly heroic, the great dog had emerged victorious from fifty pitched battles. Lord Byron only used the bottom four lines, however, and substituted a better epitaph of his own:

Near this Spot
Are deposited the Remains of one
Who possessed Beauty without Vanity
Strength without Insolence
Courage without Ferocity
And all the virtues of Man without his Vices
This praise which would be unmeaning Flattery
if inscribed over human Ashes
is but a just tribute to the Memory of
BOATSWAIN, a DOG ...

Lord Byron had a fine monument and vault constructed at Newstead, inscribed with Boatswain's epitaph. Since he had been so remarkably fond of the great dog, Byron instructed that his own remains should one day be interred in Boatswain's tomb, but this did not happen due to the poet's untimely demise in Greece. When the vault was opened for restoration purposes in 1987, some bones from a dog were found; Boatswain was still waiting for his master to join him in their Newstead tomb.

There has been much conjecture as to why Byron was inspired to write such an elaborate epitaph for his favourite dog.[10] Epitaphs for deceased pet animals, either humorous or sentimental, were actually quite popular at the time. The monumental tomb of Serpent, a favourite dog of Lady Stepney, had an epitaph dated 1750; the Earl of

86. The inscription on Boatswain's monument, from an early postcard, reproduced by permission of Nottingham City Museums and Galleries, Newstead Abbey.

Carlisle wrote a poem for the monument to a favourite spaniel; and John Gay wrote the *Elegy of a Lap-dog*. The *Poems* of G. D. Harley, published in 1796, contained a fourteen-page elegy on his Newfoundland dog Dash.

Nor was Byron the first to use the theme of contrasting human faithlessness with canine virtue; it occurs already in Matthew Prior's 1693 epitaph for True, Her Majesty's dog:

> Ye murmurers, let *True* evince,
> That Men are Beasts and Dogs have Sense.
> His Faith and Truth all *White-hall* knows,
> He ne're could fawn, or flatter those
> Whom he believ'd were *Mary's* Foes …

Dr John Arbuthnot's epitaph for Earl Temple's greyhound Signor Fido describes the dog as 'an Italian of good extraction, who came to England not to bite us, like most of his countrymen, but to gain an honest livelihood'. Fido was a perfect philosopher, a faithful friend, and an agreeable companion: 'Reader – This stone is guiltness of flattery, for he to whom it is inscribed, was not a Man, but a Greyhound.' Dr Percival's prose epitaph to Sylvia, published in the *Annual Register* for 1777, may well have inspired Byron further, since it introduces even more clearly the theme of perfect brute and imperfect man. Sylvia 'mingled in all companies, yet preserved her native simplicity of manners; and was caressed by the profligate, while she reproved their Vices ... This Monument blazons no feigned virtues of the Dead, to flatter the Vanity of the Living; for it is erected not to a Woman, but to a Spaniel.'[11]

Sir Edwin Landseer was the leading British animal painter of his time. When the rich and famous wanted portraits of their dogs, he was always ready to oblige; as a result, his output was very considerable. In 1824, he painted Mr Gosling's celebrated Newfoundland dog 'Neptune', and Mr William de Merle's 'Lion'; both dogs were portrayed in a mountainous landscape, with water nearby. In 1837, there was hubbub in the newspapers about 'Bob', a dog presumed to have been shipwrecked off the coast of England. As a stray, he became well known along the London waterfront for saving people from drowning. He was declared a distinguished member of the Royal Humane Society which not only entitled him to a medal, but also a free supply of food every day. When Landseer decided to paint Bob in 1837, the dog could not be located, and there is still debate as to whether he really existed, or if the whole thing had just been a newspaper hoax. But one day, Landseer saw a very handsome black and white Newfoundland dog walking down a street in London carrying a message for his mistress. Although there is no evidence the elusive Bob was really a Newfoundland, Landseer got a brilliant idea: he would cash in on Bob's fame by painting a substitute dog! The large Newfoundland dog, whose name was 'Paul Pry', was taken to the artist's studio to play the part of the heroic distinguished member of the Humane Society. Through bribing the great dog with various treats, Landseer persuaded him to lounge on a table, the table-top becoming the quayside. He painted the dog against a dull threatening heaven: the light falls beautifully on his white coat, and his dark head stands out against the brightest part of the sky.

When his latest masterpiece *A Distinguished Member of the Humane Society* was exhibited in 1838, Landseer's popularity increased even further. The young Queen Victoria was one of the many people impressed by his work. An avid dog fancier, she commissioned Landseer to paint portraits of several of her dogs. In 1839, he painted Princess Mary as a child, with her favourite Newfoundland dog, Nelson, balancing a biscuit on his nose. This large and handsome dog is brown and white spotted, a fur colour variation uncommon at the time, and even scarcer today. Like many of Landseer's dog portraits, it was engraved by Thomas Landseer and sold in considerable quantities.

The Earl of Dudley, a former Foreign Secretary, was extremely fond of his large black and white Newfoundland dog 'Bashaw'. Since the wealthy nobleman wanted a portrait of his dog, the ubiquitous Landseer was again called into action. In his portrait of this dog, Landseer hinted at Bashaw's life-saving abilities by showing him at the seashore, on the verge of leaping into action. It was later engraved, with the title *Off to*

87. Landseer's portrait of 'Lion'.

88. Landseer's *A Distinguished Member of the Humane Society*.

the Rescue! Landseer's portraits of these handsome early Newfoundland dogs indicate that already in those days, there was some kind of unofficial 'breed standard': very large dogs, with luxuriant fur, and elegant long tails, were preferred to the rather scrawny animals depicted by the painter Philip Reinagle, and the strange-looking Boatswain. Jean-Léon Gérôme's fine study of a Newfoundland dog from 1858, and other French and German paintings of prize Newfoundlands from that period, indicate that continental Europeans agreed.

After receiving Landseer's painting of Bashaw, the dog-loving Earl of Dudley was not done yet. He commissioned the artist Matthew Cotes Wyatt to make a statue of his favourite dog, since he thought Bashaw should live to posterity in breathing marble. The peer agreed to pay the prodigious sum of 5,000 guineas for the statue. Since the perfectionist Wyatt kept beavering away for many months, the poor dog had to be taken to more than fifty modelling sessions. Bashaw was a sturdy dog, and Wyatt became fearful that the heavy statue would collapse, since the legs would not hold it. He cleverly introduced a bronze boa constrictor, whose head is trodden on by the dog, into the image; it served as a much-needed support for the statue. Bashaw's eyes were made from precious gems, and the pupils from black lava. But after Lord Dudley had died, his heirs did not appreciate the logic of spending 5,000 guineas on the statue of a dog. After much wrangling, the disgruntled Wyatt had to keep the statue. It was exhibited as *The Faithful Friend of Man trampling underfoot his Most Insidious Enemy*

89. Landseer's *Off to the Rescue!*

at the Great Exhibition of 1851, attracting considerable praise, but no good cash offers. After Wyatt's death in 1862, nobody wanted to buy the marble dog. His son sent it to Christie's in 1887, where it fetched just 160 guineas.[12] The marble Bashaw can today be met with at the Victoria & Albert Museum. It is a majestic sight indeed, although the contrast between the sturdy, placid-looking dog and the coiling boa constrictor is an unhappy one; when aesthete John Ruskin saw the statue in 1870, he pronounced it 'the most perfectly and roundly ill-done thing I ever saw produced'.

The reader may have been surprised to see that all the Newfoundland dogs depicted in this chapter so far, Nelson, Boatswain and Bashaw included, have been black and white spotted. Today, the vast majority of Newfoundlands are solid black. Already in 1880, the dog fancier Dr William Gordon Stables proclaimed that the black Newfoundland was the 'pure' breed, whereas the black and white variety should be referred to as 'Landseer' since these dogs were so very often depicted by Sir Edwin Landseer. Other authorities on dogs went on to claim that the solid black Newfoundland was the original version, whereas the black and white variety had become popular for a little while only due to Landseer's paintings, only to sink back into obscurity. Some of them even asserted that Landseer had been a faddist, with a fanatical liking for black and white spotted Newfoundland dogs, and a distaste for solid black examples of the breed. The 'black supremacy' hypothesis, first proposed by some late Victorian dog fanciers, has been the generally accepted version of Newfoundland dog history ever since. Some fantasists have even asserted the existence of 'large black bear dogs' left behind by the Vikings to become the ancestors of Newfoundland's great indigenous breed of dog.

Over the years, a few dissenters to the 'black supremacy' hypothesis have made themselves known. Already the old dog author Rawdon B. Lee found it odd that although the Landseer Newfoundland was clearly more common than the black dogs in the early part of the nineteenth century, the late Victorian dog breeders and dog judges preferred the 'original' solid black dogs, considering even a white chest and white toes as 'disfigurement'. Nor was the distinguished dog historian Edward C. Ash particularly impressed with the bluster of the Victorian Newfoundland dog fanciers, clearly recognizing that due to selective breeding, the dogs had changed very much in the last century.[13] In 1976, American art historian Dr Emma M. Mellencamp queried why, if the black Newfoundlands were the original breed, there were so very few paintings of solid black Newfoundland dogs by Landseer and his contemporaries.[14] In 1989, English Newfoundland breeder Denis Conlon and German cynologist Christa Matenaar published a review of Newfoundland dog iconography, clearly demonstrating that prior to the mid-1800s, there were very few, if any, solid black examples of the breed.[15]

To investigate these matters further, I made use of the advertisements for lost or stolen dogs in *The Times*. For these advertisements to have the desired effect, they had to contain a good description of the animal in question, thus hopefully eliminating the bias due to carelessness or journalistic licence. Excluding the advertisements that did not describe the fur colour of the dogs in question, as well as those that concerned mongrels or were obviously confused, there was a total of 132 advertisements to recover lost or stolen Newfoundland dogs from 1785 until 1890. It turned out that prior to the year 1840, there was not a single advertisement describing a solid black Newfoundland, but numerous dogs that were obvious Landseers. There are also many representatives of Newfoundland dogs that are today referred to as 'mismarked' or 'Irish spotted': they are mainly black, but have white paws and chest, and a white tip of the tail. Brown dogs, and brown and white spotted, were few and far between. Between 1840 and 1850, a few solid black dogs begin appearing, and in the period 1850–1860 they have caught up with the other fur colour variations. In the period 1860–1890, solid black dogs are in the majority. It is quite telling that during the latter part of this period, some of the advertisements emphasized the 'purity' of the solid black dogs. This investigation thus strongly supports the arguments from the art historians quoted above: it would appear as if solid black Newfoundland dogs were very scarce in Britain prior to 1840. Landseer was no faddist who had a strong predilection for black and white Newfoundlands: he merely portrayed the dogs he came across without discrimination.

The explanation for the solid black Newfoundland dogs becoming numerous in the late 1800s lies in their fur colour genetics. Firstly, the reason brown dogs were (and still are) in a minority is that the basic colour of a Newfoundland dog is determined by what is known as the B locus, with 'Black' colour being dominant over 'brown'. Then there is the S locus, where 'Solid' colouring is dominant over 'spotted'. In the light of the data described above, and the art history studies of fur colour variation in Newfoundlands, it is reasonable to suggest that the 'Solid' gene was introduced into the British population of Newfoundland dogs sometime in the 1830s or 1840s, quite possibly through importation of solid black dogs from parts of Newfoundland. Being dominant over 'spotted', it soon made an impact on the Newfoundland dog phenotype, particularly since the solid black dogs became highly fashionable in late Victorian times, with selective breeding playing a part. Interestingly, in some Victorian illustrations of Newfoundland dogs, the solid black dogs are smaller than the Landseers, with shorter fur and a less massive head.

A more mysterious matter is how there could be so many 'mismarked' or 'Irish spotted' Newfoundland dogs in Georgian and early Victorian times, at a time when there were no solid black dogs. The current thought on these 'mismarked' dogs is that they are Solid/spotted heterozygotes, some but not all of which are supposed to exhibit white markings on the breast, face, chest and tip of the tail. This would hardly be possible, however, if there were no Solid gene available at the time. A Swiss researcher has suggested that there were several modifiers to the 'spotted' gene, causing dogs to be mostly dark (Mantel), with a black face and large black spots (Medium) or with only a few dark spots (Light).[16] This deduction makes good sense to the Newfoundland dog breeding fraternity, but is considered 'not proven' by the geneticists. Experienced dog breeders in Britain, Europe, and the United States have also recognized the 'Irish spotted' pattern, which their observations have made them presume to be dominant over Landseer, although this hypothesis lacks experimental support. The discovery of advertisements like the following, from 1785, seems to ask further questions about how the various forms of spotting are regulated in Newfoundland dogs:

LOST on Saturday last, May 28th, a large Black Newfoundland Dog, has White Feet, a little White in the Forehead, the end of his Tail White, answers to the Name of Lyon.[17]

Might there in fact be multiple modifiers to the 'spotted' gene, determining the different forms of black and white spotting in Newfoundland dogs, ranging from the 'Hereford cow' white with black patches, to the nearly pure black dogs with a few spots of white?

In Victorian times, one of the leading Newfoundland dog breeders was Mr Henry Richard Farquharson. Having made a fortune in the tea trade, he settled down at the stately Eastbury House, Tarrant Gunville. Unlike some breeders of the time, he was not convinced by the 'pure black original breed' theory, and bred both Blacks and Landseers. Not content with having just a few Newfoundland dogs, he hoarded more and more of these animals, housing them in large, purpose-built kennels. He had an advantage over other Newfoundland fanciers, since he lived not far from Poole, so he could send down carts to collect the dogs when the timber ships arrived from Newfoundland. After several years of breeding and collecting dogs, Farquharson (who was apparently quite sane) possessed a total of 125 Newfoundland dogs, one pack of 50 bitches and another of 75 dogs. Two country lads were employed full-time to look after the dogs. Twice a day, the two packs were taken for long walks, one towards Blandford Camp, the other in the opposite direction, towards Chettle. But one day, one of the lads took a wrong turning, and the packs met on Chettle Down. Since Newfoundlands have a strong pack mentality, the dogs started what must surely have been the biggest dog fight since the days of the Roman arena. Not less than forty-five dogs were either bitten to death or had to be put down; in addition, the two careless kennel boys were thrashed to within inches of their lives by the irascible Mr Farquharson.[18] In spite of the 'Battle of Chettle Down', as this epic fight became known among the locals, Farquharson continued breeding Newfoundlands: he had several champions, and his dogs were very highly regarded at the time. Later, he became a Member of Parliament and made efforts to expose the true identity of Jack the Ripper, but he was heavily fined for libelling another politician in 1892, and expired three years later.

Throughout Victorian times, Newfoundland dogs were very highly regarded, mainly due to their ability to save human lives during shipwrecks or bathing accidents. The struggle between life and death, with the helpless human in the hands of the hostile elements, when a compassionate brute creature takes his side and brings him to safety, was a subject that fascinated the Victorians. Heroic Newfoundland dogs were depicted in schoolbooks, on popular engravings, and in books on natural history. These dogs were considered not just brave and altruistic, but also extremely intelligent; a large proportion of the anecdotes of dogs told and retold by the Victorian dog fanciers were related to the extraordinary sagacity of the Newfoundland.[19]

In Victorian collections of dog stories, and children's books and magazines, wise and altruistic Newfoundland dogs make use of their superior intellects to protect children, catch thieves, and rescue people from various calamities. If an imprudent child is in danger from drowning, fire, or falling down a precipice, a sagacious Newfoundland dog is never far away. If burglars or robbers are up to mischief, the watchful Newfoundland drives them away with his fierce 'Bow-wow-wow!', or teaches them a lesson with his powerful fangs. If a yapping little dog annoys the lordly Newfoundland, he grabs it by the scruff of the neck and drops it into the water from the quayside, but he then benevolently leaps into the water himself to rescue the struggling little wretch.

The cult of the Newfoundland dog in popular culture reigned supreme throughout the nineteenth century, not just in Britain but in most European countries, even those where Newfoundland dogs were extremely scarce, like Sweden.[20] Some authors have suspected that this cult rest on far from solid foundations. Some of the unreferenced old yarns about super-intelligent Newfoundland dogs read more or less like fairy tales; were they equally devoid of factual foundation? Nor can some of the more recent stories of lifesaving Newfoundlands be taken at their face value. The oft-repeated tale of the dog 'Hero' taking a lifeline ashore and saving ninety-two people from the shipwreck of the SS *Ethie*, off the rocky shores of western Newfoundland in 1909, has been shown to be a newspaper hoax. The tale of the Newfoundland dog 'Rigel' performing heroics after the *Titanic* had sunk is equally untrue.[21]

So, how many true stories of sagacious and lifesaving Newfoundlands are there? The answer has to be: certainly very many! These dogs have a powerful instinct to retrieve objects from the water, and to save people struggling to swim. Already more than two hundred years ago, they were excellent water rescue dogs. In October 1789, a young student named William Phillips was carried out to sea when bathing at Portsmouth. Being unable to swim, he was half-drowned when a Newfoundland dog named 'Tiger' came to his aid, grabbed him by the hair, and pulled him ashore. The grateful Phillips bought the dog and renamed him 'Friend'. When Friend died in 1810 at a very advanced

90. A sagacious Newfoundland saves a drowning child, from the *Illustrated Police News*, 4 July 1868.

age, Phillips had become vicar of Eling; he erected a fine monument to the life-saving dog in the vicarage gardens, with the following inscription:

> In Memory
> of a Newfoundland dog
> Formerly called 'Tiger', afterwards 'Friend',
> Eminently qualified
> By acuteness of sight, quickness of eye,
> Strength of body, and peculiar sagacity
> For every duty of his species ...[22]

In November 1812, after the *Fantome* sloop of war had anchored in Hamoaze, eleven sailors, a woman, and a waterman rowed out to this sloop in a shore-boat. Unfortunately, this heavily loaded boat capsized and all its crew were struggling in the water. A Newfoundland dog on the quarter-deck of the sloop instantly leapt into the sea, and seized one of the men by the collar of his coat. Another boat was lowered and all the sailors were saved except the waterman. Amazingly, the dog seemed to know this individual was still missing, since he swam a wide circuit around the ship, although found nothing but an oar, which he retrieved.[23]

On 8 March 1834, two little boys aged six and nine, the sons of a Mr Horncroft, were amusing themselves by climbing a crane at the old Grosvenor Canal, Pimlico. When the youngest boy lost his footing and plunged into the water, the elder boy jumped after him, but since they were both indifferent swimmers, they soon went down. Fortunately for them, the comedian Mr Ryan came past, accompanied by his acting Newfoundland 'Nero', the favourite of Astley's Theatre. After a man who had seen the children sink threw a pebble to the spot, Nero plunged in and dived. He soon retrieved both boys, who recovered completely. As a result, Nero became quite a newspaper celebrity, something that is likely to have done his acting career no harm at all.[24]

Sometimes, the powerful lifesaving instinct of the Newfoundland dog led to unfortunate mishaps. Once, in 1839, a friend of the Pall Mall tailor Mr Ashton went to have a swim in the Serpentine, accompanied by the tailor's large Newfoundland dog. But when the dog saw the man swimming about, it presumed he was drowning, and seized him hard by the hair, elevating his head above the water. The poor man struggled with the dog for several minutes, before men from the Humane Society could save him from his overzealous canine companion, very much injured from the incisions on his scalp made by the dog's teeth. Just weeks later, another Newfoundland was in the news, for a better reason this time. When the Hon. Mr Westenra MP was returning to his residence in Bishopsgate, he was attacked by a ferocious mastiff. He defended himself with his stick, until it was broken in pieces. Fortunately, a Newfoundland dog rushed up and attacked the mastiff. After a desperate struggle, the sagacious Newfoundland killed its opponent by dragging it to a ditch and keeping it below water until it was drowned.[25]

In the 1840s, several newspapers announced that ten Newfoundland dogs were to be imported into Paris, for use as life-savers. They were to live in handsome kennels erected on the bridges across the Seine, and experienced trainers were to teach them to 'draw from the water stuffed figures of men and children'. The newspaper writers gave no explanation as to why the dogs should be trained to ignore the female inhabitants of Paris, and leave them to drown! In fact, the whole thing may well have been a newspaper *canard*, since contemporary French sources mention nothing about these alleged life-savers.[26]

In July 1868, Mrs Jane Titherleigh, the wife of a Hull ironmaster, was taking a cruise with her little son in a small sailing boat, when the boy suddenly fell overboard. Consternation ruled among the humans on board, who were all indifferent swimmers, but a Newfoundland dog leapt overboard without being prompted in any way, swum up to the young lad, and dragged him back to the vessel. The boy was none the worse for his ducking, but poor Mrs Titherleigh fell into hysterics.[27]

In June 1875, some children were sitting on the Thames embankment between Waterloo and Hungerford. A gust of wind suddenly blew a little girl into the river, where she could be seen to be struggling. A gentleman passing by unleashed his Newfoundland dog, appropriately named 'Ready', and made the dog aware of the girl's situation. Without further prompting, the dog leapt into the Thames, seized the girl by the collar of her cape, and swam to the stairs nearby. In August 1892, a youth bathing in the River Towy near Carmarthen was seen to be struggling. The local dog fancier Mr T. Davies immediately ordered his celebrated Newfoundland dog 'Picton' into the water, and the young Welsh lad seized the dog round the neck and was towed to safety.[28]

In June 1896, some children were playing on the tram lines near Daubhill Mill, Bolton. They were watched by a Newfoundland bitch named 'Princess May', lying down in front of the door of her master's house. But when the tramcar approached at a brisk pace, one of the children fell down in front of it. The driver desperately tried to rein in the horses, and people shouted with alarm, but Princess May dashed across the road, grabbed the three-year-old boy by his frock, and pulled him to safety. When some journalists were incredulous at this novel instance of Newfoundland sagacity, they were taken to task by Mr Fred Lomax, the secretary of the Bolton and District Humane Society, who had carefully collected witness testimony of the rescue. He, too, had initially doubted this extraordinary story, but four witnesses unanimously stated that Princess May had acted independently, and that she had been clearly seen to drag the boy to safety before any human rescuer could reach him. In November, Princess May appeared at a Humane Society presentation ceremony at Bolton town hall, along with eleven humans who had performed various heroics. Lord Stanley MP and the Mayor of Bolton presented them with a silver medal each; the dog also received a silver collar to be able to wear hers in a becoming manner. The next month, Princess May was the guest of honour at a grand dog show in London, walking round the ring to show off her collar and medal. She was said to be the first dog so decorated, but here the journalists would seem to have forgotten about our old friend Munito back in 1818.[29]

The Victorian Newfoundland fanciers were very proud of their breed's lifesaving heritage, none more so than the aforementioned Dr William Gordon Stables, a naval surgeon who had gone ashore to start a second career as a writer of juvenile fiction.

91. A Newfoundland dog saves a child from drowning in the Thames, from the *Illustrated Police News*, 8 September 1883.

He was a copious contributor to the *Boy's Own Paper*, sometimes writing about his Newfoundland dogs. A somewhat naive and eccentric character, he was fond of teaching his dogs various silly tricks, like imitating a circus elephant, or carrying a large sheep's head through the streets, with a placard saying 'I am starving!' Dr Stables was very fond of his sagacious Newfoundland 'Theodore Nero', the paragon of every canine virtue. At the Maidstone Dog Show of 1876, Theodore took part in the first water trials held for Newfoundlands and other dogs. But although Dr Stables had boasted that his dog would take to the water leaping from a steamer doing 15 knots, poor Theodore stood howling at the water's edge, refusing to leap in, and ignoring his master's frantic entreaties. The pair returned for the Portsmouth water trials later the same year, in which the dogs were supposed to swim out to a boat, fetch a large dummy, and bring it to shore. This time, the Newfoundlands outclassed all other entrants, the black dog 'Commodore' beating Theodore by just one second, although Dr Stables complained that the boat had drifted out to sea, so that the great Theodore had further to swim.[30]

In 1900, the Paris police prefect Louis Lépine founded the Brigade Fluviale, a police squad that would devote itself entirely to policing the Seine. In 1901, it was decided to finally act upon the idea that had been discussed in the previous century, and to provide the Brigade Fluviale with some life-saving dogs. Five animals were purchased: three Newfoundlands

92. A nasty French soldier turned rapist on the prowl? You are safe if you have a Newfoundland dog! From *La Nature* 16(1) [1888], 397-8.

ROLLED DOWN THE HILL.

DOG SAVES A CHILD'S LIFE.

93. Forgotten to lock the brakes on the pram? No danger, if there is a Newfoundland dog nearby. From the *Illustrated Police News*, 8 June 1907.

and two Newfoundland crosses. The purebred Newfoundlands cost as much as £20 each. Their main purpose would be to save drowning people, or would-be suicides jumping into the river. They should also be used to catch thieves who tried to evade the police through swimming the Seine or taking refuge on a barge. The dogs were housed in a comfortable kennel adjoining the police station at the Quai de la Tournelle. They underwent an ambitious training programme, using large floating dummies and a series of commands aiming to make the *chiens plongeurs* leap into the Seine and grasp the dummy. A 1902 illustration shows the youngest of the dogs, the Landseer bitch 'Diane', leaping into the Seine from the embankment.[31] Approvingly, the 15 March issue of the *Annuaire des Commissaires de Police* wrote that these robust Newfoundland dogs would become valuable assets to the Brigade Fluviale, since they were well suited to save drowning people, and to pursue dangerous vagabonds taking refuge near the Seine or its tributaries.

The *chiens plongeurs* were also given some basic police dog training, in order to be useful also on dry land. This part of their education was tested later in 1902, when a thief came rushing out of a shop right in front of some of the river constables. They immediately gave chase, releasing Diane and her fellow Landseer 'Félix' when the miscreant refused to stop. The great dogs were slow starters, but gradually they caught up with the exhausted thief. He suddenly veered into an alley, with the dogs in hot pursuit. The constables had high hopes of a vital success for their team, but all they found inside the alleyway were the two police dogs, who were greedily eating some bread and sausages strewn on the ground. The constables were nonplussed, but a waiter from a restaurant nearby explained that the clever thief had grabbed a large plate of bread and sausages from a table, and emptied it in front of the pursuing dogs, before running off unharmed.

A few months later, there was further farce when the black Newfoundland 'Paris', the most fierce of the river police dogs, was sent to sniff out a dangerous criminal, who was believed to be hiding on board a barge. Just seconds after the great dog had boarded the barge, a yell of pain was heard, and a man came lurching out on deck, clutching his buttocks. The river constables took him into custody, but he turned out to be the owner of the barge, who had been sleeping on board; the criminal had once more escaped.

Later in 1902, when the *chiens plongeurs* were formally tested in front of the *commissaire*, they gave a dismal account of themselves. Only Diane could be coaxed to leap into the Seine, whereas the other four dogs obstinately refused to take to the water. One of the Newfoundland crosses was sacked for being entirely uneducable; the other four dogs were grudgingly given another chance, because M. Lépine was himself a strong supporter of the river police dogs. And the police prefect's confidence in his canine life-savers seemed to have been vindicated when, on 5 June, the dog Diane plunged into the river without any word of command, and seized a man who had just thrown himself into the water. She held him by his coat until the constables arrived to pull the would-be suicide up onto the embankment. Several witnesses to this extraordinary rescue stood to attention and applauded Diane, and an old lady came up to embrace the soaking wet dog. The journalists who had previously been quite unimpressed with the *chiens plongeurs* now applauded Diane's heroism, which was not less than astonishing, they wrote, since the dog was just twenty months old. The only dissenter was the would-be suicide, not because he had really intended to destroy himself, but since he had been badly bruised by the dog's powerful jaws when hauled to safety.

The four remaining river police dogs remained active throughout 1903 and 1904. In 1905, a photograph in the *Quiver* magazine shows them all alive and well. But their performance still left much to be desired; they jumped into the river only when they wanted to, and could be very obstinate. During another review of their willingness to take to the water, the constables were asked to detail the rescues made in the last twelve months. The only success had been scored by the black Newfoundland Paris, who had once attempted to retrieve a corpse from the Seine. He had only 'rescued' the coat and hat, however, since the body sunk. More than once, the unpredictable dogs had jumped into the Seine on their own accord, to retrieve hats and sticks that mischievous individuals had thrown into the water to tempt them. On other occasions, they could not be persuaded to take to the water at all, lying down on the Seine embankment to watch a corpse float by, or a thief swim away. Diane had not performed any further rescues, but she had once retrieved valuable evidence, the constables claimed, namely a large ham stolen from a grocer. This was hardly an exacting task for a highly trained police dog, however, particularly when it turned out that she had been discovered eating it.

By this time, the river police and its unpredictable dogs had become figures of fun. On a cartoon illustrating a popular song, a red-nosed police constable and a jolly-looking Newfoundland dog stand on the Seine embankment, watching a corpse float by. There were many newspaper jokes about the bumbling police dogs, of which the following is a fair example:

A Newfoundland dog on the probationary staff of M. Lépine one day distinguished himself by rescuing a child from drowning. The grateful father presented the canine life-saver with a large, juicy beefsteak. Two days later, another child was saved by the dog in a similar manner, and then yet another one. The dog was again praised and rewarded, and the sentimentalists wanted to give it a medal. The police were busy chasing the maniac who was throwing children into the Seine. They soon found the culprit: for the sake of the beefsteaks, the Newfoundland dog had been pushing children into the river and then rescuing them! M. Lépine made sure it was dismissed in disgrace from his force of canine lifesavers.

In September 1905, when the river police dogs were briefly featured in the *Daily Mirror*, there were only two animals in the photograph, probably the Landseers Diane and Félix, indicating that the police were scaling down its force of canine life-savers. There are many fewer mentions of the life-saving dogs in 1906 and 1907, and the force may well have been entirely disbanded around these years. It turns out, however, that at least one of the *chiens plongeurs* became an ordinary police dog, patrolling the streets instead of the river embankments. In late 1909, a thief took refuge in a large indoor food market, pursued by a police constable and his large Newfoundland dog Diane. The dog was released, bounded after the fugitive with alacrity, and tackled him into a fishmonger's stall. But again there were no thanks to the gallant former

94. A rowdy song making fun of the hapless river police and their dogs.

chien plongeur: far from praising the canine thief-taker, various people pushed over by the dog demanded compensation, and the fishmonger vociferously lamented his broken stall.

Why were the life-saving dogs of Paris such a failure? After all, one rescue and one corpse nearly retrieved in more than five years of active service were not particularly favourable statistics for the dogs and their handlers. Firstly, it was unwise to leave their training to ordinary police constables, who possessed neither experience with dogs, nor any particular water rescue skills. Secondly, the river police were very much mistaken when they paid such exorbitant prices to purchase adult dogs, which were not amenable to be taught new tricks. For a Newfoundland dog to become fully competent in water rescue, the animal has to be actively taught since quite a young age. Thus it was no coincidence that Diane, the youngest of the dogs, ended up becoming the most competent of the canine life-savers. Furthermore, it was probably not a good strategy to try to make the dogs into jacks of all trades; it would seriously tax their intellects to determine whether a person swimming in the Seine was an absconding thief, or a drowning person calling for assistance. The disbanding of the river police dog force seems to have been a result of the adverse newspaper publicity, and the gradual realization that the animals were not up to the task. Mischievous people throwing coats, hats or sticks into the river to distract and tempt the unpredictable dogs cannot have done them any favour either.

Vindicating the opinion of M. Lépine back in 1901, many Newfoundlands have since been successfully trained as professional life-saving dogs. Both in France and in Italy, Newfoundland dogs have patrolled the beaches at least since the 1960s. The Italian school for lifesaving dogs has a formidable force of Labradors and Newfoundlands, some of them trained to jump out from a helicopter to save swimmers in difficulties. The United States has several Newfoundland dogs trained for water rescue. In an amazing story from 1995, vouched for by *National Geographic*, a ten-month-old Newfoundland named 'Boo' was taken out for a stroll by his master, along the Yuba River in northern California. When Boo, who entirely lacked water rescue training, saw a man desperately trying to stay afloat in the swollen current, he leapt into the water and pulled him safely to shore. The man turned out to be a deaf-mute who had fallen into the water while gold-dredging.[32]

In Britain, the Swansea division of the Royal Navy reservists has a team of life-saving dogs, trained by Mr Dave Pugh, who has also set up the charitable organization Newfound Friends to promote Newfoundland dog water training. Its leading light has been the 13-stone Newfoundland 'Whizz', who has been trained to leap into the chilly waters of the Bristol Channel, together with his two-legged sidekick, schoolgirl Ellie Bedford. The remarkably intelligent Whizz is likely to be Britain's finest professional water rescue dog. Once, when going for a walk near Clevedon, Whizz darted off into the bushes, to save an Irish setter named Topper, who had fallen into a disused water tank. Just like he had been taught, Whizz plunged into the tank, resolutely grabbed Topper by the scruff of his neck, and pulled him to safety. A dog saving the life of another is always news, at least in Britain, and Whizz was featured in the evening newspapers; in one of the photographs, a rather apprehensive-looking Topper was depicted seated next to the hulking Newfoundland. Mr Pugh and his team of dogs regularly perform at various events, being one of the headliners of the Cardiff Harbour Festival of 2009, to very considerable acclaim.[33]

Bilbo, another lifesaving Newfoundland dog, patrolling the beach at Sennen Cove in Cornwall, has been no stranger to controversy. After stopping a foreign woman from entering the surf on a windy day, through simply blocking her way, Bilbo was widely featured in the newspapers. And the benign-looking 14-stone brown Newfoundland did not look back. Already a local hero, he made celebrity appearances, and visited schools to help teach beach safety. He beat seventy human contestants in a mile-long open-water swimming race from Newlyn to Penzance. Sponsorship from a dog food company kept his food-bowl well filled, and he was invited to Crufts as a guest of honour. A film of Bilbo leaping from a raft towed by a water scooter, to save a person waving for help, became a YouTube favourite. Bilbo soon had a web site, and his own fan club; he made regular TV appearances, and his biography was published in 2008.[34]

It would appear as if some of the lifeguard bosses did not like all this publicity for a mere dog, or appreciate the newspaper hints that Bilbo was a fully trained lifeguard capable of doing the job of his two-legged colleagues. Ignoring Bilbo's good work to promote beach safety education, they decided to ban Bilbo from the Sennen Cove beach, allegedly because dogs were not allowed, and because there were health and safety concerns about the 14-stone dog riding on the back of a quad bike. Newspapers all over the country scented a good story. In tabloid press parlance, the lifeguard bosses had to be *barking* to *hound* Bilbo out of his job, and demand that this *four-legged Hasselhoff* would *bow-wow* out of *Baywoof*. All the odium in the newspapers, and thousands of people petitioning the Queen and the Prime Minister to reinstate Bilbo, finally had the desired effect: in March 2009, he was allowed to return to duty at Sennen Cove.[35]

Already the author Rawdon Lee found it peculiar that so many early Victorian authors extolled the superior intellect of the Newfoundland dog; in his opinion, they were much like other dogs. He has had support from Professor Stanley Coren's *The Intelligence of Dogs*, which ranks the Newfoundland as number 34 out of 78 breeds, with regard to obedience and working intelligence. Dr Stables and his fellow Victorian dog fanciers would have considered this an insult to their sagacious breed. Nor have some of the present-day Newfoundland breeders appreciated Professor Coren's ranking of their breed. They have objected that although the Newfoundland is hampered by its somewhat independent nature, and short attention span, the dogs are definitely cleverer than most large breeds, particularly with regard to problem solving. An anecdote in Professor Coren's book would support their case: a tired Newfoundland bitch was annoyed by a yapping little Maltese terrier wanting to play. In the end, the great black dog seized the little terrier by the scruff of the neck and walked out to the bathroom, where she deposited it into a large, empty bathtub, where it was securely confined, before contentedly returning and settling down to sleep. This not only shows a very good example of creative action in dogs, but also that some of the old stories of sagacious Newfoundlands ducking annoying little dogs in ponds or ditches may well be true.

Professor Coren also has a very low opinion of the Newfoundland as a watchdog. In my opinion, this is true for most bitches, and also many male dogs, due to their placid and friendly nature, and lack of suspicion towards strangers. Any burglar who takes on a large and alert Newfoundland male used to guarding his territory, and being protective of the other members of the household, may well be mistaken to rely too much on the professor's advice, however. It is curious to note that many of the early Newfoundland dogs in Britain, Lord Byron's Boatswain prominent among them, were known for their pugnacious nature. According to many sources, they were also excellent watch dogs: vigilant and wary of strangers. *The Times* provides many examples of burglars emerging second best from encounters with fierce Newfoundlands, and even reports of smugglers and thieves keeping Newfoundlands to set on the police and customs officers.[36]

To analyze the problem of the changing Newfoundland, it is it important to take into account the work of Professor Jasper Rine and co-workers, with regard to canine genetics.[37] A border collie is a very intelligent dog, concentrated and intense; it has a strong herding instinct: crouching and 'giving eye' when it sees some recalcitrant sheep, or sometimes even a human being it considers to require some herding. The present-day Newfoundland is friendly and easygoing, has webbed feet and loves water, and holds its tail high. Rine and his colleagues cross-bred a male border collie with a Newfoundland bitch; the union of this mismatched couple produced seven healthy puppies, which were in turn bred with each other, resulting in a third generation of twenty-three 'grandchildren'. These dogs exhibited a seemingly quite random combination of 'border collie' and 'Newfoundland' traits: for example, one of the dogs might be very intelligent but also friendly and easygoing, holding its tail high but hating water, and possessing the herding instinct to 'give eye'. It is important that the typical traits of these dogs thus appear to be inherited separately.

With these arguments in mind, let us return to the early Newfoundland dogs. These dogs were selectively bred to have webbed feet and a talent for water work, but also to be intelligent and altruistic, with a strong instinct to rescue some person falling into the water. The dogs should also be watchful and wary of strangers, not fearful to 'have a scrap', and ready to defend their masters. Understandably, these remarkable dogs were widely admired in Georgian and Victorian Britain. The stories of Newfoundland sagacity recounted in this book are only the tip of the iceberg; there is no wonder these amazing dogs were so widely featured in magazines, children's books and books of anecdotes on natural history. We will never know what genetic event triggered the development of these remarkably intelligent early Newfoundland dogs.

A recent study aimed to determine whether dogs would seek help from a bystander if their owner feigned a heart attack, or pretended to be trapped underneath a falling bookcase; they did not.[38] There is a marked contrast between these very ordinary dogs standing by uselessly when their owner was in trouble, and the heroics of the Newfoundlands described earlier in this chapter; for example, there was the extraordinary Princess May not just sensing danger to the child on the tram line, but taking appropriate action with commendable alacrity. There was clearly something special about the Newfoundland dogs in those days, something that set them apart from other breeds of dog.

With time, the Newfoundland dog fanciers valued different qualities in their dogs, and adapted their breeding accordingly. For example, since they were not used as watchdogs, there was no need for them to be watchful and wary of strangers; in recent times, the dogs have become increasingly placid and friendly, not just to their owners, but to everyone else. A calm and stolid temperament, great size and solid black fur were valued characteristics, whereas the spirit and watchfulness formerly exhibited by the dogs was no longer appreciated. The dog Boo who rescued the drowning American gold-dredger, and the remarkably intelligent Whizz, seem to be throwbacks to the earlier type. It would appear as if selective breeding in the last 150 years has led to the Newfoundland dogs losing a good deal of their pugnacity and guarding instinct along the way – and also some of the remarkable intelligence for which these amazing dogs were once rightly admired.

12

THE GREAT BARRY & SOME OTHER CURIOUS SAINT BERNARD DOGS

Where the St Bernard Pass climbs up
  Amid the Alpine snows
The far-famed Hospice crowns the heights
  With shelter and repose.

Its inmates, with their faithful dogs,
  Are truly friends in need
When snowdrifts block the traveller's way,
  And blinding storms mislead.

'The Brave Dog of St Bernard' by 'Cousin Cecil',
from *The Children's Friend*, 1 January 1874.

Bernard de Menthon was born in Savoy at the end of the tenth century AD. He was the son of a wealthy baron, and although he had studied theology in Paris, his parents demanded that he should marry a wealthy heiress. But since Bernard was determined to become a monk, he tore the bars from his window and escaped the night before the intended wedding. He went to the Augustinian cathedral at Aosta, where he entered holy orders. With time, he advanced to become Archdeacon. One night, some frightened peasants came knocking on the door, disturbing his prayers. Up in the mountains, they had been attacked by a devil named Procus, who was said to worship at the temple of Jupiter. Through a terrible snowstorm, Bernard led the peasants to the temple. Procus transformed into a dragon, but Bernard threw his stole around its neck. Through a miracle, the stole became a chain, which held the dragon down while Bernard slew it. Bernard ordered the peasants to tear down the temple of Jupiter, and instead build a hospice in the mountains, to serve as protection and shelter for travellers. Impressed with his dragon-slaying prowess, the peasants followed the command of the future Saint Bernard.

The Hospice of Great St Bernard still stands at the top of the Great St Bernard Pass in the Canton of Valais, near the border between Italy and Switzerland. This pass was, at the time, one of the most important routes across the Alps, used by a multitude of pilgrims, migrant workers, and other travellers. The hospice, standing at over 8,000 feet above sea level, is one of the highest human habitations in Europe. From an early stage, the benevolent monks considered it one of their duties to house needy or stranded travellers, and to look out for those imperilled by snowstorms or avalanches. Since the entire archives of the hospice were destroyed in a fire in 1555, not much is known about its early history. Dogs were kept at the hospice at least since the late seventeenth century. In 1695, the Neapolitan artist Salvatore Rosa painted the portraits of two large, mastiff-like dogs residing at the hospice. With their beige and white spotted bodies, and short muzzles, they rather resemble the Cane Garouf, an ancient breed of Italian mastiffs bred for protecting cattle.

It may well be that the dogs had been imported to the Hospice of Great St Bernard sometime between 1660 and 1670. With time, the monks discovered that with their highly developed sense of smell and direction, the dogs could also be useful to find travellers lost in snowstorms and avalanches. In 1707, one of the monks wrote in his journal that 'a dog has been buried by snow this day', indicating that at least by that time, the dogs were used for rescue work.[1] The year after, it was noted that another of the monks was 'making a wheel in which a dog is put to turn the spit'. Some St Bernard dog enthusiasts have tried to imagine a dog-wheel sized to suit a representative of their favourite breed, but the reader who has paid attention to the earlier chapters in this book will appreciate that this must surely have been a wheel for a small turnspit dog.[2]

Throughout the 1700s, teams of rescue dogs were kept at the Hospice of Great St Bernard, often making themselves useful in detecting stranded travellers. Most often, the monks accompanied the dogs to direct their search; at other times, the entire pack of dogs was released to search for people who were taking cover from the snow. The work was quite hazardous for both monks and dogs, and there were regular casualties, particularly in avalanches. The regular loss of dogs necessitated the keeping of quite a large pack, housed in purpose-built kennels. It was said that this formidable force of dogs more than once helped the Prior to foil gangs of burglars who were after the valuables kept at the Hospice.[3]

When Napoleon crossed the Alps in 1800, his forces of course made a halt at the Hospice of St Bernard. One of the soldiers, Jean-Roch Coignet, described how he and his equally cold and exhausted comrades in arms 'entered the house of God, where men devoted to the cause of humanity are stationed to give aid and comfort to travellers. Their dogs are always on hand to guide unfortunate creatures who may have fallen into the avalanches of snow, and conduct them to this house, where every necessary comfort is provided.' Coignet and his colleagues were given a meal of bread and Gruyère cheese, as well as a bucket of wine for every twelve men. When they departed, the grateful French soldiers shook hands with the monks 'and embraced their dogs which caressed us as if they knew us.'[4]

In 1801, a certain Pastor Bridel visited the Hospice of Great St Bernard, to see the famous dogs. Their character was very gentle, he wrote: they never bit people, and barked only rarely. They were fawn-coloured, with some white spots. They often went

95. St Bernard dogs on patrol, from an early print with text in both German and French.

alone to meet travellers and guide them to the Hospice. They had an admirable instinct to find a traveller buried underneath the snow, to know where the road was, and to find their way back home to the Hospice. These dogs loved the wintry weather very much, and enjoyed rolling about in fresh snow; they preferred the mountains to the plain. The monks were very assiduous in training the dogs, and spent much time doing so.[5]

> One noble dog, amid his kind,
>   Deserves a honoured name,
> And many an abler pen than mine
>   Records his deeds of fame
>
> Brave 'Barry' once, far down the track
>   That crossed a glacier deep
> Found buried deep beneath the snow
>   A poor boy, fast asleep.

As the poetic 'Cousin Cecil' rightly expressed it, the most famous of the Hospice dogs was Barry, who was active from 1800 until 1812. He was credited with saving at least forty lives. Like the other Hospice dogs at the time, Barry had short, thick white and brown fur, a strong and sturdy build, and a short, mastiff-like muzzle. When Barry had become old and infirm, the kindly Prior sent the famous dog to Berne, where he lived in comfortable retirement for another two years, before expiring in 1814. There is no painting or drawing of Barry while alive, but the Prior ordered that his body should be stuffed and mounted at the local museum.

> For many years brave 'Barry' lived,
>   And many a life he saved:
> On a bright collar round his neck,
>   The record was engraved.
>
> And after death his well-stuffed form,
>   In Berne's museum placed,
> Still calls to mind the noble deeds
>   By which his life was graced.

In spite of the above testimony from the generous 'Cousin Cecil', the job of stuffing and mounting Barry was not particularly well done, with the dog in a strange crouching position. Apparently, a certain Hans Caspar Rohrdorf, who worked as assistant at the museum, wanted the dog to have a humble and dispirited look. The ravages of time did not help Barry's appearance. Over the years, many people hoping to see the famous Barry must have been disappointed when they saw this queer-looking animal. Finally, in 1923, the stuffed dog was restored and remounted, gaining four inches in height and acquiring a more natural position. Barry is still standing in the foyer of the Museum of Natural History in Berne, where I saw him in 2009.

Over the years, a number of legends have grown up around this famous life-saving dog. One that is demonstrably untrue is that having saved forty people, Barry was killed by the forty-first! Barry was supposed to have run to the rescue of a frozen and confused man, alternatively described as a soldier or a hunter. Tragically, this individual mistook the dog for a wolf and killed him with his rifle (or sword). But as we know, there is ample evidence that Barry died of old age in Berne after having been retired.[6] Still, this falsehood is, even today, widely distributed in ill-researched books.

Another legend says that the wise Barry once saved a little boy by ushering the child to ride on his back. Barry carried the boy all the way back to the Hospice, where the great dog pulled the rope of the doorbell to alert the monks. This yarn turned up in the collection *Alpenrosen* just a few years after Barry died, and various paintings and prints of the child ride followed suit. Few visitors to Berne, or to the Hospice of Great St Bernard, failed to purchase a print of the noble Barry saving the child. Nor did the sentimental contemporary magazines spurn the opportunity to regurgitate this tall story, with an appropriate illustration of the great dog making his way through the snow with his lifeless burden. Indeed, the Victorian cult of the sagacious Newfoundland dog also encompassed their Alpine cousins at Great St Bernard: the tale of Barry and the child ride was retold in school books and collections of anecdotes all over Europe.

On the monument to Barry erected at the famous Cimetière des Chiens at Asnières near Paris, a shaggy-haired Barry is seen carrying a child nearly his own size, with the following epitaph: 'He saved forty people – He was killed by the forty-first!'

But St Bernard dog historian Dr Marc Nussbaumer discovered that the story of the child ride had actually originated in a sentimental old dog book by the French author Anne de Fréville. His *Histoire des Chiens Célèbres* had been published already in 1796, four full years before the hopeful young St Bernard pup Barry first saw the light of day! This implies that the story of the child ride derived from a pre-existing tradition (or fantasy) about a heroic life-saving dog.[7] Although a strong, muscular dog, Barry was much smaller than a present-day St Bernard, and it would hardly have been possible for him to carry a heavy, half-grown child. It is a similarly unlikely scenario for a small child half frozen to death to be capable of holding on to the back of a large, smooth-haired dog lurching through the mounds of snow. And it is the nature of a dog, if it wishes to bring with it some heavy object, to carry or drag it along with its teeth, not to carry it on its back.

Another cornerstone of St Bernard dog lore is of course the keg of brandy they always carried round their neck, for use in reviving stranded travellers during their treks through the snow. No illustration of a St Bernard dog, from the 1850s onwards, is complete without such a keg. Many a cartoon, and many a cheap joke, has been

96. Barry gives a ride to a child, from *The Children's Friend*, 1 February 1865.

97. Another old drawing of the 'child ride'.

inspired by the St Bernard dog and its ubiquitous keg of brandy. The important early illustrations of the Hospice dogs, Barry included, never show any such keg, however. Barry instead wore a spiked collar, to protect his neck from the bites of wolves and other predators. It is true that for a while, the stuffed dog was equipped with a large keg with a Swiss flag on it, but more historically-minded museum conservators have restored the original collar. It would hardly make any sense for the monks of St Bernard to have the dogs carry kegs of strong spirits, which would serve to render stranded Alpine travellers further disoriented. The spirits would also cause peripheral vasodilatation, causing the person the dog was supposed to save to freeze to death more quickly. As Dr Nussbaumer has proposed, the yarn about the keg of brandy is likely to have originated in some early sources on St Bernard dogs mentioning that the dogs were sometimes taught to carry a basket with bread, butter, sausages and wine, for use in reviving starving travellers. The archives of the Museum of Natural History in Berne hold an early painting of *A Dog of Saint Gotthard* carrying a small flask (or rather gourd) of wine suspended from its collar. Interestingly, the old dog writer Thomas Brown, who clearly had been to see the stuffed Barry in Berne, wrote that 'the little phial, in which he carried a reviving liquor for the distressed travellers whom he found among the mountains, is still suspended from his neck'.[8] The present-day custodians of the Museum of Natural History in Berne have no knowledge of any such 'little phial' associated with the stuffed Barry, however.

98. Barry rings the Hospice bell at his return, from *The Children's Friend*, 1 January 1874.

99. The dogs of St Bernard in action, from *The Child's Companion*, 1 August 1872.

After the tales of Barry's heroism had made the rounds of Europe, there was widespread curiosity about these extraordinary dogs. There is no evidence that any St Bernard dog had set paw in Britain prior to April 1815, when Mrs Boode, who lived at Leasowe Castle, took delivery of a dog and a bitch from the Hospice of St Bernard. They were not known as St Bernard dogs at the time, but 'Alpine mastiffs'. The dog, named 'Lion', was 76 inches long and 31 inches tall; he was claimed to be the largest dog in Britain. Lion was nearly yellow in colour, with a black muzzle and a narrow facial blaze. Lion was seen and painted by the young Edwin Landseer; an engraving of this remarkable dog sold well for several decades. Several litters were bred from Lion, with various imported bitches. His son 'Caesar' featured in yet another early Landseer painting, *Two Alpine Mastiffs Reanimating a Stranded Traveller* from 1820. He is the dog to the right; interestingly, the other dog in the picture has a small keg fastened to its collar. Might this have been the beginning of the brandy keg myth?

Many upper-class people wanted an Alpine mastiff of their own, partly due to the reputation of these famous dogs, and partly, it must be suspected, from a desire to show off that they could afford one of these rare and valuable dogs. In 1825, Mr John Crabtree, of Kirklees Hall in Yorkshire, imported two Hospice dogs, which he crossed with mastiffs. Another Alpine mastiff, named 'L'Ami', was publicly exhibited in London and the provinces from 1827 until 1829 as the largest dog in England. The earliest use of the term 'St Bernard dog' occurred in September 1828, when a newspaper article described a 'portrait of the Earl of Eglington's famous St Bernard dog'.[9]

Sir Thomas Lauder, who lived near Edinburgh, obtained a St Bernard dog from the Hospice in 1837. Named 'Bass', the dog was the largest in Scotland: 'his bark is tremendous; so loud, that I have often distinguished it when in the Meadow Walk, nearly a mile off'. Bass liked to play with the postman, but one day, this individual was ill, and another postman attended Sir Thomas's house. When the great dog came bounding up to play, the fearful postman tried to escape, but the enthusiastic Bass knocked him over and took possession of the mailbag.[10]

The Duke of Devonshire kept a fine St Bernard dog at Chatsworth, and Lord Herrington had another, which had cost him fifty guineas, at Elvaston Castle in Derbyshire.[11] The Earl of Warwick gave Prince Albert a particularly fine 'Mount St Bernard dog' named 'Greville' in 1842, but this boisterous animal seems to have been reluctant to adapt to a role as an idle royal pet. In May 1842, the royal dog-keeper Maynard took Greville and some other valuable dogs belonging to the Queen and Prince from their kennels near Windsor Castle down to the Thames, to give them a bath. After the dogs had been unleashed to have a romp in the Thames, Maynard wanted to gather them together, but Greville had other ideas. He ran off in the opposite direction, with Maynard and the other dogs in hot pursuit. Greville leapt a fence and entered a field, where he attacked and killed a large sheep. When the farmer's son tried to rescue the sheep, Greville flew at him, snapping and biting. The resourceful lad pulled up an old pistol, took aim, and fired! The bullet passed through Greville's right ear, and entered his right foreleg.

When Maynard came running up, followed by the pack of royal dogs, the farmer's son received a terrible shock: he had just shot Prince Albert's Mount St Bernard dog!

Doffing their caps, the farmer and his son humbly apologized to Maynard, assuring him that if they had known to whom the dog belonged, they would have been much less hasty in making use of firearms against the animal. The sheep was not worth very much; Maynard could settle the amount with the loose change he kept in his purse. Greville the St Bernard, estimated to be worth at least a hundred guineas, was transported back to Windsor Castle on a cart; he is said to have recovered completely from his wounds.[12] It is curious to contrast the 1842 journalist expressing relief at the 'Narrow escape of Prince Albert's Mount St Bernard dog' with the likely present-day tabloid newspaper coverage of such an event. Surely, there would have been an interview with the farmer's son, with the headline, 'I fought for my life against the Prince's Monster Dog!', and a photograph of the dead sheep, with the caption, 'Poor Flossie, murdered by the Prince's Vicious Pet!'

In spite of his violent tendencies, Greville the St Bernard remained at Windsor Castle for several years. When the Ascot gold cup was exhibited at Windsor Castle, it was noted that it was ornamented with models of some of the royal dogs: the Prince's Turnspit watching a rat, a favourite Scotch terrier, and Greville the valuable Mount St Bernard dog. A few years later, Queen Victoria, who had once stayed at the Hospice of Great St Bernard, imported two more dogs from there, a dog and a bitch named Alp and Glory respectively.[13]

As late as 1899, Queen Victoria had an amusing encounter with two St Bernard dogs. When she was taking a holiday in Switzerland, taking some fresh air in an open coach, she came across a beggar who drove a cart pulled by two large St Bernards. He doffed his cap at the Queen, before riding alongside her vehicle, the dogs easily keeping pace with the horses. When the royal coachman whipped up his team, the beggar gave a whoop, racing and easily overtaking the Queen's equipage. When the royal carriage caught up with the beggar, he received a *pourboire*; after solemnly blessing the Queen, he drove off in his cart. Queen Victoria was much amused by this singular incident, as were her two attendants, the Duchess of York and Prince Henry of Battenberg.[14]

Throughout Victorian times, the cult of the St Bernard dog continued. Just as the sagacious Newfoundland was admired for its aquatic prowess, the noble St Bernard ploughing through the Alpine snow to rescue stranded travellers was a subject of considerable fascination. No respectable annual for children, book of anecdotes about dogs, or illustrated magazine, was complete without some fanciful drawings of these remarkable dogs reanimating travellers, giving rides to children, or ringing the bell outside the Hospice to alert the monks.

As the St Bernard dogs enjoyed success as expensive and fashionable society pets in Britain, all was not well at the Hospice of Great St Bernard. More than once, after disease and avalanches had taken their toll among the dogs, cross-breeding with Pyrenean Mountain Dogs and Landseer Newfoundlands was necessary for the Hospice dogs to avoid total extinction. When a certain Mr E. A. Aglionby visited the Hospice in 1845, five large, muscular, short-haired St Bernard dogs were there; they were all reddish fawn in colour, with white markings. When another early St Bernard fancier,

REWARDED!

AMUSING INCIDENT DURING THE QUEEN'S VISIT ABROAD.

A STURDY BEGGAR RACES HIS DOGS AGAINST THE ROYAL CARRIAGE.

100. Queen Victoria races the St Bernard dog-cart, from the *Illustrated Police News*, 8 April 1899.

the novelist Albert Smith, visited the Hospice in 1854, the Prior, M. de l'Eglise, was most anxious that he and the monks would not be able to keep up the world-famous breed. Since the mortality among the dogs had been very great, only two dogs were kept at the Hospice, with some others lodged in Martigny. Smith, who already owned a pair of St Bernards himself, promised to send some puppies to the Hospice when his bitch whelped.[15]

Through interaction with Swiss and foreign St Bernard breeders, the Great St Bernard priors managed to restore their pack of dogs, although cross-breeding with Landseer Newfoundlands made the dogs heavier, with larger heads and bushier tails. The tendency for the St Bernards to have a black face-mask was also acquired in this manner. Whereas all the original St Bernards had been short-haired, there were now both rough-haired and smooth-haired versions of the breed; the latter variety were more useful as rescue dogs, since their fur and paws did not get weighed down with snow and ice. To honour the memory of the first Barry, the largest and most handsome male in the Hospice pack was named after him. Gifted with extraordinary strength and courage, Barry II saved several travellers in the early 1900s, before drowning in 1905. He was succeeded by the equally heroic Barry III, who also excelled as a rescue dog. After he had fallen down a ravine in 1910, his stuffed body was put on exhibition at the Hospice.[16]

In the mid-1800s, there was no breed standard for St Bernards. As a consequence, the dogs were still quite heterogeneous, with various influential breeders valuing different characteristics. The names 'Alpine Mastiff', 'Mount St Bernard dog' and 'St Bernard dog' were still used interchangeably. The Revd J. Cumming Macdona MP kept large kennels at his rectory in West Kirby, Cheshire. He bred pointers, setters, fox-terriers and pugs, before developing a liking for St Bernards. The wealthy and eccentric clergyman soon had a pack of twenty of these great dogs, romping together in the sea near West Kirby. His favourite was the Swiss import 'Tell', the paragon of every canine virtue, who was never defeated in the show ring. When Tell had saved a child from drowning in the River Dee, Macdona built a tall tower nearby to commemorate his heroism; when the great dog expired in 1871, his remains were interred there. A stone effigy of Tell guards the tomb, which has the following inscription:

In Memory of the St Bernard dog

TELL

Ancestor of most of the Rough-coated Champions of England,
and himself winner of every prize in the Kingdom.
He was majestic in appearance, noble in character, and of undoubted courage.
Died January, 1871.

Tell's Tower was for many years a well-known West Kirby landmark, but today it has been partly incorporated into a house.[17] 'Hope', a son of Tell, was given to the Princess of Wales, later Queen Alexandra. Macdona played an important role in helping to expand the British St Bernard population, and to improve the breed, although other influential breeders did not agree with his ideas of what a St Bernard dog should look like.

At an 1875 dog show, a *Sporting Gazette* journalist contrasted the St Bernards bred by Macdona with those exhibited by two other big-time St Bernard fanciers, Frederick Graham and A. B. Bailey: 'What is the St Bernard? Is it the dog imported by Macdona, or the extinguisher applied to it by Mr Graham, or the more recently impending snuffers of Mr Bailey?' Not entirely inappositely, the journalist compared the rival St Bernard breeders to Frankensteins flooding the world with monsters, 'which we heartily wish would emulate his and devour their creators'.[18]

It would take until 1882 for the St Bernard Club to be formed, and four more years for its members to agree on a formal breed standard. From 1882 onwards, annual St Bernard dog shows were held, first at the Duke of Wellington's riding school in Knightsbridge, then at Albert Palace, Battersea. 'Rector', a champion St Bernard of the time, stood 34 inches at the shoulder; 'Sir Bedivere', who was almost as tall and weighed 212 pounds, was sold to the United States for £1,300; he met his match in another expensive British import, the 223-pound 'Princess Florence'. As time went by, St Bernard ownership was no longer restricted to the upper classes of society: Britain had a healthy population of St Bernards, and the dogs were no longer ruinously expensive.

The author and traveller Lady Florence Dixie was an eccentric society figure in the 1880s and 1890s. She was the daughter of the equally dotty Marquess of Queensberry, the defendant in the Oscar Wilde case, and the sister of Lord Alfred Douglas. She married the wealthy Sir Beaumont Dixie in 1875 and took him with her on long journeys to Africa and South America. In early 1883, when they were back in England, Lady Florence unwisely started to meddle in Irish politics, condemning the Fenians with great vehemence. After she had allegedly received several death threats from the enraged sons of Erin, Sir Beaumont decided to purchase a large St Bernard dog, named 'Hubert', to serve as his wife's bodyguard.[19]

On 17 March 1883, Lady Florence Dixie came running up to the Fishery, their elegant Regency house near Windsor. Two men dressed as women had suddenly attacked her, she breathlessly explained, flinging her to the ground and attempting to stab her three times! When she screamed for help, the villains stuffed earth into her mouth and knocked her on the head. Her fate would have been a dreadful one indeed, had not the faithful Hubert come bounding up to pull away the man with the knife!

'I owe my life to this Mount Saint Bernard dog!' Lady Florence exclaimed when giving interviews to journalists. She and Hubert were the celebrities of the day, particularly in the anti-Irish press: attempting to murder a defenceless woman was considered just the thing to expect from these dastardly Fenians. Hubert became the most famous dog in Britain. He was praised in the newspapers for his heroism, and the *Illustrated Police News* published his portrait. A gentleman sent Hubert a silver-studded collar, and many people sent him bones, beefsteaks and other treats.[20]

A wealthy American who offered to purchase Hubert, and a showman who wanted to exhibit the hero dog in a music hall, were both turned down by the snobbish Lady Florence, although she consented to Hubert becoming the special invited guest at a dog show in Durham, where he was awarded first prize. The crowning touch in Hubert's

101. The sensational attack on Lady Florence Dixie, from the *Illustrated Police News*, 31 March 1883.

meteoric career as a four-legged celebrity came when, as a newspaper expressed it: 'To-day, Hubert, the dog to whose courage and devotion Lady Florence attributes the preservation of her life, was photographed by Mr Snooks, of Windsor, and an autographed copy was sent to H.M. the Queen.' Unless this paragon of canine virtue had added handwriting to his accomplishments, it was probably Lady Florence who supplied the autograph.

But after the police had begun to investigate the mysterious incident at the Fishery, there were serious doubts as to whether there had been any attack at all. Nobody had seen the two assassins in drag; had they used some magic spell to return to Ireland, or had Hubert eaten them? Lady Florence's dress was not dirty, and her injuries were very superficial. Nor had any of the several people near the Fishery gardens heard Lady Florence scream, as she claimed to have done. If a St Bernard dog is approached by threatening strangers, it is natural for the animal to bark, but nobody had heard Hubert utter a single yelp. And the booming bark of a fully grown St Bernard male would carry for half a mile at least in quiet Victorian times. After it turned out that an Eton master had actually seen Lady Florence return to the Fishery, looking quite unhurt, newspaper opinion quickly changed. Although several gentlemen objected that it was caddish to doubt the word of a noble lady, and although the *British Medical Journal* suggested that Lady Florence might have suffered from a hallucination, the eccentric lady and her silent four-legged accomplice both became laughing stocks. It was even suggested that she had been drunk at the time, since she was known to share her husband's predilection for the bottle; the witty Countess of Antrim had once called her and her husband 'Sir Always and Lady Sometimes Tipsy'!

Several ribald poems were written to ridicule Lady Florence, with verses such as

> Lady Florence, Lady Florence, when you cried aloud for help,
> · And when your faithful hound proclaimed his presence with a yelp –
> Why did no one hear you, in your own or neighbour's grounds?
> The public to your ladyship this problem now propounds.

Lady Florence, Lady Florence, that such want of faith should be!
The public will not presently believe the things they see.
But when you next adventures of this kind should have to tell,
Please arrange to have some witnesses upon the scene as well!

Hubert also received his fair share of ridicule. A letter to *Punch*, allegedly from the dog Toby, suggested that the two villains must have crammed dirt down Hubert's throat to prevent him from barking. Toby called on Hubert to end his silence on this mysterious matter, and to answer those who doubted the heroism of the St Bernard dogs, were it carrying half-frozen children to the monastery, or fighting armed assassins. *Funny Folks* published an amusing poem, allegedly written by someone who had seen Hubert at the Warwick dog show, beginning with

So thou art Hubert, canine stout,
    Whose teeth – good gracious, what a row! –
Put banded murderers to rout.
    (At least we're told that this was so.)
That massive throat bayed noble rage
    As at the dastard pair you flew,
Just like a dog upon the stage!
    (That is, if what's been said is true.)

Lady Florence Dixie's career took quite some time to recover after this disastrous ending to the 'Windsor mystery' of 1883. She published several more books, and became known as a proponent for equality between the sexes, rational female dress, and various kinds of medical faddism and quackery. When she expired in 1905, those who shared her views wrote approving obituaries.[21] Sir Beaumont said he was heartbroken, but a few months later he married a barmaid.

And what about that canine prodigy, Hubert the St Bernard dog? It is sad to say that he sunk back into obscurity, fading away like a shooting star that once had lit up the firmament, or some luckless reality TV contestant trudging back to his job stacking shelves in the supermarket.

In 1937, the Norwegian mariner Erling Hafto bought a pedigree St Bernard puppy as a family pet. The puppy was named 'Bamse', a Norwegian word beginning as an acronym for 'bear' and later being used also for a teddy-bear, or to signify some particularly large object. In the latter meaning, 'Bamse' was (and is) not infrequently used as a name for a particularly large dog. Young Bamse was just an ordinary dog until the Second World War broke out. When Norway expanded its navy, Hafto became a naval lieutenant, appointed to command the patrol boat *Thorodd*. Since Mrs Hafto found it difficult to cope with the boisterous Bamse, Erling took the dog with him.[22]

Although Bamse sometimes suffered from seasickness, he became a useful ship's dog. He slept in a large wicker basket on the upper deck, and became very popular with the crew of the *Thorodd*. When Nazi Germany invaded Norway in April 1940, the navy fought back, When the *Thorodd* was attacked by fighter aircraft, Bamse stood on the bow-gun platform, wearing his steel helmet, and barking angrily at the planes. When the ship transported some German prisoners of war, Bamse stood guard.

In spite of the brave resistance of the Norwegian forces, the numerical superiority of the Germans, and their brutal and uncompromising style of warfare, meant that defeat was inevitable. King Haakon of Norway went to London to set up a government in exile, and the remaining thirteen ships of the Norwegian navy limped across the North Sea to join him. Arriving safely in Scotland, the *Thorodd* was converted to a minesweeper and stationed in Dundee. Bamse remained a worthy member of the ship's company, and a great favourite of the sailors. When his master Captain Hafto was transferred to command another vessel, the crew threatened mutiny if their St Bernard mascot was taken away from them. Although Hafto was not happy about losing his dog, Bamse was allowed to remain with his friends.

Bamse lifted the morale of the ship's crew, and became well known to the local civilian population. When the *Thorodd* and its crew were stationed in Dundee, and later in Montrose, Bamse liked attending football matches, sometimes taking part in the games himself. Once, Bamse saved a drunken sailor who had fallen overboard; another time, the enthusiastic dog himself needed saving, after having leapt headlong into the open sea to retrieve a football. When one of the Norwegian officers was returning to the *Thorodd* with Bamse, walking through the docks, he was attacked by a knife-wielding robber. Bamse was again the hero of the day: the great dog fiercely attacked the miscreant and pushed him over the quayside.

After being equipped with a bus pass, Bamse liked travelling on the local buses, to visit his favourite public houses, where he could count on being given beer and other treats. He was also known for breaking up fights among his crewmates by putting his paws on their shoulders, calming them down and then leading them back to the ship. One of Bamse's tasks was to round up his crew and escort them back to the ship in time for duty or curfew. To achieve this, he travelled on the local buses unaccompanied, with the bus pass attached to his collar. He would get off at the bus stop near his crew's favourite watering hole and go in to fetch them. With time, Bamse was promoted to mascot of the Royal Norwegian Navy. Later, he was proclaimed the largest dog serving in the Allied forces, and further promoted to become the official mascot of all the Free Norwegian Forces. An iconic photograph of him wearing a Norwegian sailor's cap was used on patriotic Easter cards and Christmas cards during the war. The image of Bamse became a symbol of Norwegian resistance against the German yoke.

When Bamse died in July 1944, probably from heart failure, he was buried with full military honours. A year later, the Nazi empire was conquered, and the King of Norway returned home with his navy, the *Thorodd* included. Since Bamse had been very popular among the people of Montrose, they kept tending his grave. More than once, sailors from the *Thorodd*, or other Norwegians who knew Bamse's story, came to visit it. In 2006, Bamse's grave was restored, and a life-size bronze statue of him was unveiled by Andrew, Duke of York, a fitting tribute to one of the world's most famous St Bernard dogs.

After the St Gotthard and Simplon tunnels had been constructed, the winter traffic through the Great St Bernard Pass diminished very considerably. As a consequence, the rescue work of the Hospice dogs became less important. By the 1930s, they were little more than a tourist attraction. The visitors freely fed and spoilt the dogs, and the entire pack sometimes roamed free to scavenge in the grounds. The Swedish traveller and busybody Lizzy Lind-af-Hageby, who had been such an admirer of the Talking Dogs of Weimar, visited Great St Bernard in 1937. In a letter to the Superior, she complained that the visitors felt free to tease the dogs, although she felt sure the problem could be solved by appropriate housing of the dogs, and good care. Later the same year, however, a little girl died after an encounter with the dogs. The police admonished the monks not to allow the dogs to roam free without a guardian, and to build them a proper kennel. According to Miss Lind-af-Hageby, it was her International Humanitarian Bureau that saved the Hospice dogs from destruction, through a donation of 15,000 Swiss francs for the dogs to be properly housed.[23]

In 1949, the dogs were moved to a better kennel, at the Maison Saint-Louis. In the early 1980s, these premises were restored and enlarged. The kennel of the Hospice was registered at the Swiss Saint-Bernard Club, and noted for its fine animals; there were numerous requests for the fifteen to twenty puppies born every year. Since the monks were overwhelmed by the large amounts of tourists, they reluctantly put the dogs up for sale in 2004, the reason being that they simply lacked the time and energy to look after them properly. There was an outcry among the St Bernard lovers around the world that the famous Hospice kennel would be broken up, but the Swiss handled matters with

102. The iconic photograph of Bamse wearing a sailor's cap.

their usual efficiency and common sense. The dogs were promptly purchased by two foundations created for the purpose. The Fondation Barry bought the kennels and the facilities in Martigny and continues to support and breed the dogs with good success. One condition of the sale was that the dogs should be brought to the monastery for the summer. Travellers are likely to see them romping around the slopes. The Fondation Bernard et Caroline de Watteville set up a fine Musée des Chiens de St Bernard in Martigny, with an impressive collection of St Bernard dog memorabilia. When I visited it in 2009, a number of good-looking dogs and puppies were kept in kennels adjacent to the museum. The monastery of Great St Bernard currently houses a handful of monks on a permanent basis and serves as a spiritual centre for others on retreat. When it was recently visited by a journalist, it housed only one dog, a golden retriever used for rescue work in avalanches.[24]

103. The current Barry sitting on the Hospice stairs – a postcard from the 1930s.

13

ANNALS OF THE RAT-PITS OF LONDON & NEW YORK

To obtain some first-hand knowledge of London's mid-Victorian underworld, there is no better source than Henry Mayhew's four-volume *London Labour and the London Poor*. Mayhew was a journalist who decided to make a full-scale survey of the poor people of London. He interviewed everybody he thought would have anything interesting to tell: street musicians, dustmen, sewer-hunters, bone-grubbers, rag-gatherers, crossing-sweepers and mendicants of every description. There were street sellers of the most quaint and outlandish articles: whelks, sheep's trotters, cough drops and bird's nests. Mayhew described the dress of all these weird individuals, how and where they all lived, their entertainments and customs, and made detailed estimates of the numbers and incomes of those practising each trade. The criminal underworld, with its thieves, robbers, pimps, bawds, bullies and fancy-men, had a particular fascination for him.

For the canine historian, Mayhew's *London Labour and the London Poor* is a treasure trove. He exposed the activities of the organized gangs of dog-thieves, and their close relations with the 'dog-finders' and 'dog-restorers' who charged fees of their own for the safe return of the stolen animals. Then there were the street sellers of dogs, some of whose animals may well have been by-products of the dog-stealing racket, for which the dog-restorer had been unable to negotiate a safe return to family life. Mayhew also interviewed an exhibitor of dancing dogs, and the proprietor of a 'happy family': some particularly docile animals of different species who were supposed to live happily together in a cage. But since the dog sometimes went berserk and killed the rats, and since the hawk and the cat kept decimating the mice, the trick was really to have a plentiful supply of the animals lowest down on the food chain in this unhappy family. The street seller of dog meat had a hard life, wheeling his smelly goods round the endless streets of the metropolis for very little return; the street seller of dog collars fared little better. Lowest of the low were the 'pure-finders', street collectors of dogs' faeces. According to Mayhew, they met with a ready market for all the dogs' dung they were able to collect, for use as a siccative for bookbinding leather at the Bermondsey tan yards.

Perhaps the weirdest of all chapters in Mayhew's book concerns a visit to the rat-killing. At the Graham Arms rat-pit, the bar was well attended by cigar-smoking, beer-drinking 'sportsmen'. At nine o'clock, the rat-pit was lit up, and some rats put into it for those present to try their dogs with; some of the dogs turned out to be quite proficient in killing rats, others less so. For the evening's grand match, the rat-pit was swept and the dead rats gathered in a bag. The rat-catcher brought a large basket full of squirming rats, picked out fifty of the largest, and put them into the pit. When one of the sportsmen wanted to tease some of the rats, he was advised to take good care not to be bitten, since 'these 'ere are none of the cleanest'. Indeed, their pungent odour resembled that of an open drain. A squirming bull-terrier was put into the pit, and the timekeeper started the match. The dog flew at the scurrying rats, killing them one by one with swift bites to the neck. 'Hi, Butcher! Hi, Butcher! Good dog! Bur-r-r-r-rh!' the dog's second cheered him on, blowing on the rats to make them scatter. When one of the rats bit into the dog's nose, the fierce terrier dashed it hard against the side of the pit. 'Dead 'un! Drop it!' shouted the second when Butcher sniffed at a still twitching rat, which was slowly dying of a broken neck.

In the end, Butcher lost the match, not being able to kill all fifty rats within eight minutes. His owner, the publican, was aggrieved at this dismal performance, and threatened to sell the dog. Still, he put an end to the evening's proceedings by bonhomously promising a solid silver dog's collar to be killed for next Tuesday, with a plentiful supply of rats.[1]

When I first read Mayhew's account, more than ten years ago, I wanted to find out more about this sleazy ratting 'sport', but so little had been written on the subject that it would take a long time to track down the relevant original sources.[2]

104. Henry Mayhew's drawing of the rat-pit.

It would appear as if the sport of ratting originated as a form of eighteenth-century dog trials, where the killing instinct of young terriers was tested by giving them a few rats to kill. With time, the sport spread to London and other cities. Instead of just being dog trials, the ratting matches became increasingly competitive, with a higher amount of rats put into the pit, and a good deal of betting going on. A dog owner might announce in the newspapers that his animal was capable of killing a certain number of rats in a certain amount of time – say twenty rats in five minutes – and bets were matched as to whether the dog would be capable of this feat. After a sack of live rats had been emptied into the pit, the dog was let loose on its path of destruction. The best dogs dispatched each rodent with a swift bite, without worrying at it or carrying it around, before attacking the next rat. The rats scurried around as well as they could, sometimes piling up in the corner of the rat-pit as if to seek protection, at other times desperately fighting for their lives.

Already in the early 1800s, there were several rat-pits in London, the most famous of which was the Westminster Pit, located in Duck Lane, Orchard Street. In the 1820s, this sleazy establishment became the catalyst of the growth of London ratting, thanks to 'Billy the Raticide', the most famous ratting dog ever. He was a 'Bull and Terrier' (a cross between an Old English bulldog and some kind of terrier), bred by the famous dog breeder James Yardington, and owned by a certain Charles Dew. Billy was a muscular dog of 26 pounds' weight, mostly white in colour, with strong jaws and a fierce glare in his eye. He had already set a record in 1820, by killing twenty rats in seventy-one seconds, at the cost of being deprived of one of his own eyes by one of the infuriated rodents.[3]

In September 1822, Billy was wagered, for twenty sovereigns, to kill a hundred rats in less than twelve minutes. Since ratting of this magnitude had rarely been seen before, the Westminster Pit was completely full. The audience, nearly 2,000 strong, laid many hundreds of pounds on the outcome of the match. There was a huge cheer when Mr Dew brought the squirming, growling Billy down to the pit, and another when a huge sack of large sewer rats was carried into the arena. The gentlemen puffed hard at their cigars to escape the pungent smell of the rodents, and tankards of beer were liberally swigged

105. A print of an early ratting dog, quite possibly Billy.

from. There was a roar as the umpire and timekeeper checked their watches, and Billy was set free. To the delight of his supporters, the fierce little dog dispatched all one hundred rats in 8 minutes, 45 seconds, a new world record. One of Billy's supporters, who had probably won a healthy sum backing the dog, wrote a poem in his honour:

> Oh Billy! let me celebrate thy fame,
> Proclaim thy true blood, and exalt thy name.
> For, in these vile degenerate times,
> Thou shouldst be made conspicuous in rhymes.
> 'Tis mere instinct – antipathy in cats,
> But thou, from principle, dost strangle rats …

Next month, when a similar wager was made, for Billy to kill a hundred rats, there was again immense interest from all classes of society: having a bet at the ratting was considered very fashionable by the young London swells of the time. Again, the sack of rats was emptied, and Billy let loose to wreak havoc. After 4 minutes and 45 seconds, Mr Dew took Billy out of the pit, washed his bloody jaws, and gave him some water to refresh himself with, before putting him back into the pit. When Billy was all done, in just 7 minutes and 17 seconds, the floor of the pit was drenched in gore; dead rats were everywhere. The spectators were most uproarious. Mr Dew allowed some gentlemen to caress and fondle the fierce little dog; Billy did not bite their fingers off, but seemed genuinely pleased with the situation. The world record holder in rat-killing was given a beefsteak and a bowl of porter to wash the taste of sewer rat out of his mouth; he dispatched both with alacrity.[4]

In April 1823, Billy beat his own world record by killing a hundred rats in five and a half minutes exactly; this record would stand for nearly forty years. In 1825, when Billy was challenged to a hundred-rat match by the 'Kentish Bitch', the Westminster Pit was completely packed. But there was a dreadful anticlimax: the pit-keeper's poor grasp of arithmetics meant that too few rats had been purchased, and the umpire declared the match a 'No Go'. Deservedly, the pit-keeper was roundly booed when this dismal announcement was made. To avoid full-scale rioting, the dogs were set to work in the pit against the existing rats: Billy destroyed ninety rats in seven and a half minutes, but the Bitch took nearly nine minutes to manage just sixty-five. Billy's angry, red-faced backers screamed for the blood of the pit-keeper, whom they accused of cheating. Billy's home fans did not lose out when their champion outclassed another out-of-town challenger, the Liverpool dog 'Crib', in a hundred-rat match at the Cockpit in Tufton Street.

In his *Ingoldsby Legends*, Richard Harris Barham told the story of Bloudie Jacke, the Shropshire Bluebeard, who had murdered his wives. When the sister of his latest victim comes to make inquiries,

> But nor Jacke nor his Man
> Can see young Mary-Anne,
> She has hid herself under the stair,
> And there

> Is a horrid great Dog, I declare!
> His eyeballs are bloodshot and blear,
> Bloudie Jacke!
> He's a sad ugly cur for a pet;
> He seems of the breed
> Of that 'Billy', indeed
> Who used to kill rats for a bet
> – I forget
> How many one morning he ate.

Barham's knowledge of ratting lore seems to have been quite defective, however: Billy was not a horrid great dog, but a fierce little one. Nor did he eat any of the rodents he killed, an erroneous notion which recurs in Barham's *Life and Letters*:

> On Monday Mrs. Coutts's plate
> Was removed to Piccadilly
> And a hundred rats, for want of cats.
> Were devour'd by Crib's dog Billy.

In 1827, Billy was still going strong under his new owner and manager Charley Aistrop. A noble German tourist, Prince Hermann von Pückler-Muskau, saw Billy perform in December that year. The rat-pit had two galleries: one for the lower classes, who were quaffing from huge pots of beer in a cloud of tobacco smoke, and another one for the gentlemen, who made bets of between twenty and fifty pounds on whether Billy would be able to destroy a hundred rats in ten minutes. In a letter, the Prince described how there was an anxious, fearful pause among the betters when a strong man entered the arena carrying what looked like a sack of potatoes. As the rats were set at liberty, they scattered about the pit, as though knowing what their fate was going to be. Billy set to work with murderous fury, killing all hundred rats in nine and a quarter minutes. Charles Dew had always been careful with Billy, never allowing him to fight other dogs or bait larger animals, but Aistrop, who was keen to cash in on the old dog while he still could, lacked these finer feelings. The ratting was followed by a badger-bait, in which both the badger and Billy had a second holding the animal by the tail. Billy seized the badger fast by the ears several times, and won the match, before retiring greatly exhausted.[5]

In 1829, Charley Aistrop invested the money Billy had earned for him, becoming the new proprietor of the Westminster Pit. By this time, Billy was quite an old dog, and his teeth no longer as serviceable as in his prime. At what may well have been his final performance, on 1 February, it was remarked that the effects of old age were visible on his exertions, and that he rather failed in destroying as many rats as in his prime. Later the same month, the rats of London gave a collective squeak of relief, when Billy the Raticide breathed his last. His admirer, the sportsman Pierce Egan, published the dog's epitaph, after the manner of Charles Wolfe's poem about the funeral of Sir John Moore after Corunna:

Not a *bell* was toll'd – not a shop was shut,
Nor a searcher deign'd her *fives* to put
On the lifeless corse of the Prince of Dogs,
Whose history every history flogs.

Not a *bark* was heard – but a lively squeak
Was echoed from rat to rat a whole week,
From Whitechapel church to Piccadilly,
Of 'Long *life* to grim *Death* – for *boning* Billy!'

Charley Aistrop had Billy stuffed and put in an elegant glass case, along with details of all his ratting records. The stuffed dog was kept on exhibition at the rat-pit for many years, and was much admired. Billy was not the only famous ratter to be made immortal by the taxidermist, but certainly the most famous.

In several contemporary caricatures, King William IV was depicted as the Dog Billy. In *The Royal Dog Billy at the Westminster Pit*, a dog with the head of William IV treads on a rat with the head of the Duke of Wellington, and grabs another one, with the countenance of Sir Robert Peel, with his jaws. The latter politician, known as a law enforcement pioneer, screams 'Police!' The Royal Dog Billy is cheered on by Lord Brougham to destroy the enemies of the Reform Bill. Those who hoped to recruit the vacillating King to support the Reform Bill were highly suspicious of the German-born Queen Adelaide's influence over him. In another caricature, *Royal Dog Billy led astray by a German Bitch*, the Royal Dog Billy is seen sniffing at the heels of a canine Adelaide, as she leads him across perilous, rocky chasms.[6]

106. The caricature 'The Royal Dog Billy', from Mary Frances Sandars' *Life of Queen Adelaide*.

Throughout Georgian times, cruel baiting sports had been extremely popular. It was considered an integral part of country life to enjoy a bull roaring in pain with a fierce bulldog holding it fast by the nose, or to cheer the dogs on when they attacked a chained bear. Almost everything on four legs was baited: bulls, horses, bears and wild boar. With its tough hide, punishing bite, and reluctance to die, the badger was another target for these perverted 'sportsmen'; watching a badger with its tail nailed to the floor being harried by some fierce fox-terriers was considered very droll by the rough country bumpkins. If they had no badgers handy, these loutish sadists caught some hedgehogs instead, put them on the fire to make them unroll, and then set the dogs on them.

It was not until the 1820s that there was any determined opposition to this wholesale sadism. The Society for the Prevention of Cruelty to Animals was founded in 1822 and did good work from the start; the humanitarian Richard Martin MP and some other politicians were active in lobbying for animal baiting to be outlawed. Although the humanitarians were opposed by traditionalist country squires, and rustics of every description, they eventually won the day: in 1835, Martin's Cruelty to Animals Act laid down penalties for mistreating bulls, bears, badgers and other animals. When the irate countrymen protested by baiting bulls at country fairs in the old tradition, there was sometimes full-scale rioting; the military had to be sent in, and harsh magistrates taught the loutish country bumpkins respect for animal rights the hard way.[7]

But one baited animal could not count on any sympathy: the rat. The weird ratting sport, which had already been bolstered by Billy's much-publicized exploits in the 1820s, actually received a further boost by the Cruelty to Animals Act. Country people considered animal baiting a venerable British tradition, like playing cricket or hunting foxes; for the bumpkin who liked nothing better than to see animals fighting to the death, ratting was now the only recourse. The raffish London 'sportsmen', forbidden to stage dog-fights or badger-baits, also had to make for the rat-pit in order to try their dogs, drink some beer, and put some bets on the killing. Like loathsome fungi, the rat-pits spread all over Britain. There were rat-pits in Leeds, Liverpool, Birmingham, Derby, Bristol and Reading, and probably in other towns and cities as well. There seems to have been rather less enthusiasm for this sleazy pastime in Ireland, Wales and Scotland.

The humanitarians were of course outraged at this resurgence of a brutal and degrading blood sport, but the Society for the Prevention of Cruelty to Animals (granted its royal status as the RSPCA in 1840) was initially reluctant to prosecute the ratters, since there was no way rats could be classed as domestic animals, and since there was very little public sympathy for the hated rat. The London rat-pits were particularly disgusting, due to a combination of large and rowdy crowds, and the use of foul-smelling sewer rats. Moralists depicted them as dens of vice and depravity, where youth was perverted. Of all blood sports, they rightly pointed out, ratting was the least edifying, offering neither exercise nor fresh air, but instead ample exposure to drunkenness, betting and crime.

The leading newspaper for the Ratting Fancy, as devotees of the sport called themselves, was the broadsheet *Bell's Life in London*. This unfastidious organ of the London sporting world was published once weekly on pink paper. Its 'canine' and 'ratting' columns make it clear that by the late 1840s ratting had become almost an industry. According to Henry Mayhew, there were at least seventy regular rat-pits in London alone, nearly all of them connected with a certain public house. The Southwark, Holborn, York Minster and Admiral Vernon pits were among the largest, along with old Charley Aistrop's new pit at the Eight Bells, Denmark Street, St Giles.[8]

The godfather of the London Ratting Fancy was Jemmy Shaw, a dog fancier and publican who kept his rat-pit at the Blue Anchor, Bunhill Row, St Luke's. Jemmy had begun his career as a useful boxer in the 1830s, before purchasing his pub and rat-pit in 1846. Jemmy was proud of his little dog 'Tiny', only five and a half pounds in weight, since this fierce little terrier had once won him a large bet by killing two hundred rats in less than an hour. Jemmy had this scene engraved and printed on large silk handkerchiefs, which he sold for half a sovereign each. Another star in Jemmy's menagerie was his ratting bulldog 'Tumbler', the hero of several closely contested fifty-rat matches.

By the 1840s, the ratting matches were governed by a strict system of rules, constructed to ensure fairness for the dog owners, and fair play for the betting fraternity. There was always a match umpire, and a timekeeper as well. The dog's second was strictly forbidden to interfere with the gory proceedings in the pit, except to cheer the animal on with gestures and verbal commands. He was also allowed to take the dog out of the pit, if he felt it needed rest or refreshments, and to blow on the rats, when they had piled up in the pit corner, in order to disperse them. After some distressing incidents

107. The first of three old ratting prints: the dog is lifted into a rat-pit.

involving frenzied sewer rats running up the handler's legs and inflicting very painful bites, the dog handlers made a habit of wearing their trousers tied to their boots.

A sample of the rats was closely examined before the match, to rule out that they had been drugged with laudanum beforehand to make the dog's task easier. A dog could be disqualified for a false pick-up, or for jumping out of the pit. A badly trained dog worrying the rat after killing it, or carrying it proudly around the pit, brought a volley of oaths from its backers. A tricky question was what to do if some of the rats had been shamming dead. In a fifty-rat match, three rats, and three rats only, were allowed to 'come to life' after time had been called and the dog lifted out of the pit. The opposite party was allowed to make an appeal by calling out 'That 'un 'baint dead, guv'nor!' and pointing at the rodent in question. The umpire would then put the rat within a chalked circle on his table, and strike its tail three times with a metal rod; if the rat managed to crawl out of the circle, it was 'alive', otherwise it counted as 'dead'.

Supplying rats for London's seventy rat-pits was an industry of its own. If we assume that these establishments were each open twice a week, and that two hundred rats were destroyed at each session, this would imply that the rat-pits of London alone would require four thousand rats each day. The rodents were supplied by a network of rat-catchers, who scavenged for live rats in warehouses, hedges and ditches, and often in the sewers as well. Jemmy Shaw, who boasted that he never had less than two thousand rats on the premises, had a number of rat-catcher families dependent on him. He bought between three and seven hundred rats each week, paying two or three pence for large, well-fed specimens. Jemmy kept his rats well fed on good barley meal, not from kindness of heart but to keep them from eating each other. In spite of the relatively decent rewards, rat-catching does not appear to have been a very amusing line of work.

108. The spectators gather round the rat-pit.

109. The time-keeper holding a dog.

Henry Mayhew once spoke to one of the rat-catchers, who gave a graphic demonstration what it felt like to have your finger bitten to the bone by a large sewer rat, and showed the best technique to pull out a rat's teeth that had broken off inside a bite wound.

Jemmy Shaw and other ratting impresarios realized the importance of varying the matches. Ferrets were sometimes brought in as an alternative to the dogs. Even a badger, a 'tiger cat', a mongoose and a white hedgehog fought in the rat-pit, although the latter animal was only backed to kill two rats. Terriers of all sizes were useful ratters, and so were terrier–bulldog crosses. Sometimes, a weight handicap system was made use of: either the dogs were matched to kill as many rats as the amount of pounds they weighed, or an individual dog was backed to 'destroy its weight in vermin'. Some dogs were considered experts on three-rat matches, dashing round the pit to kill the rodents in just a matter of seconds; others were gritty, determined fighters, used in fifty- or hundred-rat matches. Sometimes, a single dog killed rats against the clock, as Billy had done, but increasingly often, two dogs competed against each other in twenty- or fifty-rat matches, one of them killing first, and the second being ready to chase down the score after the pit had been cleared of corpses and new rats supplied. There was an annual all England ratting sweepstakes at Jemmy Shaw's pit, where as many as twenty canine competitors destroying five hundred rats between them. The male ratters had 'tough' names like 'Bruiser', 'Cribb' or 'Nero'; in honour of the world record holder, quite a few of them were called 'Billy'. The female stars, who were just as lethal as their male colleagues, often had ludicrously feminine names like 'Duchess', 'Miss Jennifer' or 'Lady Gwendoline'. The Sheffield bitch 'Lassie' was a force to be reckoned with in the rat-pits up north; she once outclassed one of the aforementioned 'Billys' by 40 seconds in a twelve-rat match.

110. The rat-catcher in the sewers.

111. The Great 100 Rat Match, from Augustus Mayhew's *Paved with Gold*.

London's Mr Ratting, Jemmy Shaw, generously donated prizes for the ratting sweepstakes, and for the main event matches in his pit: a silver dog's collar or snuff box, or a live sheep. The lesser rat-pits were content with putting up a ham, a goose, or even two squirrels in a cage, to be ratted for. In contrast to the prosperous Jemmy Shaw, Billy's former owner Charley Aistrop had to face poverty in old age. He had to sell the stuffed Billy to Jemmy in early 1856; the last we hear of this famous dog is that his stuffed body was 'ratted for' at Shaw's pit later the same month.[9]

There could be serious grudge matches when two ambitious dog fanciers or rat-pit proprietors matched their best dogs against each other. Syndicates were formed to back the dogs, hundreds of pounds were betted, and crowds gathered in their thousands to back their favourites. The beer and the excitement sometimes got the better of the audience, and serious fights could break out. When a celebrated provincial ratting dog challenged one of the London stars, the atmosphere might resemble that of a present-day football game between a London club and a bitter out-of-town rival.

In 1848, the London dog 'Jack' was carried round the streets in a drunken procession after beating the Southampton bitch 'Beauty' by 106 rats to 100 in a fiercely contested encounter. In another epic ratting match, the Manchester bitch 'Miss Lily', less than eight pounds in weight, was wagered to kill a hundred large barn rats. After a frenzied effort, she narrowly lost by 1 minute, 40 seconds; still, the London sportsmen gave her a standing ovation. A certain Mr Beardmore, of Salford, had a lame, one-eyed retriever bitch named 'Nell', allegedly fifteen years old. When he backed this decrepit-looking animal to destroy sixty rats in half an hour, the Ratting Fancy of London was quick to oppose him. But as soon as the rats had been put in the pit, Nell's limp was miraculously cured; she flew round the pit like a dervish, dispatching all the rats in just twenty minutes. This time it was the Salford contingent who celebrated a great away win for their canine champion.[10]

Perhaps the greatest scandal in the annals of ratting concerned one of these controversial grudge matches. For months, Leeds dog fancier James Searles had been 'talking up' his fierce ratting bitch 'Jenny Lind' to 'destroy rats against anything breathing', as he expressed it. His offer was taken up by the London sportsman Andrew White, who backed his bitch 'Teddy' against Jenny Lind in a hundred-rat match at Jemmy Shaw's pit. In February 1851, the Ratting Fancy was much looking forward to this encounter. A formal contract was signed by the two dog owners; since Teddy was pregnant, it contained a clause that if one of the bitches died before the match, the syndicate backing it would forfeit only £1.

But Teddy delivered her puppies without complication, and was fit for the fight. She was no cuddly bear, but a lean, mean rat-killing machine. Teddy had numerous London supporters, who were backing her with hundreds of pounds. A large Leeds contingent, supporters of Jenny Lind, arrived in town and made their presence felt in the ale houses. But on the great day itself, a glum-looking Mr Searles came into Jemmy Shaw's pub, opened a large bag and lifted out a dead dog: Jenny Lind had just expired!

But Jemmy examined the dead dog closely, pointed his finger at Mr Searles, and exclaimed 'That 'baint Jenny Lind!' Several other ratting enthusiasts, who had previously made the acquaintance of the Leeds phenomenon, agreed. Mr Searles was roundly accused of having 'chickened out' of his very considerable bet, perhaps after hearing some anecdotes about Teddy's exploits in the London rat-pits. Unwilling to risk his money against such a fearsome opponent, the cunning Northerner had procured a dead dog resembling Jenny Lind, in order to cheat his way out of the match. There were 'high words' between the London and Leeds contingents: the angry Mr White blasted his opponent as a cheat, but Searles and his friends maintained that the dead dog was really Jenny Lind, although they refused to *give their words* concerning this matter. Rather surprisingly, the quarrel did not end in a fight, but in some acrimonious newspaper correspondence, with allegedly honest Leeds people providing affidavits that the dead dog was really Jenny Lind.[11]

The long-time aim for Jemmy Shaw and other dog fanciers was of course to find a dog capable of matching the exploits of Billy the Raticide. During the 1840s and 1850s, there were several attempts at beating Billy's epic hundred-rat record, but none was successful. But in 1861, Jemmy Shaw's black-and-tan Bull and Terrier 'Jacko' was spoken of as a future star in the London rat-pits. Jacko destroyed sixty rats in 2 minutes, 42 seconds, with a killing time of just 2.7 seconds per rat. In 1862, Jacko beat Billy's record, killing a hundred rats in just 5 minutes, 28 seconds. There have been claims from various 'experts' alleging that the exertions of Billy, or Jacko, or both, had been aided by some person drugging the rats beforehand. But as we have seen, there were safeguards against such skulduggery, and the matches took place before numerous and critical spectators; had the rats been drugged, they would surely have detected it.

The crowning moment of Jacko's career was the famous thousand-rat match of 1862, in which Jemmy's famous dog killed a hundred rats once weekly for ten consecutive weeks, destroying the total of a thousand rodents in less than a hundred minutes. Jacko was still alive in 1866, when he and Jemmy were guests of honour at the Crystal Palace dog show; between 1861 and 1866, Jacko had won three hundred matches, and destroyed eight thousand rats. Just like Billy, Jacko was stuffed after death; his record still stands today.[12]

There was turmoil among Manchester's Ratting Fancy after an unprecedented match in 1880. Mr Benson's fox-terrier 'Turk' was matched against Mr Lewis's monkey, in a twelve-rat match. Since the monkey was an unknown quantity, and the dog a formidable ratter, Turk was the favourite. After the dog had killed the twelve rats in very good time, the monkey was put into the rat-pit. Mr Lewis handed it a hammer, which the clever primate made good use of, bashing the rodents' heads in with alacrity and winning with time to spare. Several months later, it was still debated whether the rules of ratting should be amended to exclude monkeys wielding blunt instruments.

At the height of the Ratting Fancy, the RSPCA had been quite powerless to impede the ratters. An early attempt at prosecuting the ratters ended in dismal failure. In 1850, the Secretary of the RSPCA, Mr Thomas, applied for a summons against the proprietor of the Manor House rat-pit, for cruelty to animals. The magistrate Mr Tyrwhitt just made fun of him, declaring that the law did not extend to such mischievous vermin as rats. Showing off his knowledge of the ratting world, he added that if there had been a few more Dogs Billy

112. A ratting scene, from *Animal World*,
1 August 1871.

113. The amazing ratting monkey, from the *Illustrated Police News*, 4 September 1880.

around, the farmers would have been very glad. Jemmy Shaw wholeheartedly approved of this wise decision, and the forthright words from the magistrate, adding that since rats were not animals, but vermin, the Cruelty to Animals Act did not apply to them.[13]

To strengthen his case, Jemmy wrote a pamphlet under the pen-name 'Uncle James'. Entitled *Rat!!! Rat!!! Rat!!! A Treatise on the Nature, Fecundity and Devastating Character of the Rat, and its Cruel Cost to the Nation*, this pro-ratting diatribe was sold in his pub and rat-pit. Using some very dubious statistics, Jemmy claimed that one pair of rats, with their progeny, would in three years produce more than 600,000 rats, which would consume the food of 64,000 human beings. Had it not been for the exertions of Jemmy and his fellow ratting impresarios, the entire British Empire would have been starved out by the ravenous rodents. The Dog Tiny should receive a solid gold collar, by public subscription, for killing so many rats. It was dismal to see that mawkish do-gooder Mr Thomas of the RSPCA applying for legal means to protect man's greatest four-footed enemy, the rat. Instead, there should be more terriers, and more ratting, to allow the empire to rise to its true potential!

The humanitarians were wholly undeterred by Jemmy's blustering. In 1868, they took on the proprietor of the Globe Inn rat-pit in Birmingham. This time, the magistrate was more sympathetic, declaring that ratting was indeed a cruel sport, and that it had a brutalizing influence upon the spectators. The pit-owner was fined five shillings, and the pit was closed down. A few years later, the Ratting Fancy of Birmingham was struck another hard blow when seven people connected with a rat-pit were fined £5 each for cruelty to animals.[14]

Egged on by this triumph, the RSPCA took on the Queen's Head rat-pit, in the Haymarket. Their leading witnesses were two policemen, who had seen a dog being lifted into the rat-pit three times. When finally taken out of the pit, it was bleeding from having been bitten by the rats, and appeared greatly exhausted. The London publican had employed the barrister Montagu Williams to defend him. This eloquent gentleman said that the dog had merely followed its instincts to kill the rats. The animal was present in court, and appeared to be in good health and spirits. If ratting was cruel, then so was fox hunting! Could there be a more preposterous notion? But on the strength of the testimony of the two policemen, the magistrate fined the pit-keeper £5, since he felt there had been cruelty to the dog.[15]

In the RSPCA's magazine *Animal World*, ratting was depicted as the most degraded pastime, inflicting needless cruelty on both dogs and rats. In the 1870s, the tide was clearly turning: other newspapers spoke up against the goings-on in the rat-pits, and even Jemmy Shaw no longer openly advertised his ratting matches. Ratting had lost its fashionable London following, and the metropolitan rat-pits closed down one after another. By this time, the responsible dog breeders and dog fanciers were sneering at the sleazy rat-pits and their low, degraded clientele. Jemmy himself sold or lost his pub in 1876, and the year after, poor Jemmy was clearly 'going to the dogs' in more ways than one. A newspaper appealed for help for this once well-known London character in his hour of distress: Jemmy should be restored to 'the position of comfort which he has lost since he gave up his well-known hostelry in Soho'. It would appear as though poor Jemmy died in poverty in 1889, at the age of seventy-three.

114. Ratting in the Haymarket, from the *Illustrated Police News*, 24 December 1870.

By the 1880s, the Ratting Fancy was nearing total extinction: few rat-pits remained, and ratting had become a working man's sport well-nigh forced underground. When another Birmingham rat-pit was closed down in 1887, and its proprietors heavily fined, the newspapers deplored this brutal, degraded pastime, and its motley following of drunks, vagabonds and criminals.[16] The journalist Wentworth Day left behind a singularly unflattering description of one of London's last rat-pits:

This was a rather dirty, small place, in the middle of the Cambridge Circus, London. You went down a rotten wooden stair and entered a large, underground cellar, which was created by combining the cellars of two houses. The cellar was full of smoke, stench of rats, dogs and dirty human beings as well. The stale smell of flat beer was almost overpowering. Gas lights illuminated the centre of the cellar, a ring enclosed by wood barriers, similar to a small Roman circus arena and wooden bleachers, arranged one over the other, rose stepwise above it nearly to the ceiling. This was the pit for dog fights, cockfights and rat killing. A hundred rats were put in it, large wagers went back and forth on whose dog could kill the most rats within a minute. The dogs worked in exemplary fashion, a grip, a toss and it was all over for the rat. With especially skilful dogs, two dead rats flew through the air at the same time ...

After London's very last rat-pit, situated behind Ludgate Circus, had been permanently closed down, some die-hard ratters were reluctant to see the end of their favourite sport. They hired a Thames barge, purchased some rats and put them in the hold, placed their bets and released the dog.[17]

The amended Protection of Animals Act of 1911 provided the RSPCA with ample powers to prosecute rat-pit proprietors. The last recorded prosecution of the owner of a rat-pit happened in Leicester as late as 1912. According to *Animal World*, this relic of barbarism had been in operation for over forty years, and thousands of defenceless little rats had been done to death in merciless fashion. After this ultimate rat-pit had been closed down, the sport was permanently forced underground.[18]

It took until 1870 for ratting to be taken up in Paris. This *chasse à l'Anglaise* was considered a novel and exciting sport among the Parisian dog fanciers. There were two elements of the competition. In the first one, a rat was put underneath one of ten large flower-pots, and the dog was timed to smell it out, overturn the pot, and kill it. In the second one, five or ten rats were put into the outdoor rat-pit and the dog was timed to kill them all. There was usually a competition between several dogs, with new rats supplied for each. At a time when ratting was largely frowned upon by respectable people in Britain, it gained considerable support in France, both in Paris and in the provinces. The *Graphic* magazine published a feature on French ratting, wondering why their neighbours across the Channel had spurned boxing and cricket, instead taking up the least respectable of Britain's national sports and pastimes.[19]

It should be noted, however, that the French *concours des chiens ratiers* were much more edifying than the gory ratting matches that had flourished in London. Leading terrier breeders supported the ratting, and helped to found the Ratier Club de France.

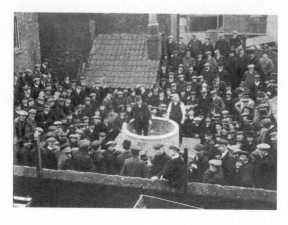

115. One of the last rat-pits in England to remain open, from *Animal World*, August 1912.

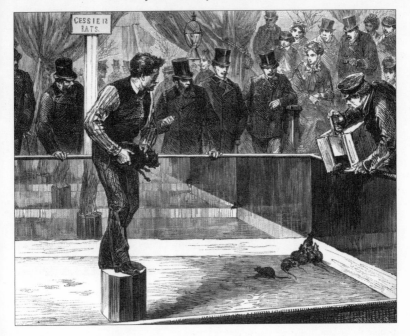

116. A Paris rat-pit.

The number of rats was limited, sewer rats were never used, and the matches were usually held outdoors in a special *ratodrôme*. If there was any betting, it was conducted with decorum. Most cities in northern France had regular ratting matches; the rats were supplied by the local rat-catcher or *dératiseur*. The sport even spread to Belgium. In 1894, *La Nature* magazine featured some hot action in the Lille *ratodrôme*, and a similar establishment in Spa flourished at the same time.[20]

In Paris, the main *ratodrôme* was situated at the Route de la Révolte, near the Porte des Ternes. In his 1910 book *A travers Paris*, historian Georges Cain pitied the poor rats put to death in this dismal *ratodrôme*. A hundred rats were killed each hour, most of them in five- or ten-rat matches where dogs competed against each other. The owner of the *ratodrôme* replenished his stock from rat-catchers and garbage collectors, paying 25 centimes for healthy specimens.

Not even the First World War could crush the French ratting sport: in 1920, the Ratier Club de France held a grand championship meeting in Paris. The French animal rights movement objected, but once more, there was no sympathy for the rat. They never succeeded in banning the ratting sport: there were matches in the Lille and Spa *ratodrômes* as late as the 1920s. The Spa *ratodrôme*, kept by the celebrated *dératiseur* Gustave Xhrouet, may well have been the last one standing.[21]

117. A French variant of ratting, with the rats hidden under flower-pots.

118. 'Concours de Chiens Ratiers' depicted in *La Nature* magazine of 1892.

Already in the days of Billy the Raticide, the Ratting Fancy spread across the oceans. There was a thriving ratting scene in Melbourne and other large Australian cities. Nor did ratting fail to establish itself in the United States. Here there was no Cruelty to Animals Act, and the ratting matches competed with dog-fights and badger-baits. Kit Burns, who kept the Sportsman's Hall saloon on Water Street in New York, was the American equivalent to Jemmy Shaw. He was notorious for his gory dog-fighting and rat-killing matches. A stout, muscular, red-faced fellow, his ugly, pock-marked features had more than a passing resemblance to those of one of his fighting bulldogs. On a shelf, he proudly exhibited the stuffed body of 'Jack', the American ratting champion, whose record of killing a hundred rats in 6 minutes and 40 seconds was still standing. Kit was also the proud owner of a fierce black bear, and the fearsome fighting dog 'Belcher' had his own 'canine boudoir' on the premises, where he ate better food than his master. Kit's son-in-law Richard Toner, known as 'Dick the Rat', was New York's champion rat-catcher. He sometimes performed in the rat-pit as well, biting the head off a mouse for a nickel and a wharf rat for a quarter.

The rat-pit occupied the first floor of the Sportsman's Hall. Kit Burns always had a stock of large grey wharf rats, which was replenished at regular intervals by the stalwart Dick the Rat. Throughout the 1850s and 1860s, the Sportsman's Hall saloon remained a notorious New York den of vice, staging dog-fights and bare-knuckle boxing prize fights. In 1868, Edward Winslow Martin left a vivid description of the rat-pit, in his *Secrets of the Great City*:

> Rats are plentiful along the East River, and Burns has no difficulty in procuring as many as he desires. These and his dogs furnish the entertainment, in which he delights. The principal room of the house is arranged as an amphitheatre. The seats are rough wooden benches, and in the centre is a ring or pit, enclosed by a circular wooden fence, several feet high. A number of rats are turned into this pit, and a dog of the best ferret stock is thrown in amongst them. The little creature at once falls to work to kill the rats, bets being made that she will destroy so many rats in a given time. The time is generally 'made' by the little animal, who is well known to, and a great favorite with, the yelling blasphemous wretches who line the benches. The performance is greeted with shouts, oaths, and other frantic demonstrations of delight. Some of the men will catch up the dog in their arms, and press it to their bosom in a frenzy of joy, or kiss it as if it were a human being, unmindful or careless of the fact that all this while the animal is smeared with the blood of its victims. The scene is disgusting beyond description.

Henry Bergh, the founder of the New York Society for the Prevention of Cruelty to Animals, decided to take Kit Burns on. He found the gory dog-fights staged at the Sportsman's Hall most brutal and degrading. It was harder for him to stir up any popular sympathy for the rat, however, and the cunning Kit only advertised his ratting matches, keeping the dog-fights as unscheduled extra events. But Henry Bergh and his friends were spying in the audience, ready to call the police when the dog-fight was started. After being prosecuted, the indignant Kit objected that rats were not animals;

they were vermin. Would that miserable Henry Bergh not have killed a rat himself, if he had found it in his cupboard, or his bed? Soon, an honest New Yorker would be prosecuted for opening and eating an oyster![22]

Henry Bergh kept pursuing Kit Burns and his cronies. In November 1870, Kit and many of his supporters were once more arrested for illicit dog-fighting and rat-killing after a successful raid on the premises had been led by Bergh in person. But Kit, whose habits were not consistent with a long and healthy existence, would be tried by a higher tribunal; he expired not long after being arrested, just before his fortieth birthday. Henry Bergh exulted that he had closed Sportsman's Hall for good. The building was rented to a mission for 'unfortunates', where the parson held his sermons standing in the former rat-pit! But by some stratagem or other, Dick the Rat managed to regain control of the premises. For some years, he competed with the West Side and Clinton Place rat-pits, but the indefatigable Henry Bergh harried all three pits with undiminished fervour. Knowing that there was much less opposition to ratting outside New York City, Dick reluctantly gave up Sportsman's Hall, which was turned into a full-time saloon.

For the remainder of the century, Dick the Rat would remain America's Mr Ratting. He and his assistants were employed by slaughterhouses and hotels, and even by the Metropolitan Opera House, to catch rats at these premises. In a newspaper feature, Dick explained the tricks of his trade. Described as a slim, clean-shaven young man with sharp black eyes, he told the journalist that after receiving a poisonous rat bite that nearly led to his festering arm being amputated, he had started using tongs of his own invention to catch the rodents. At night, Dick and his assistants put out bait for the rats, disoriented them with a flash from a lantern, and picked them up with their tongs. The rats were put in a large sack, specially designed for holding them. Once, Dick said, a 'copper' had 'necked' him as a suspected burglar. At the police station, he had been ordered to surrender the large bag which was suspected to contain various stolen goods. But when the bag was dropped on the floor, a hundred rats scurried all over the station-house![23]

Until his death in 1888, Henry Bergh kept on fighting the New York ratters. In 1879, he closed down the Clifton Place pit and had its proprietor jailed for three months. A Scotch terrier, part of the rat-pit, and two empty rat cages were exhibited among the prosecution evidence.[24] But if Bergh had hoped to stop ratting in the United States, he would have been disappointed. The country was too large, the legislation that protected animals too vague, and the 'sportsmen' who liked cruel baiting sports too numerous. The mastermind Dick the Rat went wherever there was a ratting match, supplying the rodents and sometimes entering one of his own dogs to take part. For lengthy periods of time, he settled in Chicago, where the rats were plentiful and the enthusiasm for ratting high. In 1889, he caught 460 rats at one Chicago hotel only, selling them for a nickel each.[25] In 1891, Dick supplied the rats for a ratting match in Newark, NJ, at Professor Norton's Club Rooms. The main hall of the club was packed with spectators long before the entertainment started. Dick served as master of ceremonies as several dogs were matched to kill five or ten rats: a bull pup, a little terrier, and even a 'Chinese hairless dog'. According to the *National Police Gazette*, this was 'A Brisk and Well-attended Baiting. Badgers make way for the Lively Rodents'.[26]

119. Hot action in a New Jersey rat pit, from the *National Police Gazette*.

During the 1890s, the American enthusiasm for ratting was slowly waning. A meeting in Syracuse in 1893 was a disaster due to the dogs being slow and inexperienced. When Dick the Rat arranged a meeting in Auburn the same year, the participants were met with 'expressions of disgust'. Even in Chicago, the tide was turning: a ratting match in February 1899 was stopped by the police. Although some early baseball meetings featured dog-fights or baitings of rats or badgers, American ratting was slowly but steadily forced underground.[27] In 1897, a newspaper published a good obituary for this sleazy 'sport', supplied by James B. Frazier, known as the Munchausen of Lexington, Kentucky.[28] After Frazier's duck had died, his fox-terrier 'Fanny' took an interest in sitting on the duck's eggs, he alleged. They all hatched, and the ducklings followed the dog about and regarded it as their mother: 'Fanny is a remarkable ratter, and these little ducks developed into the finest rat killers that I ever saw. I am willing to match these six ducks against six terriers for from $100 to $1000 in a rat killing contest, and I will win the match.'

14

THE BROWN DOG RIOTS

As we go walking after dark,
We turn our steps to Latchmere Park,
And there we see, to our surprise
A little Brown Dog that stands and lies!

From 'The Brown Dog Song',
written by some London medical student

In November 1907, Mr Edward Ford, a London gentleman who had recently returned from a long stay abroad, was taking a stroll in the Strand, when he perceived a large crowd of hooligans approaching him, shouting and singing. They carried the effigy of a brown dog on a high wooden pole. Mr Ford tried to avoid these rowdy miscreants, but they surrounded him singing 'Ha ha ha! Hee hee hee! Little Brown Dog don't we hate thee!', and rubbed a fluffy toy dog against his nose. A police constable stood grinning nearby without interfering. When the outraged Mr Ford managed to extricate himself from the throng, he went up to the constable and asked him why he had not taken action against these street pests. 'Why, it's only 'em Brown Doggers!' the jovial constable replied. Mr Ford, who had been away from London quite some time, did not at all understand what he meant; since the reader of this book is likely to share this predicament, we will have to start from the beginning.[1]

After suppressing the Ratting Fancy, among other well-publicized successes, the Royal Society for the Prevention of Cruelty to Animals (RSPCA) went from strength to strength. Most members of this both popular and well-supported organization were benign animal lovers, who objected to cruel dog owners, careless farmers, and the rabble attending the cock-fights and rat-pits. In late Victorian times, some radical members demanded the suppression of blood sports and vivisection. One of them, suffragette author Frances Power Cobbe, founded the Society for the Protection of Animals Liable to Vivisection in 1875. Not without reason, she and her followers objected to the Cruelty to Animals Act, which exempted vivisectors from prosecution for cruelty to animals, as long as they were registered with the Home Office to conduct experiments. This law thus allowed the killing and torturing of animals, as long as a certain class of people were responsible. One of Cobbe's protégés was the Hon. Stephen Coleridge, the dilettante son of the Lord Chief Justice of England. Having worked together for several years, they quarrelled in 1898, and he ousted her from the society's executive committee.[2]

By the time Coleridge took over the reins, the renamed National Anti-Vivisection Society had not inconsiderable public support. The majority of these supporters were kind, animal-loving humanitarians, who objected to the wholesale cruelty that was going on in the laboratories. At a time when many people bonded strongly with their pet dogs, and thought highly of their intelligence and fidelity, there was increasing opposition to the use of dogs in experimental research. After all, these were the times of the cult of the Newfoundland dog, and the beatification of that bizarre anchorite, Greyfriars Bobby. If a dog could act altruistically, and save people's lives while displaying extraordinary intelligence, or alternatively become so attached to its master as to keep vigil at the grave for twelve long years, was it not a shameful thing to reward these canine paragons of virtue with torture and an ignominious death in a laboratory?

Many educated people agreed with these sentiments. Albeit no close student of the subject, Queen Victoria herself more than once expressed herself in vague anti-vivisectionist terms. The Earl of Shaftesbury and the Archbishop of York were co-founders of Frances Power Cobbe's anti-vivisection society; poets Lord Tennyson and Robert Browning both opposed the use of higher animals in experimentation; aesthete John Ruskin resigned from his Oxford chair after he learnt the university were funding a physiology laboratory. The dapper Stephen Coleridge fitted in well with these upper-class anti-vivisectionists. Like most of them, he favoured a gradual phasing out of painful experiments on living animals, rather than an outright ban.

By the 1890s, many lower- and middle-class people were just as fond of their cats and dogs as the anti-vivisection luminaries listed above. They were fearful that their animals would be stolen by the gangs of dog-thieves infesting London and other large cities, and end up on the vivisector's bench. Their fears were not unfounded, since there were several verified instances of unscrupulous laboratories purchasing stray or stolen dogs for vivisection, or even employing dog-thieves of their own. The reason for the foundation of the Battersea Dogs' Home was to rescue stray dogs, not just from starvation and ill-treatment in the streets, but also from the vivisector's scalpel. The much-resented illicit supply of stolen dogs for vivisection was a major reason for the anti-vivisectionists receiving support from ordinary people, women as well as men.

A hard core within the anti-vivisection movement were fanatics who opposed medical science as a whole, and objected to the social and professional power of doctors. They boldly denied both the transmission of disease through infection and the existence of immunity, and objected to vaccination as being both dangerous and unnecessary. They viewed hygiene, cleanliness and fresh air as the key to human health, rather than the new-fangled discoveries of germs, bacilli and antitoxins. Some of them dabbled in spiritualism and occultism; others were quacks or proponents of 'self-healing'; yet others were vegetarians and teetotallers. Within the very considerable female contingent, many were suffragettes and propagandists for rational female dress. In 1895, the anti-vivisection *Herald of Health* magazine contained articles such as 'Stolen Dogs sold for Vivisection', 'Bad Air as Cause for Disease', 'Vaccination, the Delusion of the Century', 'Anti-Corset League's Meeting Transactions', and 'How the State may Prevent Premature Burials'. The faddists involved with this magazine were not always impressed with the foppish Stephen Coleridge; firstly, he was a meat-eating man and they were mainly vegetarian women; secondly, they deplored his gradualist approach and demanded the immediate total abolition of vivisection. It took all Coleridge's tact and suaveness to maintain good relations with the divergent factions of his organization.

One of these hardcore anti-vivisectionists was the young Swedish controversialist Emelie Louise Lind-af-Hageby, known to her friends as 'Lizzy'. Born into a minor noble family in 1878, she was in possession of considerable independent wealth. Little is known about her formal schooling, except that she attended Cheltenham Ladies' College for a while in 1896, although she never graduated.[3] As she herself later expressed it, her 'mind was turned at an early age from things young girls are supposed to enjoy, such as balls and dances. I became interested in work for women and children and prison reform and social work generally.'[4] She delivered her first public lecture in Stockholm at the age of eighteen; the subject was how to prevent premature burials. To the acute embarrassment of her family, she boldly claimed that the current signs of death were entirely useless: tens of thousands of people were still alive when six feet underground in a coffin, to die a terrible, lingering death within its unyielding walls. The only way to prevent these horrid scuffles, the alarmist young lady asserted, was to employ a recently patented signalling system that caused a bell to ring and a flag to wave on top of a pole attached to the coffin, if its still-living inmate turned a switch.[5]

120. Miss Lind-af-Hageby, from an old postcard.

In 1900, Miss Lind-af-Hageby and her friend Leisa Schartau went to Paris to study languages. Having obtained a letter of recommendation from some French magnate, they also visited the Institut Pasteur and other laboratories. Outraged by the scenes of cruelty they had been exposed to, they immediately joined the Swedish anti-vivisection movement, where their energy and single-mindedness ensured that they were soon leading lights. The year after, they went to London to meet Stephen Coleridge and other prominent anti-vivisectionists. In 1902, they enrolled as students of physiology at the London School of Medicine for Women. Taking fee-paying extra students in this manner was one of the medical school's ways of earning some much-needed extra money. One reason Lind-af-Hageby and Schartau became physiology students has been stated to be that they realized that their lack of medical knowledge would hamper their campaign against vivisection; another reason is likely to have been that they wanted to 'go undercover' as students to make observations of illegal experiments on animals. They attended many demonstrations on live animals at the University College, taking copious notes in their diaries, before giving up their studies in April 1903.

When Miss Lind-af-Hageby and her friend brought their diaries to Stephen Coleridge, it was one particular incident that galled them. On 2 February 1903, they and seventy other students had attended a demonstration of the function of the salivary glands, involving a small brown mongrel dog. Firstly, they had seen that this dog had a scar on its belly from a previous operation. Secondly, the dog did not appear to be properly anaesthetized, since it seemed to struggle throughout the experiment. Coleridge realized that these were infringements of the Cruelty to Animals Act, since it was prohibited to use the same animal for vivisection twice, or to neglect to anaesthetize it properly. A more prudent man would have made some further inquiries before taking action, for example contacting some of the other students who had been present, but Coleridge was both rash and emotional. Making a passionate speech at a grand anti-vivisection meeting on 1 May, before three thousand people, he outlined how the cruel vivisector, Dr William Bayliss, had broken the law when torturing the Brown Dog to death. Soon, the newspapers were full of these matters, and the outraged Bayliss sued for libel. A more prudent man would have been reluctant to take on a respected scientist like Bayliss, supported by the influence and wealth of the University of London, but Coleridge was defiant. He had an edited version of the diaries of his two Swedish friends published under the title *The Shambles of Science*. One chapter, entitled 'Fun' described the sad fate of the Brown Dog, and the coarse and unfeeling reaction to its sufferings by the other students.[6]

When the trial began in November 1903, Coleridge remained sanguine about his prospects, although Bayliss had employed a formidable legal team, led by the eloquent Rufus Isaacs. And indeed, the early part of the trial went quite well for the anti-vivisectionists. Miss Lind-af-Hageby and Leisa Schartau gave their evidence clearly and without contradictions, whereas the University College scientists were soon in difficulties. Professor Ernest Starling admitted that he had operated on the Brown Dog on 3 December 1902, tying one of the animal's two pancreatic ducts. The dog recovered and was quite well when again taken to the theatre on 2 February 1903. Starling once more opened the dog's abdomen to inspect the pancreas, before clamping the wound with forceps and handing the dog over to Bayliss for use in an experiment to determine whether the pressure at which saliva was excreted was higher than the blood pressure. Through another incision, Bayliss tried to stimulate the nerves of the salivary glands, but without success. After thirty minutes of futile probing, the dog was taken away by the laboratory assistant Charles Scuffle, who testified, on oath, that he had killed the dog with chloroform. But when called, research student Henry Dale testified that it was in fact he who had put an end to the Brown Dog's sufferings, by stabbing it through the heart, before taking the pancreas for microscopic examination. There was delight among Coleridge's supporters when the scientists contradicted each other, and even the pro-Bayliss *Lancet* had to admit that Starling had technically infringed the Cruelty to Animals Act.

But as the trial went on, Rufus Isaacs put his opponents under pressure. He reminded the jury that in the present case, it was the activities of Bayliss that were under scrutiny, not those of Starling. Isaacs went on to call two male and three female medical students, who all testified that the dog had not struggled, and that the anaesthesia appeared to be working well; in fact, another witness later added that the reason the salivary glands could not be stimulated was probably that the dog had been put under too deeply. The reason the Brown Dog's paws had been twitching had been canine chorea, involuntary jerking movements brought on by the anaesthesia.

Under cross-examination, the blustering Coleridge cut a sorry figure: he admitted that he had trusted Miss Lind-af-Hageby and Leisa Schartau implicitly, neither contacting Bayliss prior to his libellous lecture, nor making any other exertion to make sure his two friends were telling the truth. Successfully playing on the jury's xenophobia and sex prejudices, Isaacs went on to emphasize the youth and foreign birth of the two key witnesses, and their lack of medical knowledge; surely, Miss Lind-af-Hageby must be the most ignorant person that ever entered a lecture room for medical students! The judge, Lord Alverstone, tried his best to be even-handed when summing up, apart from condemning *The Shambles of Science* as a 'hysterical' book. Still, it took less than half an hour for the jury to unanimously find Coleridge guilty; he was fined £2,000, with £3,000 costs.[7]

Several newspapers took the side of the anti-vivisectionists, the radical *Daily News* prominent among them. After this influential paper had published an appeal, its Brown Dog Subscription Fund soon contained £5,700. Thus Coleridge got off without paying a penny in damages, and he had another £700 for his movement's fighting funds. Indeed, the much-publicized trial had created the best publicity the anti-vivisectionists could ever have dreamt of; after reading about the sad fate of the Brown Dog, many people joined up as members, or made donations. In spite of his humiliation at the hands of Rufus Isaacs, Coleridge's position as leader was stronger than ever.

Miss Lind-af-Hageby, who had decided to remain in London permanently, also became a minor celebrity. In spite of her youth and foreign birth, her wealth, energy and enthusiasm ensured that she was catapulted into becoming the country's leading female anti-vivisectionist. After the squeamish Coleridge had objected to her use of horrid drawings of fettered, terrified dogs awaiting the vivisector's knife, she founded her own

'Animal Defence and Anti-Vivisection Society' and edited the *Anti-Vivisection Review*. She rented a shop in Piccadilly and filled the window with such alarmist propaganda that many people were outraged and appalled. Still, being young and quite attractive, and a talented public speaker, 'Vivisection's Fairest Foe' toured the country to spread the word not only about the horrors of experimentation on animals, but also about other subjects on which she held equally strong views. She was a feminist, a suffragette, a proponent of rational female dress, a spiritualist and an anti-vaccinationist. As a leading member of the London Society for the Prevention of Premature Burials, she harangued her audiences with horrid tales of scratched coffin lids, entombed skeletons found in strange, contorted positions, and prematurely buried women giving birth to children inside their coffins.

The London anti-vivisectionists were determined that the Brown Dog should not be forgotten. With Miss Lind-af-Hageby's approval, wealthy do-gooder Miss Louisa Woodward commissioned the sculptor Joseph Whitehead to make a bronze statue of the Dog. They planned to mount it on a granite drinking fountain with troughs for both humans and animals, just like the monument to Greyfriars Bobby in Edinburgh. The two ladies were very pleased when they saw Whitehead's effort: the handsome, dignified-looking Brown Dog sat upright with his head held high, looking almost defiantly at his human tormentors. They supplied an inflammatory inscription for the drinking fountain:

121. The statue of the Brown Dog, from *Animal World*, November 1906.

In memory of the brown terrier dog done to death in the laboratories of University College in February 1903, after having endured vivisection extending over two months and having been handed over from one vivisector to another until death came to his release. Also in memory of the 232 dogs vivisected at the same place during the year 1902. Men and women of England, how long shall these things be?

In the early 1900s, the slum-ridden Battersea had a reputation as London's most progressive borough. Its political leader, the socialist John Burns, became one of the earliest Labour MPs. Battersea was not just known for its radicalism, but also for its pioneer Dog's Home, and its General Hospital, known as the 'Anti-Vivi' because it pledged neither to use animal experimentation, nor to employ any vivisector on its staff. Clearly, the anti-establishment Battersea municipal leaders were kindred spirits to Miss Lind-af-Hageby and her friends; they willingly accepted the drinking fountain, which was to be set up in Latchmere Park in September 1906.[8] There were angry murmurations from the direction of University College, since the inscription on the Brown Dog drinking fountain certainly stretched the truth quite a bit, although it was not libellous. The medical press, which had hoped to have heard the last of the Brown Dog, was at its most irate.[9] The pro-vivisectionist Dr Stephen Paget thought the statue and its inscription 'not much better than an indecent exhibition, obscene picture, or blasphemous oratory'; Sir William Osler considered it 'a disgraceful insult to a great teaching body and the whole profession'. The *Lancet* reminded its readers that the Brown Dog represented 'a lie which received condign punishment from a British Jury'; the *British Medical Journal* quoted Pope on another monument: 'Where London's column pointing at the skies, / Like a tall bully, lift the head, and lies!'

After such hostile remarks from the medical press, there was relief from Miss Woodward and her Battersea friends when the unveiling ceremony went off without a hitch. They knew that the University College medical luminaries were very much opposed to the 'libellous' statue of the Brown Dog, and feared that the London medical students, who were a force to be reckoned with in those days, would steal or deface the statue. These students had evolved somewhat since the times of Dickens's Bob Sawyer, but not very much: they were still rowdy, beer-swigging extroverts, known for their strong mob mentality. Their generally misogynist and reactionary views included a strong support for vivisection. Unlike the snobbish Oxford and Cambridge men, many of these London students originated from the middle classes, and were proud to be considered 'not quite gentlemen'. They were known for their 'rags' where mobs of students made themselves obnoxious to the general public, through letting off firecrackers or stink bombs, or burning the effigies of people they had taken a dislike to. There was a tradition for the police not to interfere with these shenanigans, partly since the 'Varsity Students' Rags' were considered an old London tradition, and partly because a force of several hundred students was difficult to control.

At the time, a certain William Howard Lister was active as a medical student at the University College. In late 1907, he wanted to invade Battersea and destroy the statue of the Brown Dog. His loud-mouthed, beer-swigging friends wanted to go there straight away, but Lister had read in the newspapers that an electrical alarm had been installed to protect the statue, and that Battersea workers and plain-clothes police officers were guarding it. 'Let us get a strong troop of chaps together, get some crowbars and sledgehammers, and wait until there is a proper pea-souper of a fog,' he advised. On 20 November, when Lister thought the weather conditions were just about right, he spread the word that the troops were to gather in Tottenham Court Road. He was surprised and dismayed when it turned out that only six other students were present, but after waiting for a while, they took the bus to Battersea to see what could be accomplished. When the anti-Brown Dog commando arrived, the fog was slowly lifting, but they forged ahead nevertheless. Entering Latchmere Park, Lister felt a thrill when he was finally face to face with the Brown Dog: 'There it stood before us, this famous lie about which so much had been said and planned!'[10] A student named McGillicuddy sneaked up to the statue and used his crowbar to wrench at the front legs. They were tougher than he thought, but eventually they were beginning to bend, when suddenly a shout of warning went up from some person, and the entire troop of students ran away in panic.

After having gathered their thoughts, Lister and his Brown Doggers returned to the scene of the crime, to determine whether the electrical warning system was operational. To his horror, he saw a crowd of students talking volubly nearby. The reason they had been too late to join his own party was obvious: they had been drinking at some public house. Before Lister could warn them, a student named Jones ran up to the Brown Dog and dealt it a mighty blow with a sledgehammer. He was aiming another when two plain-clothes policemen jumped out of the bushes and seized hold of him. There was a half-hearted shout of 'To the rescue!' but the drunken students did not feel up to fight the police. Lister and eight others went to Battersea police station to bail Jones out, but this proved their undoing; they were themselves arrested, and put before the magistrate Mr Paul Taylor at the South Western Police Court the following morning. Here, all ten Brown Doggers were harshly spoken to, and fined £5 each plus ten shillings for the minimal damage done to the statue; if any medical student would appear before Mr Taylor on a similar charge, he would be sent to prison for two months, with hard labour.[11]

There was widespread outrage in London's medical student world after this dismal debacle. Not only had the Brown Dog survived well-nigh unscathed, but ten of their own colleagues had been arrested by the police, and heavily fined. It was considered a particular disgrace that ten medical students had been captured by just two police constables. Old doctors wrote to the newspapers to lament the degeneration of the Anglo-Saxon race; in their day, *two* medical students had been more than a match for *ten* policemen! The assertion of the 'beak' Paul Taylor that the Brown Dog monument was perfectly legitimate was criticized not just in the student newspapers, but in the *British Medical Journal* as well, and the harsh Battersea magistrate became a marked man among the London medical students.

On 22 November, the Brown Doggers were ready to strike back. After reinforcements from Charing Cross, Guy's, King's College, London and Middlesex hospitals had arrived at University College, Lister harangued his troops with a short speech, ending with the limerick,

> There was an old beak named Paul,
> Who thought he could threaten us all,
>   But the little Brown Dog
>   Will be lost in the fog,
> Fifty-five pounds will pay for it all!

Without further ado, the entire mob of students, more than a thousand strong, made its way down Tottenham Court Road. A life-sized effigy of Paul Taylor was unveiled and put at the head of the procession: it was followed by a large effigy of the Brown Dog, dangling from a pole. As the Brown Doggers went through Oxford Street and Leicester Square, they were singing 'Ha ha ha! Hee hee hee! Little Brown Dog don't we hate thee!' and 'Let's hang Paul Taylor on a sour apple tree as we go marching along!' They rubbed brown toy dogs, some of them daubed with soot, into the faces of respectable passers-by. The police tried to stop the rioters at Trafalgar Square, but several hundred Doggers broke through and ran at full speed through Chandos Street.

The procession re-formed in the Strand, completely stopping the traffic, and made its way to King's College, the students behaving as obnoxiously as ever. They were singing a deplorable ditty specially composed for the occasion, to the tune of the 'Old Brown Jug':

122. The Brown Doggers on the charge!

> As we go walking after dark,
> We turn our steps to Latchmere Park,
> And there we see, to our surprise,
> A little Brown Dog that stands and lies!

> If we had a dog that told such fibs
> We'd ply a whip about his ribs,
> To tan him well we would not fail
> For carrying such a monstrous tale!

> Little Brown Dogs may sit and beg
> But they must not pull the public's leg,
> And if put-up stories shock the town,
> The authorities ought to pull them down!

At King's College, the effigy of Mr Taylor was set alight, but since it did not burn very well, it was dumped into Thames amid boos and catcalls. Since the anti-Brown Dog protest march was considered just another students' rag, the police presence was woefully insufficient. Feeling very pleased with the day's proceedings, all the Brown Doggers made it home safely. The medical journals expressed themselves with satisfaction that the students had come good, but the anti-vivisection newspapers were outraged. Not only were the students coarse and ungentlemanly, but openly disrespectful to the poor Brown Dog who had given his life for science. Not unreasonably, the *Daily Graphic* declared that the demonstration had been about as stupid and in about as bad taste as could possibly be conceived, whereas the *Birmingham Daily Mail* said that the students' latest escapade would earn them the reprobation of all good citizens.

There was some further horseplay in the days that followed, one incident involving three drunken students in Leicester Square shouting and yahooing, and knocking people on the head with a stuffed dog. But the budding strategist William Howard Lister had bigger plans than such minor hooliganism. He had cards distributed that stated another anti-Brown Dog protest march was planned for 10 December, when London would be full of students due to the annual Oxford versus Cambridge rugby match. The Brown Doggers would gather at Queen's Club, where the match was played, in the hope of picking up reinforcements from kindred spirits among the spectators. The main force would then march to Trafalgar Square, drawing the attention of the police, but at the same time, a smaller detachment would cross the river, steal the Brown Dog, and throw it into the Thames.

But Lister's master plan had several drawbacks. Firstly, it was not wise of him to advertise his intentions beforehand, in the *Daily Mirror* and other popular newspapers; after all, his great success on 22 November had mainly been due to the element of surprise. Nor were the snobbish Oxbridge undergraduates particularly eager to join their rowdy metropolitan counterparts; when the Doggers congregated outside the Baron's Court underground station, their number was just 250. And many of them were already

123. A newspaper photograph of an anti-vivisection rally.

quite inebriated from visiting the pubs near Queen's Club. Still, Lister had high hopes that his strategy would work, since he knew that large gangs of students from Guy's and Charing Cross hospitals were already at large in central London, keeping the police busy. Accordingly, 150 Doggers marched off to join them at Trafalgar Square, shouting and making use of their rattles, and holding their stuffed brown dogs aloft. A hundred others sneaked off towards Battersea, to deal with the Brown Dog once and for all.

Marching through Kensington on their way to Trafalgar Square, the Brown Doggers picked up new recruits along the way, some of them fellow medical students, others drunks and hooligans eager to have a scrap with the police. As they walked past St George's Hospital, the police were becoming seriously worried about this large and disorderly mob. They decided to try and scatter the Doggers, but the agile and resourceful students managed to dodge them, some boarding buses to travel to Trafalgar Square in style.

The sizeable Guy's Hospital contingent was the first to break through the thin police cordon and reach Trafalgar Square; the other Doggers followed in several waves until a mob of 400 excited youngsters were gathered under Nelson's column, where the police again tried to contain them. When the student leaders tried to climb the pedestal of the column to harangue their troops, the police pulled them down. This angered the Brown Doggers, and soon there was a pitched battle going on all over Trafalgar Square. Once a policeman was down, the students wrenched his helmet off his head, for use as a trophy. The *Daily Mirror* correspondent, who was watching from a safe distance, was reminded of the riots of the great dock strike.

The students lashed out with their fists, and used their high poles as lances, but the exasperated policemen repaid them with interest, using their formidable truncheons with good effect. At one stage, it looked like if the Doggers would overwhelm the police, but showing characteristic resilience, the tough London bobbies kept them at bay. When a student was arrested, a large troop of Doggers followed him to the Cannon Row police station, to clamour for his release. This left the main mob in Trafalgar Square depleted in numbers. When mounted police made a charge to relieve their colleagues on foot, there was some serious fighting and disorder, with several down on either side, before the Doggers retreated. Writing many years later, one of the participants described the Trafalgar Square riots as 'a terrifying affair' from which 'many were lucky to escape without injury'.[12]

After the 'Battle of Trafalgar Square', the more responsible of the Doggers went home, but a large contingent of drunken students infested the West End pubs, theatres and music halls, disturbing the shows with further hooliganism. After midnight, a force of 120 Brown Doggers reassembled at Leicester Square. When they attempted to march to Trafalgar Square, they were met by a very strong force of police; after the ugly scenes earlier in the evening, not less than 300 extra constables had been called in. There were two further arrests when the police again scattered the Doggers, this time for good.

In the meantime, William Lister and his anti-Brown Dog commando had taken up a position outside Latchmere Park. After scouts had reported that the grounds appeared unprotected, he divided his Doggers into two columns and ordered 'Charge!' But this time, the police had come well prepared, alerted by the imprudent Lister's advertisements: the Doggers were flabbergasted to see police constables jumping out from hedges and sheds. Although one student managed to break through the cordon and come close to the Brown Dog, Lister's next command appears to have been 'Run away!' His troops scattered all over Battersea, where the local workers, who had taken exception to the Doggers invading their territory, jeered them and pelted them with mud. When a drunken student fell off a bus and injured himself, the locals shouted 'That's the Brown Dog's revenge!'

Although no arrests had been made at Battersea, a plentiful troop of Brown Doggers appeared before the Bow Street magistrates' court for their part in the Trafalgar Square riots. Two of them were fined £3 each for assaulting the police; six others escaped with a fine of forty shillings each. Several who had been arrested on minor charges, such as barking like a dog or behaving disorderly, were discharged altogether by the benign magistrate. Even some of the mainstream newspapers, who had had enough of the Doggers turning central London into a battleground, contrasted these very lenient fines to what could have been expected had the rioters been working men. The medical journals defended the students, who had done right to get rid of the 'lying' Brown Dog memorial; in spite of their 'high spirits', they had really done nothing wrong. The anti-vivisectionists deplored the violence and vulgarity of it all, although conceding that the obnoxious students provided the best possible propaganda for their movement.

124. A caricature of the
Brown Dog statue, with
a gang of sinister-looking
Doggers in the background.

As the prime mover among the radical anti-vivisectionists, Miss Lind-af-Hageby had accepted an invitation to speak before the earnest ladies of the Ealing & Acton Anti-vivisection Society on 21 December, the evening after the Trafalgar Square riots. When the meeting started at 8 p.m., the organisers were alarmed to find that more than two hundred Brown Doggers had occupied the entire left side of the hall, making use of their trumpets and rattles. Some timid old ladies were put to headlong flight when the first firecrackers and stink bombs went off, but Vivisection's Fairest Foe did not budge in the slightest, even when the obnoxious Doggers blew her kisses and 'made use of the full gamut of hospital slang'. She lambasted them for their lack of compassion and their vulgar brutality, until the noise of their rattles was quite deafening. When another string of firecrackers had the timid Ealing ladies running for their lives, the 'Valkyrie of Anti-Vivisection' quietly and dignifiedly sat down to await developments.

Looking daggers at the obnoxious students, Miss Lind-af-Hageby was treated to several renditions of 'Ha ha ha! Hee hee hee!' and all three verses of the 'Brown Dog Song'. A party of Battersea workers, who had been employed to steward the meeting, tried to evict the students, but the Doggers resisted them vigorously, lashing out with their fists and walking sticks. Only when the police arrived was it possible to scatter the Doggers, minus one of their number who was arrested for head-butting one of the constables. Pursued by the police, the Doggers swiftly retreated towards Shepherd's

125. An anti-vivisection
meeting disrupted by
raucous Brown Doggers.

Bush, scattering road signs and roadworks equipment as they went. They moved with such speed that the panting constables decided to board an electric tram to be able to keep up with them. For once making use of their supposed intellectual superiority, the canny students saw this coming; they suddenly doubled back as the helpless police shot by in their vehicle. The Doggers made it all the way to Shepherd's Bush Green, where they dispersed into the underground railway entrances.

Never one to avoid a fight, the plucky Miss Lind-af-Hageby was ready to speak again five days later, on the controversial subject of 'Vivisection and Medical Students', at Caxton Hall near Parliament Square. To prevent a repeat of the Ealing & Acton fiasco, it was an all-ticket affair, but it turned out to be hard to keep a good Brown Dogger down; when Vivisection's Fairest Foe began her speech, there were at least fifty students in the audience, ready for mischief. In her usual uncompromising language, the Valkyrie of Anti-Vivisection treated them to a severe tongue-lashing: through their disgraceful insults to the Brown Dog, they had descended into brutality. The Doggers made use of their rattles, stink bombs were discharged, and a mob of students who had climbed onto the roof from a nearby hotel began banging the windows and ventilation pipes. Drawing herself up to her full height, like the heroine of a Victorian novel, Miss Lind-af-Hageby exclaimed, 'Be silent, you cads! Who will respect such ruffians as yourselves when you have taken your degrees, put up your brass plates, and assumed your bedside manners?'

The only answer to this heated tirade was another volley of fireworks, before a door was broken through at the back of the platform; amid loud cheers, another dozen students tumbled into the meeting hall. The Battersea roughs were again called into action as stewards; this time they held the numerical superiority, and went into action with a hearty goodwill. Blows and kicks were exchanged, before the outnumbered Doggers made for the doors. Singing their deplorable ditties, they tried to re-form at Trafalgar Square, but the police were wise to this trick and forced them to disperse.[13]

Two days after the Trafalgar Square disturbances, the Commissioner of Police suggested to the Mayor of Battersea that the public cost of protecting the Brown Dog monument was becoming quite prohibitive. Surely, the Battersea council itself should defray the £700 annual cost of watching the Dog all around the clock. The local worthies, who did not at all like the sound of this suggestion, debated for several months; after Miss Lind-af-Hageby and Louisa Woodward had harangued them, they finally showed some bottle and decided that the monument should remain protected at all costs. In early 1908, there was an uneasy truce between the anti-vivisectionists and the Brown Doggers. Perhaps the University College authorities had spoken to their students, reminding them that their recent hooliganism had enjoyed but counter-productive results. On the other side, Stephen Coleridge was still hoping for a peaceful solution; perhaps he, too, had been reminded by some very high authority that further rash and inflammatory speeches were not needed in the present situation.

Dr Stephen Paget, the secretary of the recently formed pro-vivisectionist Research Defence Society, suggested a compromise: the Brown Dog memorial should remain, but the inscription ought to be changed. Although his opinion of Paget was far from high, Coleridge agreed to hear his suggestion. But when he learnt that the new inscription should say that the dog had been 'happy and well' before the second set of experiments, Coleridge refused to accept it; describing a frightened, caged dog awaiting vivisection as 'happy' was simply not done. The radical element in his movement, who must have had misgivings that Coleridge would betray their aims, rejoiced in his show of determination.[14]

There was further good news for the Brown Dog's supporters when it turned out that the Prime Minister's legal advisers had made a most unusual recommendation about the controversial Latchmere Park drinking fountain. There were some monuments that some people liked and others detested, they pontificated; the Westminster statue of Oliver Cromwell was one, the Brown Dog of Battersea another. Such monuments that a minority of people wanted to deface, although they were not libellous, should rightly enjoy police protection. Whatever the Prime Minister himself thought of the Brown Dog and its supporters, he followed this advice.

After this unexpected reprieve, the Brown Dog enjoyed a peaceful and quiet existence for many months, looking enigmatically at the Battersea locals from the top of the drinking fountain, just like his distinguished Edinburgh colleague, Greyfriars Bobby. The local workers' families were proud of their Brown Dog; not only were many of them opponents of vivisection, but the Dog had become something of a local hero after the riots back in 1907. But once more, dark clouds were gathering that would seriously imperil the Brown Dog monument. The maverick politician John Burns, once the hero of the Battersea socialists, had truckled to the Liberals and accepted a cabinet post in their government. This led to widespread political unrest in Battersea: could the radicals really be trusted at all, when their leader had betrayed those who had voted for him? In November 1909, after the Battersea radicals had been severely routed in the municipal elections, their conservative successors immediately pounced on some of their faddist excesses, like the Brown Dog monument.

On 8 November 1909, a medical student named Arthur Allan sidled up to the police constable guarding the Brown Dog. He offered a bribe of £15 for the constable to turn his back while the monument was defaced, but the staunch London bobby took Allan into custody instead. Very conveniently, after such a long period of uneasy truce, this incident happened just in time to remind the new Battersea local government that the Brown Dog was still a liability. They again began deliberating: should the drinking fountain remain, should the inscription be changed, or should the Brown Dog be returned to Miss Woodward, the original donor? Miss Lind-af-Hageby and her friends found it intolerable for Battersea to lose its Brown Dog; would there have been a similar outcry, she asked, if the anti-vaccinationists had tried to steal the statue of Edward Jenner from Kensington Gardens? But in a meeting on 9 March 1910, the craven politicians decided, with forty-two votes to just four, to remove the Brown Dog monument forthwith.

Before dawn the very next day, the borough surveyor and four Battersea council workers, protected by three inspectors and fifty policemen, went into Latchmere Park and removed the Brown Dog monument. In a carefully planned raid, the workmen disconnected the electric alarm, cut off the water supply to the drinking fountain, lifted the entire monument onto a lorry, and drove off. Since the Battersea politicians were worried what legal challenges Miss Lind-af-Hageby and her friends would instigate, the monument was not destroyed; in fact, the surveyor hid it in his bicycle shed back home. When the Battersea workers came to check on the still-famous monument later on 10 March, they were appalled to find only a slight unevenness in the centre of the Latchmere recreation grounds; the sign on a fence nearby said 'No Dogs'.

There was of course outrage among the anti-vivisectionists when the kidnapping of the Brown Dog became headline news in London. At large protest meetings in Hyde Park and Trafalgar Square, thousands demanded the Dog's reinstatement. When Louisa Woodward took the Battersea borough council to court, she lost and was left with considerable legal costs. In March 1911, the politicians voted to destroy the statue of the Brown Dog, and it was accordingly removed from the surveyor's shed, smashed to pieces with a sledgehammer, and melted down.[15]

So, what happened to the main players in the drama, after the statue of the Brown Dog had been disposed of? Stephen Coleridge, who remained chairman of the National Anti-Vivisection Society until his death in 1936, never seems to have been in any way blamed for the debacle of the original Brown Dog lawsuit back in 1903. Later historians have presumed that it had been his plan from the outset to try to win a propaganda victory, something that seems far from certain. Still, Coleridge became much respected among the anti-vivisectionists for his gentlemanly demeanour and the obvious sincerity of his views. It would appear that he made a valuable contribution to his cause, through keeping the extremists at bay although not alienating them, and leaving the anti-vivisection movement open to all sympathizers, without regard to their political opinions.

Not unexpectedly, the future career of the maverick Miss Lind-af-Hageby was rather more adventurous. Speaking in favour of vegetarianism, spiritualism, feminism and anti-vivisectionism, she remained a minor celebrity, throwing her weight about in the newspapers whenever she had half a chance. In public debates against Stephen Paget and other pro-vivisectionists, she ably held her own. In 1909, she organized the first International Anti-Vivisection and Animal Protection Conference in London. Later the same year, she toured the United States, courting controversy in various public debates. She took great exception to a jocular newspaper headline exclaiming 'Vivisection's Fairest Foe: Better a Hundred Babes Die than One Dog would Suffer!' She visited the Rockefeller Institute, where transplantation pioneer Dr Alexis Carrell became another of her hate objects: what purpose would it serve, she exclaimed, to transplant white legs onto black dogs, and vice versa? To an American journalist, she exclaimed, 'Bah! One would feel happy, I should imagine, hobbling about on a leg that once belonged to an electrocuted murderer!'[16]

In 1913, a certain Dr Saleeby took exception to the horror propaganda spread by Miss Lind-af-Hageby's Piccadilly anti-vivisection shop. When he called her 'a systematic liar' in a newspaper article, she sued for libel and represented herself in court. Dubbed the 'Modern Portia' by the newspapers, she treated the court to speeches lasting several days. The *Daily Express* and other mainstream papers made fun of her filibustering with jocular headlines like '13 Hours Not Out' and 'Latest Score: 37 Hours' but more sympathetic papers recognized that she was in fact a quite talented advocate. The *Lancet* was outraged by her audacity in denying such worthies as Harvey, Pasteur and Koch any worthwhile contribution to medical science.[17] All her advocacy was in vain, however, and she was left with considerable legal costs, which the *Daily News* helped her to recoup.

Although Miss Lind-af-Hageby now held the unenviable position of being one of the few people in Britain who had it in black and white that she was a systematic liar, she returned to New York in late 1913. In a lecture, she denied the existence of immunity and the contagion theory of disease; vaccination was a both unnatural and dangerous practice, leading to 'physical degeneration'. The reason smallpox had been eradicated was not inoculation, but increase in cleanliness and sanitation. The American journalists were flabbergasted by this farrago of nonsense. Later, when attending an anti-vivisection conference in Washington, she boldly proclaimed that if it was conceded that a human idiot had a soul, there was no reason why an intelligent dog should be without one. This time, a wisecracking journalist was up to the task: his article ridiculing the dotty lady had the headline 'Miss Lind-af-Hageby says kippered herrings have souls, and warns the American people not to eat them, in case the herrings' souls come back to haunt them!' When the earnest lady objected to being so blatantly misquoted, her indignant 'I did not say that!' was met by the standard American journalist's retort 'No, but we wrote it!' Speaking to another, more sympathetic newsman, Miss Lind-af-Hageby was most indignant about these shenanigans, expressing herself with characteristically bluntness about the shortcomings of the American newspaper press.[18]

In the First World War, Miss Lind-af-Hageby earned several French decorations for supporting children's homes and sanatoria for sick war horses. But in the 1920s, her movement went into a slow decline, overtaken by the progress of medical science and the influence of the pharmaceutical industry. She lived in St Edmunds Terrace near Regent's Park, together with her old friend Leisa Schartau and two younger Swedish ladies who acted as her secretaries. She also bought a property in Switzerland, where she kept her half-bred St Bernard dog 'Barry'. The dotty lady tried to convince her dog to embrace vegetarianism, initially with good success, since Barry seemed to thrive on his new diet. The experiment continued until an angry farmer came to complain that Barry had just pulled down and eaten one of his sheep!

Together with her great friend the Duchess of Hamilton, Miss Lind-af-Hageby founded the International Bureau for the Protection of Animals in Geneva. The two ladies went to Italy to see first the Pope and then Benito Mussolini; they were proud to say that *Il Duce* turned out to be a kindred spirit, introducing stern anti-vivisection legislation in Italy. Miss Lind-af-Hageby also spoke approvingly of that great friend of animals, Adolf Hitler, who had taken similar measures in Germany. In August 1938, after she had been invited to Frankfurt-am-Main by the *Reichsführer* of German *Tierschütz*, she pointed out the giant strides made by Nazi Germany in the field of animal protection. Miss Lind-af-Hageby came very close to finding out the truth about Hitler's Germany the hard way, when her London house was blown up during the London Blitz, but fortunately she was not at home at the time.[19] Together with the Duchess, she set up a large animal sanctuary at Ferne, for pets left behind when their owners joined the armed forces, and various stray and orphaned beasts of every description. She died in December 1963, at the age of eighty-five, leaving nearly £100,000.

After winning the Brown Dog libel suit, William Bayliss donated the money to the University College, for use in supplying animals for research; this fund is still in use today. For two more decades, Bayliss continued his very distinguished career, becoming Professor of General Physiology in 1912. His pioneer work in endocrinology, and his discovery of secretin, gained him great international acclaim, as did his landmark studies of the innervation of the bowels, and the vasomotor reflexes. On a more sinister note, Bayliss was again in trouble in the 1920s, after his laboratory had been supplied with stolen dogs for vivisection; the matter was quietly hushed up, the dog thieves being used as scapegoats.[20] When knighted in 1922, the unworldly Bayliss at first refused the invitation to Buckingham Palace, since he wanted to attend a meeting at the Physiological Society instead. His friend and colleague Ernest Starling, who had performed the first operation on the Brown Dog, gained much distinction as a pioneer of cardiac physiology. Henry Dale, who stabbed the Brown Dog to death, also enjoyed a distinguished scientific career. He was knighted in 1932, and awarded the Nobel Prize in 1934 for his groundbreaking discovery of the role of acetylcholine in chemical neurotransmission. Sir Henry Dale lived on until 1968, outlasting nearly every other player in the Brown Dog drama.[21]

William Howard Lister, the bungling leader of the Brown Doggers, eventually qualified as a doctor in 1913. He took an interest in military medicine and became an officer in the Royal Army Medical Corps. In the First World War, Lister displayed exceptional skills and bravery in the trenches, leading his stretcher bearers under constant fire. He was awarded the Military Cross with two bars for gallantry in the field, and later also the Distinguished Service Order. Captain William Howard Lister was killed by a mortar bomb in 1918, aged just thirty-one.[22]

After the original Brown Dog had been destroyed, there were several appeals from the anti-vivisectionists to erect another memorial, but fearing renewed rioting, the Battersea borough council was unenthusiastic. It would take until 1985, during the final throes of the left-wing Greater London Council, for the anti-vivisectionists to raise funds for a replacement statue of the Brown Dog, and obtain permission to erect it in Battersea Park. Made by the sculptor Nicola Hicks, it was allegedly modelled on the artist's own dog.

Unlike its predecessor, the new Brown Dog does not sit proud and upright, but looks quite jolly and playful, as though interacting with some unseen human friend. There was but scattered newspaper publicity when the new Brown Dog was unveiled in December 1985. The *British Medical Journal* was not amused by the fact that the original inscription had been retained, and amended with an appeal that animal experimentation should have no place in a civilised society: the authority responsible for Battersea Park ought to 'remove this degrading, libellous, and offensive memorial'. Nobody bothered much about the new Brown Dog, however; it is still there, unmolested and well-nigh forgotten, on a little-used garden path.[23]

In early Victorian times, there was little debate about vivisection; apart from a few enthusiasts, nobody wanted to know. But from the 1860s onwards, there was growing opposition to painful experiments being performed on cats, dogs and primates. This was due to a growth of empathy towards pet animals, partially fuelled by the sentimental notions of canine fidelity that were current at the time, as well as by the illicit supply of stolen pet dogs to the physiology laboratories. By the end of the century, there was a hard core of radical anti-vivisectionists, who openly opposed modern medicine, and the social and professional power of doctors. No longer content with (rightly) claiming that the vivisection of dogs in medical experimentation was morally corrupt, they went on to (wrongly) propose that vivisection was entirely worthless and that it had done nothing to promote knowledge of human physiology. Their pet hate object was the Bad Doctor, the arrogant proponent of vivisection, hell-bent on torturing animals, and propagating the new-fangled ideas of bacteria and vaccines, when it was really clean air and a vegetarian diet that promoted human health.

The Brown Dog riots can be viewed as the inevitable clash between the medical establishment and its liberal interpretation of the Cruelty to Animals Act, and the increasing opposition to vivisection among all classes of society, fuelled by the horror propaganda distributed by the radical phalanx of the movement. This also explains the extreme hostility of the debate. Backed up by the left-wing newspapers, Miss Lind-af-Hageby blasted some of the finest scientists in the land as sadistic torturers of animals. On the other side, the London medical establishment was hell-bent on removing the hated Brown Dog, by fair means or foul. But since that time, the medical profession has changed very much, also with regard to its awareness of animal rights. Although there are still old London doctors who treasure a policeman's helmet as a relic of their rowdy student days, the present-day medical students are emphatic young women and men, averse to cruel experiments being performed on dogs, and wholly incapable of turning Trafalgar Square into a battleground. The Brown Dog riots were the last hurrah of the old-fashioned hooligan medical student.

Not the least curious aspect of the original Coleridge *v.* Bayliss libel trial is the strong suspicion that both parties lied in court. The University College contingent clearly got their stories mixed up: it was not the assistant Scuffle who had killed the Brown Dog, but the future Sir Henry Dale. Similarly, it seems likely that Miss Lind-af-Hageby and Leisa Schartau were far from truthful when they claimed that the Brown Dog had not been properly anaesthetized; surely, the other students would have reacted to such glaring incompetence, if this had really been the case. The jury is still out on whether the two ladies had been genuinely convinced the Dog had been conscious, or whether they had deliberately lied in court, reasoning that the end justified the means. As the reader will be aware, that paradigm has been taken to its logical extreme by the present-day radical animal rights activists, using terror tactics to intimidate those involved with the notorious Huntington Life Sciences. Whereas Miss Lind-af-Hageby sincerely believed that empathy for animals would ultimately prevail, her latter-day radical followers have lost their confidence in a fair society.

Another important aspect of the trial is that Coleridge had taken on the wrong men. Bayliss and Starling were among the leading scientists of their generation, and a vast number of people, dogs and other animals have directly or indirectly benefited from their groundbreaking research. Although the moralist might still object to their wholesale vivisection of dogs, the realist must admit that with the limitations of the surgical techniques of their time, they had no other choice but to use large carnivorous mammals in their research. Present-day scientists do not share the benefit of that excuse, and it is to be hoped that in a not too distant future, the phasing out of vivisection of dogs in biomedical research will be completed.

DOG CEMETERIES,
DOG GHOSTS & SOME LAST WORDS

The annals of eating dog meat reach far back into time. The Greeks and Romans occasionally ate puppies and young dogs. Hippocrates considered dog meat particularly light and wholesome food. Nor did the early Christians spurn dog meat. Well into the seventeenth century, puppy soup was considered a delicacy. 'Bow-wow sauce', a quaint Gloucestershire specialty, is today served with roast beef, but the original version involved a litter of puppies baked in a pie. In rural parts of Switzerland, there was (and perhaps still is) a tradition of making sausages from cured dog meat. With time, the eating of dog meat declined in the Western world: firstly, it did not taste very good, and secondly, people found it distasteful to eat the meat of a pet animal. During the siege of Paris in 1870, these finer feelings had to be set aside due to extreme hunger and privations: there were market stalls for dog, cat and rat meat. The British war correspondent Henry Labouchère did not care much for donkey steaks, or for salami made from rat meat, but a dish of roast spaniel met with his full approval, since it tasted something like lamb.[1]

In modern Britain, the eating of dogs is not just prohibited, but culturally taboo. In a recent newspaper article, the celebrated TV chef Hugh Fearnley-Whittingstall described how he had just selected one of his piglets for early slaughter. He also had a litter of puppies at the same time, and decided to make a 'cultural experiment', contrasting the pampered lives of pet dogs with the short and sanguinary existence of pigs bred for slaughter. Fearnley-Whittingstall joked that perhaps his free-range, outdoor-reared, organic puppy would be oven ready just in time for Christmas.[2] Had he tried this experiment live on TV, River Cottage would have been at serious risk of being razed to the ground by irate canophiles, however.

China and some other Asian countries have a long tradition of eating dog meat. The old Chinese had a whole cookery book full of recipes for boiled, stewed and roast dog, some of them dating back to the time of Confucius. In Hong Kong and Taiwan, the slaughter of dogs is prohibited, and in urban parts of China, dog-eating is sneered at by modern-minded people, but in the countryside, millions of dogs are slaughtered for food each year. The Koreans are also inveterate dog eaters, with an elaborate

126. Cat and dog meat for sale during the Paris Commune.

cuisine of dishes available. The eating of dog meat, which is believed to increase male virility, is considered a national symbol.[3] Not unreasonably, European and American humanitarians have objected to these practices. The lives of dogs bred for human consumption are unlikely to be particularly pleasant. The campaign against the eating of dog meat is not 'cultural imperialism', rather a rightful objection against a practice that is morally corrupt. Although I myself have eaten horse, reindeer, moose, bear, crocodile, kangaroo and squirrel, I have no intention of adding 'dog' to that list.

On an equally sinister note, there are many instances of human beings being eaten by dogs, either before or after death. Already in Victorian times, there were some instances of some elderly dog-owning miser expiring, and the body being eaten by the dogs. At regular intervals, this still happens today: the half-eaten remains of some friendless, reclusive wretch are found in some squalid flat, together with some half-starved dogs. In a recent case from Portugal, anatomical studies of bones found in the stomachs of the dogs, and genetic studies of their DNA content, could ascertain that the animals had eaten from the corpse of their dead master.[4] In Victorian Britain, there were some tragic instances of careless parents leaving babies unattended, only for the defenceless babes to be carried off and eaten by large dogs. This kind of thing still happens today in Africa and Australia. In the latter country, there have also been several instances of packs of feral dogs attacking and eating people. In 2009 and 2010, packs of dogs killed and ate a mentally disabled South Australian, and later also made a meal of another unfortunate tramp.[5]

Murderers have sometimes made use of pigs or minks (at mink-farms) to dispose of the dismembered bodies of their victims. There are also some instances of demented killers feeding dogs with parts of their victims, although this seems to have been motivated by perversion rather than constituting a deliberate plan to conceal their crimes. Still, a kennel full of young St Bernard dogs might be a valuable asset for the enterprising murderer, who could feed his hungry four-legged accomplices baskets full of offal, skin and meat, with some tasty bones to gnaw.

The eccentric politician Lord Avebury, a convert to Buddhism, caused some stir in the newspapers in 1987, when he declared that in his will, he had left his body to the Battersea Dogs' Home, for consumption by its four-legged inmates. Anything biodegradable should be recycled, the noble lord reasoned, and he felt sure the dogs would appreciate his nice gesture. The director of the dogs' home turned Lord Avebury down, however, saying that he ought to leave some money to buy food for the dogs instead. The London evening newspapers had a field day, with headlines like 'Pedigree chum! Make a dog's dinner of me, demands peer!' and 'Dinner is served! But peer cannot get into the doghouse!' When Lord Avebury had his photograph taken together with a grumpy-looking, elderly mongrel dog, he edified the journalist with some further words of wisdom.[6] If people followed his example and donated their dead bodies to the dogs, there would be no 'sterilization of land in our inner cities to provide graveyards'. But the great cemeteries of London would hardly be as sterile as the dismal housing estates of the 1960s and 1970s, commissioned by Lord Avebury and his fellow politicians.

The ancients sometimes showed praiseworthy zeal to honour their deceased favourite dogs. With their habitual fondness for preserving the bodies of their dead, the old Egyptians did not restrict this practice to human beings. When his favourite dog died in 2180 BC, the grieving Pharaoh ordered a fine sarcophagus made for the dog, detailing that much fine cloth, incense, and scented oils, should be used in the mummification process. Another ancient dog-lover, Alexander the Great, owned a large mastiff-like dog named 'Peritas'. When she died, Alexander led the funeral procession to the grave. He had a fine stone monument erected on the site, and ordered the locals to extol the dog's memory in annual ceremonies.

Since at least the eighteenth century, royal and noble personages had cemeteries for their beloved pets. The dog-loving Duchess of York, who kept a hundred pampered dogs at Oatlands Park, founded an elaborate dog cemetery within the grounds. The names of the dogs, and the dates of their deaths, were given on the headstones, which number sixty-three in all, one of them for our old friend Nelson, the handsome Newfoundland. Another dog, 'Jennie Gregory' lived to be twenty-six years old. Some of the headstones have verses, like that of 'Julia', who might have been a Great Dane:

> Here Julia rests, and here each day
>> Her mistress strews her grave with flowers,
> Mourning her loss whose frolic play,
>> Enlivened oft the lonesome hours.
> From Denmark did her race descend,
>> Beauteous her form, and mild her spirit,
> Companion gay, and faithful friend,
>> May ye who read this have half her merit.

In 1871, Queen Victoria visited Oatlands and expressed a wish that the dogs' tombstones should be restored, something that was duly carried out. Although Oatlands Park is today a fashionable hotel, the old dog cemetery still exists within its grounds.[7]

Queen Victoria had her own pet cemetery at Windsor Castle. Several horses and many dogs are buried there, some of them with elaborate tombs and bronze statues. There was also a small dog cemetery at Sandringham, for the pets of Edward, Prince of Wales, and his family. Among them were 'Jung', a Tibet dog given to the Prince in Nepal, and the equally exotic 'Beattie', a 'Siberian dog, for ten years the companion of H.R.H.'[8]

The Earls Spencer had their own dog cemetery on Dog Island at their Althorp estate, although the headstones were later removed to make way for the monument to Diana, Princess of Wales, who is also buried there. Lady de Grey's dog cemetery at Wrest Park, Bedfordshire, still exists. Lord Ystwyth had a private dog cemetery at Tanybwlch near Aberystwyth, where this Welsh peer put up a headstone for a very elderly dog, with the simple text 'Coronet, aged 30'. The Earls of Warrington had their dog cemetery at Dunham Abbey in Cheshire, and famous society hostess Lady Londonderry buried her dogs at Wynford Park, County Durham.[9]

In Victorian times, ordinary people were just as fond of their dogs as the wealthy princes and nobles. Whereas rural people could bury their dogs where they wanted, the only option open to middle-class urban dwellers was to throw out the remains of their departed canine friend in the rubbish, or deposit the dead dog in some river. In Paris, an average of 3,000 dead dogs were annually retrieved from the Seine; the relevant statistic for the Thames was unfortunately not recorded. Since the dogs were considered as family members, many people felt that neither of these alternatives was acceptable: the dog should have a proper burial.

In 1880, when the Duke of Cambridge was taking a stroll outside Hyde Park, his little dachshund Prince made a sudden dash into Bayswater Road, only to be run over and killed by a heavy vehicle. The grieving Duke carried the tiny corpse to Victoria Lodge nearby, where he asked the lodge-keeper to bury the dog in his garden, with an appropriate tombstone saying 'Poor Little Prince'. When another of the Duke's dogs died, it was buried in the same place. Since other upper-class people followed suit, the lodge-keeper Mr Winbridge soon had a profitable extra business as sexton to the dog cemetery. For a fee of £5, he acted as chaplain, and provided a headstone.

127. A drawing of the Hyde Park dog cemetery, from the *Westminster Budget* of 11 March 1898.

By 1893, not less than thirty-nine dogs had been buried in the Hyde Park dog cemetery.[10] Since Prince's tombstone was undated, the oldest date belonged to 'Cheri', a little Maltese terrier buried in April 1881. The stalwart Mr Winbridge still performed the burial ceremony, sometimes with a coffin, but more often with a canvas bag. The Hyde Park dog cemetery was reserved for the dogs of titled and well-to-do people. The inscriptions on the early headstones, like 'To my darling Flossie, Maudie's only love', 'The most intelligent, faithful, gentle, sweet tempered dog that ever lived: & adored by his devoted and sorrowing friend Sir H. Seton Gordon, Bart.', and the pathetic 'Balu, son of Fritz, poisoned by a cruel Swiss, Berne, 1899' leave no doubt as to the affection and sense of loss experienced by the dog owners. Some inscriptions, like

> Shall he whose name is love
> Deny our loving friends a home above?
> Nay, he who orders all things for the best
> In Paradise will surely give them rest,

clearly express a hope of future reunion in a Better Place. Reviving the old question whether animals have souls, these smug Victorian dog owners seem to have reasoned that although pests like cockroaches and houseflies lacked souls, a faithful dog might acquire one, ennobled by its close relationship with its human companions.

By 1929, the Hyde Park dog cemetery had 400 headstones: dogs, monkeys, rats and birds were buried there. Since it was nearly full, some of the dead animals had to be diverted to another, larger establishment in Molesworth, Huntington.[11] As time went by, the old dog cemetery in Hyde Park became almost entirely forgotten. It is not open to visitors, nor featured in any tourist guide, although it is still possible to glimpse the old headstones through the railings, just by the old lodge at Victoria Gate.

The aforementioned Molesworth dog cemetery remained open through the 1920s and 1930s, catering mainly to the upper classes of society: some of the graves were marked marble pedestals and fine statuary. One dog was embalmed after unexpectedly expiring during a visit to Italy, and shipped back to Molesworth for interment in a fine marble mausoleum with stained-glass windows. Today, evil times have overtaken the old cemetery, however, with long-term neglect resulting in theft and vandalism.[12]

On a happier note, another dilapidated dog cemetery in Ilford, Essex, was restored in 2007 using lottery money. Founded in 2007, it is the final resting place for some

128. The Hyde Park dog cemetery, from an old postcard.

129. The Hyde Park dog cemetery and the gate-keeper's lodge, from an old postcard.

130. The Molesworth dog cemetery.

distinguished war dogs, holders of the Victoria Cross for animals. The rescue dogs 'Peter' and 'Rip', who saved many lives through locating victims trapped under buildings destroyed in the London Blitz, are both buried here.

The main pet cemetery in France is the Cimetière des Chiens, situated in Asnières-sur-Seine, just north of Paris. In 1898, the Paris city government declared that the bodies of dead pet animals should not be taken out with the rubbish, or thrown into the Seine, but buried in hygienic graves at least 100 yards from the nearest house. The attorney Georges Harmois and the journalist Marguerite Durand thought it would be a good idea to found a cemetery for dogs and other domestic animals on the outskirts of Paris. Some riverfront land in Asnières-sur-Seine was purchased, and the Cimetière des Chiens was opened in 1899. Remaining more or less intact today, the cemetery is a most impressive sight, which canophile visitors to Paris should take good care not to miss. Over the years, not less than 40,000 animals have been buried there – not only dogs, but also cats, hamsters, mice and fish, a racehorse, a lion, and a monkey. The handsome Art Nouveau entrance to the Cimetière des Chiens, designed by Paris architect Eugène Petit, dates back to the opening of the cemetery in 1899.

The most prominent monument in the Cimetière des Chiens is that to the famous St Bernard Barry, who is depicted saving a child. The most famous dog interred there must surely be Rin Tin Tin the acting dog, whose tomb is regularly visited by American cinema buffs. Some of the other dogs are notable only for their famous owners, like Alexandre Dumas, the Princess Lobanof, and Princess Elizabeth of Romania. All dogs that are not dead and buried need to be kept on a short lead on the premises of the Cimetière des Chiens, since there is a plentiful population of cemetery cats, who like to sun themselves on the old tombs.[13]

In 1898, the *Westminster Budget* published a feature on dog cemeteries. It contrasted the well kept Hyde Park dog cemetery, and the quaint cemetery for military dogs at Edinburgh Castle, with a recent example of gross disrespect for deceased canines, emanating from Germany. An eccentric old Berliner named Vogel, known as Dog-Vogel for his great fondness for dogs, had purchased a plot of land near one of the great graveyards of Berlin, and turned it into a dog cemetery. Dogs belonging to Dog-Vogel and his friends were buried here, and also dogs that had saved a human life, or performed some other valorous act. Dog-Vogel employed a gravedigger who was also the keeper of the cemetery; he made sure that flowers were planted on the graves, and that tablets were erected to tell the tales of the dogs' heroism. A collie named 'Victor' was credited with saving six adults and nine children from drowning. After Dog-Vogel had died, his friends made sure the dog cemetery was well taken care of; they found it very appropriate that the dogs were buried just outside the great graveyard where their masters' bones would one day be laid to rest. But in 1898, some influential religious bigots found it distasteful to have a dog cemetery just outside one for human beings, and the place was levelled to the ground.[14]

Dog-Vogel's cemetery cannot have been the only one in Germany at the time, but these early German dog cemeteries still await their chronicler. There are several hints

131. The entrance to the Cimetière des Chiens in Paris.

132. The Cimetière des Chiens, from old postcards dated 1906 and 1907.

that dog cemeteries existed in that country already by the mid-1800s, but no solid evidence to that effect. In contrast, there is ample evidence that Sweden's first dog cemetery was founded already in the 1870s. August Blanche, a popular Swedish novelist and playwright, used to be very fond of his large black dog 'Nero'. After Blanche had died in late 1868, the dog was adopted by an artillery battery garrisoned at Djurgården just outside central Stockholm. When Nero himself expired, they buried him in Blanche's private gardens, with a headstone saying 'Nero, Blanche's Dog. Died in 1872'. But due to an urban development scheme in Stockholm, Blanche's house was pulled down and the garden used for the construction of a major road. The artillerymen moved Nero's remains and headstone to Kaknäs, several miles outside central Stockholm, where they rightly presumed the dog's bones would remain undisturbed by urban developers. Since Blanche had been such a fashionable author, other Swedes began burying their pets nearby. This was the origin of the well maintained Kaknäs animal cemetery, which is still open today.[15] Many dogs and cats are buried here, as well as some rabbits, parrots and tortoises, and a circus horse named Don Juan. When I visited this animal cemetery in June 2010, many of the graves were decorated with photos of the animals themselves, and also flowers, lighted candles, garden gnomes, plastic toadstools and other ornaments the former owners believed the departed animals would appreciate.

Dr Samuel Johnson was a well-known American veterinarian, and Professor of Veterinary Surgery at New York University. He was also a pioneer in the field of animal welfare, and a kindly, compassionate man. When, in 1898, a distraught woman came to see him, carrying a dead dog, he did not crack a joke about her consulting him a bit too late, but politely listened to what she had to say. It turned out that she wanted her dog to have a proper funeral, something that could not be accomplished legally in New York City, since it was prohibited to inter dogs in cemeteries intended for human beings. The kind doctor, who owned an estate in Hartsdale, Westchester County, allowed her to bury the dog in his apple orchard there. After the story had been published in a newspaper, many other New Yorkers contacted Dr Johnson asking to have their dead pets interred at Hartsdale.[16]

In 1905, when the Hartsdale animal cemetery was featured in the *New York Times*, hundreds of dogs had been buried there. It stretched out over three acres, and some of the monuments had cost hundreds of dollars. After the Hartsdale Pet Cemetery had been incorporated in 1914, business was booming. Some very wealthy and eccentric Americans arranged elaborate funerals for their dogs there.[17] The animals were sometimes buried wearing gold or silver collars, in satin-lined caskets with a crystal window in the lid. In stately processions, the coffin, covered with wreaths and flowers, was carried to the grave, as a choir sang and an organ played mournful tunes. The most expensive monument, an elaborate marble tomb, cost $25,000. The Hartsdale Pet Cemetery remains the oldest and most famous animal necropolis in the United States. It has expanded from Dr Johnson's humble apple orchard to cover nine acres of meadowland, planted with specimen trees and with large and elegant flowerbeds; there is a total of 60,000 headstones and monuments. On Memorial Day, it is visited by hundreds of mourners, who decorate the graves with wreaths and flowers.

After the success of the Hartsdale Pet Cemetery had demonstrated that such establishments could be financially profitable, animal cemeteries mushroomed all over the United States. In 1915, the rat-terrier 'Teddy Miller' had a particularly grand funeral at a Milwaukee dog cemetery, with a funeral procession of seven carriages, one of them full of floral tributes to the dog.[18] In the 1970s, Hartsdale was challenged by the fifty-acre Bubbling Well Pet Memorial Park at Napa Valley. Some of the present-day commercial animal cemeteries are downmarket affairs, with paper or plastic coffins, and rudimentary headstones with inane inscriptions like 'Beloved Zsa Zsa, God loaned us you' and 'Penny: She never knew she was a rabbit'.[19] For an extra fee, it can be made sure that a card saying 'Your little Woofy is thinking of you in heaven today, and wagging his tail' is punctiliously delivered on every anniversary. The more prestigious animal cemeteries offer a variety of religious services, with pastors of different persuasions ready to officiate; not infrequently, a white dove released at the moment of interment is to symbolize the soul of the deceased dog. Funeral technicians are employed to rearrange the stiff limbs of the dead dogs, to create an impression of calm repose, and to carefully groom the fur. The options of cremation, embalming, and taxidermy are open. A Utah company used to offer Egyptian-style embalming for both dogs and humans, with the use of fabric strips to create a mummy, and a polished bronze sarcophagus. The Long Island Funeral Home boasted a series of elaborate 'slumber rooms' for dead dogs; the oriental-style 'Ming Room' was considered particularly appropriate for Pekingeses.

There is widespread folklore concerning the ghosts of dogs. In his curious *Animal Ghosts*, the ghost-hunter Elliott O'Donnell collected many examples of spectral canines.[20] One of his stories concerned a lady named Miss Lefanu, who was followed by a strange Newfoundland dog when she walked in a country lane. She called to the dog, but it stayed at a respectful distance. Suddenly, two murderous-looking tramps jumped out from a hedge, ready to strike at her with their bludgeons. The Newfoundland uttered a low, ominous growl and flew at them. The terrified tramps fled yelling, as though the salvation of their souls depended on it. After the dog had followed Miss Lefanu home, she decoyed it into her back yard, which was surrounded by a high wall, and shut it up in there. She ordered her cook to prepare a hearty meal for the heroic dog, but when it was to be delivered, the dog was nowhere to be seen. Clearly, it must have been a ghost! Miss Lefanu later heard that on the very spot where the tramps had been lurking, a pedlar and his Newfoundland dog had been found murdered many years before. A sceptic would of course instead suspect that it had been a *real* Newfoundland dog, which had made use of its superior intellect to effect its escape from the back yard, losing out on its free meal as a result.

Another of Elliott O'Donnell's stories concerned 'The Phantom Dachshund of W-St., London, W.' Two people saw a little dachshund with a gaudy collar follow them in the street, until they came to a certain house, whereupon the dog vanished into thin air. It turned out that a gentleman living nearby had lost a dachshund, which had been allowed to roam the neighbourhood. The house where the Phantom Dachshund disappeared was the home and surgery of a German doctor with a great interest in vivisection; he was known to put out raw meat in a box to trap stray dogs for his experiments. A sceptic would have no answer to this kind of ghost story, except to find it rather silly.

A collection of railway-related ghost stories contains a tale of some Bristol railwaymen haunted by a spectral dog. One of them is reduced to a nervous wreck by the dog's spooky presence and its large staring eyes. The narrator himself also feels the presence of the ghost dog, hears its paws patting against the platform and the panting of its breath, and the soft nudge of its nose against the back of his knee. But instead of fainting, screaming or going mad with fear, the young railwayman shouts 'Bugger off, you daft brute!' This uncouth outcry seems to have frightened off the ghost dog, since although its presence was sometimes felt, it did no further mischief. This story might well seem even sillier than the previous one; the reason I have included it here is that later, a colleague of the narrator deduced that it must have been the ghost of Bristol Bob, the once-famous collecting dog that used to patrol the platform. Unlike many of his fellow collectors, Bob was never stuffed to keep working for charity; instead, he seems to have haunted the station, trying to entice the human ghosts to put some money into his collecting-box.[21]

A considerable amount of British canine ghost folklore concerns the Black Dog.[22] Some of these large, black, shaggy dog ghosts haunt certain roads or bridges; others appear in churchyards to frighten grave-robbers with their large glowing eyes and vaporous breath, or haunt certain families to whom they have taken a dislike. Most of them are silent, although some can growl, bark or even scream. Some of them are headless, others make up for this deficiency by having several heads. Some Black Dogs are helpful ghosts, warning people from unseen dangers; others have been definitely harmful. The Black Dogge of Newgate was supposed to have been the ghost of a prisoner murdered for cannibalistic purposes, haunting this ancient prison in the guise of a large black dog walking on its rear legs. Some Black Dogs were conjured up by witches or magicians. A classic ghost story is that some traveller insults some witch-like old woman, or refuses her alms. She is heard muttering a curse, but the rude or parsimonious traveller does not believe in witches. Then he is pursued through the country lanes by a shaggy Black Dog with bright shining eyes …

The Black Dog of Bungay, Suffolk, appeared in St Mary's priory church in August 1577; it ran down the nave, wrung the necks of two people, and disappeared. Within minutes, the spectral dog also appeared in the Holy Trinity church in Blythburgh, seven miles from Bungay. Again, it ran down the nave, killed two men and a boy and burnt the hand of another, before again abruptly disappearing; the church door still exhibits the claw marks of this demonic dog. There has been much speculation about the origin of this weird and violent Black Dog: had some rabid dog or out-of-place black panther been on the prowl, or had the inhabitants of Bungay and Blythburgh been hallucinating or suffering from ergotism? A recent and valuable study of Black Dogs has ascertained that there had been a great thunderstorm the day the Black Dog appeared, and that two men had died when the steeple of St Mary's priory church was struck by lightning.[23] Had the tale of the Black Dog resulted from a confused retelling of this event, or had perhaps ball lightning been involved, to represent the Dog's luminous eyes?

133. The Black Dogge of Newgate.

134. Another view of the Black Dogge of Newgate, from the 1638 pamphlet *The Discovery of a London Monster*.

A colleague of mine once had a spooky canine ghost story to tell. He lived in Richmond just outside London, with his wife and their three Newfoundland dogs. One of these dogs was not less than thirteen years old. She had problems with arthritis and seemed frustrated by not being able to play and run with her two younger friends. One day, the old dog was discovered to have died in her sleep, and she was buried in the large garden. The other two dogs did not do a 'Greyfriars Bobby' on their grandmother's grave, but instead were unseemingly hilarious, insisting on being let out at all hours, to romp in the garden barking vigorously, and even leaping a fence and digging a large hole in a neighbour's flowerbeds. When an old lady neighbour came to call, my friends believed she was about to complain about the barking dogs and the vandalized garden, but instead she turned out to be a great canophile. She had been admiring these *three* magnificent Newfoundland dogs playing in the garden, the old dog with the grey nose leading the way and playing pranks on the other two. The old lady saw the ghost dog once more, just as dusk fell; when she opened an upstairs window, the dog looked up at her, before slowly moving away. For several days, the other two dogs vainly searched for their ghostly companion.

When out ghost-hunting, Elliott O'Donnell often brought a dog with him, since he believed the canine senses were more acute even than his own when it came to indicating the presence of a ghost. And he may well have been right. In 2001, I moved from a flat in London to a large house in Wales. The place was not a little spooky with its large, empty rooms. The door to a small bedroom on the second floor seemed to open and shut without human intervention. When I had dinner with my new neighbours, they politely inquired whether there had been any ghostly manifestations in the house! It turned out that my predecessors in the house had been troubled by a resident ghost, which had been visible only to their two small dogs. The ghost liked to play with the dogs, and when their balls started rolling without human intervention, the dogs yapping and running after them, it was clearly time for a medium to be called in. This individual said that it was the ghost of a young servant girl, who had died in the house in Victorian times. By some stratagem, the medium also persuaded the ghost to behave with more decorum, something that has continued until the present time.

One theme in this book has been amazing dogs versus ordinary dogs, and amazing people versus ordinary people. When Munito, the only performing dog whose name became a by-word for canine sagacity, was seen and admired by celebrities like Charles Dickens, the Duke of York and Alexander Pushkin, it was the amazing dog who was the star, not them. Boatswain, who was a fairly ordinary dog, notable only for his pugnacious nature, was elevated to become an amazing dog through his relationship with Lord Byron, his famous epitaph written by the poet, and his monument at Newstead where Byron wanted to share his tomb. The 'American Lovers of Bobby' performed a not dissimilar duty to the obscure, perhaps apocryphal 'John Gray' when they belatedly erected his gravestone at Greyfriars; in this bizarre instance, his status as an ordinary man was elevated because of his amazing dog. With a different twist, the same argument can be applied to the chapter about Rolf, Lola and their fellow

135. A Black Dog appears in a scholar's study.

136. A Black Dog surprising the man who had conjured it.

canine intellectuals. At the time, it was presumed that these amazingly clever dogs wrote poetry and discussed philosophy and military tactics, with their ordinary owners proudly looking on; today, we instead see some fairly ordinary dogs surrounded by amazingly ignorant and bigoted German busybodies who had developed an *idée fixe* that dogs and horses possessed near-human intelligence.

Another theme has been unsolved mysteries of the canine race. Some of these received relatively straightforward solutions: for example, the tale of Saint Guinefort had its origin in a widespread medieval myth. When I started researching this book, I was inclined to disbelieve the marvellous stories of sagacious Newfoundland dogs in old dog books and collections of anecdotes. However, I found a wealth of solid evidence that these early Newfoundland dogs were capable of intelligence exceeding what we today associate with dogs, with regard to problem solving and creative action. Nor would many sceptically minded readers have credited the almost surreal tale of Don the Talking Dog and his American adventures, but again, reliable sources agree that this amazing performer could really imitate the human voice. The yarn of the faithful Greyfriars Bobby keeping vigil on his master's grave for twelve years has been accepted by the majority of historians, but it rests on very feeble foundations indeed. There is good reason to consider Bobby as one of several opportunistic 'cemetery dogs' taking advantage of the sentimental notion of the faithful dog keeping vigil on its master's grave; his story is one of human credulity rather than canine fidelity. Thus, some of the 'canine enigmas' we started with were true stories and others fabulous, but not always those the reader would have expected.

One hundred and fifty years ago, the Victorian acting dogs were 'taking the seize' on stage, and the turnspit dogs kept their dog-wheels rotating in the kitchens. A hundred years ago, Owney and other canine globe-trotters were touring the world, and every major English railway station had its own collecting dog. So, what aspects of present-day dog–human interactions are going to strike future historians as bizarre or amazing? What will they think of the present-day yobs and thugs with their aggressive fighting bull terriers on the lead; will they not seem as absurd and brutal as the rabble surrounding the rat-pits in Victorian times? And how will the present-day Paris Hilton wannabes carrying their pampered Chihuahuas in custom-made Gucci handbags compare with the Victorian gentlemen paying vast sums of money for pedigree Newfoundlands or St Bernards, and ordering expensive paintings and monuments to immortalize their favourites? Will there ever be another 'learned' dog to challenge the great Munito, or another talking dog to rival Don? How long will the reprehensible practice of breeding dogs for human consumption be allowed to continue? And will there one day be another Brown Dog with sharper teeth, capable of putting an end to the vivisection and killing of dogs in experimental research?

NOTES

1
Introduction

1. See the papers by C. Manwell & C. M. A. Baker (*Zeitschrift für Tierzüchtung und Züchtungsbiologie* 101 [1984], 241–56), C. Vila *et al.* (*Science* 276 [1997], 1687–9), P. Savolainen *et al.* (*Science* 298 [2002], 1610–3) and J. A. Leonard *et al.* (*Science* 298 [2002], 1613–6); also the very useful overview of canine evolution given by A. Miklosi, *Dog Behaviour, Evolution, and Cognition* (Oxford 2009), 95–133.

2. M. Hilzheimer (*Antiquity* 6 [1932], 411–9); S. J. Crookford (ed.), *Dogs through Time* (London 2000); D. Brewer *et al.*, *Dogs in Antiquity* (Warminster 2001).

3. M. Zedda *et al.* (*Anatomy Histology & Embryology* 35 [2006], 319–24)

4. J. Caius, *Of English Dogges* (London 1576).

5. U. Aldrovandi, *De quadripedibus digitatis viviparis libri tres* (Bologna 1645), 482–563.

6. C. Paullini, *Cynographia Curiosa* (Nuremberg 1685).

7. C. Linnaeus, *Cynographia* [Resp. Erik M. Lindecrantz] (Upsala 1753). It was later translated into Swedish as *Beskrifning om Hunden* (Sigtuna 1962), but has never been published in English; see also N. Palmborg, *Under Hundstjärnan* (Stockholm 1965), 83–96.

8. H. Dalziel, *British Dogs* (London 1887); H. Ritvo (*Victorian Studies* 29 [1986], 227–53).

9. There are many good modern books on the history of dogs. On canine ethnology, see M. Leach, *God had a Dog* (New Brunswick NJ 1961) and P. Dale-Green, *Dog* (London 1966). On canine intelligence and cognition, see S. Coren, *How to Speak Dog* (London 2000), *How Dogs Think* (London 2005), and *The Intelligence of Dogs* (London 2006); also V. Csanyi, *If Dogs could Talk* (Stroud 2006) and A. Miklosi, *Dog Behaviour, Evolution, and Cognition* (Oxford 2009).

On dogs in art, see W. Secord, *Dog Painting 1840–1910* (Woodbridge 1992), *Dog Painting, The European Breeds* (Woodbridge 2000) and *A Breed Apart* (Woodbridge

2001), C. d'Athenaise, *Vies de Chiens* (Paris 2000) and C. Jones, *Dogs: History, Myth, Art* (London 2008).

On general canine history, see E. C. Ash, *Dogs, their History and Development*, 2 vols (London 1927) and *Practical Dog Book* (London 1931); also C. L. B. Hubbard, *Dogs in Britain* (London 1948), F. Mery, *The Life, History and Magic of the Dog* (New York 1970), M. Villemont, *Le Grand Livre du Chien*, 2 vols (Paris 1970), C. I. A. Ritchie, *The British Dog* (London 1981), A. Patmore, *Your Obedient Servant* (London 1984), M. E. Thurston, *The Lost History of the Canine Race* (Kansas City 1996), M. Garber, *Dog Love* (New York 1996), K. McDonogh, *Reigning Cats and Dogs* (London 1998), J. Moinault, *Histoire du Chien et des Hommes* (Paris 1998), S. Coren, *Pawprints of History* (New York 2002), S. McHugh, *Dog* (London 2004), and M.-P. Daniels-Moulin, *Le Grand Livre de l'Histoire du Chien* (Paris 2004).

I wish to thank the following libraries and repositories: in the UK, the British Library, the Wellcome Institute Library, the Bodleian Library, the National Library of Scotland and Edinburgh Central Library; in France, the Bibliothèque Nationale; in Germany, the Staatsbibliothek of Berlin; in Sweden, the Royal Library of Stockholm and Lund University Library.

2

The Great Munito & The Learned English Dog

1. *Country Journal*, 13 September 1729; *General Advertiser*, 4 January 1752.
2. There is much information about the French and English learned dogs in Lysons' *Collectana*, kept in the British Library. On the French Dog, see also *Old England*, 13 July 1751 and *Daily Advertiser*, 26 November 1751.
3. *The Exercises of the Chien Savant; or, Learn'd French Dog* (London 1751).
4. On the English Dog, see *General Advertiser*, 4 January 1752, *Daily Advertiser*, 11 April 1752.
5. Reprinted in *Miscellaneous and Fugitive Pieces* (London 1774), vol. 3, 81–6.
6. The dog's tours can be reconstructed from cuttings in Lysons' *Collectana*; see also *Morning Chronicle*, 6 September 1827.
7. Anon., *On en parlera longtemps … dans une des séances du célèbre Munito* (Paris 1817); *L'Hermite de Londres* (London 1817), vol. 3, 194–205; *Literary Gazette* 11 [1817], 170; *Weekly Entertainer* 57 [1817], 389–90; *New Monthly Magazine* 8 [1817], 292–3; *Hampshire Telegraph*, 10 November 1817. Short accounts of Munito have been given by M. Christopher, *Panorama of Magic* (New York 1962), 35–7; P. Bräuning, *Circus und autverwandte Künste* (Königstein 1990), 361; S. Oettermann, *Ankündigungs-Zettel von Kunst-Reitern* (Wiesbaden 1993), No. 536. The three major published sources on the Wonderful Dog are S. Hirn in *Hufvudstadsbladet*, 27 March 1970 and *Den Gastronomiska Hästen* (Helsinki 2002), 58–9, 218; R. Jay, *Jay's Journal of Anomalies* (New York 2001), 4–8, 165; and J. Bondeson, *The Cat Orchestra and the Elephant Butler* (Stroud 2006), 47–62.

8. There is primary material about the Wonderful Dog in Lysons' *Collectanea* and in the Fillinham Collection of Cuttings from Newspapers; see also *The Times*, 25 May 1817 la and 15 March 1819 le.

9. Ch. de Ribelle, *Histoire des Animaux Célèbres* (Paris 1858), 105–6; E. Richebourg, *Histoire des Chiens Célèbres* (Paris 1867), 351–2.

10. Anon., *Notice historique sur la vie et les talens du savant chien Munito* (Paris 1820).

11. *Stockholms-Posten*, 15 May 1830; see also Hirn, *Den Gastronomiska Hästen*, 58.

12. A.-A. de Berruyer, *Epître à M. le Marquis de La Londe, par Munito, Chien Savant* (Versailles 1827), Anon., *Levons-nous en masse! Proclamation de Bianco et Fido, écrite sous leur dictée, par un élève de Munito* (Paris 1830).

13. J.-F. Bertachon, *Notice sur les Chiens Munito* (Nantes 1836).

14. *The Courier* (Hobart Town), 18 and 25 November 1842, 13 January 1843, 10 March 1847.

15. *All the Year Round* 17 [1867], 105–6.

16. E. de Tarade, *Education du Chien* (Paris 1866).

17. Birger Schöldström, *Brokiga Bilder* (Norrköping 1892), 51–3.

18. On other learned dogs, see Revd C. Williams, *Dogs and Their Ways* (London 1868), 356–76, E. Jesse, *Anecdotes of Dogs* (London 1873), 331–6 and A. Lehmann, *Tiere als Artisten* (Wittenberg 1956), 168–79.

3
Some Canine Intellectuals

1. Some similar tricks were actually performed already by the extraordinary sixteenth-century learned horse Marocco; see J. Bondeson, *The Cat Orchestra and the Elephant Butler* (Stroud 2006), 13–28.

2. O. Pfungst, *Clever Hans* (reissued New York 2009).

3. K. Krall, *Denkende Tiere* (Leipzig 1912). The best English-language account of Krall's activities is D. K. Candland, *Feral Children and Clever Animals* (Oxford 1983). See also M. Gardner (*Semiotica* 38 [1982], 357–67), G. H. Hövelmann (*Semiotica* 73 [1989], 199–217) and R. Kressley-Mba (*History of Psychiatry* 9 [2006], 55–74). The recent PhD thesis by B. von den Berg, *Die „Neue Tierpsychologie" und ihre wissenschaftlichen Vertreter* (Hannover 2008) provides much useful information from various German sources.

4. P. Moekel, *Mein Hund Rolf* (Stuttgart 1919). There were articles about Rolf by P. Moekel, K. Gruber, L. Wilsner and W. Mackenzie in *Tierseele* 1 [1914], 193–200, 250–1, 251–3, and 323–3; see also *Mitteilungen der Gesellschaft für Tierpsychologie* 2(1) [1914], 3–16, 4(1) [1916], 1–11 and NS1(1) [1920], 1–12; *Djurens Rätt* 1916(3/4), 4–31; also the articles by E. Claparède (*Archives de Psychologie* 13 [1913], 312, 377–9) and H. Pièran (*L'Année Psychologique* 20 [1913], 218–28) and W. Sheard, *The Glory of the Dog* (London n.d.), 94–104.

5. Moekel, *Mein Hund Rolf*, 86.

6. Frau Moekel's obituary was in the *Mitteilungen der Gesellschaft für Tierpsychologie* 4(1) [1916], 1.

7. P. Moekel (ed.), *Briefe und Erinnerungen des Hundes Rolf* (Stuttgart 1920).

8. H. Kindermann, *Lola, or the Thought and Speech of Animals* (London 1922). There was a critical review of this book in *Journal of Mental Science* 69 [1923], 374–6.

9. von den Berg, *Die „Neue Tierpsychologie"*, 74–133; A. Arluke & B. Sax (*Anthrozoos* 5 [1992], 6–31).

10. *Sunday Dispatch*, 11 April 1937 and *Manchester Guardian*, 15 April 1937; L. Plate (*Zoologischer Anzeiger* 95 [1931], 250–4) and H. Graupner (*Der Zoologische Garten* 5 [1932], 150).

11. O. Wulf, *Kuno von Schwertberg genannt Kurwenal, der zahlsprechende Teckel* (Stuttgart 1933). See also the articles by O. Renner (*Natur und Geist* 3 [1935], 105–9); L. Plate (*Archiv für Rassen- und Gesellschaftsbiologie* 30 [1936], 312–40); also *Time* 14 March 1938, *Das Kalenderblatt in Bayern*, 16 January 2006 and the article by L. Olsson and U. Hossfeld in the Swedish magazine *Folkvett* 2008(2).

12. M. Müller (*Tierärtliche Mitteilungen* 24 [1943], 71–2); A. Arluke & B. Sax (*Anthrozoos* 5 [1992], 6–31); von den Berg, *Die „Neue Tierpsychologie"*, 124–5.

13. H. Jutzler-Kindermann, *Können Tiere denken? Ja!* (Schopfheim 1954).

14. E. Mann Borgese, *The White Snake* (London 1966); *Washington Post*, 3 April 1966; the dog's poems were published in the literary magazine *Brick* 76, Winter 2005.

15. C. J. Warden & L. H. Warner, *Quarterly Review of Biology* 3 [1928], 1–28.

16. On Rico, see the articles by J. Kaminski *et al.* (*Science* 304 [2004], 1682–3), P. Bloom (*Science* 304 [2004], 1605–6) and E. M. Markman & M. Abelev (*Trends in Cognitive Sciences* 8 [2004], 479–81). The average ordinary dog knows only around thirty words, according to the estimation of their owners; see P. Pongrácz *et al.* (*Current Psychology of Cognition* 20 [2001], 87–107).

17. Betsy was featured in the March 2008 issue of *National Geographic* magazine.

18. A. Miklosi *et al.* (*Animal Cognition* 1 [1998], 113–21 and *Animal Behaviour* 67 [2004], 995–1004); B. Hare *et al.* (*Science* 298 [2002], 1634–6); B. Hare & M. Tomasello (*Trends in Cognitive Sciences* 9 [2005], 439–44; M. A. R Udell & C. D. L. Wynne (*Journal of the Experimental Analysis of Behaviour* 89 [2008], 247–61).

19. N. Schultz (*New Scientist* 200 [2008], 12).

20. K. Douglas (*New Scientist* 199 [2008], 33–6).

21. A. P. Rossi & C. Ades (*Animal Cognition* 11 [2008], 329–338).

22. W. Neumann, *Mensch und Tier* (Heidelberg 1928), 18–32.

23. T. A. Seboek (*Semiotica* 57 [1985], 117–24).

4

Some Celebrated Talking Dogs

1. *Histoire de l'Academie Royale des Sciences* (1715), 3.

2. C. Kornholt (ed.), *Recueil de diverses pieces sur la Philosophie, les Mathematiques, l'Histoire &c. par M. de Leibniz* (Hamburg 1734), 53; *Curiositäten der physisch-*

literarisch-artistisch-historischen Vor- und Mitwelt 2(1) [1812], 74–6; K. Krall, *Denkende Tiere* (Leipzig 1912), 212–5.

3. *Daily Courant*, 16 May 1718; *Weekly Packet*, 14 June 1718.
4. *Weekly Irish Times*, 19 November 1887; *Notes and Queries* 9s 3 [1899], 378–9.
5. Some are quoted by P. Scheller, *Der sprechende Hund* (Berlin 1911).
6. *San Fransisco Call*, 27 November 1910; *New York Times*, 20 and 27 November, 11 December 1910.
7. Scheller, *Der sprechende Hund*.
8. J. Vosseler, *'Don' der sprechende Hund* (Hamburg 1911).
9. *New York Times*, 2 April 1911.
10. *Penny Illustrated Paper*, 26 August 1911.
11. *New York Times*, 16 May, 27–28 June 1912.
12. Vosseler, *'Don' der sprechende Hund*.
13. *Sechste Beilage zur Possischen Zeitung*, 27 April 1911.
14. *Bericht über den V. Kongress für experimentelle Psychologie* (Leipzig 1912), 241–5.
15. H. M. Johnson, *Science* NS 35 [1912], 749–51.
16. Vincent Sheean, *The Amazing Oscar Hammerstein* (London 1956), 113; J. Traub, *The Devil's Playground* (New York 2004), 22–23.
17. *New York Times*, 11 July 1912, 16; *New York Tribune*, 21 July 1912, 3; *Pittsburgh Press*, 29 July 1912.
18. *Pittsburgh Press*, 22 December 1912; *New York Times*, 22 July 1913; *Brooklyn Daily Eagle*, 28 August 1913, 7.
19. *Syracuse Journal*, 11 September 1913, 8.
20. *New York Times*, 9 November 1913, 3 August 1914.
21. M. Müller (*Tierärztliche Mitteilungen* 24 [1943], 71–2).
22. *Daily Mirror*, 11 November 1910.
23. *New York Times*, 29 December 1910, 23 June 1912; A. Lehmann, *Tiere als Artisten* (Wittenberg 1956); O. Prochnow, *Annalen der Natur- und Kulturphilosophie* 12 [1913], 50–61. On performing cats in general, see J. Bondeson, *The Cat Orchestra and the Elephant Butler* (Stroud 2006), 7–11.
24. There are only scattered newspaper reports of this extraordinary dog, in the *New York Times*, 21 February 1928, *Oswego Palladium-Times*, 21 February 1928; *Daily Mirror*, 24 February 1928; *Brooklyn Daily Eagle*, 16 October 1934; *Canberra Times*, 21 Dec 1935.
25. *Daily Mirror*, 10, 12, 13, 14, 26 and 27 August 1946, and 11 August 1947; *Time*, 26 August 1946.
26. *Daily Express*, 19 January 1950.
27. *Evening Standard*, 17 January 1953, 4.
28. *Daily Mirror*, 19 January 1962; Pepe was described by C. A. Lambert in *Fate* 143 [Sept 1966], 80–4.
29. Vosseler, *'Don' der sprechende Hund*; O. Prochnow, *Annalen der Natur- und Kulturphilosophie* 12 [1913], 50–61.
30. T. Adler in *Scientific American*, 10 June 2009.

5

Doggy Drama: Some Celebrated Canine Thespians

1. Onstage canines and their significance is discussed by L.B. Wright (*PMLA* 42 [1927], 656–69), M. Dobson (*Performance Research* 5(2) [2000], 116–24), M. Peterson (*The Drama Review* 51(1) [2007], 33–48), and T. Grant in B. Boehrer (ed.), *A Cultural History of Animals* 3 [2007], 95–117. Other articles of relevance to onstage animals are those by S Duffy (*British Art Journal* 3(3) [2002], 25–35), J. Stokes (*NTQ* 20 [2004], 138–54) and M. Pomerance in B. K. Grant (ed.), *The Schirmer Encyclopedia of Film* (New York 2007), vol. 1, 79–84.

2. *Morning Chronicle*, 15 December 1803; *Derby Mercury*, 15 December 1803; *Hampshire Telegraph*, 16 January and 29 February 1804; *Spirit of the Public Journals* for 1804, 42–3; J. Boaden, *The Life of Mrs Jordan* (London 1831), vol. 2, 149–51; also the useful homepage www.dogdrama.com.

3. *The Times*, 6 December 1803 3d, 7 December 1803 3b, 16 December 1803 3b and 5 November 1804 2f.

4. E. Fenwick, *The Life of the Famous Dog Carlo* (London 1809); *Sporting Magazine* 1804; see also *Dublin University Magazine* 58 [1861], 224–5 where Carlo is described as 'a splendid specimen of the Newfoundland breed'.

5. *Morning Chronicle*, 12 October 1805; *New York Times*, 11 December 1898.

6. M. D. George, *Catalogue of Political and Personal Satires* (London 1978), vol. 8, 232–3, 251–2, 270, 379, 573, 702–3, 881.

7. *Bentley's Miscellany* 13 [1843], 372.

8. *The Times*, 31 May 1811 3b.

9. *Weekly Entertainer* 59 [1819], 415–8. There are short accounts of Victorian dog drama in H. Chance Newton, *Crime and the Drama* (London 1927), 84–6, and M. R. Booth, *English Melodrama* (London 1965), 86–7.

10. *The Times*, 11 April 1820 2c and 26 March 1821 3b.

11. A. H. Saxon, *Enter Foot and Horse* (New Haven 1968); M. Kwint (*Past & Present* 174 [2002], 72–115.

12. P. Fitzgerald, *The World behind the Scenes* (London 1881), 80–2.

13. *Age*, 8 October 1826, 591.

14. *The Times*, 18 March 1828 3c; *Era*, 18 March 1828.

15. *Harlequin*, 13 June 1829, 13; *The Times*, 19 January 1829 4a, 3 November 1830 6c, 6 December 1830 5c, 17 December 1830 2e and 26 October 1831 2b.

16. On Cony and Blanchard, see M. Morley, *The Old Marylebone Theatre* (London 1960), 3–17; M. H. Winter, *Theatre of Marvels* (London 1964), 175–89; G. Odell, *Annals of the New York Stage*, various entries in volumes 5–9; G. Morice (*Notes and Queries* 188 [1945], 250–2); *Caledonian Mercury*, 13 June 1842; *The Times*, 8 July 1846 4a; *Theatrical Journal* 3 [1842], 204, 4 [1843], 268 and 7 [1846], 401. See also www.dogdrama.com and various texts at www.circushistory.org.

17. *Era*, 18 October 1840, 5.

18. F. Dolman, *English Illustrated Magazine* 21 [1899], 521–8.

19. Both Rin Tin Tin and Lassie have useful web sites; see also R. Lee, *Not so Dumb* (New York 1970), D. Rothel, *Great Show Business Animals* (San Diego 1980), 66–183, and A. Lloyd, *Hollywood Dogs* (London 2004).

6

Railway Jack, Owney & Some Other Canine Globetrotters

1. Some early sources on Railway Jack are *Funny Folks*, 10 September 1881, 282; *Sporting Gazette*, 15 November 1884; *Hampshire Telegraph*, 5 August 1882 and 12 July 1883; *Girl's Own Paper*, 29 January 1882, 282; *Chatterbox* 30 December 1882, 44; *Liverpool Mercury*, 5 November 1881, 6, and 20 January 1882, 7; *Daily News*, 17 January 1882, 5 and *Graphic*, 4 February 1882, 99. See also the article by J. G. Wood in *Leisure Hour*, June 1885, 393–401.

2. *Bristol Mercury*, 12 July 1883; *Penny Illustrated Paper*, 12 August 1882, 111.

3. Railway Jack's obituary was in *Pall Mall Gazette*, 30 October 1890, 6 and *Oswego Palladium*, 20 November 1890. Later notices of Railway Jack were in the *Daily Mirror*, 15 October 1926, 11, *New Zealand Railways Magazine* 1(8) 1927 and *Sussex Express*, 29 April 2004.

4. These other travelling dogs were mentioned in *Hampshire Telegraph*, 1 April 1882; *Girl's Own Paper*, 16 February 1884, 315; *Liverpool Mercury*, 7 December 1895; *Newcastle Courant*, 13 June 1896, 2.

5. On Railroad Jack, see *New York Times*, 18 August 1892 and 16 June 1893; also *Malone Palladium*, 6 April, 22 and 29 June 1893.

6. The two major sources of reliable information about Owney are the valuable article by Dr C. A. Huguenin in *New York History* 38 [1957], 29–50, and J. Bruns, *Owney: Mascot of the Railway Mail Service*, published by the Smithsonian in 1998. There were contemporary UK newspaper articles about Owney in *Supplement to the Hampshire Telegraph*, 4 January and 30 May 1896 and *Leeds Mercury Weekly Supplement*, 20 June 1896. The *New York Times* covered his activities in some detail: 3 October 1892, 29 July 1894, 27 October, 24 and 31 December 1895, 7 April 1897 and 10 March 1910. See also *Brooklyn Daily Eagle*, 19 August 1895, 12, and 27 July 1902, 37; *Malone Palladium*, 6 April 1893, 4 March and 17 June 1897; *Norwood News*, 22 January 1897; *Chateaugay Journal*, 4 February and 20 April 1897; also *Pulaski Democrat*, 27 September 1956, *Guardian*, 20 July 2004 and *Deseret Morning News*, 22 April 2006.

7. Barlettani's book remains the leading source on Lampo and his career. Lampo's obituary was in the *Daily Mirror*, 6 March 1962. See also *L'Unita*, 22 November 2002 and *Guardian*, 29 Oct 2003. The chapters on Lampo and Owney in R. Gordon, *It takes a Dog to raise a Village* (Minocqua, Wisconsin 2000) add little that is new or interesting, but this book introduces some other eccentric, ownerless American dogs.

8. *Il Terrino*, 21 January, 20 February, 6 July and 20 August 2006.

9. The modern instances of travelling dogs were in the *Northern Echo*, 29 July 2006, the *Sun*, 11 April 2009 and the *Daily Mirror*, 7 April 2010.

7

Some Canine Philanthropists

1. On the murderer Rayner, see L. Stratmann, *Death of a Salesman* (Stroud 2004); the collecting dog is described in the *Illustrated Police Budget* of 13 April 1907.
2. Collecting dogs have not attracted much attention from the historians; the sole exception is the brief article by H. Christian & P. Morris (*Railway World* 48 [1987], 729–30).
3. *The Children's Friend*, 1 January 1863, 15–6.
4. *Kind Words*, 30 July 1868, 242.
5. On 'Help', see *Leeds Mercury Weekly Supplement*, 13 October 1883, 6; *Young England*, 1 March 1884, 227; *The Friendly Companion*, 1 January 1892, 12.
6. *Country Life Illustrated*, 24 June 1899, 798–9.
7. 'Brake' is described in *Animal World* 19 [1883], 152 and *Penny Illustrated Paper*, 20 December 1884, 406.
8. *Graphic*, 16 May 1883, 486.
9. *Bristol Mercury*, 4 February 1893 and 16 December 1898; *Lancet* ii [1900], 913.
10. *Daily News*, 18 August 1899, 3, and 28 August 1899, 7; also *Lloyd's Weekly Newspaper*, 3 September 1899, 13.
11. *Animal World* NS 1 [1906], 59–60 and NS 4 [1909], 75; *Scotsman*, 30 December 1905, 11; *Illustrated Police Budget*, 28 September 1907; *Daily Mirror*, 4 June 1907, 4, 15 August 1907, 13, 14 September 1907, 9, and 30 June 1933, 23; *Manchester Guardian*, 27 December 1929; *Daily Express*, 20 May 1936.
12. *The Times*, 27 August 1912 4e; *Daily Mirror*, 23 March 1912, 10, and 22 April 1913, 3.
13. *The Times*, 12 December 1924 16a, 29 October 1925 11a, 7 February 1934 16a and 3 September 1934 17d; *Daily Mirror*, 19 November 1924, 3, and 7 February 1934, 11; *Observer*, 7 November 1937.
14. *The Times*, 12 July 1900 7a.
15. Mrs de Courcy Laffan is in the *Oxford Dictionary of National Biography*; see also the article by S. Bailey (*Olympika* 6 [1997], 51–64).
16. *Penny Illustrated Paper*, 4 December 1909, 363 and *Daily Mirror*, 14 October 1910, 5–8, 3 December 1910, 5, and 4 February 1911, 1.
17. *MDA Annual Report* (2002), 8–9.
18. *Our Dogs*, October 2003; in early 2010, London Jack was removed from Tring and put into storage.

8

Guinefort the Dog Saint & Some Other Holy Dogs

1. L. Hosgood-Osler, *Holy Dogs and Asses* (Chicago 2008), 89–98.
2. A. Vayssière, *Annales de la Société de l'Emulation de l'Ain* 12 [1879], 94–108, 209–21.

3. J.-C. Schmitt, *The Holy Greyhound* (Cambridge 1983); see also the comments by J. Dubois (*Journal des Scavans* 1980(1), 141–55), J. Van Engen (*Historian* 47 [1985], 416), S. Dickman (*Speculum* 59 [1984], 699–700) and M. Albert-Llorca (*Archives des Sciences Sociales des Religions* 130 [2005], 2–4).

4. As discussed by Schmitt, *The Holy Greyhound*, 91–123.

5. Both Spencer's poem and another lengthy poem about Gelert by Richard Horne are quoted by R. M. Leonard, *The Dog in British Poetry* (London 1893), 26–9, 59–67.

6. S. Baring-Gould, *Curious Myths of the Middle Ages*, 1st Series (London 1877). See also the papers by M. B. Emereau (*Proceedings of the American Oriental Society* 83 [1940], 503–13 and *Journal of the American Oriental Society* 61 [1941], 1–17).

7. I. Taylor, *Words and Places* (London 1865), 339; D. E. Jenkins, *Bedd Gelert* (Bedd Gelert 1899), 56–74.

8. G. Borrow, *Wild Wales*, chapter 46.

9. Jenkins, *Bedd Gelert*, 56–74.

10. J. Bondeson, *The Prolific Countess* (Loosduinen 1996) and *The Two-Headed Boy and other Medical Marvels* (Ithaca NY 2000), 64–119.

11. *Daily News of Los Angeles*, 26 August 1988.

12. *Palm Beach Daily News*, 29 September 2002.

13. Quoted by S. Blackburn (*Bulletin of the School of Oriental and African Studies* 59 [1996], 494–507).

9

Greyfriars Bobby & Some Other Faithful Dogs

1. There were magazine articles about Greyfriars Bobby in *Chatterbox*, 22 June 1867 and 5 June 1886, in *The Children's Treasury*, 18 November 1876, and in *Chambers's Journal* 18 [1884], 285–7 and 114 [1900], 154–7. The fictional accounts of Greyfriars Bobby are worthless for the serious historian, but the books by Forbes Macgregor, *Authenticated Facts relating to Greyfriars Bobby* (Edinburgh 1981) and *Greyfriars Bobby, the Real Story at last* (London 2002) are valuable sources, as are J. Mackay, *The Illustrated True Story of Greyfriars Bobby* (Glasgow 1986) and G. Robinson, *The Greyfriars Bobby A–Z* (Edinburgh 2008). See also the article by J. U. Thomson (*Scotland's Magazine* 67(11) [1971], 15–7), F. Macgregor (*Scots Magazine* 130 [1989], 357–63), S. Stevenson (*Book of the Old Edinburgh Club* NS 4 [1997], 85–8), H. Kean (*Society & Animals* 11 [2003], 353–73 and K. Kete (ed.), *Cultural History of Animals* 5 [2007], 25–46), and some recent newspaper features in *Glasgow Herald*, 11 July 2001, *Edinburgh Evening News*, 29 November 2003 and *Independent*, 4 February 2006.

2. *Scotsman*, 13 April 1867; *Aberdeen Journal*, 15 May 1867.

3. *Scotsman*, 16 August 1934, 11.

4. *Aberdeen Journal*, 24 July 1867.

5. *Scotsman*, 18 April 1867; Macgregor, *Authenticated Facts*.

6. Edinburgh City Archives, Town Council Record vol. 300, 30 November 1869, ff. 451–2.

7. *Scotsman*, 13 August 1934; Macgregor, *Authenticated Facts*.

8. *Edinburgh Evening Dispatch*, 11 June 1955; *Edinburgh Evening News*, 10 and 27 May 1971.

9. F. L. Lederer (*Journal of the Illinois State Historical Society* 68 [1975], 308–18); see also www.eleanoratkinson.org.

10. Mackay, *Illustrated True Story*, 44–7; B. J. Beacock (*Bobby's Bothy* 1(3) [2001], 4–5 and *Greyfriars Bobby Magazine* March–May 2006, 6–8); M. Hubbard (*Media Education Journal* 41 [2007], 34–7).

11. *Inverness Advertiser*, 10 May 1864.

12. These versions are in *Scotsman*, 13 April 1867 and Macgregor, *Authenticated Facts*, 55.

13. Macgregor, *Greyfriars Bobby*, 60–2.

14. Macgregor, *Greyfriars Bobby*, 9–26; for more information about Gray the policeman, see *Greyfriars Bobby Magazine*, Sept–Nov 2003, 6–8 and March–May 2009, 2–4.

15. *Sunday Herald*, 26 March 2000; *Daily Mail*, 24 May 1999 and *Edinburgh Evening News*, 2 March 2000.

16. F. C. Woodworth, *Stories about Animals* (Boston 1851), 5.

17. H. Coupin, *Les Animaux Excentriques*, 4th edn (Paris n.d.), 384–5; the poem is translated in *Fraser's Magazine* 10 [1834], 677–8.

18. K. Kete, *The Beast in the Boudoir* (Berkeley CA 1994), 22–35.

19. On Fidèle, see the articles by G. Jungmarker (*Samfundet Sankt Eriks Årsbok* 1983, 165–76) and H. Öjmyr (*Blick – Stockholm då och nu* 3 [2006–2007], 24–7).

20. *Cottager's Monthly Visitor* 10 [1830], 79–83; *The Children's Friend*, 1 May 1824.

21. *Caledonian Mercury*, 7 April 1834; E. Jesse, *Gleanings in Natural History*, 3rd series (London 1835), 34; F. Power Cobbe, *The Friend of Man* (London 1889), 89–110; C. Williams, *Dogs and their Ways* (London 1893), 70–6; *Animal's Guardian* 3 [1893], 203.

22. Rollo is featured on the Freerepublic discussion forum; the story of Old Shep is given on the Roadsideamerica website, and in the *Fort Benton River Press*, 6 July 2005.

23. *Glasgow Herald*, 23 November 1871.

24. T. Wilson Read, *Gabrielle Stuart* (Edinburgh 1882), vol. 1, 227–8 and vol. 2, 5–9.

25. *Pall Mall Gazette*, 7 February 1889; *Scotsman*, 8 February 1889; *Edinburgh Evening News*, 14 February 1889.

26. F. Haley (*North West Monthly* 1(10) [1950], 7–11; J. Michell & R. J. M. Rickard, *Living Wonders* (London 1982), 127.

27. *Buffalo Evening News*, 13 February 1930; *Milwaukee Sentinel*, 14 June 1931.

28. *Bath and West Evening Chronicle*, 18 and 23 October 1978; M. Burton, *Just like an Animal* (London 1978), 78–87; Michell & Rickard, *Living Wonders*, 127–30.

10

The Turnspit Dog & Some Other Extinct Breeds

1. D. J. Eveleigh, *Firegrates and Kitchen Ranges* (Shire 1983) and *The English Tradition of Open-Fire Roasting* (Leeds 1990).
2. Not much scholarship has been devoted to turnspit dogs, apart from the efforts of C. I. A. Ritchie, *The British Dog* (London 1981), 141–4; J. Cunliffe (*Kennel Gazette* 113(4) [1991], 20–1); and M. E. Thurston, *The Lost History of the Canine Race* (Kansas City 1996), 122–5.
3. Eveleigh, *Tradition of Open-Fire Roasting*, 8–10; P. Mundy, *Travels in Europe and Asia 1608–1667* (Hakluyt Society 2s 55 [1925], 11).
4. Carl von Linné, *Beskrifning om Hunden* (Sigtuna 1962), 46.
5. *Osvego Valley News*, 9 July 1975; *Evening Recorder* (Amsterdam NY), 3 December 1949, 26; J. Schinto in *Gastronomica* 4(1), 2004.
6. R. Southey, *Letters from England* (Gloucester 1984), 473.
7. E. Jesse, *Anecdotes of Dogs* (London 1873), 418–20; R. Chambers, *The Book of Days* (London 1886), vol. 1, 489–91.
8. *London Dispatch*, 7 April 1839; J. Schinto in *Gastronomica* 4(1), 2004.
9. Eveleigh, *Tradition of Open-Fire Roasting*, 8.
10. J. P. Phillips (*Notes and Queries* 3s 2 [1862], 255–6).
11. *Notes and Queries* 3s 2 [1862], 219 and 6s 10 [1884], 271; E. Wilson, *A Three Weeks Scamper through the Spas of Germany and Belgium* (London 1858), 283–4.
12. *Notes and Queries* 3s 2 [1862], 255–6 and 3s 5 [1864], 164; S. Baring-Gould, *A Book of South Wales* (London 1905), 271.
13. *Notes and Queries* 3s 2 [1862], 149, and 10s 12 [1909], 315; *Wellington Weekly News*, 29 September 2004.
14. *The Lady's Newspaper*, 9 February 1850.
15. *Notes and Queries* 3s 2 [1862], 149, and 6s 10 [1884], 271.
16. *The Times*, 14 April 1961 16f and 13 February 1967 12e.
17. B. von Rosen (*Hundsport* No. 10 [1971], 8–9, 50–1).
18. J. Betts (*Notes and Queries* 35 [1988], 167–9; Thurston, *Lost History*, 125–7, 135–45.
19. *Daily Mail*, 25 April 1901; *The Times*, 14 April 1961 16f.

11

Lord Byron's Boatswain & Some Other Remarkable Newfoundland Dogs

1. On the history of Newfoundland dogs, see E. C. Ash, *Dogs, their History and Development* (London 1927), 565–87, M. Booth Chern, *The Complete Newfoundland* (Richmond, Va 1955), 11–45 and C. Cooper, *The Newfoundland* (Pontypool 1982), 1–17.
2. H. G. Parker *et al.* (*Science* 304 [2004], 1160–4).
3. *The Times*, 29 February 2008.

4. *The Times*, 8 April 1803 3a; 28 April 1803 2d.

5. This painting was exhibited at Gainsborough House, Sudbury, in the 1980s, and sold at Sothebys in 1999. M. Symes (*Garden History* 9 [1981], 136–56); H. Belsey (*Burlington Magazine* 129 [1987], 735–6); J. Egerton, *George Stubbs, Painter* (New Haven 2007), 92–4, 616–7.

6. *Daily Mirror*, 14 November 1903, 5.

7. T. Moore, *Letters and Journals of Lord Byron* (London 1901), 38, 44, 80.

8. C. Smith (*Kennel Gazette* 113(8) [1991], 48–9); C. Kenyon-Jones (*Byron Journal* 28 [2000], 85–8).

9. *Sunday Times*, 22 June 2008.

10. R. Lloyd-Jones (*Byron Journal* 26 [1998], 91–7) and A. M. Stauffer (*Byron Journal* 26 [1998], 82–90).

11. *Chambers's Journal*, 3 May 1884; B. R. McElderry Jr (*Modern Language Notes* 58 [1943], 553–4); see also N. B. Penny (*Connoisseur* 192 [1976], 298–303), C. Kenyon-Jones, *Kindred Brutes* (Aldershot 2001), 23–50, K. Guthke (*Zeitschrift für Volkskunde* 99 [2003], 1–28) and I. H. Tague (*Eighteenth-Century Studies* 41 [2008], 289–306).

12. J. Harris, *Country Life* 122 [1957], 1085.

13. R. D. Lee, *A History and Description of the Modern Dogs of Great Britain* and Ireland (London 1894), chapter 3; see also Ash, *Dogs*, vol. 2, 565–87.

14. E. H. Mellencamp (*Newf Tides* 7(4) 1976 and 9(1) 1978).

15. D. Conlon and C. Matenaar in the *Zuchtbuch Nr. 2* of the Deutscher Landseer Club (Pfungstadt 1989), 14–55 and 57–200 respectively.

16. H. Pape (*Genetica* 80 [1990], 115–28). On Newfoundland dog fur colour genetics, see also C. C. Little, *The Inheritance of Coat Colour in Dogs* (New York 1957), and the papers by E. K. Karlsson *et al.* (*Nature Genetics* 39 [2007]. 1321–6) and S. M. Schmutz *et al.* (*Journal of Heredity* 100 [2009], S66–S74).

17. *The Times*, 21 May 1785 4b.

18. R. Guttridge, *The Evening Echo Book of Heritage in Dorset and the New Forest* (Southampton 1991), 32–3.

19. E. Jesse, *Anecdotes of Dogs* (London 1873), 133–84; W. H. G. Kingston, *Stories of Animal Sagacity* (London 1874); Revd C. Williams, *Dogs and their Ways* (London 1893), 154–72.

20. L. Johannesson in H. Brander Jonsson *et al.* (eds.), *Historiens Vingslag* (Stockholm 1987), 232–60; see also *Lee, History and Description of the Modern Dogs*, chapter 3 and Ash, *Dogs*, vol. 2, 565–87.

21. M. Bridson (*Newfoundland Quarterly*, Spring 2003); B. Ricketts, *The SS Ethie and the Hero Dog* (Quebec 2005). C. Jamesson, *The Legand of Rigel, Hero Dog of the Titanic* (New York 2005); B. Hynes, *The Noble Newfoundland Dog* (Halifax NS 2005), 48–54, 108–10.

22. *Animal World*, NS 3 [1908], 87.

23. *The Times*, 5 November 1812 4a.

24. *Morning Post*, 11 March 1834.

25. *The Times*, 14 September and 9 October 1839.

26. Ash, *Dogs*, vol. 2, 571–3.

27. *Illustrated Police News*, 4 July 1868.

28. *Star*, 17 June 1875 and *Western Mail*, 8 August 1892, respectively.

29. *Freeman's Journal*, 10 November 1896; *Lloyd's Weekly Newspaper*, 15 November 1896; *Daily News*, 16 December 1896.

30. W. G. Stables in *Fancier's Gazette*, 25 March 1875 and *Boy's Own Paper*, 1 May 1880; see also Ash, *Dogs*, vol. 2, 578–83.

31. *Petit Parisien* No. 678, 1902; H. B. Philpott (*Quiver* 137 [1905], 573–8); *Daily Mirror*, 7 September 1905, 8; *Colonist*, 18 May 1908. A later article about the Paris police (*Almanach Pratique du 'Petit Parisien'* 1911, 17–25) has a section about police dogs, but does not mention any *chiens plongeurs*.

32. *Daily Mirror*, 22 July 1975, 16; *EasyJet Magazine* 84 (December 2008), 47–51; *National Geographic*, 7 February 2003.

33. *Sun*, 2 February and 8 August 2007; *Daily Mail*, 8 August 2007; *South Wales Echo*, 29 August 2009.

34. S. Jamieson & J. Hevizi, *The True Story of Bilbo* (Penwyn 2008).

35. *Daily Express*, 22 July 2006, 3; *Daily Mirror*, 28 February 2008, 55, and 19 May 2008, 29; *Independent*, 28 March 2009.

36. *The Times*, 7 January 1805 4a, 9 June 1806 3a, 27 September 1824 3e.

37. R. Mestel (*Discover*, 10 January 1994); D. McCraig (*Smithsonian* 27(8) [1996], 126–35); M. W. Neff *et al.* (*Genetics* 151 [1999], 803–20); E. A. Ostrander *et al.* (*Trends in Genetics* 16 [2000], 117–24).

38. K. Macpherson and W. A. Roberts (*Journal of Comparative Psychology* 120 [2006], 113–9).

12

The Great Barry & Some Other Curious Saint Bernard Dogs

1. A good overview of St Bernard breed history is provided by H. Kay, *Man and Mastiff* (New York 1967) and R. & R. Beaver, *All about the St Bernard* (London 1988). See also R. B. Lee, *A History and Description of the Modern Dogs of Great Britain and Ireland* (London 1894), chapter 2, and E. C. Ash, *Dogs: Their History and Development* (London 1927), vol. 2, 588–95. Recent continental books on the subject include M. Marquis, *Grand Saint Bernard* (Genova 1988), M. Nussbaumer, *Barry* (Berne 2000) and I. Kürscher, *Barry* (Baden 2008).

2. In spite of the fanciful drawing reproduced by Marquis, *Grand Saint Bernard*, 15.

3. Lee, *History and Description*, chapter 2; Beaver, *St Bernard*, 22.

4. L. Larchey (ed.), *The Narrative of Captain Coignet* (New York 1890), 61.

5. Marquis, *Grand Saint Bernard*, 51.

6. On the first Barry, see the article by A. Heim in *Schweizerisches Hundestammbuch* 32 [1932], and Nussbaumer, *Barry*.

7. Nussbaumer, *Barry*, 47–51.

8. Nussbaumer, *Barry*, 51–6; T. Brown, *Biographical Sketches and Authentic Anecdotes of Dogs* (Edinburgh 1829), 280–1.

9. *Caledonian Mercury*, 8 September 1828.

10. *Cleeve's Penny Gazette*, 27 February 1841.

11. *Derby Mercury*, 26 November 1851.

12. *Bell's Life in London*, 29 May 1842.

13. *Caledonian Mercury*, 11 June 1842; Beaver, *St Bernard*, 24, 31.

14. *Illustrated Police News*, 8 April 1899.

15. *Sporting Gazette*, 18 December 1875; Beaver, *St Bernard*, 31–3.

16. Marquis, *Grand Saint Bernard*, 46–8.

17. Beaver, *St Bernard*, 34. Tell's obituary was in the *Daily News*, 1 February 1871; see also *Chums*, 11 May 1898. There is a confused local tradition that Tell had been a German Shepherd who saved his master and then died himself from exhaustion.

18. *Sporting Gazette*, 11 December 1875.

19. On Lady Florence Dixie and the 'Windsor mystery', see H. Wyndham, *Victorian Parade* (London 1934), 69–108 and *Consider Your Verdict* (London 1946), 88–104; see also B. Roberts, *Ladies in the Veldt* (London 1965), 77–181, and H. Davenport (*Windlesora* 17 [1999], 5–10).

20. *The Times*, 19 March 1883 6c, and 22 March 1883 7g; *Illustrated Police News*, 31 March 1883; *Penny Illustrated Paper*, 24 March 1883.

21. Lady Florence Dixie received a long obituary in *The Times*, 8 November 1905 9f; see also *Scotsman*, 23 May 2005 and the *Oxford DNB*.

22. A. Whitson & A. Orr, *Bamse* (Edinburgh 2009).

23. Marquis, *Grand Saint Bernard*, 69–73; press cuttings among the Lind-af-Hageby papers in the Swedish Riksarkivet (SE/RA/720283).

24. Kürscher, *Barry*, 39–50; I. Fisher in the *New York Times*, 29 October 2004.

13

Annals of the Rat-Pits of London & New York

1. P. Quennell (ed.), *Mayhew's London* (London n.d.), 298–306. On Mayhew and ratting, see also the articles by R. Maxwell (*Journal of British Studies* 17 [1978], 87–105), C. Herbert (*Representations* 23 [1988], 1–24) and M. Ellmann (*Critical Quarterly* 46 [2004], 59–76).

2. There is no definite history of ratting, but the books by E .S. Turner, *All Heaven in a Rage* (London 1964), 151–6, D. Flieg, *History of Fighting Dogs* (New York 1996), 105–12, and M. Homan, *A Complete History of Fighting Dogs* (New York 2000), 121–31, all make worthwhile contributions.

3. *Annals of Sporting* 2 [1822], 265.

4. *Bristol Mercury*, 9 September 1822; *Caledonian Mercury*, 2 November 1822; *Annals of Sporting* 2 [1822], 415; *Sporting Magazine*, October 1822.

5. E. M. Butler, *A Regency Visitor* (London 1957), 215–6.

6. Pierce Egan's *Weekly Courier*, 1 February and 1 March 1829; Pierce Egan's *Book of Sports* (London 1832), 212. The caricatures are listed by M. D. George, *Catalogue of Political and Personal Satires*, (London 1954), vol. 11, 110–1, 467–70, 628, 633.

7. Turner, *All Heaven in a Rage*, 131–51.

8. Many London rat-pits were listed in *Bell's Life in London*, 2 February and 19 November 1848.

9. *Bell's Life in London*, 30 November 1855.

10. These encounters were reported in *Bell's Life in London*, 2 July and 19 November 1848, and in *Era*, 11 August 1848.

11. The Jenny Lind scandal is discussed in *Era*, 5 January 1851, and *Bell's Life in London*, 17 November 1850, 16 and 23 February 1851.

12. *Bell's Life in London*, 16 and 30 March 1862; *Era*, 15 July 1866.

13. *Bell's Life in London*, 9 June 1850.

14. *Birmingham Daily Post*, 26 September 1868 and 24 December 1872.

15. *Illustrated Police News*, 24 December 1870.

16. *Birmingham Daily Post*, 13 October 1887.

17. *Toronto Star*, 22 March 1986.

18. *Animal World*, NS 7 [1912], 156.

19. *Graphic*, 9 July 1870.

20. *La Nature* 20 [1892], 327–8.

21. G. Spailier in *Les Cahiers Ardennais* of 1935; see also the website www.sparealities.com.

22. M. and H. J. Kaufman (*New York Folklore Quarterly* 28 [1972], 15–29; R. Sullivan, *Rats* (London 2005), 76–85; *New York Times*, 22 November 1870 and *New York Spirit of the Times* (1870), 411.

23. *New York Times*, 30 January 1876.

24. *New York Times*, 6 April 1879, 21 March 1881.

25. *Milwaukee Journal*, 13 April 1889; *Pittsburgh Press*, 12 January 1902.

26. G. and J. B. Smith (eds.), *The National Police Gazette* (New York 1972), 130, 207–8.

27. *Syracuse Evening Herald*, 16 January 1893; *Auburn Weekly News*, 17 February 1893; *Chicago Tribune*, 28 February 1899; see also M. Gripshower (*Baseball Research Journal* 36 [2007], 91–4).

28. *Ottawa Citizen*, 29 January 1897.

14

The Brown Dog Riots

1. There are three full-length studies of the Brown Dog affair. C. Lansbury, *The Old Brown Dog* (Madison, WI 1985) is a wayward study containing many errors; P. Mason, *The Brown Dog Affair* (London 1997) is an admirably succinct factual account; there is also a very useful study in Swedish: L. Gålmark, *Shambles of Science: Lizzy Lind-af-Hageby & Leisa Schartau, antivivisektionister* (Stockholm

1997). H. Kean, *Animal Rights* (London 1998) puts the Brown Dog riots into their historical context. See also the articles by J. H. Baron (*British Medical Journal* ii [1956], 547–8), M. Daly (*History Today* 37(5) [1987], 7–9) and H. Kean (*Society & Animals* 11 [2003], 353–73), as well as archival material in the Wellcome Institute Library (GC/199/4/1–2).

2. E. Westacott, *A Century of Vivisection and Anti-Vivisection* (Ashingdon 1949); N. A. Rupke (ed.), *Vivisection in Historical Perspective* (London 1990); see also the articles by D. Weinbren (*History Workshop Journal* 38 [1994], 86–105, H. Kean (*History Workshop Journal* 40 [1995], 16–38), E. M. Tansey (*Advances in Physiology Education* 19 [1998], S18–S33) and L. Leneman (*Women's History Review* 6 [1997], 271–87).

3. School records from Cheltenham Ladies' College; the *Oxford DNB* wrongly claims that she graduated.

4. *Daily Express*, 3 April 1913, 6.

5. On her background, see *Djurens Rätt* 7/8 [1913], 103–22 and Gålmark, *Shambles of Science*. For more details about her efforts to prevent premature burials, see J. Bondeson, *Buried Alive* (New York 2001), 195–7.

6. L. Lind-af-Hageby & L. K. Schartau, *The Shambles of Science* (London 1903).

7. *Daily Mirror*, 14, 18 and 19 November 1903; *Lancet* ii [1903], 1614; Mason, *The Brown Dog Affair*, 7–22.

8. *Daily Mirror*, 17 September 1906.

9. *British Medical Journal*, 292 [1986], 683.

10. Lister's own manuscript account of his activities is in W. Seton, *William Howard Lister* (London 1919), 17–24.

11. *Daily Mirror*, 26 November 1907; Mason, *The Brown Dog Affair*, 47–60.

12. *Daily Mirror*, 11 December 1907; *Daily Express*, 12 December 1907; C. Morson (*British Medical Journal* ii [1956], 827.

13. *Daily Mirror*, 17 December 1907; *The Times*, 17 December 1907 9e.

14. *Daily Express*, 8 and 9 January 1908.

15. M. F. M. Martin (*British Medical Journal* ii [1956], 661; Mason, *The Brown Dog Affair*, 82–6.

16. Press cuttings in the Lind-af-Hageby private archives, held by the Swedish Riksarkivet (SE/RA/720283).

17. *Daily Express*, 2–11 April 1913; *Lancet* i [1913], 1176–7.

18. *Brooklyn Daily Eagle*, 15 December 1913; *New York Tribune*, 29 November 1913 and 4 January 1914; Riksarkivet (SE/RA/720283).

19. Riksarkivet (SE/RA/720283).

20. *The Times*, 23 December 1926 7c; Westacott, *A Century of Vivisection*, 402, 507, 536–7.

21. A. V. Hill (*Journal of Physiology* 204 [1969], 1–13); I. M. Modlin (*Regulatory Peptides* 93 [2000], 109–23); S. Jones (*Daily Telegraph*, 12 November 2003).

22. Seton, *William Howard Lister*.

23. *British Medical Journal* 292 [1986], 683; H. Kean (*Society & Animals* 11 [2003], 353–73).

15

Dog Cemeteries, Dog Ghosts & Some Last Words

1. P. Lund-Simmonds, *The Curiosities of Food* (London 2001), 54–8; I. Crofton, *Brewer's Cabinet of Curiosities* (London 2006), 242–4.
2. Quoted by S. Leith, *Dead Pets* (Edinburgh 2005), 133–5.
3. F. H. Wu (*Gastronomica* 2 [2002], 38–45); A. L. Podbersiek (*Journal of Social Issues* 65 [2009], 615–32).
4. A. Serra *et al.* (*Forensic Science International: Genetics Supplement Series* 2 [2009], 210–2).
5. *Daily Telegraph* (Australia), 20 August 2008; *Adelaide Now*, 22 September 2009.
6. *Daily Express*, 22 January 1987; *Daily Mirror*, 22 and 23 January 1987.
7. J. North, *The Chronicles of Oatlands* (Oatlands 1875), 64–6; *Fishing Gazette*, 1 July 1893; J. W. Lindus Forge in *Wilton and Weybridge Local History Society Monograph* 18, (1974). On dog cemeteries in general, see M. E. Thurston, *The Lost History of the Canine Race* (Kansas City 1996), 251–66, and the articles by P. Howell (*Ethics, Place and Environment* 5 [2002], 5–22) and D. F. Morey (*Journal of Archaeological Science* 33 [2006], 158–75).
8. *Chums*, 20 October 1897.
9. *Daily Mirror*, 6 July 1998, 14–5; *The Times*, 23 December 1937; L. Lambton, *Beastly Buildings* (London 1985), 165, 175.
10. E. A. Brayley Hodgetts (*Strand Magazine* 6 [1893], 625–33); *Reynolds's Newspaper*, 12 August 1894.
11. *Rochester Democrat and Chronicle*, 3 June 1929.
12. Thurston, *Lost History*, 264.
13. E. Charles (*Strand Magazine* 22 [1901], 714–20); P. Eudel, *De tout un peu* (Paris 1912), 285–90; Anon., *Le Cimetière des Chiens* (Paris 2007).
14. *Westminster Budget*, 11 March 1898.
15. *Jönköpingsbladet*, 11 June 1872; *Dagens Nyheter*, 25 September 1995; A. Petersson, *The Presence of the Absent* (Lund 2004), 54–7.
16. E. Martin Jr, *Dr Johnson's Apple Orchard* (New York 1997); see also the website www.petcem.com.
17. *New York Times*, 29 September 1907 and 19 August 1917.
18. *Oswego Semi-Weekly Palladium*, 19 January 1915, 7.
19. T. Engelhardt (*Harper's Magazine* 253 [1976], 26–8).
20. E. O'Donnell, *Animal Ghosts* (London 1913).
21. J. A. Brooks, *Railway Ghosts* (Norwich 1985), 110–5.
22. On Black Dogs, see P. Dale-Green, *Dog* (London 1966), 47–53; J. and C. Bord, *Alien Animals* (London 1980), 77–111; C. Stubbs (*Fortean Times* 195 [2005], 30–5).
23. D. Waldron and C. Reeve, *Shock! The Black Dog of Bungay* (Bungay 2010).

INDEX

Index

Also available from Amberley Publishing

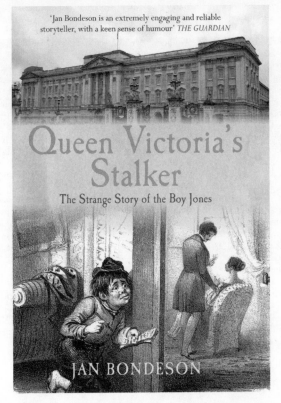

'Jan Bondeson is an extremely engaging and reliable storyteller, with a keen sense of humour' THE GUARDIAN

Queen Victoria's Stalker

The Strange Story of the Boy Jones

JAN BONDESON

The remarkable tale of Queen Victoria's teenage stalker

'The amazing story of the first celebrity stalker' THE SUN

'The lovesick stalker who stole Victoria's bloomers' THE DAILY MAIL

'Intriguing' THE DAILY TELEGRAPH

'A remarkable story… vividly depict[s] a world in which a young boy could enter the queen's rooms and end up a celebrity' KATE WILLIAMS, author of *Becoming Queen*

£16.99 Hardback
47 illustrations
160 pages
978-1-84868-863-6

Also available as an ebook
Available from all good bookshops or to order direct
Please call **01453-847-800**
www.amberleybooks.com

Available August 2013 from Amberley Publishing

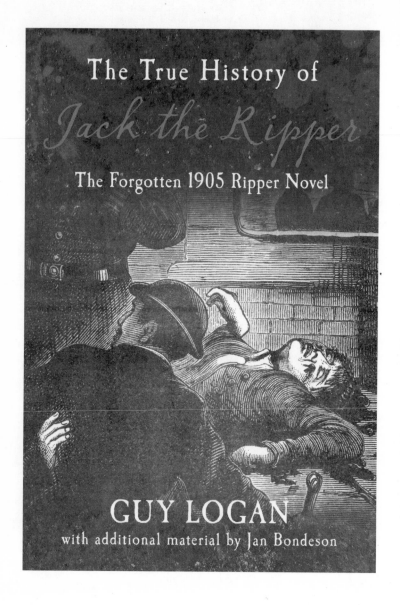

The True History of

Jack the Ripper

The Forgotten 1905 Ripper Novel

GUY LOGAN

with additional material by Jan Bondeson